W9-CEF-901

**Collaborationism in France
during the Second World War**

Collaborationism in France during the Second World War

BERTRAM M. GORDON

Cornell University Press | Ithaca and London

Cornell University Press gratefully acknowledges a grant from the Andrew W. Mellon Foundation that aided in bringing this book to publication.

First published 1980 by Cornell University Press.
Published in the United Kingdom by Cornell University Press Ltd.,
2–4 Brook Street, London W1Y 1AA.

International Standard Book Number 0-8014-1263-3
Library of Congress Catalog Card Number 79-25281
Printed in the United States of America
Librarians: Library of Congress cataloging information
appears on the last page of the book.

To Clio

Contents

7

Preface

Until recently, French collaboration with Nazi Germany during World War II was little studied in France. More than thirty years after the war, it still evokes passionate controversy there. The silence has now ended but the controversy continues. Sparked by Marcel Ophuls' film *The Sorrow and the Pity,* the French have begun to reexamine Vichy and the collaboration. The Comité d'Histoire de la Deuxième Guerre Mondiale, a government-sponsored research group studying the history of World War II in France, has led the historians' community away from the official postwar view, which had pictured almost all of France in the Resistance with but a handful of desperadoes on the other side. Scholars under the sponsorship of the Comité have begun a systematic exploration of all aspects of life under the German occupation, including the collaboration. During the years I have been working on this book, literature on the collaboration has increased significantly, as is evident in the Bibliographical Note.

Beyond the scholarly community, a new vogue of nostalgia for the days of the occupation has gripped at least part of the French reading public. Romanticized accounts of the collaboration, several concerned particularly with the French volunteers in the German armed forces, have appeared and sold well. Mementoes of the occupation disappear quickly from flea markets and antiquarian shops. The 1970's brought several films dealing with the occupation and portraying pro-Axis Frenchmen in ways inconceivable a few years earlier.

Why nostalgia for a period little mourned by so many who lived through it? The answer may be found in the coming of age of a new generation, which did not know firsthand the privations of the occupation and the cruelties of the Germans. Histories of World War II have become popular in a West that has entered a prosaic so-called postindustrial age. Perhaps there is boredom with the apparently

9

pedestrian nature of modern life, reminiscent of that which led adventure-seeking romantics to fascism in the first place. The taboo nature of the collaboration attracts some seekers of shock value in contemporary France. Fascism, in the forms it took before 1945, may be gone, but the romantic yearning for causes that led many middle-class Europeans into the politically militant but socially conservative fascist movements of interwar Europe is not. There is still a radical Right in France. Silenced for years after 1945, it has found its voice again.

Now a tiny minority, the radical Right continues to resist absorption by the larger moderate Right and awaits the crisis it hopes will drive the majority of the middle-class French into its arms. Current economic difficulties combined with the presence of non-European workers may provide its opportunity. The potential for economic trouble, a perceived threat from the Left, and the desire of some for pseudorevolutionary political activism offer it possible openings. In a France bereft of her empire, reduced to lesser power status, and preoccupied increasingly with technology and economic development, the fascist style and the adventures of World War II hold a certain appeal. To the credit of France, the collaborators were and their subsequent acolytes remain a small minority of the population. They stand as a reminder of the dangers inherent when inhumane remedies are adopted to resolve the economic, political, and spiritual deficiencies of modern civilization.

This book would have been impossible to write without the help of many people. Not all of them can be named here. I have respected the wish for confidentiality of many of the former collaborators I interviewed. Others, willing to go public, are thanked in the footnotes.

Special thanks must go to Milorad Drachkovich of the Hoover Institution of War and Peace at Stanford University and Jean Mabire and Nicholas Tandler in France, who were helpful in my work there. Without Gérard Le Marec and Gérard Silvain in Paris, I would not have become aware of the *French Basic Handbook*, a mine of useful information on the collaboration. Also of invaluable assistance in Paris were the staff of the Centre de Documentation Juive Contemporaine, especially its archivist, Ulrich Hessel; and the Comité d'Histoire de la Deuxième Guerre Mondiale, particularly Henri Michel and Claude

Lévy. Thanks are also due the staffs at the Hoover Institution and the Bibliothèque de Documentation Internationale et Contemporaine at the University of Paris X in Nanterre.

Several intellectual debts can hardly be repaid. Robert Soucy read parts of the manuscript at an early stage and he provided invaluable criticism, as did Robert Paxton during the course of making commentaries on related papers I presented at conferences. The reader may recognize in my extensive use of microfilmed captured German war documents Paxton's method in researching his book on Vichy France. Emily Goodman gave me useful suggestions about some of my early work on Marcel Déat, and Anna Nicolai helped in the early research on Déat and his Rassemblement National Populaire. Gratefully welcoming the collaboration of fellow historians in preparing this book on a less pleasing sort of collaboration, I nonetheless accept sole responsibility for any errors and faults of judgment readers may find in it. All translations from the French and German are mine unless otherwise noted.

Financial support, essential for the investigator in distant places, was provided by the National Endowment for the Humanities, the American Philosophical Society, and the Faculty Research Grants Committee and Trustees of Mills College. To all of these sources I am grateful. Special thanks are also due Bernhard Kendler and Kay Scheuer, editors at Cornell University Press, who presided over the transformation from manuscript to book. I am indebted for secretarial help to Beth Gaffney and Haleen Potts.

I could not have written the book without the forbearance of Karen and Andrew, born long after the events it considers. How does one explain fascism to one's children? Finally, to be married to a writer is not an easy lot. By following her own star, Sherry has contributed more to the book than she could have in any other way.

BERTRAM M. GORDON

Oakland, California

Abbreviations

BDIC: Bibliothèque de Documentation Internationale et Contemporaine (a library specializing in twentieth-century political history and located at the University of Paris X, Nanterre).

BN: Bibliothèque Nationale, Paris.

CDJC: Centre de Documentation Juive Contemporaine (Center for Contemporary Jewish Documentation, specializing in materials relating to the Holocaust, in Paris).

CGQJ: Commissariat Général des Questions Juives (Vichy government's special department of Jewish affairs).

CGT: Confédération Générale du Travail (France's major labor organization, dissolved during the occupation).

CSAR: Comité Secret d'Action Révolutionnaire (Eugène Deloncle's secret organization, which planned a right-wing coup in the late 1930's; also known as the *Cagoule*).

CUAR: Comité d'Unité d'Action Révolutionnaire (the united committee representing the leaders of the collaborationist groups in Tunisia after the Allied landings of 1942).

DWStK: Deutsche Waffenstillstandskommission (the German Armistice Commission in Wiesbaden).

FRN: Front Révolutionnaire National (Marcel Déat's abortive attempt to unite the collaborationist parties in 1942).

IEQJ: Institute d'Etude des Questions Juives (anti-Semitic racist "study" group, supported by the Germans in Paris).

JEN: Jeunesse de l'Europe Nouvelle (Groupe Collaboration's youth affiliate, led by Jacques Schweizer).

LVF: Légion des Volontaires Français contre le Bolchévisme (Anti-Bolshevik Legion).

Abbreviations

MSR: Mouvement Social Révolutionnaire (led by Deloncle).

PFNC: Parti Français National-Collectiviste (Pierre Clémenti's tiny radical Right party, formed in the thirties, later a collaborationist group).

PPF: Parti Populaire Français (Jacques Doriot's party).

PSF: Parti Social Français (Colonel François de la Rocque's right-wing party, the successor to his Croix de Feu after the dissolution of the paramilitary leagues by the Popular Front government).

RNP: Rassemblement National Populaire (Déat's party).

SOL: Service d'Ordre Légionnaire (the more politically activist element of Vichy's Légion Française des Combattants and the seed in 1943 of Joseph Darnand's Milice).

**Collaborationism in France
during the Second World War**

Introduction: Fascism and Fragmentation in France

The time is past when the revolutionary flame burned solely among the proletariat. The revolution has changed its meaning and today this word "nation" has more revolutionary virtue than all words referring to class.
—Marcel Déat, speech to congress of the Parti Socialiste de France, 1934

We have inhibited the rise to power of political groups and ideologies related to us and with it the energizing of political life in France in the direction of the National Socialist revolution. We have wanted instead a government to preserve peace and order, the most efficient contribution of labor, the highest possible production for our war needs. This has greatly weakened the development of the groups ideologically close to us.
—Rudolf Schleier, report to the German Foreign Ministry, 1943

In 1940, France suffered at the hands of Nazi Germany her most total defeat in modern times. The four-year German occupation that followed is still often referred to as "four years to strike from our history." It is not surprising that France, a pluralistic society, produced many different responses to the disaster of 1940. One of the most important yet least understood was the phenomenon of collaborationism, the ideological acceptance of fascism. Many Frenchmen collaborated with the Germans during the summer of 1940 when their country's defeat seemed final and the defeat of Britain imminent. When the tide of the war turned in 1942, many who had collaborated during and after 1940 began to have second thoughts. The Resistance attracted some, whereas others tried to slip back into the anonymity of private life.

There were Frenchmen, however, who continued to support the Axis long after they recognized the growing dubiousness of their cause. Some remained loyal collaborationists in German exile even after the liberation of France in 1944. Others joined collaborationist movements only when the German defeat at Stalingrad seemed to pose a danger that Communism would sweep the Continent. Many viewed themselves as disinterested partisans of Franco-German rec-

17

onciliation and the Nazi European New Order. They called themselves "collaborationists," a term they ostentatiously contrasted to
"collaborators," who trafficked with the Germans solely for material
gain or personal advancement. It was possible, according to their
argument, to have been a collaborationist without ever having personally dealt with any Germans.

The collaborator-collaborationist distinction often fails in practice,
for many sincere partisans of the Axis cause made personal fortunes
and careers during the occupation. Fernand de Brinon and Jean
Luchaire were Germanophile journalists who parlayed their political
views into influence and prestige after 1940. Pro-German before
Hitler's rise to power, de Brinon became Vichy's ambassador to the
occupied northern zone and Luchaire headed the Press Corporation
in Paris after 1940. The Press Corporation was in theory an expression of Vichyite corporatism in which all those engaged in one indus-
try were included in a single organization. In practice it became a
personal fiefdom for Luchaire. Political convictions maintained at
propitious times have often enriched their holders. There is, however, validity to the collaborator-collaborationist differentiation even
if the motivations of individuals are not always clear. Those French
who sought financial gain, adventure, or revenge against personal
enemies by working in the notorious German police office on the rue
Lauriston in Paris were often nonideological, if not nonpolitical. Collaborationists in contrast possessed at least a rudimentary political
ideology. To confuse them with pure opportunists overlooks those
who continued to support the Axis cause long after it had become
apparent even to many of them that Germany could not win the war.
Hitler's last defenders in late April and early May 1945 included
French volunteers in the Waffen-SS. [1]

Stanley Hoffmann has pointed out that there were as many forms
of collaboration as there were collaborators. [2] The Vichy regime was
forced to collaborate on issues such as the use of French labor in

[1]"What could have been the 'material' base of Doriotism? What 'interests' could
Doriot have been defending when in 1945, after France had been liberated, he
continued to direct frenetic appeals from Germany to the French people?" ask Jean
Plumyène and Raymond Lasierra, Les fascismes français, 1923–63 (Paris: Seuil,
1963), p. 152.
[2]Stanley Hoffmann, "Collaborationism in France during World War II," Journal
of Modern History, 40 (September 1968), 375.

German factories because it existed largely on German sufferance. The practical needs of administering occupied France led to collaboration on many levels between French administrative and police personnel on one hand and the occupation authorities on the other. Vichy itself was in large measure a reaction against the French parliamentary past and many of its officials, starting with Pierre Laval, especially during his tenure in power in 1940, were ready to collaborate in a wide variety of areas. In addition to what might be called political collaboration, there was the economic collaboration of French business interests which saw enlarged opportunities in German-dominated Europe. Technocratic and business interests came to the fore under Admiral Jean-François Darlan, and their form of collaboration was illustrated by Jean Bichelonne, who negotiated production agreements with Albert Speer in 1942. Political and economic collaboration were joined by the cultural collaboration of many prominent French men of letters, the theater, and the cinema, who looked with favor upon the art forms of Nazi Germany and often traveled to Berlin for direct inspiration. Otto Abetz, Germany's ambassador to occupied France, was later able to name many of the most prominent cultural figures among those with whom he had been on friendly terms during his tenure in Paris.[3]

What separated the collaborationists from others in the pro-Axis camp was their desire to restructure France politically in the image of the Axis powers. Enthusiastically committed to the New Order, they joined the half dozen political movements that are the subject of this book. The most radical and ideological supporters of the New Order, they comprised the "Ultra" or collaborationist parties, the manifestations of fascism in occupied France. In the words of one recent student of the collaboration, not all French fascists in 1940 became collaborators, but by 1944 all collaborationists had become fascists.[4]

As the fascists of occupied France, the collaborationists were a kind of alter ego of the Vichy regime. They sought to lead France further in the direction of the one-party state, mass mobilization in

[3]Testimony of Otto Abetz during his trial, November 21, 1945, in République Française, Ministère de l'Intérieur, Direction Générale de la Police Nationale, No. 204/35; Centre de Documentation Juive Contemporaine (abbreviated hereafter as CDJC), document LXXI, 113.

[4]Pascal Ory, *Les collaborateurs, 1940–1945* (Paris: Seuil, 1976), p. 270.

the fascist manner, and alliance with the Axis than Vichy was willing to go. In the end, with the intensification of civil strife and growing German pressure, Vichy bowed and accepted several leading collaborationists into its administration. The polarization of France between Resistance and collaboration pushed Vichy in the direction of the latter. Collaborationists openly embraced fascism, whereas Vichy was impelled toward it by force of circumstances. The governments of Laval and Admiral Darlan were denounced by the collaborationists as "attentiste," too cautious, following a policy of "wait and see" before committing France to Hitler's Europe. Vichy refused to create the single mass party that the collaborationists wanted. They also denounced Vichy as reactionary, too heavily oriented toward clerical and royalist and later business interests and not sufficiently willing to move France toward a totalitarian society in the image of the Axis powers. Vichy, they said, was too soft in its purge of those connected with the parliamentary life of the Third Republic. Politicians of the prewar political Left were blamed for the "decadence" of France which collaborationists saw as having been revealed by the defeat of 1940. Some of the differences between the collaborationists and the men of Vichy were of temperament and style: the former were "harder." In strident tones they demanded a rejuvenation of defeated and humiliated France by adoption of fascist models.

Collaborationists and members of the Resistance in occupied France represented two poles in the larger civil war between fascist and antifascist coalitions, both products of the Western cultural and political tradition. A defining characteristic of European history from 1919 to 1945, fascism appeared in virtually all European countries as well as some beyond the seas. French fascism shared the contradictions of fascism elsewhere, grouping together those who feared liberalism and Marxism as agents of modernization and others who sought that very modernization but through alternatives to liberalism and Marxism. World War I and the economic dislocations that followed discredited liberalism in the eyes of many. The failure of Marxism to deal with nationalism during the First World War and the phenomenon of a nonrevolutionary proletariat in many European countries discredited it in the eyes of many as did the apparent subservience of Communist parties to the Soviet Union.[5]

[5] A. James Gregor, *The Fascist Persuasion in Radical Politics* (Princeton, N.J.: Princeton University Press, 1974), pp. 140 and 179–180.

The radical Right in France was characterized by such a mix of modernizers and antimodernizers. From a variety of social classes, they shared a disinclination for social revolution, preferring instead to rally round the flag. The collaborationist movements included youthful elements who denounced what they called the effete bourgeois mores of their elders but who sought no more of a social revolution than did the older more establishmentarian conservative elites. Like fascists in other countries, the collaborationists spoke and wrote of "revolution" and "socialism." Theirs, however, was a defensive reaction in which they sought to preserve the interests of the artisanal and white-collar middle classes and peasants from the forces of modernization represented by large-scale capitalism and international Communism. They also fought Jews and Freemasons, who were agents of modernization, but their chief enemy even during the period of the 1939–1941 Ribbentrop-Molotov pact was Communism. Ernst Nolte, one of the foremost students of fascism, has defined it as anti-Marxism utilizing the revolutionary tactics of Marxist movements in order to defeat them. The French collaborationists acted in Europe's counterrevolutionary rather than its revolutionary tradition.[6]

Like those in other counterrevolutionary movements, the French collaborationists masked their basic social conservatism in revolutionary rhetoric and style. Their imitation of the fascist style was more than just the attempt to ape the conquerors of 1940. It reflected the desire of fascist movements everywhere to capture the excitement and camaraderie of the revolutionary style minus the social revolutionary content of Marxism.

Uniforms were prominent among the collaborationists of occupied France; when they were unavailable, colored shirts sufficed. The martial spirit represented commitment to a paramilitarized society of men and women toughened in the crucible of World War I and led by a chivalric warrior elite. Many of the younger recruits, who were

---

[6]For a discussion of the counterrevolutionary nature of fascism, see Arno J. Mayer, *Dynamics of Counterrevolution in Europe, 1870–1956: An Analytic Framework* (New York: Harper Torchbooks, 1971), and Barrington Moore, Jr., *Social Origins of Dictatorship and Democracy* (Boston: Beacon, 1966). The argument that fascism was characteristic of the 1919–1945 era is offered by Ernst Nolte, *Three Faces of Fascism: Action Française, Italian Fascism, National Socialism,* trans. Leila Vennewitz (London: Weidenfeld & Nicolson, 1965), pp. 3–9.

attracted by a paramilitary mystique, had never before been politically active. The uniform gave them an identity.[7]

Virtually all the collaborationists claimed to want "socialism" for France. Under the harsh conditions of the occupation, the term itself connoted a pulling together and social solidarity in the face of adversity. As elsewhere in Europe, "socialism" became a term utilized by many who felt threatened by large-scale capitalism. Anticapitalist elements of the lower middle classes appropriated the word "socialism" from earlier working-class movements in the hope that in doing so they would also inherit the solidarity and sense of belonging that they felt the workers possessed. The experiences of the First World War provided the leavening agent in the transformation of the meaning of socialism. As in German National Socialism, the socialism of the collaborationists was that of the battlefield, a feeling of egalitarianism in that all had been exposed equally to the bullets at the front. This egalitarianism was combined with the hierarchy of military merit, symbolized by the uniform and the colored shirt.

The battlefield experience of World War I was a legacy shared by many French fascists with their confreres across the Continent and passed down to younger brothers and sons, often children during the first war.[8] Their socialism sought a new and vaguely communitarian spirit, a reaction against what many across Europe felt to be the dehumanizing quality of life in modern industrial capitalist society together with a mystique glorifying the camaraderie of the trenches of the First World War. Collaborationist socialism drew upon the French radical Right tradition of lower-middle-class anticapitalism. As such it was eminently conservative, despite its strident denunciations of "plutocratic capitalism."

The frenetic, sometimes nihilistic, dynamism of the fascist style was present in the collaborationist movements and alienated them

[7]The identification with the uniform was made graphically clear by one veteran of the PPF who wore his party blue shirt when he received me for an interview in 1974. On fascism as a manifestation of masculine fright and the appeal of uniforms, see Peter Nathan, *The Psychology of Fascism* (London: Faber & Faber, 1943), pp. 52–53 and 131–132, respectively.

[8]The impact of World War I and its attendant privations upon the children of Germany who grew up to be young adults during the 1930's and 1940's is examined by Peter Loewenberg, "The Psychohistorical Origins of the Nazi Youth Cohort," *American Historical Review*, 76 (December 1971), 1457–1502.

still further from the more traditionalist circles at Vichy. Kept far removed from political power, the collaborationists became increasingly desperate and irresponsible. The energizing turbulence of incipient fascism became increasingly prominent among them as the war drew on. Experience in Italy and Germany showed that fascism in power had to make political compromises, which meant dispensing with more radical millenarian elements such as Ernst Roehm and his SA in 1934 in Germany. These movements regained their millenarian dynamism only in defeat, as illustrated by Mussolini's return to his leftist origins at Salò in 1943 and the increasingly strong SS orientation of German National Socialism in the latter stages of the war. The "pseudoradical anti-capitalism" of the French collaborationists, to use the phrase of one student of fascism, was never really put to the test.[9]

Their divorce from the compromises and realities of power was combined with the strong ideological tradition of most French political parties to render the collaborationists incapable of making the kinds of political compromises necessary to gain and hold power. To win support from within the middle classes, they needed to espouse order and authority, which brought them into conflict with the romantic spirit of revolt characterizing their more militant members. The denial of power to them and the growing sense of isolation and ostracism they felt when the war began to turn against the Germans induced an increased recklessness especially among those who remained faithful to their cause. The level of violence increased in France with armed combat against the Resistance. Frustrated at home, many of the more militant collaborationists left to fight the various enemies of the Axis, above all the Russians, on the battlefronts.

Despite its own collaboration with the occupying power, the Vichy government opposed ideological collaborationism. Pétain fought tenaciously for a modicum of French independence in Hitler's New Europe by attempting to keep communications open to the United States. The National Revolution meant many different things to different people. Some collaborationists, not wishing and others not

---

[9]The term "pseudoradical anti-capitalism" is used by Moore, *Social Origins*, p. 450.

daring to attack the vast personal prestige of Marshal Pétain, tried to picture the head of state as a leader in the fascist manner. Pétain, however, looked to the tradition of conservative agrarian France, which corresponded more closely to society in the unoccupied southern zone. With less interest in rallying the masses of the French to a fascist ideal or a single mass party, he shunned the turbulent collaborationists whenever possible and admitted a few of them to his government only under German duress when the situation changed in 1940. Laval, who in 1940 sought to accommodate France to Hitler's New Order, flirted briefly with the idea of a single party and then abandoned it during that summer. Fired by Pétain in December 1940, Laval returned to head the government again in April 1942, but he had become more cautious in view of the evolving war situation, and the gulf between him and the collaborationists widened with the passage of time. Admiral Darlan, who headed the Vichy government during most of 1941, brought many of the young technocrats into office who would later reemerge in de Gaulle's Fifth Republic, but the admiral too shied away from the collaborationists. [10]

The Germans also played a significant role in keeping their would-be allies out of power in France. Hitler and his chief aides recognized that the collaborationists lacked the respectability that Vichy held in France and that they could not match the popularity and esteem of Marshal Pétain. German policy required a tranquil and orderly France whose economic resources might be readily exploited for the German war effort. A staunchly collaborationist French government might appear to many of the French as too submissive to Germany, dividing France and producing the very disorder that the Germans wished to avoid. Hitler's contempt for France is well known, and it was strengthened by the French collapse of 1940. He did not believe that the French were suited for fascism and was content for France to be led by a regime willing to maintain domestic order and accept a subordinate role in the New Europe. National Socialist doctrine preached German superiority, and there was always the possibility that a rejuvenated fascist France might one day emerge to challenge German domination of the Continent, just as Nazi Ger-

[10]Continuities particularly in regard to technocracy in Vichy and the Fifth Republic are discussed by Robert O. Paxton, *Vichy France: Old Guard and New Order, 1940–1944* (New York: Knopf, 1972), pp. 352–357.

many had overthrown the order created by the Versailles peace treaty. Hitler wanted no rival, even a fascist one, in Europe. Collaborationists were useful as a threat to induce official Vichy to toe the line, but he had no intention of helping them to power.

To function at all, especially in the occupied zone, the collaborationists were dependent upon German support, and yet this backing was measured carefully to prevent them from seriously menacing the Vichy government. To prove their fidelity to the cause of collaboration, its supporters were obliged to identify themselves with ever more repressive and brutal German policies as the war situation deteriorated for the Axis. In so doing the collaborationists alienated increasing numbers of the French population without gaining additional German support until the war was lost. Their growing isolation was not unwelcome to Hitler, who preferred to see his French supporters compromised in respect to public opinion at home. The more compromised they were, the more dependent upon Hitler's aid and the more likely they were to fight by his side to the end.[11]

Even as the military situation worsened for the Germans, many collaborationists optimistically believed that the increased pressure put upon the Germans would force them to rely more upon their European allies and that this would open the door for a more prominent French presence in German-dominated Europe. When the German military position deteriorated sufficiently for them to seek more help from their non-German supporters, however, they were on their way toward losing the war. The victorious Germans in 1940 and 1941 had evinced little interest in a collaborationist France. Caught in a vicious circle of "heads I win, tails you lose," the collaborationists progressively boxed themselves into a political position so deeply compromised that there would be no escape after the liberation of 1944. By their own political logic, they had to subscribe to the "Europeanism" preached by German propaganda, but as Hitler and his top aides made abundantly clear, their "Europeanism" meant little more than German dominion. By the end of the occupation the collaborationist position had been reduced to total subservience to the Reich. When the Germans were forced out of France in August 1944, many of the collaborationist leaders and their supporters fol-

[11]Eberhard Jäckel, *Frankreich in Hitlers Europa. Die Deutsche Frankreichpolitik im zweiten Weltkrieg* (Stuttgart: Deutsche Verlags-Anstalt, 1966), p. 276.

lowed them to a temporary exile in Germany, where the last hopeless act in the drama was played out. The Germans finally recognized the claims to power of the Ultra movements when they were no longer in France. When French volunteers were accepted as equals in the elite Waffen-SS it was so that they could be decimated in some of the Reich's final battles against the Soviet onslaught.

Hitler was content to see several rival collaborationist groups emerge, enabling him to follow his customary policy of divide and conquer. The German bureaucracy in occupied France was itself split into rival services: the foreign ministry, the Wehrmacht, and the police and SS. Each supported different collaborationist factions at different times. As in Germany herself, the various services engaged in rampant rivalries and empire building in occupied Europe. These internecine German rivalries very much complicated the history of the French collaboration and impeded the emergence of one unified movement. Laval was also a master at subsidizing several of the Ultra movements in order to undermine their independence and thereby reduce the possible threat to his own position.

An irony in the history of the French collaboration was the existence of some half dozen political movements, each claiming to be the single party with the single leader who alone could bring a rejuvenated France into the New Europe. These factions often rose to prominence and then fell back toward obscurity with meteoric rapidity. Although Vichy and the German agencies in France helped intensify the splits within the collaborationist camp, these fissures represented real differences in the political origins and sometimes the social backgrounds of their members. Sharing allegiance to similar fascist doctrines, the diverse collaborationist factions exhibited differences in temperament, nuance, and style. All were oppositional, but a progressively increased virulence and sense of desperation can be seen in the emergence of the three major movements, one after another, as the situation of the Germans deteriorated and the frustrations of pro-Axis elements mounted in France.

The first of these movements, the Rassemblement National Populaire (RNP), was founded early in 1941 by Marcel Déat in reaction to his failure to achieve a single party during the summer of 1940 and the dismissal of Laval in December. Déat, who had broken away from the Socialist party in 1933, sought in 1941 to build a mass totalitarian party of trade-union and radical Right elements. The coalition failed to hold, however, and by the end of the year Déat was left the leader of a rump faction. The failure of the RNP was followed by the emergence in 1942 of the Parti Populaire Français (PPF), which, unlike Déat's party, had existed prior to the war and in 1937 had claimed a quarter million supporters. It had declined after alienating many of its members by supporting the Munich appeasement policy of 1938. Headed by the former Communist mayor of the Paris suburb of Saint-Denis, Jacques Doriot, the PPF was marked by a virulent anti-Communism which it found expedient to subdue between the fall of France and the German invasion of the Soviet Union. After June 1941, however, the party was able to intensify its anti-Communism and throw itself fully into the cause of collaboration. In November 1942, Doriot spoke openly of seizing power from Laval but was unable to do so without German support.

The failure of the PPF, whose tactics and tone were more strident than those of Déat's RNP, led directly to the creation of the Milice, an agency under the Vichy government that functioned as a paramilitary force in repression of the maquis and also as a collaborationist party to rival the RNP and PPF, both of which were centered in Paris. Laval was the nominal head of the Milice but he soon lost effective control over it to Joseph Darnand, a military hero of both world wars. Darnand led it into pitched battles against the maquis in 1944.

Each of the three major collaborationist movements came to prominence at a different phase of the war. The RNP blossomed during the period of Axis ascendancy. Although it continued through the end of the war, its vigor and potential were greatest before its Left and Right split in November 1941. Organized before the German invasion of Russia, the RNP was more significant on the French political stage during the spring of 1941 than after the USSR entered the war. Doriot's PPF, on the other hand, was galvanized by the attack on the Soviet Union. It emerged in 1942 as the leading collaborationist force, perceived as a real threat by Laval in November of that year. The emergence of the PPF coincided with the turning of the war. German *Blitzkrieg* did not defeat Russia, and the Reich had to shift to a total war effort in 1942. Final German victory seemed less certain than at the time of the appearance of the RNP. Successful Allied landings in French North Africa, occurring at the very moment of the PPF "congress of power" in November 1942, brought the war closer to home and intensified growing French doubts about final Axis victory.

The landings in North Africa, followed by the scuttling of the French fleet and the total occupation of the country, deprived Vichy of the limited independence it had held. As German exactions increased, Vichy assumed the characteristics of a satellite state. Public opinion shifted toward the Allies, the Resistance intensified, and the PPF chafed under its inability to direct the course of events. Its failure to attain power in 1942 led to increasingly reckless acts by frustrated militants in growing isolation from the majority of their compatriots. The Milice was the product of declining German power. German and French police forces could no longer maintain order without resorting to a paramilitary fascist league created as a government agency by Laval. The weakening of the German position and the increasing desperation of the French collaborationists armed in the Milice in 1944 brought on the final stage of civil war.

This book follows the pattern of the developing collaborationist movements. After examining the emergence of the regime in Vichy and the collaborationist community in Paris in 1940, it treats the three major movements in turn. It then discusses three lesser movements, each comprising a portion of the fascist community in occupied France. Finally, attention is given the participants in the military collaboration, the entry of several Ultra leaders into the government, the Liberation, and the last act played out in German exile. The ultimate failure of ideological collaboration is attributed to the failure of fascism to sink deep roots into the French political community before or after 1940.

France by the early twentieth century had produced a "stalled" or "stalemate" society built upon a broad consensus of the middle classes and based upon the prerevolutionary bourgeois values of "stability, harmony, permanence," and "resistance to the machine age."[12] This

---

[12]Stanley Hoffmann, "Paradoxes of the French Political Community," in Hoffmann, et al., *In Search of France: The Economy, Society, and Political System in the Twentieth Century* (New York: Harper Torchbooks, 1965 [1963]), p. 6. The "stalled" or "stagnated" society is also discussed by Pierre Sorlin, *La société française, 1914–1968* (Paris: Arthaud, 1971), 2:11, and is considered at length in Michel Crozier,

political consensus, expressed in the many cabinets of the Third Republic, was shaken but not destroyed by economic and political crises in the interwar years. The economic backwardness of France between the wars spared her the extreme dislocations suffered by Germany and thus also the extreme solutions embraced by the Germans.[13] Victors in the First World War, the French were a satisfied power lacking the keen edge of resentment produced by the myths of the *Dolchstoss* (stab in the back) in Germany and the "mutilated peace" in Italy. A strong tradition of civic education that identified French national ideals with the universalist aspirations of the 1789 Revolution also impeded the spread of fascism.

The strength of the political consensus in France was manifested in the moderation of many in the radical Right whose demonstrations in February 1934 appeared to challenge the foundations of the Republic. Most of the demonstrators were satisfied with the appointment of the conservative Gaston Doumergue to replace Edouard Daladier as premier. There was little real threat to the Republic, which instead was strengthened by the reaction of the Left to form the Popular Front that came to power in 1936.

The French political community, however, faced major challenges which threatened the stalemate society during the interwar years. A declining birthrate, stagnating economy, and the terrible exhaustion that followed World War I threatened the political cohesion and sense of purpose that had existed in 1914. The twin crises of economic depression and foreign threat exacerbated social tension and strengthened those who questioned the basic political consensus in France. Although the Republic survived until the debacle of 1940, the crisis atmosphere of 1934 and 1936 provided the terrain for the growth of political dissidence from which the collaborationists later came.

The paralysis of parliament in the early 1930's discredited it in the

---

The Stalled Society (New York: Viking, 1973), the English translation of his *La société bloquée*, 1970.

[13] French economic backwardness and its role in retarding the development of the radical Right is discussed by Charles S. Maier, *Recasting Bourgeois Europe: Stabilization in France, Germany, and Italy in the Decade after World War I* (Princeton, N.J.: Princeton University Press, 1975), p. 591. See also Sorlin, pp. 80 and 138, and Nathanael Greene, *From Versailles to Vichy: The Third Republic, 1919–1940* (New York: Crowell, 1970), pp. 74–75.

eyes of many in the middle classes, who began to consider authoritarian alternatives. Parliamentary credibility was further strained by the Stavisky scandal, in which prominent members of parliament were accused of covering up financial chicanery, intensifying the radical Right attack on the government as both corrupt and inept. Hitler's accession to power in 1933 added fuel to the right-wing denunciations of the government, which was increasingly blamed for dissipating the fruits of the 1918 victory. With the formation of the Popular Front and its rise to power in 1936, the radical Right's preoccupation shifted from Berlin to Moscow. A wave of strikes during the spring of 1936 scared many into the belief that strong measures were needed to meet an imminent revolution orchestrated by Moscow.

Whether as an alternative to the Marxist pattern of modernization or in reaction against the modernization represented by Marxism, the radical Right was fueled by anti-Communism. Frustrated young middle-class Frenchmen, impatient with their elders who seemed unable to control parliamentary stagnation and demographic and economic decline, turned in growing numbers to the longstanding French tradition of the counterrevolutionary Right. Action Française and the Jeunesses Patriotes attracted increased support, and the growth of Colonel François de la Rocque's Croix de Feu was meteoric. Some began to look toward the authoritarian solutions of France's neighbors.

The growth of the right-wing paramilitary leagues in the mid-thirties reflected a weakening of the stalemate consensus, brought about in part by the introduction of many younger and previously nonpolitical people into the political arena. They were mobilized by new issues for which most of the preexisting French political parties were unprepared. Most parties in France had not been formed around questions of economic and social balance or foreign affairs because these issues had constituted the basis of the consensus. When they became major political issues in the 1930's, the parties were unable to deal effectively with them, unable to formulate coherent policies or obtain agreement among their own members.[14] The result was formation of dissident groups such as the Jeunesses Pat-

[14]Hoffmann, "Paradoxes," p. 25.

riotes and Croix de Feu, along with the growth of the older Action Française on the far Right and the Neo-Socialists and Frontistes on the Left. None of these groups were fascist, although Action Française has sometimes been considered so. With the exception of Action Française, none of these challenged the Republic itself. What they wanted was a stronger executive and an end to parliamentary immobilism.

French fascist movements were reactive in a double sense. First, they were reactions against the stalled society and its republican consensus. Second, even within the more traditional protest groups during the interwar years, dissident factions formed which began to look for answers in a fascist reconstruction. The result was a continuing process of fracture among the dissident movements in which ever more radical groups appeared without, however, undermining the republican consensus against which all of them fought. The Munich accords of 1938, splitting the French fascists between nationalism and ideological solidarity, contributed to the fracturing process. With the defeat of 1940, the antiparliamentary dissidents were split yet again over the issue of collaboration with or resistance to the German occupiers. The formation of the collaborationist groups was part of a continuing process of fissure within dissident movements that had begun during the crises of the interwar years. They became minorities within the minorities.

Stanley Hoffmann has pointed out that many of those who embraced collaborationism after 1940 knew very little about Nazi Germany. Instead they chose it as a way to gain an upper hand in longstanding quarrels with domestic political enemies. Frustrated for so long in their oppositional politics, they saw in the German victory a chance for revenge. What Hoffmann calls a "Franco-French" civil war erupted violently in 1944.[15]

The three major collaborationist movements had different pedigrees, but all of them resulted from what Eugen Weber has called the impatience of a new generation of political leaders, a search for something new.[16] Spokesmen for all the factions took great pains to point out their antecedents in pre-1940 France. Doriot's PPF and Marcel

[15]Hoffmann, "Collaborationism," pp. 376–377.
[16]See Eugen Weber, *Varieties of Fascism* (New York: Van Nostrand Reinhold, 1964), pp. 138–139.

Bucard's Francistes predated the war. Déat repeatedly invoked his interwar departure from Marxist socialism in his espousal of national socialism after 1940, and Eugène Deloncle viewed his Mouvement Social Révolutionnaire (MSR) in 1940 as a continuation of his interwar activities in the extremely Rightist *Cagoulard* organization. Darnand and many of his close aides in the Milice were dissidents from Action Française, as was Deloncle.

The PPF originated among a group of Communist dissidents. Doriot had led the Communist street fighters in the 1934 February Days and had called for unity of the Left in advance of Moscow's adoption of the Popular Front line. Expelled from the party for breach of discipline the same year, Doriot took with him much of his personal backing in Saint-Denis and two years later founded the PPF. He had always been more attuned to local French audiences than was party head Maurice Thorez, whose orientation was more clearly toward Moscow. The PPF claimed to focus upon the nation rather than the proletariat, and Doriot's resentment against the Communists for expelling him and then adopting his strategy helped color the new party in strongly anticommunist hues. As had Mussolini earlier, Doriot turned away from a Marxism he believed outdated in its neglect of the nation and its failure to rally the lower middle classes and peasantry. His evolution toward fascism was completed only after 1940 but in 1936 the PPF was already attracting fascist intellectuals such as Pierre Drieu la Rochelle, who expounded a personality cult of Doriot as a charismatic fascist chieftain. Drieu helped elaborate a party doctrine emphasizing nationalism, corporatism, and the youth cult characteristic of interwar fascist movements elsewhere in Europe.[17]

As Doriot moved away from his Communist views and the PPF

[17]Plumyène and Lasierra, p. 110, contend that the PPF was the only authentic French fascist party in the 1930's. In a more detailed analysis of Doriot and the PPF, Dieter Wolf argues that although literary supporters such as Drieu la Rochelle openly embraced fascism during the PPF's early years, Doriot did not take an openly fascist stance until after 1940. See Wolf, *Die Doriot-Bewegung, Ein Beitrag zur Geschichte der französischen Faschismus* (Stuttgart: Deutsche Verlags-Anstalt, 1967), pp. 224–225. See also Gilbert D. Allardyce, "The Political Transition of Jacques Doriot," in Walter Laqueur and George L. Mosse, eds., *International Fascism, 1920–1945* (New York: Harper Torchbooks, 1966), pp. 73–74. Doriot is seen as a fascist chieftain in Drieu la Rochelle, *Avec Doriot* (Paris: Gallimard, 1937).

32

adopted openly fascist positions, it began to attract men with large business interests, such as the steel magnate Pierre Pucheu, who wanted to use the new party as a vehicle to move the "stalled" society in a technocratic direction. It also attracted some members from the lower middle classes, the "losers" in the modernization process, to use the term of one historian. They were drawn to the PPF as Doriot increasingly championed their interests, which they saw threatened by the Popular Front government.[18] The PPF claimed nearly 300,000 members in January 1938, grouping together mutually antagonistic big-business and lower-middle-class interests in a mix typical of most fascist movements. Added to this was the contingent of Communist cadres and followers taken by Doriot from Saint-Denis.[19]

The interwar fragmentation of the French Left was reproduced in part, in inverted form and smaller scale, in the rivalry between Doriot and Déat for leadership of the collaborationist camp. A former Socialist, Déat had criticized the party of Léon Blum for focusing exclusively on the proletariat at the expense of the rest of the French community. In a book, *Perspectives Socialistes*, published in 1930 by the former Faisceau leader Georges Valois, Déat argued for a broad coalition of all "anticapitalist" social strata, presaging the Popular Front. Like Doriot, he was searching for something new, different from the seemingly outdated proletarian orientation of the Marxist parties. He found it in the Saint-Simonian economic planning theories of the Belgian Socialist Henri de Man.

Criticizing the Socialist party for too narrowly addressing only the proletariat, Déat urged instead a more centrist coalition with the Radicals in 1933. Together with Barthélemy Montagnon and Adrien Marquet, Déat challenged Blum for ignoring potentially "an-

[18]The higher proportion of *employés* and middle-class elements in Doriot's PPF following in Saint-Denis compared to his earlier Communist following there is brought out in Jean-Paul Brunet, "Réflexions sur la scission de Doriot (février-juin 1934)," *Le Mouvement Social*, 70 (January–March 1970), 47. See also Wolf, p. 162. Fascist appeal to the "losers" in the modernization process is analyzed by Wolfgang Sauer, "National Socialism: Totalitarianism or Fascism?" *American Historical Review*, 73 (December 1967), 417. For the role of big business support of French fascist movements in general and Pucheu's interest in the PPF during the 1930's, see Klaus-Jürgen Müller, "French Fascism and Modernization," *Journal of Contemporary History*, 11 (October 1976), 85–86.

[19]PPF party membership claims for the interwar years are given in Wolf, p. 159.

ticapitalist" peasants and lower middle classes. In November 1933, Déat, Montagnon, Marquet, and twenty-four other likeminded deputies were expelled from the Socialist party. They established the Parti Socialiste de France, better known as the Neo-Socialists, as a centrist-leaning splinter group from the Socialists.

The Neo-Socialists also criticized the internationalism of Blum and the Socialists, especially with the formation of the Popular Front and its link to the Communists. Committed to what they called "pacifism"—specifically, opposition to another war with Germany— the Neo-Socialist leaders and many others from all shades of the French political spectrum charged that the Popular Front was risking a French war with Germany for the sake of Moscow. By the time of Munich in 1938, the French political community from Left to Right was split among so-called "bellicistes," hawks in today's parlance, those who believed France had to resist the growing Axis threat, and "pacifists," who wanted at all costs to avoid another war with Germany. Many of the "pacifists," who opposed war with Nazi Germany in the 1930's were later quite willing to fight against the Soviet Union.

By the late 1930's, Déat and Doriot, despite temperamental and programmatic differences, typified many in France who sought to overcome economic stagnation by means of a stronger executive vis-à-vis the parliament,[20] while avoiding all risk of war with Germany. Déat remained a supporter of the Third Republic up to 1940 and defended the concept of an authoritarian republic even afterward, but his articles and books after 1936 paid more attention to order than to liberty, and he began to flirt with the idea of corporatism. In May 1939, his widely publicized newspaper article entitled "Faut-il mourir pour Dantzig?" (Must one die for Danzig?) expressed the

[20]Doriot's decision to work through legal channels within the parliamentary system is discussed by Wolf, p. 222 and the similar tendency of most of those in the interwar French radical Right by Müller, pp. 94–95. The basis of Déat's Neo-Socialist ideas was laid out in the *Perspectives socialistes* (Paris: Valois, 1930). For the sequence of events surrounding the Neos' split from the Socialist party, see Charles Bloch, *Die Dritte Französische Republik. Entwicklung und Kampf einer Parlamentarischen Demokratie (1870–1940)* (Stuttgart: K. F. Koehler, 1972), pp. 397–398. See also Philippe Machefer, *Ligues et fascismes en France (1919–1939)* (Paris: Presses Universitaires de France, 1974), pp. 17–18. Machefer's book appears in the series Dossiers Clio.

feelings of a significant segment of French opinion, which in 1939 lacked the unity and élan of 1914.

After 1940, Déat drew support mainly from those who had been aligned against the Popular Front for its cooperation with Communists at home and its anti-Axis stance abroad. These included former Neo-Socialists and non-Communist members of the Confédération Générale du Travail (CGT), who had sometimes lost positions in that organization upon the reintegration of Communist trade unions into it at the time of the formation of the Popular Front. When the CGT was banned under the occupation, some of its anti-Communist members joined René Belin in working for the Vichy government, but others with their base of support in the northern zone found Déat more congenial.[21] Déat also attracted support after the armistice, as did Doriot, from lower-middle-class elements drawn by his rhetoric, which championed their interests against Vichy-supported trusts. Having feared the 1936 strikes as harbingers of "Red" revolution, they looked to Déat as an alternative to big business and big labor.

The move toward "pacifism" was the first step away from Germanophobia for many who were to accept full collaboration after 1940. During the occupation Déat repeatedly invoked the tradition of Jaurès and Briand, whose commitments to individual liberty he overlooked in an attempt to root Germanophile politics in the French Socialist past. Steeped in the thought of Kant, Hegel, and Marx, Déat and some of his ex-Socialist backers remembered the preeminence of the German Social Democratic party within the Second International prior to the 1917 Revolution in Russia.[22]

The same process of fission that splintered an already fragmented Left after 1934 was also at work within the French Right. The parliamentary Right was confronted by the rise of an extraparliamentary new Right in the form of paramilitary leagues including the Croix de Feu and the Jeunesses Patriotes. Old and new Right were both stridently nationalist and socially conservative. After the Popular Front government dissolved the leagues in 1936, they were

[21]Paxton, p. 277.
[22]Deat's Germanophile intellectual proclivities of the years between the wars were discussed in an interview accorded me by one of his supporter's in the RNP, July 13, 1973.

converted into political parties which emerged to challenge the older Fédération Républicaine for domination of the right-wing camp.[23]

Several factors went into the protest of the new Right. The First World War had raised expectations among the soldiers for a better life after their many sacrifices. France, however, emerged poorer after 1918 than she had been four years earlier. After the war, veterans began to organize to defend their interests. Some, although a distinct minority, militarized by their years in the trenches, joined the radical Right paramilitary leagues. While most veterans maintained the centrist political leanings they had held earlier as civilians, a few such as Marcel Bucard, Eugène Deloncle, and Joseph Darnand emerged as leaders of the radical Right. The Stavisky scandal of 1934 discredited parliament in their eyes, and the strikes of 1936 seemed to portend Communist revolution. Significantly, the first Rightist leagues after the Dreyfus years developed contemporaneously with the Cartel des Gauches, the leftist government of 1924.[24]

A minority of French businessmen, representing rapidly modernizing industries such as oil, electricity, and automobiles, supported the leagues. Movements such as Valois' Faisceau were seen as vehicles to open the stalled society to the structural changes needed to facilitate the expansion of newer and more dynamic industries. Ernest Mercier and other industrialists organized to effect changes in the technocratic tradition of Saint-Simon and supported the politicization of the veterans' groups. François Coty and Jean Hennessy, perfume and liquor magnates, respectively, gave financial support to the right-wing leagues, and the interest of Pucheu in Doriot's PPF has been mentioned. Eugène Schueller of L'Oréal perfumes backed the far Right political activities of Deloncle before and after 1940. A naval engineer, Deloncle exemplified the technocratic tradition in French fascism. For a brief time in 1941 he joined Déat at the head of the collaborationist RNP. Despite their differing political origins, both

[23]William D. Irvine, "French Conservatives and the 'New Right' during the 1930s," *French Historical Studies*, 8 (Fall 1974), 559.
[24]Hoffmann, "Paradoxes," p. 25. The veterans and their political orientation are examined by René Rémond, "Les anciens combattants et la Politique," *Revue française de science politique*, 5 (April–June 1955), 274–275, and Robert J. Soucy, France: Veterans' Politics Between the Wars," in Stephen R. Ward, ed., *The War Generation: Veterans of the First World War* (Port Washington, N.Y.: Kennikat Press, 1975), pp. 97 and 99.

men were able to agree on a program of anti-Communist industrial modernization.[25]

The fragmentation of the Right in interwar France was compounded by a series of splits within Charles Maurras' Action Française, itself the most extreme right-wing movement in France in 1918. Despite the continued virulence of its anti-Republican propaganda between the wars, Action Française was weakened by several factors, not the least being the aging of its leadership. Younger members often turned against Maurras' preoccupation with rhetoric at the expense of action, especially after his failure to effect a counter-revolutionary coup in February 1934. Those who sought modernization under the authoritarian Right were often dissidents from Action Française, as shown by Valois in the mid-twenties and Deloncle a decade later. Maurras and his movement seemed to them as stagnant as the Republic against which they rebelled. Another dissident from Action Française was the war hero Darnand. Militarized by his experiences in the trenches, Darnand became the incarnation of a latter-day crusader whose authoritarian military spirit and anti-Communism led him to the leadership of Vichy's collaborationist Milice in 1943.

The process of continual fragmentation at the fringes that splintered the Left in the interwar years also destroyed any chance for unity on the Right. Among the lower middle classes hurt by the depression, the business leadership in search of a vehicle for modernization, and discontented youth seeking to emulate its elders among the war veterans, it was not unusual for an individual to join and then leave a succession of right-wing leagues. The continuing process of fission reflected the French political community of many small ideological parties against which the protest from the far Right was being made. It also shaped the history of the collaborationist camp, afflicted with a continuing fragmentation that destroyed any remote possibility of effective political action under the occupation.[26]

---

[25]French business "outsiders" and their influence in the modernizing tendencies of the interwar radical Right are considered in Müller, pp. 82–84. See also Claude Willard, "Quelques aspects du fascisme en France avant le 6 février 1934," in Jacques Chambaz, *Le Front Populaire pour le pain, la liberté et la paix* (Paris: Editions Sociales, 1961), pp. 195–196.

[26]Bloch, pp. 386–387. See also Stanley Hoffmann, "Protest in Modern France,"

The tide of the radical Right crested in 1936 and 1937 with the rise of the Popular Front. There was no problem for the French Right in supporting Franco in the Spanish Civil War in 1936, but the Munich crisis two years later gravely weakened it. Doriot's PPF was badly split between those who supported appeasement at Munich for ideological reasons and those whose sense of nationalism prevented them from conceding what they perceived as essential French interests. When Doriot came out for appeasement in 1938, many of his leading backers left and his party entered a period of dormancy from which it was revived only by the German occupation.

In addition to the foreign policy dilemma, the radical Right movements were weakened in 1938 by the Daladier government, which practiced what has been called "de la Rocquism without de la Rocque."[27] Daladier's policy satisfied most of the radical Rightists who, as in February 1934, wanted only a more authoritarian executive and a conservative social policy. The Croix de Feu and the Jeunesses Patriotes, the largest of the interwar paramilitary leagues, more conservative than fascist, and transformed into political parties after the dissolution of the leagues, were satisfied by the Daladier cabinet in 1938 and 1939. It took the shock of 1940 to sever the attachment of the middle classes to the republican consensus and revive the possibilities of the radical Right.[28]

With the defeat of 1940, the "pacifist" dissidents were given new political life. Many arrested as "defeatists" by the Daladier government after the outbreak of the war reemerged as self-proclaimed Cassandras in July 1940. The occupation and the disappearance of the Republic facilitated the emergence of a new French fascism based on old dissidences and provided the opportunity for the settlement of some personal political scores. The defeat, which discredited the Republican parliamentary elite, opened the way to those who had been outsiders during the interwar years. To many of the collaborationists the events of 1940 showed the emergence of a new superior German man produced by fascism, a toughened virile *homo fascista,* according to the fascist writer Robert Brasillach. Some of

in Morton A. Kaplan, ed., *The Revolution in World Politics* (New York: Wiley, 1962), p. 77.

[27]See Hoffmann, "Protest," p. 78, n. 11, and Bloch, p. 504.

[28]Müller, p. 98 and Sorlin, pp. 139–140.

those who later enlisted in German military formations, the Waffen-SS in particular, wished to prove that Frenchmen could equal the exploits of the smartly uniformed young German warriors they had seen parade in victory down the Champs-Elysées in June 1940. They believed that they were reasserting the existence of a virile French manhood that would form the elite corps of a new fascist France, very different fron the stagnant society of the interwar years. During the early years of the occupation, collaborationists could combine their romantic fascist identification with a feeling of political realism. Loyalty to the New Europe, they believed, might win tor defeated France a place of preeminence in German-dominated Europe. Many hoped that a collaborationist France would supplant Italy as second-in-command in the New Order. In Vichy and in Paris there was much discussion of France's mission in administering North Africa on behalf of Europe. Collaborationists wished to forestall Italian designs on Nice, Corsica, and Tunisia by bringing France eagerly into Germany's New Europe.[29]

During their turbulent history, the collaborationists tried repeatedly to rouse the masses to the kind of fever pitch they associated with the mass rallies of Italy and Germany. Most of their popular support was urban and they flourished primarily in Paris, not only because of German protection, but because of the relatively larger numbers of the dislocated and alienated there as opposed to the more agrarian unoccupied southern zone controlled by Vichy. There were more unemployed in the Paris region than in the countryside and many of these joined radical Right movements before and after 1940. An estimate in 1935 showed 10 percent of the work force unemployed in the departments of Seine and Seine-et-Oise. A third of France's unemployed were found in Paris and its environs. Other large cities followed.[30] None of the collaborationist movements were able to sink substantial roots into the countryside in France. There was no follow-up after 1940 to the Green Shirt peasant movement led by

[29]On the personal qualities of twentieth-century *homo fascista,* see Robert Brasillach, *Notre avant-guerre* (Paris: Plon, 1941), p. 235, Maurice Bardèche, *Qu'est-ce que le fascisme?* (Paris: Les Sept Couleurs, 1961), pp. 191–192, and the discussion in Robert J. Soucy, "The Nature of Fascism in France," in Laqueur and Mosse, pp. 49–51.

[30]Sorlin, p. 108.

Henri Dorgères in the mid-1930's and described by one historian as "quasi-fascist." Dorgères had claimed 35,000 followers before the war, but after 1940 most of these were attracted to Marshal Pétain and offical Vichy's emphasis upon the virtues of rural life. Dorgères himself became a fervent supporter of the marshal, and when eventually he turned away from Vichy it was in the direction of the Resistance. Ideologically similar to fascism, the Green Shirt movement had distrusted all politicians during the 1930's and maintained a certain distance from the right-wing leagues. Dorgères and Doriot had appeared together at a few rallies but the peasant leader refused to allow any of his associates to join Doriot's Front de la Liberté, the PPF leader's attempt to unify the interwar Right.[31]

Continually mistrustful of "politicians" and refractory to political organization, the peasants stayed away from the collaborationist parties. Those who collaborated or in any way favored Germany preferred to do so in their traditional individualistic way. There was no organized peasant collaborationism. By the latter stages of the war, peasants were in a better position than were some of their urban compatriots to see clearly how much of France's natural and human resources was being used to feed Germans and support the Axis war effort.

It is hardly surprising that many should choose collaboration in 1940. The entire French social, political, and intellectual order had been put in question by the defeat, and the attitude of many was epitomized in the archcollaborationist book *Les décombres* by Lucien Rebatet, published in 1942. Thousands of French men and women joined the various collaborationist factions and thousands more sympathized. Several thousand young men volunteered to serve in the Anti-Bolshevik Legion, created by the Ultra groups in 1941, the Waffen-SS, and other German military formations. They were willing to give their lives in German uniforms, fighting for Hitler's New

[31] Dorgères and his Green Shirts are discussed by Gordon Wright, *Rural Revolution in France: The Peasantry in the Twentieth Century* (Stanford, Cal.: Stanford University Press, 1968 [original edition, 1964]), pp. 51–52, where he calls the Green Shirts "quasi-fascist," and 76, where he discusses the devotion of Dorgères to Pétain. See also Pascal Ory, "Le Dorgérisme: institution et discours d'une colère paysanne (1929–1939)," *Revue d'histoire moderne et contemporaine,* 22 (April–June 1975), 175 for a discussion of Dorgères' relations with Doriot before 1939, and 182 for consideration of the peasant leader's strong *Maréchaliste* position after the armistice.

Order on the frozen battlefields of the Soviet Union, firm in their conviction that in fighting for Hitler they were also fighting for France.

As political parties the collaborationist movements were small. Except for the Groupe Collaboration headed by the writer Alphonse de Châteaubriant, which claimed approximately 100,000, it is unlikely that any of them possessed more than 30,000 members at any one time during the occupation. The Groupe Collaboration was more a cultural organization than a political party seeking power. Except for the Communists, French political parties have traditionally been small, and it is impossible to gauge with precision the numbers of sympathizers for the various Ultra factions. Taken together, they formed a small but by no means insignificant minority of the French population between 1940 and 1944. A recent French study of the collaboration points out that after the Liberation there were almost as many cases brought before the special courts created to try collaborators as there were cards given out officially certifying membership in the Resistance.[32] Their potential strength, however, was blunted by the continuing process of fission which produced half a dozen competing political groups.

For all their weaknesses, divisions, and internal contradictions, the collaborationists represented one response of a proud people to a profound humiliation. It was the response of those among the French population who even before the war were turning toward fascism to move the stalled society. Frustrated politically during the interwar years, they sought help from a powerful new ally, the enemy of 1939, with whom France remained legally at war after the signing of the armistice in 1940. They became so thoroughly identified with the losing side and the brutality of German occupation policies in France, "dirtying their hands" in close affiliation with the Nazi regime, that for years they received scant attention from French historians.

Literary figures such as Drieu la Rochelle and Robert Brasillach have attracted significant scholarly study. The publicity with which these writers wore their fascism, together with the accessibility of their writings, which are highly personal and psychologically revealing, has made them fruitful sources for historical inquiry. Less prom-

[32]Ory, *Les collaborateurs*, p. 271.

inent but no less significant were the political leaders and their followings to whom the German occupation opened a new scope for action. These movements comprised the expression in France of the "epoch of fascism" that swept Europe and unleashed within the Western world a bloody and destructive civil war. It is time for a closer look at the losers in the French theater of the 1939–1945 world upheaval. [33]

[33]A full discussion of the literature on the collaboration is provided in the Bibliographical Note at the end of the book.

1 The Gathering:
Vichy, July 1940

Pierre Laval told us calmly, as if he were quite unconscious of the enormity he was relating, that he had offered the Field-Marshal the entry of France into the war against England. Von Brauschitch had received this offer with contempt. "We have no need of your assistance, which would in any case be of little account."

—Paul Baudouin, *Private Diaries*, August 30, 1940

As the victorious German army moved south through France in June of 1940, millions of Frenchmen preceded them in panic-stricken droves. Having abandoned Paris to the enemy, the government also migrated south, first to Bordeaux, then during the early days of July to the small resort town of Vichy. Marshal Pétain, the last premier of the Third Republic, had negotiated with the Germans an armistice by which three-fifths of France, including Paris and most of the more industrial north, lay under direct German military occupation. The southern two-fifths of the country were to remain free of German occupation forces and Vichy, in the unoccupied zone, was chosen as the provisional capital.

In July 1940, Vichy, a small town known for its mineral water, was jammed with government officials trying to adjust to new working routines and the defeat and occupation. They were joined by all sorts of politicians and would-be politicians attempting to determine their role in the new National Revolution being enunciated by the government of Marshal Pétain. Having obtained an armistice, the Pétain government next addressed the task of developing a new political structure for France. Few at Vichy dared to speak out in defense of the Third Republic, which had drawn widespread opprobrium following the defeat. Pétain, the victor at Verdun in 1916, had in his own words "made a gift of his person" to the French, who hoped that somehow his great personal prestige would shield them from the more severe exactions of the Germans. Pétain had served the Republic loyally but he had been no friend of the parliamentary system with its

43

many political parties which, he believed, had gravely weakened France in the face of a united and determined enemy. To many in France the National Revolution meant Pétain, and in the confusion and despair of July 1940, they were satisfied to give him free rein.[1]

It soon became apparent that the eighty-four year old marshal was going to be heavily dependent on those around him. These people shared the marshal's antipathy to the parliamentary Republic. Justice Minister Raphaël Alibert was a royalist of Action Française. General Maxime Weygand, the commander of the army, and Admiral Jean-François Darlan, raised to a new importance by the undefeated status of the navy and its role as the only military service left intact to France by the terms of the armistice, both favored authoritarian regimes. The most important role in the creation of the new French state was played by Pierre Laval. Unlike the others, Laval had functioned successfully in parliament and had twice been premier under the Third Republic. He threatened and cajoled the members of the National Assembly gathered in Vichy and was the driving force behind the combined 569 to 80 vote of the Senate and Chamber of Deputies on July 10, giving Pétain the power to draw up a new constitution, based upon "labor, family, fatherland."

The new French state was to be authoritarian. It was to be "social" as well, and the Vichy Labor Charter of 1941 was an attempt to move France in a corporatist direction, to avoid class conflict, and to defuse Marxist revolutionary movements. Vichy corporatism went back to the early nineteenth-century romanticization of medieval society and resembled Fascist doctrine in Italy. Late nineteenth- and early twentieth-century Christian social thought, largely but not exclusively Catholic, had also borrowed heavily from the romanticized corporatist tradition. Corporatism tended to magnify the roles of the artisan and peasant classes in society. It was embraced by the leadership of a National Revolution that sought solace and renewed strength in the traditional values of family, village, and soil. Yet it also offered big business a way to rationalize the economy without disturbing existing social relationships. The National Revolution

[1] For discussions of Pétain's personality and political ideas, see Henri Michel, *Vichy année 40* (Paris: Robert Laffont, 1966), pp. 107–115, and Robert Aron, *The Vichy Regime, 1940–44*, trans. Humphrey Hare (Boston: Beacon, 1969 [original French edition: 1955]) pp. 122–123.

wished to appropriate the strengths of the totalitarian powers but also create a conservative rather than a fascist France under the benevolent rule of Pétain the Father.

Not all who gathered in Vichy in July, 1940, shared the marshal's view of the National Revolution. Former Interior Minister Georges Mandel had wished to continue the struggle against the Axis from French North Africa, but a departure on June 21 for Casablanca had been aborted politically by Laval.[2] Others paid the usual compliments to the marshal but wished to push France further in the direction of Hitler's New Order. A manifesto signed by sixty-nine, including many members of parliament, was read at the session of July 9. Denouncing the Third Republic, the manifesto called for the establishment of a single mass party led by parliamentarians who had opposed the war in 1939. Similar to the single parties in Germany, Italy, Spain, and the Soviet Union, this party was to incorporate people of all political origins to serve as an intermediary between the marshal and the people. The manifesto was written by Gaston Bergery and the parliamentary lobbying for it led by Marcel Déat.[3]

Bergery, a former Radical, like Déat had been repudiated by his own party for attempting to create a unified Left in the immediate aftermath of the February 1934 riots. Isolated, he had later created a movement of his own, Frontisme (Frontism), which he represented alone in the Chamber of Deputies. Bergery published a newspaper, La Flèche, in which he criticized the parliamentary regime and called for unity against both capitalists and Communists. In September 1939 he was the only deputy to vote against the war credits sought by the Daladier government.[4]

Déat was a talented political columnist and a highly literate man of ideas. An Auvergnat, he had been graduated from the Ecole Normale Supérieure and through the study of Kantian and Hegelian philosophy had been drawn intellectually to socialism. He had served with distinction during the First World War, rising to the rank of captain,

[2]Aron, p. 51.

[3]Henri Du Moulin de Labarthète, Le temps des illusions: souvenirs (juillet 1940–avril 1942) (Brussels: Cheval Ailé, 1946), p. 30. See also Michel, pp. 64–65 and 105–106.

[4]For discussion of Bergery see Paxton, p. 214 and p. 214n, and also William L. Shirer, The Collapse of the Third Republic (New York: Simon & Schuster, 1966), p. 231.

and emerging with five citations. After World War I, Déat turned to teaching, married one of his students, and was subsequently elected as a Socialist to the Chamber of Deputies. His deviation from Socialist orthodoxy and his break with Léon Blum had led to the formation of Neo-Socialism. The Neos remained with the political Left, and Déat served as aviation minister in the brief Albert Sarraut government early in 1936.

Déat spent the 1930's in and out of the Chamber of Deputies, winning elections in several constituencies and representing Angoulême at the time of the outbreak of hostilities in 1939. Like Bergery he had supported the Munich accords of 1938 on the grounds that even unsatisfactory negotiations were preferable to good wars. What brought him to public prominence, however, was his article entitled "Faut-il mourir pour Dantzig?" published in the May 4, 1939 issue of L'Œuvre, a daily newspaper in Paris. Called by one historian "the most explosive article published in the world press between 1919 and 1939," it was a decided step toward the collaborationist position Déat was later to take.[5] With the declaration of war in September, Déat tried to enlist for service at the front, but found that to do so he would have had to resign his parliamentary seat. The collapse found him with his constituents in Angoulême from whence he made his way to Vichy when the government settled there in July 1940.

The impressive German military performance of 1940 convinced Déat that National Socialism had united the energies of the German people and had given her armies a revolutionary élan that had carried them to victory in the West. The revolution which the French had been incapable of making for themselves would now be imposed upon them by the conditions of life in a new Europe. Many times during the war Déat would compare the armies of Hitler to those of the First French Republic, spreading their revolutionary spirit across the Continent. The universalist ideal of liberty also spread across Europe by the French Revolution took second place in Déat's value system to the

---

[5]André Brissaud, *La dernière année de Vichy* (Paris: Librairie Académique Perrin, 1965), p. 93. See also Claude Varennes, *Le destin de Marcel Déat* (Paris: Janmaray, 1948), pp. 20–22. Varennes is the *nom de plume* for Georges Albertini, the secretary-general of Déat's Rassemblement National Populaire after 1941. For Déat's attitude toward the Popular Front, see his small book, *Le Front Populaire au tournant* (Paris: Edition du Journal La Concorde, 1937).

élan and community he sensed in German National Socialism. Demoralized by the divisiveness within the French body politic, Déat
and the other collaborationists clearly envied the sense of community
they felt National Socialism had given to the German people. It
appeared to have transcended social classes in the way that the interwar Neo-Socialists, PPF, and radical Right movements had sought to
do in France.

As the war progressed, Déat's support for National Socialism
deepened, but the basic commitment had been made during the first
days of the occupation. He would later repeat that from Neo-
Socialism to National Socialism was not, after all, so great a leap.
Convinced that Germany had won the war, Déat in his first newspaper column after the armistice called upon his compatriots to draw
requisite lessons from their recent experience and collaborate with
"revolutionary" Germany. The 1940 collapse seemed to offer Déat a
chance for the power to realize the *planisme* he had outlined a decade
earlier.[6] With singular purpose and determination, Déat would pro-
pound collaborationism in some 1,200 daily editorial columns over
the next four years.

During the early days of July, Déat took the lead in the campaign
to introduce a single-party system into France. The success of his
quest depended on the views of Marshal Pétain, who alone had the
legal and moral power to remake the French state. The effort to
establish a single party was launched amid favorable auspices but
by August it had been blocked effectively by a combination of interests
which held the marshal's ear. Pétain told Déat that a party would be
divisive and that he wished to govern all of France, not just part of it.
Henri Du Moulin de Labarthète, Pétain's *chef de cabinet*, advised the
marshal against accepting a proposal that would make France openly
fascist. In his memoirs Du Moulin recalls having advised Pétain to
defuse the single-party movement by sending its spokesmen as *missi
dominici*, in the fashion of Charlemagne, to study and report back to
Vichy on the morale in the various parts of France. Déat saw through
Du Moulin's scheme but others including Bergery and René Château,
the Socialist deputy from Charente, departed. The movement to create
a single party was broken.[7]

[6]Déat, "Au pied du mur," *L'Œuvre*, July 5, 1940.
[7]De Moulin de Labarthète, pp. 31–32.

Déat's plan also had other powerful antagonists. General Weygand opposed it as did Colonel de la Rocque, who aligned his Parti Social Français against it. Charles Maurras was also against the idea, and Action Française possessed a strong and growing influence in Vichy circles. Most important in derailing the single party was Laval, who in the early days of July had led Déat to believe that the plan would have his support. As Laval secured his own power base, however, the prospect of a strong single party which he might be unable to control appeared less attractive. Both Déat and Laval faced yet another opponent in the person of Jacques Doriot. The Parti Populaire Français had been France's largest profascist party before the war but it was sorely in need of a shot in the arm after its post-Munich decline. The collapse of the Republic presented it with new opportunities. Like Déat, Doriot envisioned a single party, his own, to govern France. None of the factions wanting a single party in the summer of 1940 were sufficiently powerful to impose their own control upon it, and to Pétain and Laval a single party could entail only the diminution of their own power. To avoid offending the Déat-Bergery group and possibly the Germans as well, they put the Du Moulin suggestion into operation. By August 1940 the weakness of those who wished to create a totalitarian France had become apparent.[8]

The failure of the single-party movement revealed to Déat the gap between his conception of the National Revolution and that held by official Vichy. On September 6, Pétain's cabinet was reshuffled and, with Laval the only exception, all its ex-parliamentary members were removed. Included in this group was Adrien Marquet, mayor of Bordeaux and one of the founders of the Neo-Socialists, who had been chosen as Vichy's first interior minister. Even Marquet had been unable to prevent extensive censorship by Vichy authorities of Déat's

[8]Publicly Déat blamed the PSF of de la Rocque and Action Française for the failure of the single-party project; see Déat interviewed by M. Dan, a Japanese correspondent, December 21, 1940, typescript in the Bibliothèque de Documentation Internationale et Contemporaine (BDIC) at the University of Paris X in Nanterre, Q pièce 600 Rés. In private, however, Déat blamed Laval; see Jean Berthelot, *Sur les rails du pouvoir (1938–1942)* (Paris: Robert Laffont, 1968), p. 96. De la Rocque's rejection of the single party is mentioned in Maurice Martin du Gard, *La chronique de Vichy, 1940–1944* (Paris: Flammarion, 1948), p. 71. See also Emily H. Goodman, "The Socialism of Marcel Déat," Ph.D., Stanford University, 1973), pp. 297 and 297, n. 7.

early columns in *L'Œuvre,* when the paper was being published temporarily in unoccupied Clermont-Ferrand.

Marquet's dismissal was a clear sign to Déat that Vichy would offer inhospitable soil for the realization of his goals for a new France. He moved to occupied Paris and the newspaper *L'Œuvre* shortly followed him there. With German help he was able to become political director of the paper, which before the armistice had been a paper of the moderate Left. For the next four years *L'Œuvre* served as the personal vehicle for Déat, who conducted a one-man editorial war against Vichy. Sparing only Pétain, Déat's biting articles rivaled in their intensity anything produced by the Resistance. In six editorial columns per week, Déat touched on all subjects with a constant anti-Vichy tone that became ever more strident and bitter as his frustration grew with the passing years.[9]

On October 11, 1940, a speech by Pétain temporarily rekindled Déat's optimism with respect to Vichy. Written at Pétain's request by Bergery, the speech called for collaboration with Germany and domestic reforms that would facilitate such collaboration. Anticapitalist in tone, the speech promised the creation of a strong France, social and authoritarian. The October 11 speech was part of an orchestrated campaign by Pétain to bring about an interview with Hitler, which took place at Montoire on the twenty-fourth of that month. The single-party idea was taken up by the government but transformed into the establishment of the Légion Française des Combattants, a veterans' league that was to collect the supposed elite of France into one organization, but a heterogeneous one with little political significance. Bergery was named ambassador to the Soviet Union. After the German invasion of the USSR, Vichy severed diplomatic ties to Moscow and Bergery was moved to the embassy in Ankara. With Déat in Paris and Bergery abroad, the single-party movement was for the time being quashed.[10]

---

[9]Picot, "Bericht über die deutsche Tätigkeit in Paris nach dem Stande von Mitte Oktober d. J. [1940]," Microcopy T-120/Serial 475/frame 229318. Materials from the collection of captured German war documentation are cited: microcopy number/ serial number/frame number in the footnotes that follow.

[10]Laval turned against Bergery in October 1940 when he learned that Bergery was proposing a single party that would exclude him. Laval blamed Bergery's plotting against him and his loquaciousness on this subject for the failure to see the message of October 11 translated into concrete action. See J. -M. Aimot, deposition in *France*

Déat and Bergery looked back to the Jacobin tradition of an authoritarian republic that mobilized popular enthusiasm around the national ideal but left intact property rights and the social structure of France. Déat especially stressed the totalitarian quality of the radical phase of the French Revolution. To Jacques Doriot, whose political career as a Communist and then as PPF leader had kept him outside the Republican establishment, Déat and Bergery were opportunists trying to thwart real change by maintaining in power those responsible for the debacle of 1940. Throughout the period of the occupation Doriot was to chide Déat for softness in promoting drastic changes and sweeping purges. Déat riposted in kind, charging Doriot with having been so corrupted by Communist agitprop tactics that he could only disrupt the "national" camp.

In the chaotic political situation of June 1940 in Paris, Doriot and his associate Marcel Marschall, the PPF mayor of Saint-Denis, attempted to make contact with the Germans. They approached Rudolf Schleier, an official of the German Foreign Ministry attached to the Wehrmacht in Paris. In his history of the PPF, Dieter Wolf indicates that nothing definite is known of the conversations and speculates that Doriot may have been testing German reaction to a possible PPF coup in Vichy. Finding no satisfaction in Paris, Doriot went to Vichy where the National Assembly was busy delegating constituent powers to Pétain. There Doriot denounced the influence of the parliamentarians, Déat and Bergery, in the committee among the proponents of the single party. The split between the hard-line Doriot and the more moderate Déat formed a mirror image of the Communist-Socialist split that had fractured the interwar French Left. More closely tied to the parliamentary past than any of his collaborationist rivals, Déat was never willing to go as far as they in the purge of "old regime" officials.[11]

Unlike the other leaders of the collaboration, Doriot came from working-class origins. The son of a blacksmith from Brittany, Doriot

during the German Occupation, 1940–1944: A Collection of 292 Statements on the Government of Maréchal Pétain and Pierre Laval, collected by Josée and René de Chambrun, trans. Philip W. Whitcomb, 3 vols. (Stanford, Cal.: Hoover Institution, 1957), 3:1098.

[11]Wolf, pp. 232–235. For one of Doriot's many broadsides against not only Déat and Bergery but also de la Rocque and Action Française, see Doriot, *Je suis un homme du maréchal* (*notes à leur date*) (Paris: Bernard Grasset, 1941), pp. 93–94.

was a tall, robust, impressive-looking man and a powerful public speaker with an element of charisma totally lacking in Déat. He became active at a young age in Communist politics and rose to be head of the French Communist Youth and to membership in both the Comintern and the Central Committee of the French Communist party. His fiery outbursts both in and out of the Chamber of Deputies led one French journalist to describe Doriot as "the living incarnation in France of the man with a dagger clenched between his teeth."[12]

By the early 1930's Doriot was bridling under what he felt to be the too rigid leadership of party head Maurice Thorez. Like Déat and Bergery, Doriot reacted to the February 1934 riots by seeking a broader popular base for an antifascist coalition than was furnished by his own party. Communist parties, however, were still under Moscow's order to oppose alliances with the non-Communist Left. When Doriot refused to toe the line he was summoned to Moscow. Whether Moscow was ready to offer him Thorez's place as the price for obedience, as rumors went, is questionable. Doriot refused the summons and was expelled from the party. When the Communists changed strategies and joined the Popular Front, Doriot found himself politically isolated on the Left. The result was the creation of the PPF, whose tendencies toward fascism have already been described. While the Communist party shifted to an antifascist stand by supporting the Popular Front, Doriot remained true to its earlier tactic of "revolutionary defeatism," which in the mid-1930's meant conciliation of Germany. Doriot's tactics survived his personal transformation but his goals did not. The same energy that he had given to the Left was now poured into efforts on behalf of the counterrevolutionary Right. Gravely weakened by Doriot's support of the Munich accords, the party was further sapped in 1938 by revelations of Italian financial aid. Doriot's support of Munich alienated some, including Drieu la Rochelle, who hoped that France might embrace fascism to mobilize her own resources more effectively against a growing threat from the Axis powers.[13]

---

[12]Jean Maze, *La Flèche,* March 21, 1936, cited in Allardyce, "The Political Transition of Jacques Doriot," p. 56.

[13]Drieu la Rochelle, "Mourir en démocrates ou survivre en fascistes?" October 28, 1938, in Drieu la Rochelle, *Chronique politique 1934–1942* (Paris: Gallimard, 1943), pp. 190–193.

51

During the summer months of 1940, Doriot repeatedly denounced the interwar leaders of the Third Republic and demanded their chastisement. The English attack on the French fleet at Mers-el-Kébir in Algeria on July 5 helped turn frustrated French anger against Great Britain, and Doriot called for swift reprisals against the English. He hoped that a strong anti-British move by France might induce the Germans to release at least some of the million and a half French prisoners they had taken during the May-June campaign. Professing loyalty to Marshal Pétain, Doriot established a Rassemblement pour la Révolution Nationale (Assembly for the National Revolution), the nucleus of a single party of his own. This movement included the rightist president of the Paris Municipal Council, Charles Trochu, and Marcel Gitton, the deputy from Pantin, secretary of the Communist party, and a member of its political bureau in 1939. Gitton and others had left the Communist party after the August 1939 Nazi-Soviet pact and they now joined previously disillusioned ex-Communists around Doriot.[14]

Unlike Marcel Déat, Doriot in the summer of 1940 had in his PPF a preexisting organization with which to work. He was, however, in an anomalous position. The Germans had forbidden political party activity in the occupied zone and the demarcation line, which the Germans used to seal off communications, made it difficult to coordinate any political activity between the two zones. In 1941 Vichy Interior Minister Pierre Pucheu, who had left the PPF for its pro-Munich stand, cracked down on nonofficial political activity in the southern zone and the party had to overcome legal impediments to its operation there. The PPF had had a particularly strong base before the war in Marseilles. Victor Barthélemy, another disillusioned ex-Communist who had joined Doriot in 1936, reorganized the party in the unoccupied zone after the armistice. The secretary-general of the PPF, Barthélemy had also represented Doriot on the committee for

<hr />

[14]Saint-Paulien, *Histoire de la Collaboration* (Paris: L'Esprit Nouveau, 1964), pp. 158-160. Saint-Paulien is the *nom de plume* for Maurice-Ivan Sicard, a member of the PPF political bureau during the war. For Doriot's earliest attempts to contact the Germans, see "Der Vertreter des Auswärtigen Amts bei dem Militärbefehlshaber in Paris an den Chef der Militärverwaltung Frankreich," Paris, July 15, 1940, in *Akten zur deutschen Auswärtigen Politik 1918–1945. Aus den Archiv des deutschen Auswärtigen Amts*, Series D, 1937–1945, vol. 10 (Frankfurt am Main: Keppler Verlag, 1963), document no. 170, p. 177.

the single party at Vichy. In the unoccupied zone and in French North Africa, which had seen especially strong PPF activity before the war, Barthélemy reorganized the party under the sobriquet "Les Amis de *l'Emancipation Nationale"* (Friends of *"Emancipation Nationale,"* a PPF newspaper published after the armistice in Marseilles). In the occupied northern zone PPF activity was reorganized under the name "Les Amis du Maréchal" (Friends of the Marshal). [15]

The relationship of Doriot and his party to the Germans in the summer of 1940 and before the German invasion of the Soviet Union has been described by Barthélemy as one of "prudent collaboration." The occupation provided Doriot and his partisans with opportunities to seek personal revenge on their political enemies, and Doriot is said to have threatened the life of Marx Dormoy, the Popular Front interior minister who had had Doriot removed from the mayoralty of Saint-Denis. In July 1941, Dormoy was assassinated and suspicion fell upon the PPF. The political opportunities provided by the occupation together with the ideological affinities between the PPF and National Socialist Germany impelled Doriot toward collaboration. However, there were serious impediments. German fears were repeated at intervals that Doriot was too uncontrollable for the purpose of keeping occupied France quiet.

A growing power in Paris during the summer of 1940 was Otto Abetz, Ribbentrop's representative on the Wehrmacht staff in Paris who was later named German ambassador to France. A Socialist prior to Hitler's accession to power, Abetz preferred politicians of the type of Laval and Déat to Doriot, whom he kept at arm's length. The Nazi-Soviet pact was also a problem for Doriot, to whom a burning anti-Communism was the most basic political issue. Some of the post-1939 recruits of the PPF were former Communists such as Gitton, who had left the party in opposition to the Nazi-Soviet pact so Doriot had to move cautiously. To Doriot the Communists played the villain's role in much the same way the Jews did for Hitler. Doriot had evidenced no signs of anti-Semitism before the war although this changed after the defeat of 1940.

During the early days of the occupation, the French Communists had reason to believe that they would receive aid from the Germans

[15]Author's interview with Victor Barthélemy, July 9, 1974.

and applied to them for permission to publish openly *L'Humanité,* which had been driven underground by the last Daladier government. German anti-Communism had been muted by the Nazi-Soviet pact and there were some in Berlin who had believed that Communist opposition to the war effort in France could be utilized for German aims. With the rapid defeat of France, however, German desires for France changed from disorder to stability and the Germans quickly lost interest in the French Communists. They might have been willing to allow the reappearance of *L'Humanité* in the early days of the occupation, but the project was blocked immediately by Vichy. The public pronouncements of Doriot and other PPF spokesmen openly embraced collaboration as soon as the armistice had been signed, but caution was necessary. Because of the Nazi-Soviet pact, Doriot and his friends could not give full expression to their anti-Communist wrath. Caught between the passionate anti-Communism of his supporters and German reserve on the issue in July 1940, Doriot turned his fire on the parliamentary leaders of the Third Republic and the Jews.[16]

It has been the nature of the counterrevolutionary Right to attempt to paper over deep social cleavages by creating the spirit rather than the substance of revolutionary change. To do this during the interwar and wartime years, "crusades" were continually being launched, whether Mussolini's "battle for grain" or some "mission" abroad. Such campaigns offered the appearance of militant revolutionary action to those who craved this excitement, especially in the dreary conditions of occupied France, but had no real interest in revolutionary change. These movements succeeded so well in creating the image of revolutionary action that they misled many of their own members, the "Left" fascists: Rocca in Italy, Roehm and the Strassers in Germany, and Drieu in the PPF. To keep the attention of his millenarian following, Doriot found new targets to attack when temporarily deprived of the Communists. Meanwhile he waited for Pétain to summon him to initiate the "real" National Revolution.[17]

[16]The account of Doriot's activities is from my interview with Victor Barthélemy, July 9, 1974. In this interview Barthélemy described himself as having been a professional revolutionary.

[17]The National Socialists were obliged to keep German society at a fever pitch in order to prevent the various antagonistic interests from recognizing their mutual

Like Déat, Doriot was finding Vichy a poor setting for his political activities in the late summer of 1940. The move toward a single party had failed and de la Rocque had ordered his supporters to back the marshal and eschew the Ultras. The colonel now became an object of scorn for collaborationists, who called him a tired reactionary. Convinced that Germany had won the war, Doriot was determined to stake out the collaborationist political ground for himself, anticipating that Laval and the others at Vichy would discredit themselves in the eyes of the Germans. On the international scene Doriot was frustrated in his attempts to produce a French reprisal against England after Mers-el-Kébir. Paul Baudouin, Vichy's foreign minister, told him in an interview that there were no plans to fight against England. Doriot was not told, of course, that the marshal's government was maintaining contacts with the British throughout the autumn of 1940.[18] With the failure of his plans in Vichy, Doriot returned to Paris in October and established the daily newspaper *Le Cri du Peuple* to express PPF political views. *L'Emancipation Nationale* was already performing the same function in Marseilles.

What united Doriot and Déat ideologically if not politically was their desire to end the stagnancy of French society. During the 1930's the Neo-Socialists and the PPF had become convinced that the Marxian concept of class conflict with revolution tied exclusively to the fortunes of the proletariat had grown obsolete. The Marxist Left, they felt, had failed to adjust to the new realities of France in the 1930's with its many millions of white-collar professionals of all types, artisans and small merchants and *employés,* peasants, and war veterans. What was needed, they argued, was solidarity, not polarization. The dissidents of the 1930's shared with many others the belief that France was growing old, that her fecundity, already in decline by 1914, had been dealt a crippling if not mortal blow by the First World War. In Italy and Germany they saw countries that appeared united with a sense of purpose. The German victory of 1940 convinced them that they had been right. The key to Axis success, according to the

hostility and tearing German society apart through social warfare. See David Schoenbaum, *Hitler's Social Revolution: Class and Status in Nazi Germany, 1933–1939* (New York: Anchor Books, 1967), p. 275; also Nolte, pp. 20–21.

[18]Paul Baudouin, *Neuf mois au government; mémoires* (Paris: La Table Ronde, 1948), pp. 293ff. Cited in Wolf, pp. 237, n. 788.

Ultras, was the one-party system which had united the Axis powers and mobilized their people. Openly imitative of their single-party neighbors, collaborationist spokesmen still looked to gallicize their movements. Early on, Déat wrote that the one-party French state would take its place in the German-dominated European New Order and that in time French civilization would smooth out the rough edges and soften the sharp totalitarianism of the New Europe. [19]

The rejection of the parliamentary tradition by both the new and the reemerging Ultra factions in 1940 was represented as a generational revolt against aging leadership. A gerontocracy was held to be at the helm of the Republic, many of whose leaders were old men such as Gaston Doumergue and Pétain. But although the groups formed by dissidents from the interwar Left tried to picture themselves as leaders of a new generation in revolt, there is little to indicate their success in capturing a significant segment of French youth. Nonetheless, in the name of youth they criticized not only the leaders of the Republic, but also the leaders of the established parties of the Left, particularly the Socialists.

A parallel phenomenon existed on the extreme Right. It was almost impossible to be involved in far Right French politics during the period between the wars without in some way having been influenced by Charles Maurras and the Action Française. An outgrowth of right-wing reaction to the Dreyfus Affair at the turn of the century, Action Française had been molded by Maurras and Léon Daudet into one of the major ideological forces of twentieth-century French political life. Aggressively royalist and clericalist, Maurras and Daudet welded traditional monarchism and federalism to a new urban nationalism and anti-Semitism. The integral nationalism that Maurras preached could be expressed, he argued, only in a restoration of the monarchy that over the centuries had built France into a great state. Looking to traditional France, Maurras combined his political doctrine with an emphasis on logic and classicism, traits which he believed characterized the eternal genius of France. Nourished by the *revanchiste* spirit of a France that had lost Alsace and Lorraine in 1871, Action Française castigated everything German, including the

[19]Déat, "L'étape totalitaire" and "Vocation de la France," L'Œuvre, August 22 and 23, 1940, respectively.

spirit of romanticism to which it referred as German obscurantism. Yet the classicism of Action Française coexisted in uneasy tension with the romantic spirit of many of its youthful militants. Action Française appealed to a nationalist middle-class intelligentsia and was particularly influential among the students in the Latin Quarter of Paris.

Because of the boldness with which Maurras attacked the Third Republic and its prominent figures and the violence of its militants, particularly in the universities, Action Française in its early years was able to muster an influence far beyond that warranted by its numbers. Things began to change after World War I. Maurras, who had been able to unite so many behind the demand for the return of Alsace and Lorraine, was deprived of his major rallying point when the provinces were restored to France. Middle age also began to cool his passion for action and although his columns in the newspaper *Action Française* remained as vitriolic as ever, the movement was increasingly passing from action to rhetoric. In 1925 Georges Valois broke away from Action Française to found the openly fascist Faisceau. The inactivity of Maurras during the February Days of 1934 confirmed the trend of the young away from his movement.[20]

The same process of stagnation and fragmentation that disrupted the interwar Left produced a succession of right-wing offshoots from Action Française. Valois was followed by Deloncle and Darnand. After the failure of his Faisceau in the late 1920's, Valois turned toward the Left. He died in a German concentration camp during the war. The later dissidents who quit Maurras after the 1934 Days were more inclined toward collaborationism. The collaborationist careers of Darnand and Deloncle contrasted sharply, however, in that the former continued Maurras' Germanophobic tradition into 1941 and turned only gradually toward collaboration. Only in 1943 when he emerged as leader of the Milice, did Darnand embrace full collaboration. Deloncle, on the other hand, came out immediately for collaboration in the summer of 1940 and moved away from it after 1942. He was to die in 1944 at the hands of the German police.

[20]For the break between Valois and Action Française, see Plumyène and Lasierra, pp. 36–38, and for a discussion of their differences after 1925, see Eugen Weber, *Action Française: Royalism and Reaction in Twentieth-Century France* (Stanford, Cal.: Stanford University Press, 1962), pp. 209–210.

A naval engineer, Deloncle had been an artillery officer during World War I and had been wounded and cited for bravery. In 1934 he joined Action Française, in which he became vice president of the relatively strong section in La Muette, Paris's sixteenth district. A staunch anti-Communist, Deloncle chafed under what he felt was the inactivity of Action Française, and in 1936 he established a secret organization, known by a number of names, whose steering committee was called the Comité Secret d'Action Révolutionnaire or CSAR.[21] The CSAR held that France was faced by an imminent threat from the Communists, against which Action Française had been insufficiently active. Secret, with elaborate initiation rites resembling those of the Freemasons, the CSAR was responsible for a wave of widely publicized political assassinations. Best known was the 1937 murder of the Roselli brothers, anti-Fascist refugees from Italy. Action Française tolerated no dissidence, and Maurice Pujo, one of its leaders, dubbed the CSAR the *cagoule* or "hood," as in hooded men. The reference was to the American Ku Klux Klan and the appellation stuck.

During 1936 and 1937 the CSAR was the talk of France. It shared with Action Française an admiration and support for Mussolini but the tactics of the two organizations were radically different. While Action Française kept up its war of words against the Republic, the CSAR engaged in assassinations and bombings and stockpiled arms in secret caches throughout Paris. It maintained very close ties with high ranking figures in the army and by 1937 was in contact with

[21]A useful account of Deloncle's political peregrinations after quitting Action Française is found in Bernard Voiron, "Deloncle Chef de la Cagoule fut abattu en janvier 1944 par la police allemande," *Europe-Amérique,* October 31, 1948, p. 24. Deloncle and some friends had created an ephemeral Parti National Révolutionnaire et Social, which was soon joined with other right-wing elements to form the Union des Comités d'Action Defénsive (UCAD) directed by General Edmond Duseigneur. The CSAR was apparently the steering committee for a larger movement called the Mouvement Social d'Action Révolutionnaire, a name strikingly familiar to the collaborationist Mouvement Social Révolutionnaire that was to figure prominently in the history of the Ultras after 1940. See the account of Col. Georges Groussard, *Chemins secrets* (Paris: Bader-Dufour, 1948), 1: 37–38. One last name by which the *Cagoulards* were known was Organisation Secrète d'Action Révolutionnaire Nationale (OSARN): see J. -H. Morin, "Vrais débuts du procès de la Cagoule," *Libération,* October 14, 1948. In organizations as clandestine as those headed by Deloncle, even the names are sometimes difficult to ascertain. They are, however, suggestive of the political direction taken by Deloncle and his associates.

Commander Georges Loustaunau-Lacau, who had organized an anti-Communist intelligence network known as "Corvignolles" within the French army.

The purpose of the Corvignolles was to root Communist subversion out of the army, but its leaders plotted with Deloncle's men to overthrow the Popular Front government then in power. The Communists were to be enticed into making a first strike, after which the CSAR and Corvignolles would respond with a countercoup and seize state power. Marshal Pétain was approached but remained cool to the project. Undaunted, the CSAR secured weapons and funds in preparation for a coup d'état. There were betrayals, however, within the CSAR, and police infiltration was able to block its plans by the end of 1937. *Cagoulard* leaders either were captured, sought refuge in hiding, or left for foreign exile. A surprised French public began to learn in part the intricate story of the *Cagoulard* conspiracies, assassinations, and arms stockpiles. The CSAR leaders, however, were not tried at the time and the occupation precluded a trial from being held. Only in 1948 were some of the surviving members brought to trial. Much of the history of the CSAR is still shrouded in mystery.[22]

With the outbreak of war in September 1939, many of the former *Cagoulards* were released from prison and others returned from exile to serve in the French war effort. Deloncle was attached to the navy where he served unenthusiastically in the 1939–1940 campaign. With the defeat and the armistice, Deloncle, like Doriot, Déat, and so many others, made his way to Vichy. The discrediting of the old political institutions and parties, which enabled some of the previously minoritarian factions from the prewar Left to move into the mainstream of French politics, provided similar possibilities for the Right. Deloncle was in Vichy to explore the various political options open to him there. A fervent anti-Communist, not ideologically oriented, and primarily concerned with action, he brought to the

---

[22]On the subject of CSAR assassinations, see "La Cagoule à Bagnoles-de-l'Orne," *Libération,* October 21, 1948. For the relationship between the CSAR and the army, see Commander Georges Loustaunau-Lacau, *Mémoires d'un Français rebelle, 1914–48* (Paris: Robert Laffont, 1948), pp. 114ff., and Philippe Bourdrel, *La Cagoule. 30 ans de complots* (Paris: Albin Michel, 1970), pp. 146ff. For Pétain's reaction to the conspiracies, see Jacques Szaluta, "Marshal Pétain's Ambassadorship to Spain: Conspiratorial or Providential Rise toward Power?" *French Historical Studies,* 8 (Fall 1974), 518–519 and 527.

political community at Vichy a temperament far different from that of the theoretician Déat.

As with the prewar PPF and Neo-Socialists, however, not all former associates of Deloncle in the *Cagoule* turned to collaboration after the 1940 armistice. The CSAR had taken a well-known anti-German stance during the thirties and one of its purposes in seeking to rid the army of Communist subversion had always been better to resist the German threat. The issue of "bellicism" and "pacifism" with respect to Germany during the 1930's had cut across party lines. Many on the Right retained their Germanophobia and blamed the Popular Front for weakening France in the face of the German danger. Action Française was pro-Latin, supporting Mussolini, Franco, and Salazar, but remained firmly anti-German, and many of Deloncle's associates had shared his own political origins in the movement of Charles Maurras. When Deloncle gathered many of his old supporters together in Vichy he found them split into three groups. Some opted for anti-German resistance and made their way to London where they joined General de Gaulle. Others told Deloncle that fidelity obliged them to follow Marshal Pétain and they would do what they could to strengthen France and resist the Germans by working within the marshal's government. Only a minority was willing to follow Deloncle, who was convinced that the Germans had won the war and chose open collaboration.

Deloncle had several options. Loustaunau-Lacau had moved to Vichy and had decided to resist the Germans from within the French military. He asked Deloncle to join him in procuring military intelligence on the Germans for the Vichy government. According to the account of Loustaunau-Lacau, who later joined the Resistance and ultimately survived the Mauthausen concentration camp, Deloncle was offered a signed paper stating that at Loustaunau-Lacau's order he was working for the Germans. Deloncle by this time had achieved a well-deserved reputation for his conspiratorial abilities. He hesitated, telling Loustaunau-Lacau that the Germans had already won the war and that it made more sense to work with them than against them. Loustaunau-Lacau never again saw Deloncle.[23]

[23]Loustaunau-Lacau, pp. 200–201, and Joseph Désert, *Toute la vérité sur l'affaire de la Cagoule: sa trahison, ses crimes, ses hommes* (Paris: Librairie des Sciences et des

If Deloncle had been coy in talking with Loustaunau-Lacau, he had been far more open in a letter to his wife, revealing his profound joy at witnessing the demise of the Republic and its leaders who had, he wrote, persecuted him. To this he added that he had played a not insignificant role in the demise but he made no specific reference. It is not clear whether he had in mind prewar *Cagoulard* activities; his orders of September 1939 telling his backers not to fight the Germans too vigorously; or something else. The British attack on the French fleet at Mers-el-Kébir particularly angered Deloncle, a navy man. The Mers-el-Kébir incident, his conviction that Germany had won the war, and his accumulated resentments led him to the path of collaboration. [24]

In the general sorting out of French political figures at Vichy, Deloncle flirted briefly with Doriot. The two men were seen together during the summer of 1940 but they fell out after several weeks. Deloncle could never forget that Doriot had been a Communist and his own *Cagoulard* conspiratorial past made him an object of suspicion to the PPF leader. In addition, each wished to be sole leader of the single party that was expected to result from the discussions of July and August 1940. Deloncle was also unsuccessful in his quest for a government post in Vichy. Pétain's justice minister, Raphaël Alibert, was a member of Action Française and shared its mistrust of the ex-*Cagoulard* chieftain. In a classic case of hostility between old and new Right, Alibert used his influence to keep Deloncle far removed from any possible influence in the government. He called Deloncle a bomb likely to explode at any time, bringing destruction to his allies. His evaluation of Deloncle was not inaccurate. Because the doors to government were closed to him and the prospects for successful political action in Vichy were bleak, Deloncle, like Doriot and Déat, left

---

Arts, 1946), pp. 60–61. The division of the *Cagoulards* after the armistice into London, Vichy, and Paris political directions is discussed in Bourdrel, pp. 214–242.

   [24]The letter from Deloncle to Madame Deloncle was revealed during the postwar *Cagoule* trial: see "Le 10 juillet 1940, Deloncle écrivait 'Mon rêve est à demi réalisé, la République n'est plus,'" *Libération,* November 17, 1948. At the same time his order to his Nice supporters to go easy in fighting the Germans was also brought out. See "Grand Chef de la Cagoule et du MSR Jacques Corrèze se défend âprement," *Libération,* October 7, 1948. For Deloncle's reaction to the Mers-el-Kébir incident, see Henry Charbonneau, *Les mémoires de Porthos,* 2 vols. (Paris: Editions du Clan, 1967), 1:334–335.

the provisional capital in September and returned to Paris. A number of his former lieutenants in the *Cagoule* remained in Vichy where they organized protection squads, which served as an elite praetorian guard for the marshal.[25]

By autumn 1940, Deloncle, Doriot, and Déat had returned to Paris, with Déat determined not to go back to Vichy until France had a new government. "Vichy," in the words of the historian Robert O. Paxton, "was not the triumph of the prewar leagues."[26] As Paxton points out, many of the ideas if not the leaders of the prewar leagues triumphed in 1940. Official Vichy, however, disdained the idea of the single party and Maurrasian Germanophobia was also felt there. Collaborationists spoke of a reversal of alliances with France joining the Tripartite Pact but Pétain, more cautious, sought in 1940 to keep a channel open to Britain. Pétain's government evolved through several phases during the four-year occupation. At first Maurrasian and highly traditionalist, the government in 1941 under Darlan shifted toward technocracy and economic collaboration. Only during the last few months of the occupation in 1944, when Resistance activity had greatly intensified, were any Ultras accepted into the cabinet and then only under German pressure. The familiar French pattern of political fragmentation assumed a new geographic form with Paris pitted against Vichy.

Denied power in Vichy, the Ultras returned to Paris where they established fascist movements. In Paris they might hope for support from the German occupation authorities. With its millions of citizens cut off from their traditional political attachments as a consequence of the German refusal to allow the leading parties of the Third Republic to operate, Paris offered a wide open political field to the Ultra leaders. The Ultras returned to a Paris that was seeking after the mass exodus of June to reconstruct as normal an urban life as possible in the presence of German occupation forces.

[25]Groussard, p. 110. On Alibert see Robert Aron, *The Vichy Regime,* p. 63.
[26]Paxton, p. 257.

2 Paris, 1940

Collaboration means: Give me your wristwatch, I will tell you the time.
—Jean Galtier-Boissière, *Mon journal pendant l'occupation*, December 30, 1940

While the men of Vichy were remaking the French state, the Germans installed their occupation services in many of the large hotels in Paris. Many who in June 1940 had fled the capital and northern France returned to their homes during the fall. Returning to Paris from the unoccupied zone in September, Jean Guéhenno described the capital as a dead city. The quais along the Seine, usually bustling with people, were desolate and the streets were deserted. He had come back, he wrote, to Thebes or Memphis rather than the Paris he had known. Even the birds were gone, killed by the burning of nearby oil and gasoline stocks which had spread a heavy black smoke over the city with the approach of the Germans. To the desolation of the streets was added a strange and depressing stillness in the trees and gardens. [1]

The German soliders had received strict orders to behave correctly toward the local population and as the weeks went by, the Parisians' initial fears began to subside. Contacts increased on both official and nonofficial levels as Germans and French attempted to define patterns of dealing with each other. Many in France expected a quick German victory over England, which they believed would shorten the duration of the armistice and hasten its replacement by a treaty of peace. If France played her cards right, they argued, she might receive a far better deal in the final peace treaty, a possibility Hitler kept tantalizingly in view. The German leader led the French to believe that if they cooperated in the defeat of the English, the impending settlement would be made at British expense. France might be allowed to slip off the hook. If the French proved recalcitrant, a compromise peace might be arranged between Germany and England

[1] Jean Guéhenno, *Journal des années noires* (*1940–1944*) (Paris: Gallimard, 1947), p. 47.

at the expense of France. As the victor, Germany was not to be expected to pay for the war.

While the Germans dangled various diplomatic scenarios before the French, they also began to organize the occupied zone to draw the maximum possible from it for their war effort and to use it as a base for the coming attack on England. According to the provisions of the armistice, the administrative jurisdiction of the Vichy government extended into the occupied zone, but the Germans rapidly excluded Vichy from any effective control there. The Nord and Pas-de-Calais departments were detached from the northern zone and placed under the administrative authority of the Brussels Wehrmacht command to facilitate coordination of invasion plans against the British Isles. Despite armistice stipulations that French territorial integrity was to be left intact, the departments comprising the Alsace-Lorraine territory taken by Germany in 1871 were annexed to the Reich, a move against which Abetz protested in vain. A Franco-German commission was established in Wiesbaden to implement the terms of the armistice but French protests often fell on deaf ears. Apart from the so-called "forbidden zone" of Nord and Pas-de-Calais, the occupied zone was administered by the Militärbefehlshaber in Frankreich (Military commander in France), first General Streccius, succeeded by General Otto von Stülpnagel. Theoretically the Militärbefehlshaber was concerned only with military matters relating to the security of the Wehrmacht in France and the planning of future campaigns. In reality, however, such a mandate gave the German military authorities power to intervene in virtually all aspects of French life. The Abwehr, the German military intelligence network, was established throughout both zones of France. In Paris, matters were complicated still further by the presence of Otto Abetz as Foreign Minister Ribbentrop's representative on the staff of the military command. In August, Ribbentrop elevated Abetz to the rank of German ambassador to France, but instead of establishing his embassy near the French government in Vichy Abetz remained in Paris.

There was also a propaganda staff, attached to the military command in Paris but taking its orders and receiving its material support from the foreign section of Goebbels' Propaganda Ministry in Berlin. Last but not least in importance was the SS of Reinhard Heydrich, who headed the RSHA (Reichssicherheitshauptamt), the umbrella

64

organization for all the German police services. Heydrich's representative in occupied France and Belgium was SS-Standartenführer Max
Thomas, one of whose subordinates, Karltheo Dannecker, was placed
in charge of an anti-Jewish department.[2]

As in Germany herself, the various administrations of Hitler's government competed for power in occupied France, and this meant that
different German services worked with different groups of French
collaborationists. The rivalry among the German services exacerbated
the fragmentation already present among the French Ultras. A
French party dissatisfied with one branch of the occupation authority
might receive better treatment from another. In turn, a German agency
might support a given Ultra faction in the hope of extending its own
influence within the German state apparatus. Each side could play
off the divisions within the other. Because the collaborationists were
dependent upon the Germans, however, they invariably came off
second best. To balance the objective advantage held by the Germans,
the collaborationists would have had to present a united front. The
fragmented French political tradition did not permit this. Furthermore, the Germans were fully cognizant of the splits within the
French political community and exploited them thoroughly. The
Ultra groups were occasionally able to use personal connections to
save friends from German detention and worse, but they could not
alter basic German policy toward occupied France. Since their reason
for existence was collaboration, the Ultra parties were not prepared
to confront the occupation authorities on even minor issues. Indeed
because of their own divisions, they tended to bargain for favors to
strengthen their own organizations against their rivals within the
collaborationist camp. Thus they gave away in advance any bargaining leverage they may have possessed.

Apart from the advantage held by the Germans as a consequence of
their military superiority, they also had a point of unity in their
government at Berlin. German policy was set by Hitler, and the
machinations of the German agencies in Paris and elsewhere occurred within parameters laid down from above. There was no simi-

---

[2]Michel, *Année 40*, pp. 167–174, describes the various German services stationed
in Paris. For the organization of the German police system during the war, see
George H. Stein, *The Waffen-SS: Hitler's Elite Guard at War, 1939–1945* (Ithaca:
Cornell University Press 1966), pp. xxvii–xxix.

lar unifying control over the Ultras in Paris despite Laval's efforts to
exert some influence upon them by subsidizing some of them at least
until March 1944.[3] Despite their repeated assertions that a collaborationist France would receive generous treatment from the
Germans, the Ultras were building castles in the air.

Hitler needed tranquillity in France during the summer of 1940
when France was to be a staging area for Operation Sea Lion against
England. After Sea Lion was called off, Berlin still wanted a tranquil
France for help in the continuing German war effort. German policy
of keeping the Ultras, especially Doriot after 1942, as a threat with
which to obtain concessions from Vichy was enunciated many times
by high German leaders during the war. In July 1940, Abetz recom-
mended against the formation of a strong united France. He
suggested instead that the Germans encourage many French newspapers, radio broadcasters, and propagandists. They should be
allowed to polemicize against one another, the future ambassador
wrote. He made clear his opposition to any sort of united French front
that might at some future time seek revenge against Germany.[4]

The appointment of Abetz as ambassador to France was in itself a
provocative move by the German government. Before the war he had
been a counselor to the German embassy in Paris, but had been
expelled from France in 1939 by the Daladier government, which
suspected him of espionage. A Social Democratic sympathizer prior to
the rise of Nazism in Germany, Abetz had attended Franco-German
youth congresses as early as 1930. At one of these he met the young
Frenchman Jean Luchaire, with whom he developed a lasting friendship. He subsequently married Luchaire's secretary, Suzanne de
Brouckère, and in 1940, at the age of thirty-seven, returned in
triumph with her to be feted by "tout Paris." Luchaire also had

[3] Jean Tracou, *Le maréchal aux liens* (Paris: André Bonne, 1948), pp. 188 and 192.
Tracou was Pétain's *chef du cabinet* in 1944.

[4] Otto Abetz, "Abschrift," July 30, 1940, CDJC document LXXI, 28. See also
Joseph Goebbels, Memorandum, July 9, 1940 in *The Secret Conferences of Dr. Goebbels, October 1939–March, 1943*, ed. Willi A. Boelcke (London: Weidenfeld & Nicolson, 1967), p. 65. For Hitler's coolness to the idea of collaboration, especially after
the removal of Laval, see the entry of January 28, 1941, in Franz Halder's diary,
which is cited in *Akten zur deutschen Auswärtigen Politik*, series D, vol. XI, p. 1012.
The Nazi attitude toward the exploitation of the economies of occupied countries,
France in particular, is discussed by Alan S. Milward, *The New Order and the French
Economy* (Oxford: Clarendon Press, 1970), pp. 1, 21, and 269.

Socialist origins. (The scion of a prominent French literary family, he made journalism his career. Long a partisan of Franco-German reconciliation, Luchaire accepted subsidies for his newspaper *Notre Temps* from Briand after 1927 and continued to draw government funds through the next decade.) In 1940 he was one of three intermediaries who introduced Laval to Abetz. The others were Jean Fontenoy, a journalist and a future supporter of Deloncle, and Fernand de Brinon, the first French journalist to interview Hitler after his accession to power and a founder, in 1935, of the Comité France-Allemagne, a Franco-German reconciliation committee established in France with an analogue, the Deutsch-Französische Gesellschaft, in Germany.

Abetz had joined the Nazi party in 1937 and had acquired a reputation in the German Foreign Ministry as an expert in French affairs. In the jockeying for position among the German services, he represented Ribbentrop and the Foreign Ministry. He was gradually to lose influence after 1942, when the SS and SD (Sicherheitsdienst: Security Service) establishment became more prominent. Laval would later pay for having placed too much trust in Abetz's ability to influence Berlin. During the summer and autumn of 1940, however, Abetz was a presence with whom to be reckoned in France, and he and Laval soon found their personal collaboration of mutual benefit. By conducting negotiations with the German ambassador in Paris rather than Vichy, Laval began to make Franco-German relations his own private preserve. He shortcircuited both Paul Baudouin, Vichy's foreign minister, and the Franco-German Armistice Commission in Wiesbaden. Abetz was able to enhance his own stature and make himself temporarily an indispensable figure. During the summer of 1940, Abetz became a "Laval man." He might later occasionally lend support to some of the Ultras but never in conflict with Laval.[5]

---

[5]Abetz, *Das offene Problem. Ein Rückblick auf zwei Jahrzehnte deutscher Frankreichpolitik* (Cologne: Greven, 1951), pp. 275–276, discusses his preference for a Laval government as opposed to one led by Doriot after 1942. See also Martin du Gard, p. 78. For the activities of Jean Luchaire before and after the armistice see *Procès de Collaboration* (Paris: Albin Michel, 1948), trial of Luchaire, audience of January 21, 1946, pp. 353–357. An obviously more sympathetic account, which also captures something of the spirit of the new times and the new people of "tout Paris," is that of Luchaire's movie-starlet daughter. See Corinne Luchaire, *Ma drôle de vie* (Paris: Sun, 1949).

September 1940 witnessed the transfer of the major locus of Ultra activity from Vichy to Paris. Deloncle organized his Mouvement Social Révolutionnaire in Paris on September 1 to prod the Vichy government into a more vigorous application of the National Revolution through sweeping purges and the elimination of all vestiges of the Third Republic. Because of the semi-secret nature of political activity in Paris during the fall of 1940, parties not yet officially being allowed by the occupation authorities, the dates of events are often difficult to ascertain for this period. The destruction of membership lists and other documents relating to the Ultras at the time of the Liberation also creates difficulties. Deloncle's MSR, however, was certainly one of the earliest if not the first of the new Ultra factions established after the armistice. The movement represented, in Deloncle's words, "the visible projection of the secret organization that I had established in 1936–1937."[6]

The MSR, however, was more than the old *Cagoule*. It claimed to be both nationalist and socialist, called for an authoritarian revolution in Vichy, and unlike the CSAR, supported close collaboration with the Germans. Anti-Jewish and anti-Masonic, the new party denounced everything in which it saw legacies of the parliamentary Republican past. But despite Deloncle's statements that the MSR was to be an organization open to the public, the secrecy and violent tendencies of the *Cagoule* were carried over. Conspiratorial and se-

[6]Quoted in Henry Coston, *Dictionnaire de la politique française* (Paris: La Librairie Française, 1967), p. 735. Coston's *La Libre Parole*, the revived version of Drumont's old newspaper, was not allowed to publish by the Germans during the occupation. See also Michèle Cotta, *La collaboration, 1940–1944* (Paris: Armand Colin, 1964), p. 243. For the date of the creation of the MSR, see Deloncle, "Les idées et l'action. Conférence fait 28 février 1941" (Paris: MSR, 1941), p. 17. September 1940 is also given as the time of the establishment of the MSR in a memorandum entitled "Note sur le Mouvement Social Révolutionnaire," which was found in the archives gathered together for the postwar Nuremberg trials. Dated May 23, 1942, this document of several typewritten pages contains no other identifying information but it is a mine of information on the MSR. From internal evidence it appears to be a French translation of a German report or possibly a report of a pro-German French agent to the German police. It is to be found in the CDJC archive, document XIXa, 15. Cotta, p. 254, inaccurately states that the MSR was founded "toward the end of the year 1940." A twenty-five point manifesto of the MSR was drawn up under the heading "Charte du Mouvement Social Révolutionnaire pour la Révolution Nationale," a copy of which is available in the library of the Comité d'Histoire de la Deuxième Guerre Mondiale in Paris.

cretive by nature, Deloncle was a talented organizer who had demonstrated physical courage during the First World War. His organizational talent and boldness reminded an interwar aide of Napoleon.[7] Du Moulin de Labarthète, who met him in the fall of 1940 at Vichy, characterized the MSR chieftain as follows:

> An old Polytechnic student, a naval engineer, administrator of the Penhoët shipyards—head erect, blue eyes with a strange gleam—possessed of the taste for figures and the passion for intrigue, he gave the impression of a sort of statistician of darkness, a Fouché of nomography . . . a moon dreamer who perhaps was not a criminal but who was led astray by the taste for plots, for obscure processes, for muffled deflagrations. Why does the theme of the "sword of Malchus" come to mind when I think of Deloncle?[8]

Deloncle had come to Vichy to visit the marshal in an attempt to solicit his aid against Doriot in Paris. Having fallen out with Doriot at Vichy, Deloncle had now turned against him. Deloncle made contact with the SS in Paris, which even in 1940 he believed to be the most important German representative in France. Du Moulin told Deloncle very plainly that he had no interest in such contacts. Deloncle returned empty handed once more from Vichy and renewed his ties to SS-Standartenführer Thomas, whose help had contributed to the creation of the MSR.[9]

Deloncle attracted a diverse group of supporters to the fledgling MSR. His second-in-command was Jean Fontenoy, a talented journalist who had been something of a specialist in Russian and Chinese affairs. A large, blond, and physically striking man, Fontenoy had studied at the Ecole des Langues Orientales and had briefly belonged to the Communist party during the early thirties. After leaving the party in disillusionment, he served as correspondent for the Havas News Agency in Moscow and later in China, where he established a newspaper, the *Journal de Shanghaï*. He returned to France in 1936, joined Doriot's PPF and served on the editorial board of its prewar

[7]Author's interview with one of Deloncle's prewar aides who chose to remain in government service at Vichy in 1940, June 27, 1974.
[8]Du Moulin de Labarthète, pp. 301–302.
[9]Michel, *Année 40*, p. 172. See also Du Moulin de Labarthète, pp. 301–302.

Paris paper, *L'Emancipation Nationale*. At the same time he published several novels including *Shanghaï secret* in 1938, which one writer compared favorably with the China tableaux of Pearl Buck and André Malraux.[10] A bold romantic, Fontenoy was emotionally and intellectually set for the fascist adventures that were created by the war situation. In 1939 he volunteered for service with the Finnish army against the Russians during the Winter War and was seriously wounded in combat. There is an unsubstantiated possibility that he suffered brain damage on the frozen battlefields of Finland. With the defeat of Finland he returned to France where, in July 1940, he became the first go-between for Abetz and Laval, both of whom he knew personally. Later he brought Laval together with Deloncle, although their collaboration, while Laval was out of office, was brief.

An inveterate crusader, Fontenoy took great personal risks in illegally crossing the German demarcation line in France. One was never quite sure of what he was doing or where he was. A hard drinker and possibly a user of other drugs, Fontenoy has been described variously as an "intellectual gangster" and a morphine addict. He had twice attempted suicide by 1943 when his wife, the well-known aviatrix Madeleine Charnaux, died. Fontenoy told Maurice Martin du Gard the same year that he was going to stop trying to commit suicide because he had been sick for six months after each attempt! He may have been unbalanced after 1940 but no one could question his sincerity or the disinterestedness of his actions. Eventually he directed the Office Français d'Information (OFI), a press agency operating during the occupation. After the German attack on the USSR, Fontenoy joined the Anti-Bolshevik Legion and fought on the Russian front. He met his death either fighting or as a suicide in Berlin during the last days of the Reich in May 1945. Robert Aron has pointed out that among Fontenoy, Luchaire, and de Brinon, the three journalists who had brought Laval and Abetz together, only Fontenoy did not profit materially from his personal connections. Jean Fontenoy was a

[10]Jean Quéval [*nom de plume* of Jacques Dormeuil] *Première page, cinquième colonne* (Paris: Fayard, 1945), pp. 71–72. Dormeuil had been a journalist with the Inter-France news agency during the war and his book takes a strong anticollaborationist position. For an account of Fontenoy's brief flirtation with Doriot, see Saint-Paulien, *Histoire de la collaboration*, p. 145.

medieval *chevalier* gone haywire in the middle of the twentieth century.[11]

Fontenoy had a falling out with Doriot during the fall of 1940, at about the same time Deloncle had turned against the PPF leader. Doriot seems to have objected to Fontenoy's activities in bringing Laval and Abetz together in an alliance that threatened the PPF. Fontenoy now began to publish a bi-weekly magazine, *Lectures 40*, independently of Doriot, further angering the PPF chieftain. By September, Fontenoy had joined forces with Deloncle and was firmly in the MSR camp. Although in the autumn of 1940 the PPF and the MSR exhibited close similarities in their collaborationist ideology, there were important differences between the two. Doriot was a major political leader still limited in his enthusiasm for Germany by the Nazi-Soviet pact, whereas Deloncle was assiduously cultivating contacts within the German services, especially the SS. Deloncle remained in spirit the leader of the prewar *Cagoule* conspiracy and was out of his element in the politics of mass rallies and demonstrations in which Doriot excelled. Personal jealousies intensified their political suspicions. When Fontenoy reacted against the discipline of Doriot and the PPF in 1940, he turned to Deloncle.

Having joined Deloncle as one of the leaders of the MSR, Fontenoy edited *Rassemblement* and *Révolution Nationale*, successive weeklies expressing the party's viewpoints. Later during the occupation period, *Révolution Nationale* became more independent of the MSR and attracted articles from some of the leading literary lights of the French collaboration, although by then Fontenoy had left for service with the Anti-Bolshevik Legion in Russia. *Lectures 40*, which lasted only into early 1941, contained a series of articles written by Eugène Schueller, the self-made magnate of L'Oréal perfumes. Schueller had met Deloncle, whom he considered a potential modernizer of the stalemate society, before the war. Both had opposed the Popular Front. In several articles and books Schueller argued for a more adventurous French managerial elite, willing to take the economic risks necessary to modernize the industrial system. He also supported

---

[11]Aron, *The Vichy Regime*, p. 191. For the description of Fontenoy as an "intellectual gangster," see Martin du Gard, p. 389.

a replacement of hourly wages for labor by piece-work salaries in which he saw a way to help stimulate the increased production France would need to rebuild after the defeat of 1940. Schueller's scheme revived nineteenth-century conservative corporatism to "absorb" the proletariat into the rest of society. For leadership of his corporate state Schueller looked to the new chivalric elite of the MSR, which alone had the dynamism and technical expertise to effect the political and social changes he wanted. Deloncle and his aides met often in Schueller's offices, and he supported the MSR financially as well.[12] By December 1940 the MSR had become a force in the politics of the occupied zone with bold, even daring, leadership. Seeing themselves as a new warrior elite, the members now felt ready to move toward establishing the organization as the single party which had not been born in Vichy. The ultimate failure of the MSR was due largely to Deloncle's inveterate penchant for intrigue and conspiracy, which alienated many of his aides and backers. Deloncle was eventually to achieve the dubious distinction of being expelled from three different Ultra organizations by the end of 1942.

While Deloncle was trying to build his MSR into the single party, Doriot made similar plans for his PPF but found himself in a different situation. By September 1940 the PPF had been split in two ways. It had not recovered from the defections that followed the Munich crisis and the revelations of Italian financial aid in 1938. What was left of the party was divided again in 1940 by the demarcation line, which severely hampered the activities of all French associations, political or not. Nonetheless, there existed among the PPF faithful a feeling of vindication, a belief that their opposition to the Republic and to war with Germany had been proven correct by recent events. This feeling found expression in the eruption of an anti-Semitism made all the more virulent by the enforced moderation of PPF anti-Communism in 1940. Doriot had taken no anti-Semitic stands before the armistice but anti-Jewish feeling did exist in party circles, especially in North Africa.

[12]Eugène Schueller, *La révolution de l'économie* (Paris: Denoël, 1941), p. 7. This book, Schueller's major wartime opus, puts together ideas he had developed in a series of articles he had written for *Lectures 40* between October 1940 and January 1941. For a brief biographical sketch of Schueller, see Coston, *Dictionnaire de la politique française,* pp. 966–967; also Charbonneau, 1:344.

PPF anti-Semitism reflected an increasing wave of hostility toward Jews among many segments of the French population. France was the country of Edouard Drumont and the Dreyfus Affair, as well as the anti-Semitic preachings of Charles Maurras and Maurice Barrès, so anti-Semitism was not new in 1940. Lower-middle-class and factory-worker anticapitalism was sometimes shifted to anti-Semitism against the Rothschilds and other prominent Franco-Jewish financial families. For a period before 1936 French anti-Semitism had been more or less latent, but it was revived by the election of the Popular Front government headed by the Jewish premier Léon Blum and by an increasing wave of Jewish refugees from Central and Eastern Europe. Many in France felt that the refugees were attempting to use France as instrument against Hitler in matters of no real concern to the French. Blum was said to be advised by Jewish refugee circles to intervene against the Nationalists in Spain and embroil France in a war with the Axis powers. Anti-Semitism and anti-Communism coalesced around the Popular Front government.

With the search for scapegoats in 1940, it became tempting to blame Jews and Communists for leading France into a war against her own better interests and for failing to have prepared her adequately for that war. On August 20, some sixty members of the Garde Française rampaged along the Champs-Elysées, smashing the windows of shops owned by Jews. The Garde Française was the paramilitary wing of the Parti Français National-Collectiviste, a small profascist movement founded before the war by a hero of World War I, Pierre Clémenti. Led by Charles Lefebvre, the Garde Française mobilized youths and men in their thirties for their adventure on the Champs-Elysées. Deloncle had also been in on the planning. German reaction was one of consternation, even suspecting the whole affair to have been organized by *agents provocateurs* seeking to turn French popular feeling against the occupation authorities, who would naturally be blamed for having instigated the outburst. After receiving statements from Lefebvre and Deloncle, German officials in Paris made very clear the fact that the operation had been entirely a French affair.

The anti-Semitic reaction to the defeat of 1940 produced among many of the Ultras demands for punishment of Jewish "warmongers." Named most frequently were Blum, former Interior

Minister Georges Mandel, and former Education Minister Jean Zay. All found themselves the targets of verbal abuse, and Mandel and Zay were to be assassinated by Miliciens in 1944. French anti-Semitism had been kept alive before 1936 by journalists such as Henry Coston, who had attempted to revive Drumont's newspaper, *La Libre Parole*. Coston and like-minded witch-hunters had also sought explanations of world historical events in the occult influences of Freemasonry. The Freemasons, who had long been the subject of intense suspicion on the part of clericalists and other Rightists, came into prominence again as scapegoats after 1940. On October 3, 1940, legislation enacted by Vichy excluded Jews, except for some war veterans, from posts in the government and public media. This legislation was attacked in wide segments of the Ultra press and at party meetings for failing to go far enough in the exclusion of the Jews from French national life. [13]

Gangs of PPF militants threatened and attacked Jews during the summer of 1940. On the night of August 14–15 a gang of party activists demonstrated against Freemasons and Jews in Vichy and threatened to burn down a local synagogue. According to Léon Blum, the members of the National Assembly had panicked into voting constituent powers to Pétain in part because of their fear of roving gangs of Doriotists in the streets. A true fascist chieftain led rather than followed his troops and Doriot needed new villains in 1940. The Jews became a target for the outraged moralism of the PPF and its collaborationist rivals. During the summer, Doriot appeared with his

[13]A good example of PPF anti-Jewish propaganda during the autumn of 1940 is the tract "Parti Populaire Français aux Parisiens," which among other things states: "The Jews are responsible for all our misfortunes. They must pay." Shades of Streicher's *Der Stürmer*. A copy of this tract is available in the BDIC, Q pièce 4084.

The August 1940 incident involving the Garde Française is revealed in a group of letters, statements, and reports kept together as CDJC document LXXV, 144. The brief history of the Garde Française of Lefebvre is given in *French Basic Handbook*, Part III (London: Foreign Office, 1944), p. 153. The *Basic Handbook* was one of a series prepared by British intelligence and the Foreign Office to ready the British forces and services for what they would meet in liberated countries. The *French Basic Handbook*, parts III and IV, was prepared as classified material in January 1944. Used in conjunction with French and German materials, the *Basic Handbook* is an invaluable source of information about virtually all facets of French life during the occupation. A copy of this relatively hard-to-find book was graciously made available to me by Gérard Le Marec and Gérard Silvain in Paris.

supporters in the streets of Vichy in scenes such as the following:

> Three o'clock. In front of the restoration [Vichy's spa], Doriot passes in blue, enormous, a priest at his debut with two Sbirri [Italian police officials prior to the introduction of the Carabinieri—used figuratively here], with a calm and self-assured step. Half an hour later a great uproar and crowd a hundred meters from the Ministry of the Interior. The effigy of a Freemason leader has been hung from a tree and all around a small group attempts to create disorder: "Down with the Freemasons! Down with the Jews!"[14]

Like Mussolini, who in 1938 had felt the need to reinvigorate his aging Fascist movement in Italy, Doriot found the answer in racism. The anticipation of German support for an anti-Semitic PPF unquestionably played a role, but anti-Semitism filled deep-seated PPF needs after the armistice and it was embraced with an ardor that exceeded opportunism.

Doriot's strategy during the autumn of 1940 was to make the PPF the sole viable political formation of the collaboration. This he attempted by adopting extremist stands for the transformation of France into a fascist state. Denouncing Laval as a holdover from the Republic Doriot gave strong support to Marshal Pétain in the hope of nudging the marshal toward the PPF conception of the National Revolution. The same intense hostility manifested against the Jews and Freemasons was also directed against all parliamentary leaders of the Third Republic. Doriot was attempting to remove all possible competition from the Ultra stage, particularly Laval and the newly emerging rival Déat. Both were castigated as old republican ministers who needed to be eliminated if France was to make a reality of the National Revolution. Attacking Laval was also an indirect attack on Abetz, who was staking his personal position on Laval's success. As Abetz's coolness toward Doriot became more evident, the latter began to extend his contacts into other German services in France. Abetz had frustrated his attempt to reach the pre-1939 Communist leadership with a *Nouvelle Humanité,* and the PPF leader turned to Goebbels' propaganda staff for help in launching a new daily, *Le Cri du*

[14]Martin du Gard, pp. 91–92. For Blum's statement about fear of the PPF in Vichy, see Aron, *The Vichy Regime,* p. 98.

Peuple, in October. PPF contacts were also initiated with SD circles in Paris, through Thomas in March 1941.[15]

Doriot's political positions were elaborated in articles written for *Le Cri du Peuple* and republished in the book, *Je suis un homme du maréchal.* He attacked de la Rocque and Maurras for their opposition to the single-party idea. Déat and Laval were considered tainted by their parliamentary past and the book is replete with calls for sweeping purges. When Vichy began to replace elected town mayors with appointees of its own choosing and Déat objected on legal grounds, Doriot asked where the legal scruples had been in 1937 when he had been removed from the mayoralty of Saint-Denis. The PPF leader meant to take his full measure of revenge.[16] The economy was to be refashioned on an anti-liberal basis of autarchy, made possible by the possession of a large empire in Africa. Educational doctrines were to be revised by new cadres under the control of the state.

Doriot insisted that Pétain was ready to lead France toward a real regeneration, but that his actions were being impeded by a coterie of bureaucrats and timid men surrounding him in Vichy. This theme, enunciated early in the history of the occupation, was repeated often by Ultras, who dared not attack the marshal but sought instead to clothe their own factions and goals in his mantle. The vagueness of many of Pétain's statements and his devious political ploys opened the door to the collaborationists. Doriot was well aware that the collaborationist camp, his PPF included, represented but a small fraction of the French population and required the prestige of Pétain. The elitism shared by the PPF with its rivals was in part the col-

[15]Wolf, pp. 244–245. For Wolf's evidence of Doriot's contact with the *Sicherheitsdienst,* see p. 347, n. 813. For an attack against the Rothschild and Lazare banks, see Doriot, *Homme du maréchal,* p. 33. On p. 42 of the same book he denounces Jews and Freemasons for having led France to defeat in 1940. Castigating the Parisian youth who staged the first significant anti-German demonstration on November 11, 1940, at the Arc de Triomphe, Doriot called them "jeunesse dorée," gilded youth, a term evoking plebeian hostility to the gilded counterrevolutionary youth gangs who had terrorized revolutionaries in the streets of Paris after the downfall of Robespierre and the Jacobins in 1794. Doriot reminded his readers of the wealth of the family of General de Gaulle.

[16]Doriot, *Homme du maréchal,* p. 78. For Doriot's comments on de la Rocque, his PSF, and Action Française, see ibid., p. 73. Anti-Déat remarks are to be found in Doriot, "La Révolution Nationale. Détails historiques sur le parti unique," *Le Cri du Peuple,* December 18, 1940.

laborationists' recognition that they would never attain power through the will of the majority of their compatriots. PPF spokesmen did not refer to their party as the "knights" of the New Order in the manner of Deloncle's MSR but the idea was there. Doriot argued in 1941 that collaborationists more than any other political grouping needed the protective covering of the marshal. The one chance for proponents of the New Order in France was to steer Pétain toward their course. The PPF, wrote Doriot, would give its total support to Marshal Pétain.[17]

Publicly Doriot defended collaboration but he was troubled by the reserve of Abetz toward the PPF and by the Nazi-Soviet pact. Some of the most recent recruits to Doriot were ex-Communist luminaries who had left the party precisely because of their opposition to the pact. These included Marcel Gitton, the former senator Jean-Marie Clamamus, and Marcel Capron, a former Communist deputy from Charenton. Nonetheless, Doriot gave full public support to the collaboration policy announced by Marshal Pétain after his meeting of October 24 with Hitler at Montoire. Not only Doriot but virtually all the Ultras pictured Montoire as a turning point in French history. But whereas Déat heaped editorial praise upon Laval and Pétain for the meeting, Doriot was careful to attribute it solely to the marshal. Little was said about Laval, whose role had been crucial in bringing it about.

For Doriot the fall months of 1940 were a time to reorganize the party and stake out a position clearly in advance of potential rivals in the Ultra camp. He had learned his tactics well from the Communists. As late as February 1941, however, he considered before rejecting an offer by Colonel Georges Groussard to join an anti-German movement in French North Africa. It seems hardly likely that the prospect of illegal political activity deterred Doriot, with his Communist background, as it did others in France. But the military situation still looked favorable to Germany in February 1941 and he had plans for the PPF, so the prospect of resistance in North Africa did not entice him. Important to Doriot, a man of deep and longstanding political grudges, was his aversion to any kind of activity that might help restore to power the men and institutions of the Third

[17]Doriot, *Homme du maréchal*, pp. 109 and 119.

Republic. The Groussard episode, together with Doriot's expressed fear that the Germans might suspect him of involvement in the coup of December 13 against Laval, show that the PPF was not yet the important force for collaboration it would become after the German attack on the Soviet Union in June 1941.[18]

Any doubts Doriot held on the wisdom of collaboration were not shared by Marcel Déat, who emerged during the fall of 1940 as the leading collaborationist spokesman. Unlike Doriot, Déat was not supported by a preexisting organized political party. Journalism was his source of influence even after he became a party leader in his own right. On September 21, the newspaper *L'Œuvre* returned to Paris from Clermont-Ferrand, whence it had moved during the June exodus. Aware of Déat's collaborationist position, the Germans made sure the owners of the paper gave him a leading role. When they threatened confiscation and replaced some printing equipment with inferior machines, Déat received a free hand at *L'Œuvre*.[19]

Déat was an ideologue and his collaboration with Germany was basically intellectual. During the first few months of the occupation he elaborated his political stance, and he persevered in it with a single-minded determination that was the wonder of friend and foe alike. An aloof and lonely ascetic, Déat neither smoked nor drank and socialized very little despite the diversions available to collaborationist leaders in occupied Paris. He appeared able to inspire his fellow man personally only by the example of his morally blameless character—whether in the trenches of World War I or as the incorruptible Ultra leader during the second war. Although an effective speaker, he possessed none of Doriot's personal magnetism. His vehicle was the written word.

Déat had long argued that the age of individualism was over, and the German victory of 1940 reinforced the statist ideas that had informed his Neo-Socialism. To his Neo-Socialism he added, after 1940, the concepts of the single party and the charismatic leader. He compared the Nazis to the revolutionaries of Danton's day and placed Hitler's Germany squarely in the tradition of Rousseau and the radi-

---

[18]Groussard, p. 199. See also Wolf, p. 247. For Doriot's discussion of Montoire, see *Homme du maréchal*, p. 10.

[19]Déat, "Librement," *L'Œuvre*, September 21–24, 1940. See also Chap. 1, n. 9, above.

cal phase of the French Revolution. Déat desired order and solidarity and his experiences in 1914–1918 taught him to value the French military tradition. He saw even the Soviet Union as a one-party state evolving toward a form of National Socialism although this picture was drastically redrawn after June 1941.[20]

The magnitude of the German victory of 1940 made it impossible for Déat and many other Ultras to see that Germany might one day be defeated in turn by a more powerful coalition. One of his closest associates after 1941 said that Déat, once having taken a stand, foreclosed all other options. Advised by friends such as Colonel Michel Alerme and contacts in the Japanese diplomatic corps in Paris, Déat consistently misread the changing military situation during the course of the war. Access to other than German-supplied information was difficult at best for all Parisians during the war but Déat's isolation was compounded by an inner spiritual emigration that did not allow him to evaluate critically even the information he had. The fear of Allied victory and the social disorder he expected from a Resistance triumphant paralyzed his critical faculties. The man who did not want France under English tutelage could not see what the Germans were doing to France, especially during the latter stages of the war. Unwilling to die for Danzig in 1939, Déat was more willing to die, or at least to see his compatriots die, for it in 1943. Robert Brasillach, executed in 1945 for collaboration, argued two years earlier that the same French national interest that should have been indifferent to the fate of Danzig before the outbreak of war should have remained so four years later. As the Russians moved toward Danzig in 1943 and Déat supported German efforts to retain it, Brasillach suggested that Déat had moved so far in his course of

[20]For a discussion by Déat of de Man and class solidarity with a spirit of sacrifice, see "Solidaires dans l'épreuve," *L'Œuvre,* October 20, 1940. On April 17, 1941, Déat compared German élan to "Anglo-American materialism," in "Victoire de la Révolution," and, ironically on June 21, 1941 in "Communistes et gaullistes," he wrote favorably of the one-party Soviet system. All these articles appeared in *L'Œuvre.* For his later comparison of German National Socialism to the First French Republic, see Déat, *Révolution Française et Révolution Allemande, 1793–1943* (Paris: RNP, 1943). Déat's public respect for Pétain as the hero of Verdun was expressed in "Le Maréchal et son gouvernement," *L'Œuvre,* September 27, 1940. The admiration of the literary collaborationists for the "new German man" is discussed by Soucy, "The Nature of Fascism in France," p. 52.

ideological solidarity with German National Socialism that he had completely lost sight of French national interests.[21]

In October 1940, Déat wrote that France had become a nation of old people because her youth had been cut down during the First World War. Such a carnage should never again be permitted. A closed union of old politicians of the pre-1914 generation had maintained themselves in office and kept out all fresh blood. France, Déat continued, had stagnated after 1918. Unlike his rivals, Déat was a former cabinet minister and did not condemn all ex-parliamentarians. He felt obliged to defend his past against the denunciations of Doriot who had also served as a deputy under the Third Republic. Never a minister, Doriot had been more the outsider and now regarded Déat as a *parvenu* opportunist. Déat replied that the PPF was not up to the task of rebuilding France. He also defended Laval and the Republican mayors who were being removed from their offices by Vichy.[22]

Déat's rivals within the Ultra camp were not the only targets of his biting editorial columns. Increasingly exasperated with the conservative spirit reigning at Vichy, Déat leveled his pen, or more literally his typewriter, at the pervasive influence of Action Française. He blamed Action Française for sabotaging the single-party movement and charged it with being in league with the steel trust (Comité des Forges) to suppress the workers' unions. High finance, he wrote, was playing a far more nefarious role than any "so-called Freemason conspiracy" in France. Not daring to denounce Pétain, Déat wrote that the marshal was being misled by his advisers, who were heavily influenced by big corporations and Action Française. Déat continually argued that the National Revolution was yet to be achieved. Even after the Liberation he continued to argue that Vichy had lost all popularity because of its unwillingness to break with France's past and make the changes he had prescribed.[23]

---

[21]Brasillach, *Journal d'un homme occupé* (Paris: Les Sept Couleurs, 1955), p. 284. For Déat's basic stance on Franco-German relations, see "Quand la France ignorait l'Europe," *L'Œuvre*, October 2, 1940. In "De Dantzig à Dakar," *L'Œuvre*, October 28, 1940, Déat explains that never had he been a conscientious objector, for peace at any price. This was most certainly true!

[22]Déat, "Mais où sont les hommes nouveaux?" October 1, 1940. For his defense of Laval, see "Le fil de la légalité," September 28, 1940, and for his defense of the Republican mayors, "Ne touchez pas aux maires," October 19, 1940. All three articles appeared in *L'Œuvre*.

[23]Déat, "Toujours les mêmes," *L'Œuvre*, November 9, 1940.

The corollary of Déat's critique of Vichy's domestic policy was his continual prodding of the government to move ever further toward full-scale collaboration with Germany. Frustrated by his interwar political failures, Déat in 1940 saw a new chance to implement his Neo-Socialist ideas and at the same time satisfy his personal political ambitions. It meant emphasizing the statist and authoritarian components of his interwar thought at the expense of his more liberal and humane proclivities. It also meant following a course that would be perceived by many as treasonous, since after the armistice France remained in a state of war with Germany. To attain part of his program, Déat had to sacrifice another in 1940. He shared with his fellow collaborationists the dilemma that their vision of France and the newly emerging Frenchman could be realized only in subservience to a cruel and increasingly pitiless enemy.

Déat's case is of special interest because of the sincerity with which he embraced collaborationist ideals and the eloquence with which he articulated them. He constructed a collaborationist doctrine with Cartesian logic in 1940 and adhered to it thereafter with an inflexible persistence. Several dubious premises lay at the base of Déat's political geometry. He argued that Hitler was not an old-style ruler in the manner of the Hohenzollerns and would therefore not impose a vindictive peace on France. Accordingly, Déat welcomed the Montoire meetings. Hitler and the Germans, he reasoned, had learned from their own experience with the Versailles treaty that a harsh peace forced upon a defeated nation could not last and that the vanquished people would eventually rise again. He repeated that Germany could be prosperous only if France were also. Once the French showed their readiness to collaborate, the Germans would see it in their own interest to accept the proffered hand. The German annexation of Alsace and Lorraine and their moves to control the French economy did not affect Déat's thinking.

By November 1940, Déat was asserting that like it or not, France was part of the war. In a quest for *engagement* that had clear parallels among some early members of the Resistance, he argued that France could not be a neutral spectator when two vastly differing political systems and conceptions of man were contending for supremacy. Germany, he wrote, did not need French military help to win the war and he did not suggest that France enter the war militarily on the side of the Axis. But the immediate tasks of feeding France, easing the burden of the demarcation line, and attempting to repatriate the one and one-half million French prisoners in German *Oflags* and *Stalags* did necessitate immediate collaboration, according to Déat. He denied the existence of a neutrality option, which was gaining many adherents who hoped that at the right moment France might step in and mediate a compromise peace between Germany and England. To the neutralists Déat applied the term "Attentistes," a sobriquet that gained currency among impatient Ultras in their attacks on Vichy. Déat blamed Vichyite *attentisme* on international capitalism, the "City," referring to the London financial center, and "plutocracy," the collaborationist description of England and later America.

He also attacked the traditional Germanophobia of Action Française and the *revanchard* sentiments of generals of the Armistice Army, who had not yet accepted the defeat of 1940. Déat's denunciations of the French military establishment were particularly vexing to Pétain and led the marshal to have him arrested at the time of Laval's firing in December 1940. By then Déat had emerged as the most articulate and polemical of the Ultra spokesmen in Paris. It remained to be seen whether he would be able to transform the force of his editorial barrage into the political power he would need to bend Vichy to his view of the National Revolution and to overcome his rivals within the Ultra camp in Paris. [24]

During the fall of 1940, Déat was supported on *L'Œuvre* by a number of ex-Socialist politicians. His opposition to the blanket criticism of the Third Republic can be explained in large part by the presence in *L'Œuvre* of articles written by René Brunet, Charles Spinasse, and Jean-Michel Renaitour. Brunet had been undersecretary in the Finance Ministry under Blum and Spinasse had been economics minister in Blum's cabinet. Renaitour, a former deputy, also wrote for the stridently anti-Semitic *Pilori*. Other former Socialists writing for *L'Œuvre* included Jean Piot, the former administrator of the National Radio, and Alexandre Zevacs, once a friend of Jaurès. Contributors to the paper included Pierre-Etienne Flandin, premier in 1934–1935 and a leading prewar "pacifist," Barthélemy Montagnon, who had helped Déat establish the Neo-Socialist party, and Eugène Frot and Georges Bloch. Frot had been a Socialist and

[24]Déat, "L'aube d'une ère nouvelle," October 26, 1940; "Vers l'Europe," October 30, 1940; and "Un gouvernement fort," November 21, 1940; all in *L'Œuvre*.

Bloch, an ex-Communist, had signed the peace manifesto of a group of members of the National Assembly calling for immediate peace prior to the German offensive of 1940.

Like the men of Vichy, Déat feared possible German support of the French Communists in 1940. He wanted to make sure that the French with whom the occupation authorities collaborated were his supporters rather than the men of Moscow. The former Socialists who joined Déat and Montagnon in 1940 were those whose desire for economic planning and social solidarity and whose anti-Communism transcended their attachment to individual liberty and the parliamentary regime. Just as Vichy provided political opportunities to the frustrated radical Right after 1940, the conditions in occupied Paris gave a similar chance to the disgruntled figures of the fragmented Left. Neo-Socialists who would follow Déat to collaboration might have a chance at last for political power if they were willing to pay the price. Collaborationism also offered them the opportunity to defend the interests of their former middle- and lower-middle-class constituencies against the big-business orientation of Vichy. The ideological evolution of the former Neo-Socialists, their own past personal resentments, and the apparent availability of a leaderless political clientele in the occupied zone in 1940 all led a sizable proportion of them to accept Nazi protestations of "socialism" and "Europeanism" at face value. In his perceptions of the German Reich Déat may have been extreme but he was by no means alone.[25]

Abetz and representatives of the other German services in Paris saw to it that Déat had rivals, especially in the journalistic world of the capital. The Propagandastaffel (Goebbels' propaganda staff) assiduously did its best to see that Paris and the occupied zone were flooded with German-controlled media. Determined to penetrate the Paris media as quickly as possible, the Propagandastaffel helped launch several newspapers immediately after the armistice. In June dailies such as Le Matin, Les Dernières Nouvelles de Paris, Paris-Soir, and La France au Travail appeared. Many of the senior staff members

[25]"Bericht über die deutsche Tätigkeit in Paris," October 1940; T-120/475/229319. See also Cotta, p. 322. For an excellent discussion of the parliamentary Left at Vichy, which also bears upon the Ultras in Paris, see Françoise Laurent, "Les hommes de gauche," typewritten manuscript in collection Le Gouvernement de Vichy et la Révolution Nationale, 1940–1942. Fondation Nationale des Sciences Politiques. Colloque des 6 et 7 mars 1970, in the BDIC, F Rés. 293/19.

of these new papers were friends of Abetz from his prewar days in France. *Le Matin* passed into the hands of Maurice Bunau-Varilla, whose brother Philippe had been financially involved in the Panamanian coup which had enabled the United States to begin work on the canal in 1904. Jean Luchaire, editor-in-chief of *Le Matin*, left that paper in November to direct the *Nouveaux Temps*, which he hoped would succeed the well-established *Temps* as the principal evening daily of Paris. *Le Temps* had taken refuge at Lyons in the unoccupied zone. *Les Dernières Nouvelles de Paris*, directed by Louis Burelle, was oriented toward financial affairs but lasted only a matter of weeks. *Paris-Soir*, a daily which was published all through occupation had as its first director someone named Schisselé, who had been promoted by a German officer from elevator operator of the building that housed the paper's offices. A wide variety of opportunities seemed to open up in 1940 for all sorts of journalists and businessmen who might want to make their fortunes or careers in the Paris press. *La France au Travail* was intended to capture the former readers of the Communist *L'Humanité*. Its director, Charles Dieudonné, whose real name was Oltramare, was a transplanted Swiss with a history of profascist agitation in his native country. He had been involved in rioting in Geneva in 1936. The newspaper also attracted Jacques Dyssord, an acquaintance of Abetz, described as an unpublished poet from the bohemian community of Paris. Jean Fontenoy was likewise involved briefly on the editorial board of *La France au Travail*, which began publication on the last day of June 1940 and ceased the following May.

All of these papers depended on the Propagandastaffel not only for many of their news sources—virtually all concerning the progress of the war—but also for the physical materials needed to publish. Offices, equipment, and paper were made available by the Germans and as the war progressed and such materials became more scarce, the control of the newsprint supply became a potent weapon in the hands of the occupation authorities. These authorities were able to bestow upon their favorites funds, the lifting of travel restrictions (especially the interzonal), gasoline, free health care, and a variety of other perquisites.[26]

[26]"Bericht über die deutsche Tätigkeit in Paris," October 1940; T-120/475/229314-15. See also Cotta, pp. 321-322 and Quéval, pp. 24ff. Statistics on the

During the fall of 1940, several other newspapers, less obviously fed by the Propagandastaffel, were established in Paris. More professional journalists had returned from the June exodus and there was substantial shifting around of personnel among the various papers. In addition to *L'Œuvre,* there appeared *Aujourd'jui, Petit Parisien, Le Cri du Peuple,* and Luchaire's *Nouveaux Temps. Le Cri du Peuple* was the organ of Doriot and the PPF. Like *L'Œuvre, Petit Parisien* was a previously well established newspaper which reappeared under new management after the 1940 defeat. One of its editors had been active in the PPF before the war and the paper after 1940 had distinct Doriotist tendencies. All the papers received the same news sources from the German services with the same restrictions. It was, for example, forbidden to discuss German activities in Alsace and Lorraine in any of the Paris papers.

A brief exception to the stridently pro-German tone of the Paris press was *Aujourd'hui* under the editorship of Henri Jeanson and Robert Perrier during the autumn of 1940. *Aujourd'hui* was oriented toward a literary and theater clientele. A pacifist before the war, Jeanson had not taken a pro-German stance. He had even written in defense of Herschel Grynzspan, the young Jew who had assassinated the German consular official Ernst von Rath in Paris, a murder used as a pretext for the Crystal Night violence in Germany. Jeanson, however, had opposed war with Germany. He had been arrested in 1939 for "defeatism." After the armistice, he joined the chorus of those who blamed the leaders of the Third Republic for the 1940 disaster and was particularly critical of Daladier. Jeanson was far more reticent, however, on the question of Franco-German collaboration and did not approve of Pétain and Laval meeting with Hitler at Montoire. When Déat and *L'Œuvre* returned in September 1940 to Paris, Jeanson took them to task in his columns. In possession of the obviously more pro-German ground, Déat won the war of words, and German pressure forced Jeanson off the editorial staff of *Aujourd'hui.* He was succeeded by the more pliable Georges Suarez, who brought

number of issues printed of the various Paris newspapers during the occupation period are published by Gérard Walter, *La vie à Paris sous l'occupation, 1940–1944* (Paris: Armand Colin [Kiosque series], 1960), p. 244. The figures give an idea of the directions the Propagandastaffel took at different times during the course of the occupation. They give little indication, however, of the relative strength of the various political movements nor of their composition.

the paper into closer alignment with the remainder of the Paris press. The defeat of Jeanson was Déat's first major victory in his battle for supremacy in the journalistic and political world of occupied Paris. By helping to eliminate his opposition on the moderate side, however, Déat opened himself up to charges similar to those he had leveled at Jeanson. He was made to look relatively "softer" in contrast to the PPF and the intransigents of the extreme Right.[27]

Among the weeklies that appeared shortly after the armistice were Fontenoy's La Vie Nationale and La Gerbe, directed by Alphonse de Châteaubriant, whose lyrical eulogy of Hitler, La gerbe des forces, in 1937 had won for its author a place unique among the ranks of those committed to Franco-German reconciliation. La Gerbe was the only paper actually created by the embassy Châteaubriant was joined on its staff by Camille Fégy, who had worked for L'Humanité and then the Doriotist Emancipation Nationale before the war. A number of Châteaubriant's associates came from academic circles, including Abel Bonnard, Georges Montandon, and Bernard Faÿ. Bonnard, the author of a biography of Saint Francis of Assisi, had a romantic aesthetic conception of Christianity which he transferred to National Socialist Germany. In 1942 he was named education minister at Vichy. Montandon, an anthropologist, brought his expertise to bear upon the elaboration of theories of racial difference between Aryans and Jews, which helped in the preparation of anti-Semitic expositions held in various parts of France during the occupation. Faÿ became the administrative director of the Bibliothèque Nationale and a self-appointed watchdog against Freemasonry, over which he was to cross swords editorially in 1941 with Déat.[28]

[27]Déat, "Calomniez, calomniez . . . ," L'Œuvre, October 29, 1940. For the view of an anti-German who praises Jeanson and attacks Suarez, see Jean Galtier-Boissière, Mon journal pendant l'occupation (Paris: La Jeune Parque, 1944), p. 23. The entire Déat-Jeanson controversy is recounted in Quéval, pp. 96–101 and 107, and passim; also "Bericht über die deutsche Tätigkeit in Paris," October 1940; T-120/475/229317.

[28]"Bericht über die deutsche Tätigkeit in Paris," October, 1940; T-120/475/229318. For discussions of the ideas of Châteaubriant and Bonnard, see Paul Sérant, Le romantisme fasciste: étude sur l'oeuvre politique de quelques écrivains français (Paris: Fasquelle, 1959), pp. 119 and 115 respectively. The role of the German embassy in the creation of La Gerbe is discussed by Rudolf Rahn, "Interrogatoire, Procès-Verbal. Tribunal Général de Gouvernement Militaire pour la Zone Française d'Occupation en Allemagne," Dachau, February 28, 1947; CDJC document XCVI, 93.

The most brutally anti-Semitic weekly in Paris was *Au Pilori,* modeled in part after Julius Streicher's obscenely racial *Der Stürmer* in Germany. Created as a monthly before the war by Henri Robert Petit, *Pilori* had been closed down by government decree in April 1939; Petit received German approval to publish the paper again in July 1940. Initially he was assisted by Jean Lestandi and Robert Pierret, but they soon ousted him over financial matters. Petit had been imprisoned before the war for bankruptcy and was also accused of having abandoned his family. The occupation authorities preferred journalistic allies who were morally blameless for greater credence among the public. The sale of *Pilori* in the streets of Paris produced violent confrontations between Jews and supporters of the newspaper. A longstanding anti-Semite, Lestandi had been secretary-general of Le Grand Pavois, a literary club created in 1935. An inveterate joiner, he was also affiliated with the Comité France-Allemagne, in which Abetz and de Brinon had been active before the war. He had participated in an anti-Soviet rally and had lectured before groups of the Croix de Feu. Lestandi came from a banking family of some wealth and it was he who brought Pierret into *Pilori.* Also a journalist and an anti-Semite, Pierret had at various times before the war been affiliated with the right-wing Solidarité Française movement of Jean-Pierre Renaud, Doriot's PPF, and the CSAR of Deloncle.[29] Lestandi and Pierret were joined on the editorial staff by Roger Vauquelin, a Public Health Ministry lecturer during the 1930's. Having become interested in politics, Vauquelin had joined Marcel Bucard's Francistes and done propaganda work among the few but very active Franciste university students. With the dissolution of the leagues, including the Francistes, in 1936, Vauquelin drifted through several rightist fringe organizations and wound up in

[29]The history of *Au Pilori* is furnished in a report of the same name, June 12, 1941, drawn up for the Commissariat Général des Questions Juives (CGQJ), Vichy's government department created to deal with the "Jewish question." Many of the documents related to CGQJ affairs are available at the CJDC. The report on *Pilori* is CDJC document CCCLXXIX, 79. German apprehensions with regard to Petit were expressed in a report, apparently of SD origin, to Dr. Best of the Wehrmacht staff (Militärverwaltungsrat), August 28, 1940, p. 3; document LXXIXa, 1a in the CDJC. See also the unfavorable opinion expressed on Petit by Captain Paul Sézille, the secretary-general of the anti-Semitic Institute d'Etude des Questions Juives (IEQJ) in Paris. Sézille, Letter to Ernst Achenbach, a counselor on Abetz's staff, June 4, 1942; CDJC document XI, 198.

the PPF, again working in the area of propaganda. During the occupation he was eventually to head the PPF youth organization.

Many of the journalists active in the Paris press after 1940 came from the movements of the interwar extreme Right, which had formed a subculture in the larger French society. The disappearance of the interwar press in 1940 offered new opportunities to inveterate financial schemers such as Bunau-Varilla, racist and other fringe journalists such as those represented on the *Pilori* staff, as well as Fontenoy, Vauquelin, and other restless activists in search of crusades.[30]

Most significant from the literary point of view was the reappearance in February 1941 of the weekly *Je suis partout,* which had functioned before the war as the literary vehicle for a group of talented dissidents from Action Française. This publication was run by Charles Lesca and Robert Brasillach, the latter becoming chief editor after returning to France in 1941 from a German prisoner-of-war camp. *Je suis partout* collected articles from many of the premier literary figures of the collaboration, including Brasillach himself; Lucien Rebatet, the author of the searing *Les décombres,* which denounced nearly all varieties of French politics including Vichy from an Ultra perspective; Pierre-Antoine Cousteau, Alain Laubreaux, and the writer Georges Blond. Cousteau and Laubreaux were both journalists with right-wing backgrounds, and Blond was a well-known novelist of the interwar period. *Je suis partout* joined Châteaubriant's *La Gerbe* as an unofficial organ of the intellectual Ultra community. The style of the Parisian newspapers varied from the coarse witch-hunting *Pilori* to the more subtle and intellectually refined *La Gerbe* and *Je suis partout,* and from those that appeared in June and July, which were usually little more than French translations of the German press, to the more independent *Œuvre* and *Cri du Peuple* of Déat and Doriot respectively. The political content was very much the same in all. Windows to the outside world were closed; the Propagandastaffel was both source for news and censor when needed.[31]

[30]Report, "Au Pilori," June 12, 1941.

[31]"Bericht über die deutsche Tätigkeit in Paris," October 1940; T-120/475/ 229322; and Jean Fontenoy, letter to de Brinon, December 23, 1940, CDJC document III, 3. For a fuller discussion of the mechanics by which German information and directives were fed into the Paris press, see R. G. Nobécourt, *Les secrets de la*

By the end of 1940 a whole new world had been created in occupied Paris. The arrival of the Germans turned the political scene in France upside down. The fringe and dissident groups of the thirties now held center stage. Yet France had not really changed. The ideological fragmentation of the interwar years persisted. A brief and shallow consensus of support for Pétain masked deep political divisions. Within the collaborationist community common hostility to Vichy and the regime it had replaced was insufficient to forge unity. Paris and the occupied zone were treated to the nearly comical sight of continued acerbic infighting by journalists, politicians, and factions all espousing ideological collaboration.

Autumn 1940 was a time of hope for the Ultras. German soldiers emphasized correct behavior toward the French civilians, stories abounded of Wehrmacht soldiers giving their seats to French women in the Paris *métro,* and German propaganda featured stories of the Wehrmacht helping returning French civilians to reconstruct damaged homes they had left in panic several months before. Flushed with victory, the Germans expected a quick defeat of England and many of the French, General Weygand among them, agreed. German economic exploitation of conquered France had not yet been felt as it would be later in the war. The labor draft for German factories and the yellow star for Jews were still in the future. The handshake of Hitler and Pétain at Montoire might be expected to herald the end to the recurring series of Franco-German bloodbaths every generation.

On December 13, 1940, a split in Vichy intruded upon the development of the collaborationists in Paris. Pétain summarily dismissed Laval, the architect of the Montoire policy. The sacking of Laval was a major turning point in the history of the occupation and the collaboration, for it led directly to the rise of the Rassemblement National Populaire. Déat, the guiding force creating the party, seemed for a brief time in 1941 to have the single mass movement he had failed to obtain the previous summer.

---

propagande en France occupé (Paris: Fayard, 1962), pp. 25ff. On the subject of *Je suis partout,* see Quéval, pp. 305ff. and the more recent study by Pierre-Marie Dioudonnat, *Je suis partout, 1930–1944: les Maurrassiens devant la tentation fasciste* (Paris: La Table Ronde, 1973). The appeal of fascism to the *Je suis partout* clan is discussed within the context of fascism's appeal to intellectuals throughout Europe in Alastair Hamilton, *The Appeal of Fascism* (New York: Avon Books, 1973 [1971]), pp. 203–290.

3 Springtime in the New Order: The Rassemblement National Populaire

The Führer has decided that he does not wish to have Laval in the French government. He should remain in Paris to be used as a counterweight against Pétain.
—Franz Halder, *Tagebuch*, January 28, 1941

On December 13, 1940, with no advance warning, Pierre Laval was dismissed from the cabinet by Marshal Pétain. Several hours after his dismissal, Laval was arrested and communications between Vichy and the outside world were cut. Laval was detained by the Vichy praetorian guards, the Groupes de Protection, veterans of Deloncle's CSAR led by François Méténier and Dr. Henri Martin. Pétain had several reasons for dispensing with Laval's services. He had voiced repeated complaints that Laval had turned the entire complex of Franco-German relations into his own personal fief in his relationship to Abetz, and that he, Pétain, was being kept in the dark on the content of Laval-Abetz negotiations in Paris. As vice president of the Council of Ministers, Laval had received no special mandate for foreign policy, yet it was he who prepared the Montoire meetings. Only after the meetings at Montoire had he been named foreign minister. Pétain had wanted to meet Hitler and had put out feelers of his own, but his meeting with the German leader came only after Hitler had met Laval. Robert Paxton has observed that the issue between Pétain and Laval was not collaboration per se, for both were convinced of its wisdom, although neither wanted to bring France into the war against England. Cobelligerancy was not what the Germans wanted from defeated France.

Pétain feared that Laval might negotiate an agreement by which Vichy forces would seek to retake the French colonies which had gone over to de Gaulle. France might become involved in a colonial war with England, imperiling the fleet, the last military card Vichy had left to play. Pétain had kept open contacts in Madrid with the British, who were showing unexpected strength resisting the German war machine in the late months of 1940. With the failure of their air attack to reduce England to submission and the postponement of invasion plans against the British Isles, the Germans thought for several months of a Mediterranean strategy in which France and her fleet would play an important role. Pétain, Weygand, and Darlan all feared risking the fleet in a premature move caused by Laval.

In addition to Pétain's suspicions of Laval's Paris negotiations, the marshal also felt that a change in personnel might get more concessions from the Germans, who had as yet released very few of the French prisoners they held and who had not appreciably eased restrictions on communications between the two zones. Justice Minister Alibert and others under the influence of Action Française had little sympathy for Laval, who remained the last cabinet holdover from the National Assembly. The personal styles of Pétain and Laval were entirely antithetical, the old, austere, and cautious marshal never totally comfortable in the presence of the earthy, ebullient, cigarette-smoking Laval. Pétain and Laval's successors made very clear by their words as well as their acts that Laval's dismissal did not in any way imply a repudiation of collaboration with Germany.

Under any circumstances dismissing Laval was a risky step for Vichy because he was identified in the minds of most German leaders with the Montoire policy. By a coincidence most unfortunate for the Vichy government, his dismissal came two days before an extravaganza Hitler had planned: the return of the ashes of Napoleon's son to Paris. December 15, 1940 was to be the one hundred and fiftieth anniversary of the birth of the Duke of Reichstadt, Napoleon's son, whose remains had been interred in Vienna's Kapuzinergruft. As a grandiloquent gesture of magnanimity which would also enable him to bask in the borrowed glory of Napoleon, Hitler suggested reburial of the body in a ceremony at the Invalides. Both he and Pétain were to be present. The details were being worked out in Paris by Abetz and Laval. De Brinon was commissioned to bring the official German invitation to Pétain in Vichy. Pétain would attend unaccompanied by any members of his cabinet except for Laval, who was to meet him in Paris. Pétain had wanted the entire government to move back to Paris but he feared being isolated in the company of Laval and Hitler. Suspecting that a trap was being set for him, he became all the more determined to get rid of Laval and declined the

91

German invitation, which was taken as an insult by Hitler. The ceremony took place as scheduled but neither Hitler nor Pétain was present. Instead Abetz and some non-cabinet representatives of Vichy presided.

The most violent German reaction to the sacking of Laval came from Abetz. Official German policy might regard Laval's dismissal as a setback, but for Abetz it threatened a personal disaster, for he had built his own position around Laval. He had hardly finished with the reburial of the Duke of Reichstadt when he appeared surrounded by armed guards in Vichy, furiously threatening any French officials who had the bad luck to cross his path. In several stormy sessions with Pétain, Abetz was unable to convince him to take Laval back into his former post, but he did secure Laval's release and returned with him to Paris. Hitler was unwilling to take the chance of provoking Pétain's resignation by insisting he take back Laval. In Paris Laval might be used as a threat to exact concessions from Vichy and there was briefly some talk of establishing a rival government in the northern zone.

Most significant was the change in German strategic planning from a Mediterranean to an Eastern orientation. By December 1940 the German leaders were already planning Operation Barbarossa, the attack on the Soviet Union. With their new perspective in mind, they lost interest in France and were content to let matters lie. Hitler had no wish to challenge the personal prestige of Marshal Pétain, whom he saw as the best guarantee of a tranquil France at Germany's rear as she turned toward the confrontation with Soviet Russia. Flandin, Laval's successor, was unable to break through the icy wall of suspicion placed before him by the Germans but when Admiral Darlan emerged as the leader of the government in February 1941, he found the Germans ready to discuss economic collaboration. When Hitler made clear to the German Foreign Ministry his desire to see Laval out of office, at least temporarily, Abetz advised Laval to raise his conditions for reentering the government sufficiently high to preclude any offers from Pétain. Laval followed Abetz's advice.[1]

[1]The story of the events of December 13, 1940 has been recounted many times, most notably by Du Moulin de Labarthète, pp. 59ff. Du Moulin's account makes very clear the suspicions harbored by Pétain and his advisers in Vichy against Laval. For Abetz's account of the affair and his role in it, see his telegram no. 1556,

A spinoff of Laval's dismissal was the arrest of Déat in Paris. Déat's press campaign against Vichy had made him powerful enemies, including Alibert, who suggested that the move against Laval would also be a good opportunity to get rid of him also. Pétain could not abide Déat's denunciations of the military leaders at Vichy and incorrectly believed that Déat was serving as Laval's mouthpiece. It seemed a good idea to kill two birds with one stone. As soon as Abetz found out what had occurred, he ordered Déat released and the journalist was back home within hours of his arrest. He continued writing his editorial columns attacking Vichy in *L'Œuvre,* but the

---

December 18, 1940, in Abetz, *Pétain et les allemands: Mémorandum d'Abetz sur les Rapports Franco-Allemands* (Paris: Gaucher, 1948), pp. 44ff. and p. 53 where he blames Action Française for the removal of Laval and suggests that Germany press for his return to the government. See also Reinecke, "Vorgänge um Laval," a report of Abetz to the Foreign Ministry, January 27, 1941, CDJC document CLXXXIV, 9. Other useful accounts of the December crisis include Michel, *Vichy année 40*, pp. 359ff. and Paxton, pp. 92ff., the latter account especially valuable in showing that by no means was the move against Laval to be interpreted as a turning away by Vichy from collaboration.

For Abetz's fear of a resignation by Pétain in the event of too much pressure to restore Laval, see his telegram of December 26, 1940 to Ribbentrop in *Mémorandum d'Abetz,* pp. 65–66. The same collection also contains interpreter Paul Schmidt's account of the Hitler-Darlan meeting of December 25 at Beauvais, in which Darlan reiterated the desire of the French government to maintain the Montoire policy; see ibid., pp. 56–62. In a letter to Mussolini, Hitler told the Duce that he did not believe the official French explanations of Laval's dismissal. Hitler blamed the pressure placed upon Vichy by General Weygand for the sacking of Laval. Weygand was fearful that Laval had been following too pro-German a course, which might eventually result in the loss of French North Africa to the dissidents and the English. Hitler still trusted Pétain but felt that Weygand's influence was too strong; see Hitler, letter to Mussolini, December 31, 1940, in *Akten zur deutschen Auswärtigen Politik,* series D, XI, pp. 825–826. For the rumors that Laval was considering forming a rival regime in Paris, see Abetz, report to Ribbentrop, January 19, 1941, in ibid., p. 944. In this report Abetz also made the suggestion that Laval might be named interior minister but suggested that he remain in Paris where his safety could be guaranteed by the Germans. Hitler's decision to oppose an immediate return of Laval to power and to use him instead as a threat to Vichy is made clear in Halder, *Kriegstagebuch,* II, pp. 261–262, in which appears a report of Abetz to the Army Command, January 28, 1941, cited in *Akten zur deutschen Auswärtigen Politik,* D, XI, pp. 1012–1013, n. This report appears to be the one from Abetz to Reinecke cited above, CDJC document CLXXXIV, 9. For Abetz's advice to Laval to stay out of the government, see his report to Ribbentrop, January 31, 1941, *Akten zur deutschen Auswärtigen Politik,* D, XI, pp. 1026–1027, and for Laval's cooperation in this strategy, see Abetz, reports to Ribbentrop, February 4 and 8, 1941, *Akten zur deutschen Auswärtigen Politik,* D, XII, pp. 14–15 and 44–45 respectively.

Germans imposed a blanket censorship on the entire Paris press with regard to the affair of December 13. Paris readers did not learn anything about the events of December 13–14 from their newspapers until more than a month later, and even then they were provided only the sketchiest accounts.[2]

The evolving situation deepened the special relationship between Abetz and Laval, a kind of mini-collaboration within the larger context of Franco-German collaboration. It also brought Laval and Déat, victims of the same Vichy coalition, together in Paris. The events of December 13–14 led directly to the birth on February 1 of the Rassemblement National Populaire, which became along with the PPF one of the two major Ultra movements of the northern zone and was potentially in 1941 the mass single party Déat had tried to create the previous summer.

The birth of the RNP was announced on February 1 in a radio speech delivered by Jean Fontenoy. In a strongly worded statement, Fontenoy called anew for collaboration with Germany and the achievement of a revolution both "national and social" in France. The new party emerged with a directorate of five leaders whose past political careers showed enormous variation. From MSR circles came Fontenoy, Eugène Deloncle, and Jean Vanor (a pseudonym for Van Ormelingen). Little was known about Vanor except that he had connections in the SS. Also in the directorate was Jean Goy, president of the Union Nationale des Combattants a veterans' organization which had supported the moderate Right in the interwar years. Abetz had made contact with Goy as early as July 1940 and had reported back to Berlin that Goy headed an organization of one million veterans.

The fifth member of the directorate was Déat, who assumed the role of titular leader of the new movement. The RNP represented to Déat a new opportunity to create a single mass party by combining his

---

[2]The German order to release Déat is given in a military communiqué by the head of the Paris military administrative district to the Police Prefect of Paris [Langeron], Paris, December 14, 1940, CDJC document LXXIX, 14/15. For Déat's reaction to his arrest, see Aron, *The Vichy Regime*, p. 244. See also Varennes, pp. 77–78. On the role of Alibert in the arrest of Déat, see Abetz, report to Ribbentrop, December 21, 1940, *Akten zur deutschen Auswärtigen Politik*, D, XI, p. 766. See also Martin du Gard, p. 123. Déat's most virulent broadsides against Vichy, "Leur Sainte-Alliance" and "Il faut les chasser," were published in *L'Œuvre*, December 1 and 2, respectively, 1940.

leftist support with Deloncle's from the Right. Former Socialists and trade unionists might find it difficult at first to work with ex-*Cagoulards* in one political party, Déat admitted, but mass totalitarian parties, he wrote, had always unified the Left and Right into a higher national synthesis. The creation of the RNP marked the culmination of Déat's continuing efforts to combine socialism with nationalsim, which had led him out of the Socialist party and to the creation of the Neo-Socialists in 1933. Moving progressively from the Left to the Right, Déat followed the path of Briand and Laval, who had also attempted conciliatory policies toward Germany.

Two interwar splinter groups came together in the RNP. Deloncle brought a small contingent of mainly lower-middle-class far Right activists, many of whom had left Action Française in protest over its inaction in 1934 and thereafter. Anti-Communist, anti-Semitic, and anti-Republican, they knew only that they wanted a militarized authoritarian right-wing regime that would create a strong industrialized France, providing at the same time scope for heroic military action and security for the various strata of the middle classes. In 1941 they were willing to let Déat work out the doctrine. Déat brought a group of ex-Socialists, labor leaders, and others from the interwar Left who had argued that the crises of the thirties had rendered obsolete Marxist proletarian sectarianism. In forming the Neo-Socialist organization in 1933, Déat and his associates moved toward concern with the nation and adopted the concept of state intervention in economic planning espoused by de Man. By the late 1930's Déat had accepted corporatism as a way to pull France out of the depression and the Neo-Socialists attracted some from the Left whose anti-Communism turned them against the Popular Front and its anti-Axis stance. Both Deloncle and Déat headed factions that after having been denied power under the Third Republic were cast into the political wilderness by Vichy. Laval was instrumental in bringing the factions together. Fontenoy was a friend of his and the two introduced Deloncle to Déat. The whole affair had the blessing of Abetz.[3]

[3]Abetz's role in the creation of the RNP is discussed in his telegram, no. 379, to Ribbentrop, February 1, 1941 in *Mémorandum d'Abetz*, p. 75. For the RNP manifesto see "Exposé fait par Jean Fontenoy, Chef de la propagande du RNP au déjeuner hebdomadaire de la presse américaine, 7 février 1941," CDJC Library no.

For a brief time during the spring of 1941, the combination of Left and Right gave the RNP the potential of an important political force. Formed when German military prospects still looked bright, before the invasion of the Soviet Union galvanized the PPF and changed the character of the war, the RNP might have been a realistic alternative to Vichy. From the outset, however, the new party was inhibited by its own expressed goal of returning Laval to the government. RNP leaders did not know Hitler had decided provisionally that Laval should stay out of the government, a decision Laval accepted. Because of German directives and his own mistrust of Deloncle, Laval quickly moved away from the party. Its continuing campaign to return him to the government in 1941 became a costly waste, clouding the political direction of the new movement and dissipating its energies. Too heavily committed to Laval, the RNP did not plan a total takeover, the only possible path to power for it in 1941. Instead, Deloncle planned a march on Vichy where he expected to restore Laval to power, forcibly if necessary. Deloncle headed the RNP's paramilitary formation, the Légion National Populaire, which was mainly his following from the MSR. To Deloncle the field of action must have seemed much wider for him in the RNP, allied with Déat, Laval, and Abetz, than it would have been had he confined his activities to the more isolated MSR. The RNP was a better bet than the MSR to become a party of the masses. In addition, the RNP offered greater prospects of German support. Although Deloncle had made contacts with SS circles in 1940, the SS presence in France was not yet what it would be after 1942 when it became the major force in the German establishment there. Abetz never trusted Deloncle, whose *Cagoulard* and Germanophobic past made him suspect in the eyes of the German ambassador. Deloncle may also have been influenced in his decision to join Déat by Admiral Darlan, with whom his ties dated from his active days as a naval engineer.

Deloncle made his plans to march on Vichy much in the manner of the Fascist march on Rome of October 1922. Once in Vichy, he and his Légion National Populaire would liberate the provisional capital

---

8085. For Abetz's appraisal of Jean Goy, see Der Vertreter des Auswärtigen Amts bei dem Militärbefehlshaber in Paris, note to Chef der Militärverwaltung Frankreich," July 15, 1940 in *Akten zur deutschen Auswärtigen Politik,* D, X, p. 177. Although unsigned, the report was most certainly written by Abetz.

from the nefarious influence of the Maurrasians there. Maurras, living in Lyons, feared for his life and asked the local police prefect for protection against a possible attack by Deloncle's men. Deloncle's planned raid, however, ran into German opposition. They did not want to back an operation that might have led to the resignation of Pétain, and at the time were not even interested in returning Laval to power. Practical politician that he was, Laval was attracted to neither the conspiratorial adventures of Deloncle nor the abstract doctrinaire preachings of Déat. Put simply, the RNP was not playing the game of Abetz and Laval, and although they continued to lend moderate support to it at times, for them the party's chief importance lay in its nuisance value, as irritant and threat to official Vichy.[4]

The RNP was faced with a number of serious problems in the spring of 1941. It had taken a position on Laval in opposition to that of Hitler, Abetz, and Laval himself. Rivals within the Ultra camp, notably Doriot and his PPF, had to be either absorbed or eliminated but German policy opposed the creation of a strong single party in France and their help could not be expected in any attempt to quash the PPF. The multiplicity of German services in France also worked against the RNP's eliminating its rivals. While Déat schemed with Laval and Abetz, Doriot assiduously courted German officials in the Wehrmacht and SS. Since Vichy refused to let any political parties operate in the unoccupied zone, the RNP was confined to the northern zone until after the total German occupation of France in November 1942. The PPF had faced the same restriction on its

[4]See "Cour Nationale de Justice de Lyon. Ministère Public C/MM. Maurras et Pujo," a typewritten stenographic account of the trial, BDIC, Q 51 Rés, fascicle 3, audience of January 25, 1945, pp. 58–60. There has been some confusion in the timing because Alexandre Angeli, the prefect of Lyons, and Pujo associated the projected march on Vichy with the assassination of Dormoy, which occurred on July 25, 1941. In *Action Française*, p. 473, Eugen Weber suggests that the Delonclist threat against Maurras and Pujo followed the Dormoy assassination, whereas another account has the projected march being planned earlier. See Jean Galtier-Boissière, "Histoire de la Guerre, 1939–1945," published as special issues of *Crapouillot*, 5 vols. (1948), 4:266. The earlier timing squares more with the fact that Laval's interest in the RNP was of relatively short duration. See also Georges Albertini, "Marcel Déat and the Rassemblement National Poplaire," deposition in *France during the German Occupation*, 3:1209. By July 1941, Deloncle's preoccupations were very different from those of Laval, whose activities after December 13, 1940 are discussed by Paxton, pp. 104–108.

activity in the southern zone, but it had the remnants of its prewar organization on which to build whereas the RNP had none. In addition, there was tension within the leadership of the RNP where Deloncle and Déat coexisted uneasily. Nonetheless the movement was launched amid great fanfare and high hopes. A meeting at the Salle Wagram in Paris attracted a crowd of five or six thousand. Jean Guéhenno, an anticollaboration witness, attended the meeting out of curiosity and described in his diary what he saw.

There were, he wrote, no workers. The audience was composed of *employés* (clerks, petty employees, white- as opposed to blue-collar workers), shopkeepers, and "false intellectuals," people who before the war had supported Deloncle's CSAR and de la Rocque's Croix de Feu. Guéhenno found the crowd in no way representative of the French people, neither "nationally" nor "socially," as he put it. It was, he wrote, almost exclusively lower middle class. Since much of the Parisian population could be described as lower middle class, the crowd was perhaps more representative of the city's population than Guéhenno wished to admit. Jean Goy spoke first and was followed on the podium by a Breton spokesman. Guéhenno found all the speakers mediocre with the exception of Déat, whose energy singled him out from among the others in the group. Déat intrigued but also frightened Guéhenno, who devoted several lines in the diary to a description of the RNP leader:

> I dare not think about his faith, his sincerity. Without doubt he has the sincerity of his profession: for twenty years he has aspired to power; he still does. A political man should want to exercise power, he says to justify himself. He wants to be a leader, he will be one in German if he cannot be in French. He will be Führer if this is the language of the new Europe. What do the flock matter to him as long as he is the herdsman? One passion alone inspired him yesterday: hatred of the Vichy government which did not make him a minister.[5]

The apparent destruction of party membership lists at the time of the Liberation makes it impossible to give precise figures for the size of the collaborationist parties. An intense membership drive was launched during the spring of 1941 by the RNP. In a speech at the

[5]Guéhenno, pp. 121–122.

first party congress in June, Vanor, the secretary-general, claimed more than half a million members. Within several days of its establishment, the party had attracted 16,000 members, according to him. French political parties, except for the Communists, have been traditionally small and the figures given by Vanor seem quite impressive. Undoubtedly they were inflated. Since Goy and Deloncle were members of the RNP, Vanor simply included as members of the party the members of Goy's veterans' association and Deloncle's MSR. Goy did not control the members of his organization, however, and not all members of the MSR joined the RNP, so Vanor's figures are subject to question. Leaders of trade unions or other organizations upon joining the RNP were often considered to have brought their entire membership into the movement when membership figures were added up. In many cases the membership figures given by Ultra parties included individuals who were simultaneously members of several such organizations. One man in Auray, for example, had joined both MSR and RNP as well as the anti-Semitic Communauté Française. He was waiting to see which would prove the most dynamic in helping achieve what he called the French renovation. There is no record available of his final choice.[6]

The figures for the circulation of *L'Œuvre* do not help in gauging the membership of the RNP because the quantities of newspapers printed depended mainly upon the Propagandastaffel, and the purchase of a newspaper by an individual did not necessarily indicate membership in the movement. After 1942 the RNP was allowed to circulate free but not sell a weekly party organ, *National Populaire*, whose distribution was roughly 30,000 weekly. Many copies of the *National Populaire* were sent to prospective as well as actual party members. The party organ during the first half of 1941 was the weekly *Rassemblement*, edited by Fontenoy with a tone more MSR than Déatist. One cannot know how many persons read a copy of one newspaper, which also makes party influence difficult to assess. The large party rallies attracted the faithful but also the curious. Many spectators at the Salle Wagram in February 1941 were curiosity-seekers such as Guéhenno, bored with the curfews and grim conditions of life in occupied Paris and merely looking for entertainment.

[6]Letter dated April 22, 1941, CDJC document XIa, 227.

An anti-German observer found it relatively easy for enemies, such as Gaullists and Communists, to infiltrate the RNP. According to her account, the RNP was able to enroll only about three thousand members in the first two weeks of its existence. To show more recruits than it had, it employed the common political tactic of stamping a high number on its first membership card and counting up from it. There was also talk of pressure on civil servants to join the party or face loss of their jobs. Women sometimes joined in the hope that party influence might induce the Germans to release a family member from a prisoner-of-war camp.[7]

In addition to the Légion National Populaire, the RNP established several other affiliated organizations, to organize and politicize as many aspects of French life as possible. By June there existed a territorial network of local organizations headed by Goy, an association for the families of prisoners of war, and an association concerned with affairs in the overseas empire. An organization directed toward industrial workers drew its leadership from former Socialist and trade-union elements close to Déat. These included Georges Dumoulin, formerly of the CGT, and the other labor leaders Gabriel Lafaye and René Mesnard. Both RNP and PPF competed for workers' support now "available" in the absence of the traditional labor organizations. Déat argued repeatedly that workers' unions should have a status equal to that of employers' associations in Vichy's corporative structure, a point which the government of Darlan was unwilling to grant. Collaborationist castigation of Vichy as reactionary had a geographical base in that the occupied zone was far more industrial and the problems of the workers more pressing there than in the unoccupied zone. The southern zone, over which Vichy held sway, was more agrarian and this fact combined with the rural predilections of many Vichyites gave the government a greater orientation toward agricultural problems and peasant life.

[7]The inflated figures for RNP membership were given by Jean Vanor, *RNP: Origines, Structures, Buts* (Paris: RNP, 1941), p. 5. This pamphlet is the text of Vanor's speech to the first party congress, June 14–15, 1941. The smaller figure is given by Madeleine Gex Le Verrier, *France in Torment*, trans. Eden and Cedar Paul (London: Hamish Hamilton, 1942), p. 73. For this reference I am indebted to Colin Youlden of Merton College, Oxford University. Figures for the circulation of the leading newspapers in occupied Paris may be found in Gérard Walter, p. 75.

The RNP and PPF tried to attract working-class support but their efforts were directed more toward attempting to win the workers over to the New Order than toward basic social reform. Although the moralism and pretensions to "spiritual" values brought in some anti-Communist union leaders such as Dumoulin, they were followed into collaborationism by relatively few workers. Most French workers were aware of the suppression of independent workers' organizations in Germany after 1933 and they could see a similar development in France after the establishment of the Vichy government. With material conditions worsening as France had to pay the costs of the occupation, few workers came out for collaboration. Lacking support among the workers and peasants, the collaborationist movements depended more upon white-collar, *employé,* artisan, and petty merchant strata of society: broadly speaking, the lower middle classes. The RNP did not ignore the peasantry but, like the Green Shirt leader Dorgères, peasants preferred the more openly agrarian orientation of Vichy. Like all parties inspired to a degree by the New Order, the RNP had an active propaganda section. This was headed in June 1941 by Fontenoy. Second in command was Michel Brille, who later became a vice-president of the party. Rounding out the party structure was a youth movement, the Jeunesse National Populaire, which did not really get off the ground until later.[8]

From the outset the RNP found itself in an insoluble dilemma that affected all of the collaborationist parties during the occupation. Because neither Vichy nor the Germans wanted the Ultras in power, their calls for action and revolution sounded increasingly vain and hollow. There were no electoral battles to be waged in occupied France and the Ultras were not interested in elections anyway. Frustrated in their desires for quick action, the Ultra parties were forced to play a waiting game, competing with one another for influence among the German services in France and for popular support among a limited French clientele. The thirst for action and adventure motivating many younger party militants had to be appeased somehow, and this often took the form of anti-Semitic demonstrations such as the one in which Doriot was involved with his PPF in Vichy. Battles between members of rival Ultra factions were frequent, espe-

[8]Vanor, *RNP: Origines, Structures, Buts,* pp. 4–9.

cially when hawkers of competing newspapers met in the streets, although these confrontations seldom got out of hand. The later history of the MSR and the RNP would show that violent clashes between factions of a single party were also not ruled out. Some of the more impatient among the Ultras eventually joined organizations whose scope for action was broader. Within France they turned to the Milice of Joseph Darnand. For service beyond the borders they joined the Anti-Bolshevik Legion, the Phalange Africaine—a volunteer unit formed to fight the Allies in Tunisia in early 1943—and ultimately the Waffen-SS.

The spring of 1941 was an optimistic period for the RNP, which was engaged in setting up its various offices and affiliates. The Légion National Populaire, led by Deloncle and his aides, mounted several paramilitary operations, seizing apartments and properties of departed Jews. The Paris apartment of former Interior Minister Georges Mandel was taken over by the party. Such operations were carried out in accord with the German authorities. In Paris the party was able to get for its use offices that had belonged to the Ligue Internationale contre l'Antisémétisme and similar takeovers were organized in other French cities. An "Ordre de Mission," dated June 16, 1941 describes in detail plans for the seizure of shops in the town of Troyes, in the Aube department. In some cases operations were supervised personally by Deloncle; in others subordinate party members took charge. Captured apartments, such as Mandel's, were sometimes used as party offices. One plan included the seizure of a building in the second *arrondissement* of Paris, to establish there a "Restaurant Populaire" for use by party militants of that district. The initials RNP were to be given a culinary as well as a political significance.[9]

Despite public shows of solidarity, tension existed within the RNP almost from the very beginning. Déat had difficulties in getting some of his friends from the Left to accept Deloncle. Comparing the *Cagoule's* spirit of risk-taking and camaraderie to that of the French

[9]CDJC document XIg, 3. For Deloncle's involvement in the seizure of LICA property see CDJC document CCCLXX, 113, dated March 26, 1941; the plan for the seizures in Troyes, which were to occur on June 17, are elaborated in a letter of the day before, CDJC document CCCLXX, 66, the "Ordre de Mission." See also CCCLXX, 62 and 65, all in the CDJC.

troops at Verdun in 1916, Déat overlooked dissensions that had led some *Cagoulards* to mysterious deaths in the 1930's. He tried to relate his own interwar career to Deloncle's by saying that both had fought Communism. Alarmed at the growing activity of Deloncle within the new RNP, many of Déat's ex-parliamentary associates beat hasty retreats. To join a celebrated terrorist such as Deloncle was more than they could accept. Laval lost interest, as did his associates Adrien Marquet, a supporter of the single-party movement during the summer of 1940, and Pierre Cathala, finance minister during Laval's second tenure in office after 1942, who quickly left the RNP.[10]

Deloncle, the technician adventurer, was little suited for compatibility with the cold, doctrinaire, philosophically oriented *Normalien* Déat. Both wanted to be sole leader, and the fact that Déat presided over the five-man directorate rankled Deloncle. Most of the dynamism of the early RNP came from the Légion National Populaire, which was staffed with Deloncle's cohorts from the MSR. Despite repeated urging on the part of Déat, Deloncle refused to disband the MSR, which continued its independent existence under his control, giving rise to suspicions as to where his real allegiance lay. A series of events beginning in the middle of June provoked an open break between the two that resulted ultimately in the expulsion of Deloncle and his supporters from the RNP.

The first RNP party congress was held on June 14 and 15 amid extensive publicity and press coverage in Paris. A week later followed the German invasion of the Soviet Union. Each of these events contributed to the emerging split in the RNP leadership. The party congress was carried off with a great public show of harmony and on the surface all seemed well. Each of the five members of the directorate made a speech and had his moment of prominence. Deloncle gave a report on behalf of the Légion National Populaire in which he recounted the story of an attempted incursion into RNP offices by a gang of toughs from the rival PPF. The intruders, according to Deloncle, had been searching for RNP membership lists but had been foiled and captured by a detachment of LNP on guard. The PPF invaders were subjected to the indignity of having their own party membership cards taken and were also photographed before being

[10]*French Basic Handbook,* p. 146. See also Déat, "Retrouver les hommes," *L'Œuvre,* March 3, 1941.

released. Deloncle and later Déat used the incident to deliver sarcastic denunciations of Doriot and the PPF. The incursion actually served both parties well by enabling some of their more hotheaded activists to work off excess energy in an adventure in which no real damage was done to either movement. Similar scenes were to recur frequently during the occupation.[11]

As president of the directing committee, Déat delivered the last speech, a grand finale which summarized the results of the congress. A more effective speaker than Deloncle, Déat left a definite impression of being in charge. While Deloncle pondered his future in the RNP, the German attack launched on June 22 against the Soviet Union changed the situation of the Ultras in occupied France. The new "crusade of the West" gave the Ultras something more positive in which to become involved, and Deloncle immediately demanded the creation of a unit of French volunteers to join the Germans in their struggle against Communism. He fired off a letter calling for the establishment of a volunteer unit to Marshal Pétain, who was willing to see French volunteers fight in the East but only as a private, not as a government initiative.

Early in July the Anti-Bolshevik Legion of Volunteers (Légion des Volontaires Français contre le Bolchévisme) was established in Paris. It was a rare example of concerted action by the various Ultra factions for Deloncle was joined by Déat, Doriot, and leaders of some of the smaller collaborationist groups. The PPF was ultimately to dominate the legion, but Deloncle became the first president of its steering committee. A rally was held on July 18 at the Vélodrome d'hiver in Paris in order to stimulate recruitment. All five members of the RNP directorate volunteered to serve in the Anti-Bolshevik Legion. As news of striking German advances into Russia poured in during the summer of 1941 many expected their service to entail little more than participation in a German victory parade in Moscow. Of the five RNP directors who "volunteered," Fontenoy was the only one ever actually to see action at the front.

Deeply involved in the formation of the Anti-Bolshevik Legion, Deloncle did not lose sight of the leadership of the RNP which he apparently felt was slipping increasingly in the direction of Déat.

[11]A full report of the June RNP party congress is given in *Rassemblement,* no. 2, June 22, 1941.

Although much in the story of the events leading to the final break may never be known, by all accounts the rupture was initiated by Deloncle. Déat also had reasons to wish to be rid of Deloncle. He seemed uncomfortable with some of the pillaging expeditions organized by Deloncle's men. In 1935 Déat had shared a speaker's platform with the chief rabbi of Paris and had publicly condemned German anti-Semitism. Even in 1941 he was denounced as "philosemitic" and he continually had to fend off charges leveled at him by other Ultras of softness on Freemasonry. Deloncle's refusal to dissolve the MSR did not please Déat, who also suspected that Deloncle had known in advance of the German attack against the USSR but had not let him into the secret. Kept well informed by Darlan, Deloncle might have spared Déat the gaffe of writing the day before the attack that Stalin and Hitler would never go to war.[12]

Deloncle meanwhile had developed an elaborate scheme for taking control of the RNP. The Germans in 1941 had not yet started to draft Western European labor for their war machine, but the manpower need was felt and French volunteers were being encouraged to work in Germany. Sincere Ultras would find it difficult to avoid answering the call and Deloncle tried to arrange to have Déat's supporters within the RNP sent off as volunteer workers to Germany. His own backers would remain solidly entrenched in the RNP and the MSR, making it easier for him to take control. (This ploy was later used by Laval to denude the Ultra parties.) The remnants of Déat's following within the RNP were to be eliminated in a purge orchestrated by

[12]Déat, "Communistes et gaullistes," *L'Œuvre*, June 21, 1941. For Deloncle's connections with Admiral Darlan and Déat's awareness of them, see Jean-Raymond Tournoux, *L'histoire secrète* (Paris: Plon, 1962), pp. 145–146. Déat's announced doctrinal positions were often more extreme than he was willing to go in practice; see, for example, Varennes, p. 104, discussing Déat's Republicanism and on Déat in general, p. 223. See also Brissaud, p. 105. For Déat's defense of the rights of German Jews in 1935, see the pamphlet "Discours de Protestation contre les Atteintes Portées en Allemagne à la Dignité de la personne humaine, à la Liberté de conscience chrétienne et laïque, et aux droits humains et civiques des israélites," published in 1937 and available as CDJC document CCXXI, 50. Sharing the platform on the occasion with Déat were, among others, Pastor Marc Boegner, president of the Protestant Federation of France; Julien Weil, Grand Rabbi of Paris; and Paul Reynaud. The 1941 denunciation of Déat as philosemitic came from René Gérard, head of the anti-Semitic Institute d'Etude des Questions Juives, in a letter to *L'Œuvre*, June 13, 1941, CDJC document XId, 62. I am grateful to Joseph Billig for having drawn this letter to my attention.

Deloncle, and Déat would be removed in an "automobile accident." Deloncle's *Cagoulard* past furnished ample reason to take his plot seriously. [13]

Deloncle's plans were thwarted on August 27, 1941 by an assassination attempt made against Laval and Déat. Participating in ceremonies marking the departure of the first Anti-Bolshevik Legion volunteers for the East, Laval and Déat were both seriously wounded by the young Paul Colette, who sprayed bullets into the gathering of notables at the Borgnis-Desbordes barracks in Versailles. Colette, arrested on the spot, claimed to have acted as a member of the Resistance and was so honored after the war in a telegram from General de Gaulle. Déat and Laval owed their lives to the small caliber of the gun used, 6.35 millimeters. Both blamed Deloncle, whom they viewed as the secret instigator of the attack. Colette claimed to have joined the legion merely for the opportunity to shoot a prominent collaborator at close range. But the suspicions harbored by Déat, who later changed his view, and Laval, who did not, bear eloquent witness to the character of Deloncle and the level of tension that existed within the RNP leadership. Only a month before the Borgnis-Desbordes incident, Marx Dormoy, the Popular Front interior minister who in 1937 had exposed the various *Cagoulard* conspiracies, had been assassinated in a crime that had the distinct characteristics of a *Cagoulard* affair. [14]

At Laval's request Colette's life was spared but Colette stuck to his story that he had acted alone in a gesture of resistance. No conspiracy was ever proven but the incident provoked the final breach within the RNP. Déat was warned about an MSR plot against his leadership of the RNP by Tonia Masse, a Belgian woman who had been in Léon

[13]"A verser au dossier de la Cagoule/Mme. Masse victime du duel Déat-Deloncle," *Dissidence 40,* October 24 and 31, 1948. Voiron, p. 25 argues that Vanor, whom he calls a "professional killer," was involved with Deloncle in the conspiracy against Déat.

[14]As with so many crimes involving *Cagoulards,* the responsibility for the assassination of Dormoy has never been fully determined. See the discussion in Bourdrel, pp. 254–256. Laval's continuing suspicion of Deloncle's part in the August 27 assassination attempt was expressed during the cabinet meeting of July 12, 1944; see Tracou, p. 334. Colette's account of the incident and the honor paid him by General de Gaulle is given in "De Gaulle écrit à l'homme qui tira sur Pierre Laval," *France Dimanche,* December 15, 1946. There is confusion even in the spelling of Colette's name which sometimes appears as Collette, the spelling used by Bourdrel.

Degrelle's Rexist movement before the war and then been a secretary to Deloncle. She also headed a women's welfare section of the MSR, which existed on paper only. Madame Masse's reasons for having turned against Deloncle are not clear. She accused him of having embezzled party funds but may also have had more personal reasons to wish to frustrate him. In any case she warned Déat, who was convalescing with Laval in a Paris hospital. Whether Madame Masse went to see Déat is uncertain but her message got through and she was murdered several days later, most certainly by men of the MSR.[15]

Even before he learned of Masse's death, Déat determined that the time had come for swift action against Deloncle. He called a war council of RNP men he could trust and they organized a preventive coup to remove Deloncle and his supporters from the party. Déat's intimates included Jean Goy and Barthélemy Montagnon's brother Paul. In a neighboring bed, Laval concurred in the new course of action. The image of Déat planning a coup is at some variance with most descriptions portraying him solely as a doctrinaire ideologue. He had amply demonstrated physical courage, however, during the First World War and would show it again during the course of two subsequent assassination attempts. He could act swiftly and decisively even if he did not always project this quality through his cold pedantry. The decision was made to create a new Légion National Populaire of Déatists and with it mount an attack against the offices of the RNP to rid them of Delonclists. Contacts were used to secure German nonintervention.[16]

Déat next ordered the MSR group out of the RNP. Deloncle's men were to vacate all party installations, and all members of the RNP were given the choice of leaving with Deloncle or remaining in a party that was to be refashioned by Déat. To forestall resistance from

___

[15]"A verser au dossier de la Cagoule." Déat later recalled having met with Madame Masse who appeared, accompanied by Vanor (presumably to keep her quiet), in his hospital room. Désert, p. 57 claims that Masse discovered that Deloncle had misappropriated 300,000 francs of MSR funds and that she had threatened to expose him, although there is no indication to whom. Désert also contends that Masse was lured to her death by one of Deloncle's henchmen, whose mistress he says she was.

[16]"A verser au dossier de la Cagoule." This account has been further substantiated by several former MSR members and friends who were kind enough to give interviews to me.

Deloncle's backers, Déat named Paul Montagnon to succeed Deloncle as head of the Légion National Populaire. Montagnon was dispatched with a squadron of supporters to "recapture" the LNP offices from Deloncle's men entrenched there. The description of Montagnon's men laying siege to the offices of their own party has an almost comic-opera flavor. Passers-by in the streets of Paris could only wonder at the destination of the squad of uniformed men they encountered. A noncommissioned reserve officer, Montagnon led his troupe to the party headquarters at 128 rue du Faubourg Saint-Honoré. A contemporary journalist described their march: "Montagnon, always in the lead, hurrying most handsomely, waves his black cape in place of a flag. The men wind their leather belts around their fists, taking good care to allow the copper buckles to hang. . . . There will be some sport," Once there, the invaders took possession of the offices and barricaded themselves against any counterattack. Jacques Corrèze, representing Deloncle's forces, appeared upon the scene sometime later and attempted negotiation but Montagnon would have none of it. Deloncle and Vanor may have approached the German SD for help but the Déat group had done its homework and the Germans remained on the sidelines, as did the Paris police. Deloncle's expulsion from the RNP pleased Abetz, who in 1941 was still a person to be reckoned with in France. Vanor and Fontenoy followed Deloncle out of the RNP while Goy, having sided with Déat, remained a member but played a decreasingly important role until 1942 when he was removed from the party after Laval had been returned to power.[17]

The expulsion of Deloncle and his followers from the RNP was a victory won at great cost for Déat. Once again he had failed to build a mass totalitarian single party. The RNP had possessed an ideological unity but the legacy of the fragmented political past was too strong to overcome. The grand united party in the fascist style came apart. Technocrats and modernizing businessmen such as Schueller left with the romantic crusaders and conspirators of Deloncle. Déat retained those among his Neo-Socialist and trade-union friends who

[17]This account and the quotation comes from "A verser au dossier de la Cagoule." See also Varennes, pp. 80–81. A good synopsis of the public positions taken by Déat and Deloncle on the subject of the split within the RNP is given in Cotta, pp. 256–258.

had not been totally disaffected by the Deloncle interlude. They brought a few workers into his rump movement. The base of the party, insofar as it retained a popular following, remained the lower middle classes of Paris and some of the smaller towns of the occupied zone, as described in February 1941 by Guéhenno. United the partisans of Déat and Deloncle formed the nucleus of a fascist movement; divided each one was a fragment with fascist characteristics. Deloncle's reconstituted MSR remained a band of adventurers which split repeatedly until the movement died.

By the end of 1941 the RNP was turning into a pressure group of some disparate interests coalescing around the verbiage of fascism and collaboration to nudge France's stalled society. A few businessmen interested in social engineering remained, and they together with some dissident trade-union leaders from the disbanded CGT, sought modernization, although with different priorities. White-collar and lower-middle-class members had their own interests to preserve against Vichyite agrarian and big-business proclivities and Communist revolution and found the combination of fascist mystique and possible German support attractive. Still publicly committed to the return of Laval to the government, the party could not openly call for "revolution" with quite the intensity of its PPF rival. It suffered a drain of its most militarized members to the MSR and later the PPF, Milice, and military formations fighting in the east, whose goals were less ambiguous. Although estimates of RNP losses to Deloncle in the fall of 1941 vary from numerically minimal to two-thirds, there can be no doubt of the loss in verve and dynamism suffered by Déat's movement.[18]

The new leaders of the RNP were former Neo-Socialists and anti-Communist trade unionists whom Déat felt he could trust. They

[18]Varennes, p. 80, asserts that two-thirds of the RNP membership followed Deloncle out of the party. The *French Basic Handbook,* p. 146, in contrast, holds that relatively few RNP people followed Deloncle into the MSR and that of these many ultimately returned to Déat. Actually the losses Déat suffered to the MSR in November 1941 varied in different localities. In the Loiret, for example, a new RNP committee had to be organized with a new leader designated by the central party office in Paris. The section at Gien passed in its entirety to the MSR. See Yves Durand and David Bohbot, "La collaboration politique dans les pays de la Loire moyenne: étude historique et socio-politique du R.N.P. en Indre-et-Loire et dans le Loiret," *Revue d'histoire de la deuxième guerre mondiale,* 23 (July 1973), 58–59.

included Dumoulin and Lafaye, formerly of the CGT, Ludovic Zoretti of a CGT-affiliated teachers' union, and Kléber Legay of the northern miners' organization. The RNP attempted to assert a proprietary interest in the French labor movement against the oft denounced "reactionary" circles in Vichy. The party's uncontested leader after November 1941, Déat has been described by one historian as a man whose "practice was always better than his theory." He attracted trade-union cadres who had been Republican but antiparliamentarian. [19] These men included former Socialists such as Zoretti and Georges Albertini; adherents of the economic planning theories of de Man and Déat during the interwar years, they were moderate social-reforming "New Deal" types who were led by anti-Communism and their prior support of Déat to accept the fascism of the RNP made necessary by the changed political conditions of the German occupation. Wishing to move France to a more modern planned industrial society, they followed Déat in embracing what in National Socialism approximated their earlier Neo-Socialist ideas, ignoring the rest.

A teacher, Albertini had headed the RNP section at Troyes. Following Deloncle's departure, he was named secretary-general for the entire RNP organization. Zoretti had been active in a workers' education center for the CGT prior to the war and he now created the Union de l'Enseignement, a teachers' association under the aegis of the RNP. [20] Michel Brille, a lawyer, became a vice-president of the reorganized RNP. Déat's new appointees had almost all been opposed to war with Germany in the late 1930's. They had shared with him the criticism of the fragmentation of parliamentary activity after 1934 and had wanted to make Socialism less sectarian and proletarian and more palatable to the middle classes during the interwar years. [21]

Déat never made anti-Semitism a major part of his platform, and the virulence of his anti-Semitism after 1940 did not approach that of others in France, such as those associated with the anti-Semitic

[19]See the description of Déat in Eugen Weber, "Nationalism, Socialism, and National-Socialism in France," *French Historical Studies,* 2 (1962), 304.

[20]Varennes, p. 84. See also the typewritten stenographic trial account, *"Ministère Public C/M. Georges Albertini,"* p. 22; available in the BDIC, Q 50 1–4 Rés.

[21]Laurent, "Les hommes de gauche," p. 36. For the account of a visit to the Soviet Union by a miner who returned disillusioned, see Kléber Legay, *Un mineur français chez les Russes* (Paris: Pierre Tisné, 1937).

Institute d'Etude des Questions Juives. By the end of 1940, however, Déat saw Jews behind de Gaulle in London and the "reactionaries" who had arrested him and ousted Laval two weeks earlier. "Ideologies are of little account," wrote Déat in regard to Jews, "when it's a question of safeguarding the main thing, which is money."[22]

During the fall of 1941, Déat was attacked by Bernard Faÿ, director of the Bibliothèque Nationale and a staunch foe of Freemasonry. Replying directly to Faÿ but also to the Delonclists then on their way out of the RNP, Déat contended that the National Revolution transcended hatred of Jews, Freemasons, or parliament. He had given lectures to groups of Freemasons before the war but had not joined the organization.[23]

By the summer of 1942, Déat was arguing that the Jews were an alien race. Contradicting his own prewar stand, the RNP leader reflected a French anti-Semitism that had intensified during the late 1930's in reaction against the Popular Front and the influx of Jewish refugees from Central Europe. He suggested a whosesale transfer of Europe's Jewish population to a remote place, perhaps Madagascar, frequently mentioned as a possible Jewish resettlement center prior to the adoption of the "Final Solution" by the Germans. Even in August 1942, however, Déat was ready to make exceptions indicating that his conversion to racism was not complete. Jewish war veterans were to be viewed as "honorable allies," a position Déat borrowed from Louis-Charles Lecoc, the general propaganda delegate of the Comité d'Action Anti-bolchévique, founded by the historian Paul Chack, whose popular histories of the navy were well known in France. Too deeply steeped in the political values of Republican France to indulge in the wildly anti-Semitic and anti-Masonic outbursts of his rivals, Déat was still forced by the logic of his position to

---

[22]Déat, "Cet autre cagoulard," *L'Œuvre*, December 28, 1940.

[23]Déat, "Réponse à un jésuite déguisé en bibliothécaire," *L'Œuvre*, October 7, 1941. For attacks on Déat's alleged Freemasonry, see the MSR newspaper, *Révolution Nationale*, October 12, 1941, cited in Cotta, p. 257. That he lectured before groups of Freemasons, but had never joined the society, I was told during the course of an interview with Henry Coston, June 26, 1974. Coston devoted monumental energy during and after the war to the exposure of Freemasons. A German view of the polemics exchanged between Déat and Faÿ is available in the SD report, Bezirkschef C, Verwaltungsstab, Verwaltungsabteilung—Az. VA 202/2, Jgb. Nr. 227/41 geh.; November 7, 1941, Dijon; addressed to Beauftragten des Chefs der Sicherheitspolizei und des Aussenstelle Dijon; CDJC document LXXV, 217.

embrace anti-Semitism. This did not prevent his being denounced repeatedly by less inhibited rivals. [24]

Some of Déat's Republican traits never left him despite his pretensions as leader of the RNP. Toward the end of the occupation when he was minister of labor and national solidarity, he complained to Abetz that general policy issues were not being discussed during French cabinet meetings under the presidency of Laval. Abetz replied that discussions might lead to division within the government. In view of the growing intensity of civil strife, governmental division might be particularly dangerous for France. He asked Déat how such splits would be resolved. Déat replied that votes could settle any division of opinion, to which Abetz responded that voting seemed an odd recommendation from a national socialist such as Déat. It was not the way dictatorships functioned. [25]

Déat often defended the Republic, though not its parliament, and took great pains to connect his evolving national socialism back to his Neo-Socialist thought. Despite his Republican proclivities, his basic political positions increasingly approximated those of his collaborationist rivals as the war progressed. His hardening stand can be followed in his quarrels with Jeanson in 1940 and subsequently with Spinasse and Château, men of the Left who started down the road of collaboration but proved unwilling to follow Déat all the way. [26]

Déat attacked Charles Spinasse over the latter's refusal to support a single-party state. A Socialist before the war, Spinasse had served as minister of national economy in Blum's Popular Front government and had rallied to the National Revolution in July 1940. Shortly thereafter he became director of the newspaper *L'Effort* in the unoccupied zone. In November 1941 he came to Paris and with another

---

[24]Déat, *Le parti unique*, (Paris: Aux Armes de France, 1942), pp. 129–131. This book was a collection of articles published by Déat in the summer of 1942 in *L'Œuvre*. The racial concept of the Jew is elaborated further by Déat in "L'antisémitisme et l'église" and "Catholicisme et racisme," *L'Œuvre*, July 26 and 27, respectively, 1943.

[25]The story is told by Tracou, p. 333, and repeated by him in deposition no. 68 in *France during the German Occupation 1940–1944*, 3:1506. See Chap. 10, below, n. 37.

[26]See Stanley Grossmann, "L'évolution de Marcel Déat," *Revue d'histoire de la deuxième guerre mondiale*, 25 (January 1975), 25. For Déat's own discussion of the continuity in his thought before and after 1940, see Déat, "De l'émeute à la défaite," *L'Œuvre*, February 9, 1941.

former Socialist, Paul Rives, established a weekly paper, *Le Rouge et le Bleu*. The new venture lasted until August of the following year. Forced to give up *Le Rouge et le Bleu* in part because of his quarrel with Déat, Spinasse returned to the unoccupied zone. After the Liberation he was tried for collaboration but acquitted. *Le Rouge et le Bleu* was launched as a newspaper defending Socialism in occupied France. Spinasse renounced none of his Republican past and argued that France must avoid imitation of foreign models. For his efforts he became the target of shrill denunciations from the Right, including a suggestion by Pierre Costantini, founder of the arch-collaborationist and anti-English Ligue Française, that he be incarcerated in a concentration camp.[27]

When Spinasse came out publicly against the idea of a single-party state, Déat was added to his growing list of enemies. During the summer of 1942 the RNP chief was involved in one of his many efforts to launch a single party, and Spinasse's opposition was most inopportune. Attacked from all sides, Spinasse found himself totally isolated. Déat's criticisms seem to have surprised him for he apparently expected kinder treatment from his old parliamentary colleague. Without support in Paris, Spinasse was obliged to cease publication of his paper and suspend all political activity there.[28]

Déat also quarreled with René Château, one of his closest associates in the RNP. Château had been a Socialist and a staunch pacifist prior to the war. He had been drawn to Déat in 1940. Deputy from the Charante, Château had actively supported Déat's attempt to create a single party during the summer of 1940 in Vichy. Like Déat a philosophy professor—"these dreamers are capable of anything," he later wrote—Château was encouraged by the Montoire meeting to believe that the longstanding Franco-German enmity had finally been buried. Both Déat and Château shared in the Socialist Germanophile viewpoint, born in the years before 1917, and both were steeped in the German philosophical tradition. Château joined in establishing the RNP and contributed articles to *L'Œuvre*. When Déat was incapacitated following the August 1941 assassination attempt at Ver-

[27]Costantini, in *L'Appel*, party organ of the Ligue Française, August 8, 1942, quoted in Cotta, pp. 30–31. Cotta also cites a diatribe of Robert Brasillach against Spinasse in *L'Appel*, November 1, 1941, in ibid., p. 30.

[28]See Déat, *Le parti unique*, p. 35; also Varennes, pp. 94 and 97.

sailles, Château filled in for him as the paper's political editorialist. [29]

Gradually Déat and Château drew apart, largely because of differing conceptions of "pacifism." Château was truer to the more universal meaning of the term. Their split was sealed in 1943 by the question of militias for the collaborationist parties. Déat suggested that all collaborationist parties of the northern zone form militias which would then act jointly and perhaps pave the way for eventual unity of the various factions, but Château objected. To support his objections to Déat's militia, Château formed the Ligue de la Pensée Française, which argued for a softer collaborationist line, defended the Republican past, and was attacked by Costantini and others for protecting Freemasons. Given his pretensions to be the sole leader of a future single party for France, Déat would brook no rivals and Château was expelled from the RNP. Like Spinasse, Château had defended the political pluralism of the Republican tradition and as a pacifist had argued against the creation of party militias. His independence cost him his liberty. Arrested and imprisoned by the Germans, he was arrested again after the war and charged with collaboration by the postwar government. Like Spinasse, Château learned that as the war progressed and the German grip on occupied France tightened, French political figures whose devotion to the New Order was less than total were a luxury the Germans did not wish to afford. [30]

Although the RNP resembled its rivals in doctrine, there were differences in its emphasis and tone which reflected the Socialist and trade-union origins of many of its leaders after the departure of Deloncle. Ludovic Zoretti's Union de l'Enseignement, functioning under the aegis of the RNP, opposed Vichyite clericalism in matters of education. Maurice Collombier and Francis Desphelippon both

[29]Château's own version of his relationship with Déat is given in the autobiographical account of his postwar incarceration, written under the pseudonym Jean-Pierre Abel, *L'age de Caïn* (Paris: Les Editions Nouvelles, 1947), p. 147. For Château's involvement in Déat's effort to create a single party at Vichy, see Du Moulin de Labarthète, p. 32.

[30]Abel, p. 147. Déat wrote a number of articles in March and April 1943 attacking the position taken by Château. See in particular, Déat, "Utilité d'une polémique," *L'Œuvre*, March 17, 1943. Complaints against Château by right-wing French circles were made to the German law professor, Friedrich Grimm, during one of his lecture tours of France. See Grimm's report of March 3, 1943 to the German Foreign Ministry; T-120/6442H/E481205-6. For the Ligue de la Pensée Française, see *French Basic Handbook*, pp. 147 and 153.

came from the CGT to take active roles in the Front Social du Travail, a labor front organized under the umbrella of the RNP. Desphelippon, a former Communist who had turned to Socialism prior to the war and then to the RNP during the occupation, headed the organization and Collombier became its secretary-general. Modeled after the German Labor Front, the Front Social du Travail grouped together by trade those workers already committed to the RNP.[31]

An independent labor group with close personal ties to Déat's movement was the Centre Syndicaliste de Propagande, led by Lafaye, Dumoulin, and René Mesnard. The primary task of the CSP was to represent labor unions in the battle against a Vichy regime that they saw as too closely identified with big business. Lafaye and Mesnard published a weekly newspaper, *L'Atelier,* whose point of view was very close to that of the RNP. In 1942, 50,000 copies of each L'Atelier issue were published. The Germans found the CSP particularly useful because it supported collaboration and, although small, included prestigious labor leaders: the chairman of the Textile Workers' Federation, Roger Paul; a former CGT leader, Aimé Rey; plus those already named. Rather than create a new organizational structure for French labor, the CSP worked within the already existing unions. The Germans found the CSP methods effective and supported it financially. It organized rallies in Paris and several of its leaders visited factories employing French workers in Germany. In November 1941 a congress of the CSP drew a thousand delegates from both zones of France. The Germans were particularly pleased by CSP arguments blaming low wages and short food supplies on the government in Vichy and not the occupation authorities. In 1943 the organization leadership gave public support to the newly formed Milice of Joseph Darnand. Raoul Petit, who sat on the CSP steering committee, also took charge of social questions for the Milice. By 1944 the CSP had been largely absorbed into the structure

---

[31]Much of the background material on the RNP leaders was provided me by the former leader of the Paris section of the RNP youth affiliate in an interview, August 25, 1973. The most thorough listing of the RNP officials in the national office in Paris and on the departmental and regional level is provided by the party's *Bulletin des Cadres,* nos. 1 and 2 (September and October 1943). For Zoretti, see Varennes, p. 84.

of the RNP, and Dumoulin, Lafaye, Mesnard, and Paul were included in the party's permanent commission.[32]

Déat's labor support came mainly from areas that had been Socialist rather than Communist during the interwar years. Some of his supporters had been Neo-Socialists, others had lost positions in their trade unions when the Communists had been brought into the CGT. They shared a growing disenchantment with the parliamentary system before 1940 and a sharp hostility toward the Popular Front. RNP labor strength came in large part from the industrial north and the miners' organizations, which had been particularly resistant to Communism in the interwar years. A party network extending into the so-called "forbidden zone," the two northern departments administered by the German Army Command in Brussels, was created by René Hanote and Kléber Legay. Legay had been a CGT Miners' Federation leader and a Socialist before the war. He had returned disillusioned from a trip to the Soviet Union in 1937 and argued strongly against Socialist cooperation with the Communists in France. Legay opposed the drift toward war with Germany in the late thirties and in 1940 backed Marshal Pétain.[33]

The RNP leadership was also marked by a middle-class academic character. No other collaborationist party paid more attention than

[32]See Grimm, report, July 27, 1943; T-120/6442H/E481245, for discussion of the Centre Syndicaliste de Propagande. The CSP and *L'Atelier* are discussed in a German embassy report, October 30, 1942; T-120/6442H/E481034-7. This report also discusses the RNP's Front Social du Travail and the government sponsored Comité d'Information Ouvrière et Syndicale, headed by Gabriel Lafaye. For discussion of Georges Dumoulin, *L'Atelier,* and the RNP, see also Schleier, Durchschlag, German embassy, Paris, April 23, 1941; T-120/4645H/E209426-7. A CSP convention is described and a list of the delegates given in Grosse, Report, Pol. 10272/42, Paris, December 1, 1942; T-120/4645H/E209394-6. A later report by Grosse, March 1943; T-120/4645H/209397-8 discusses the role of Raoul Petit, who linked the CSP to Darnand's Milice.

[33]For information on Legay, I am indebted to Georges Albertini, interview, July 2, 1974. See also Legay's book, n. 21, above. A special northern edition of the RNP party organ *Le National Populaire* was published by René Hanote in Bruay-en-Artois. The first issue, dated March 1944, is available at the Institute Française d'Histoire Sociale, Paris. For reference to anti-Communist trade unionists who chose collaboration with the Germans instead, see Abetz, telegram, Paris embassy to German Foreign Ministry, December 13, 1940; T-120/4645H/E209454. See also Paxton, p. 277. The anti-Communist attitudes of northern labor are discussed by Georges Lefranc, *Les Gauches en France (1789–1972)* (Paris: Payot, 1973), pp. 205–206.

the RNP, with its affiliated Union de l'Enseignement, to questions of education. From Déat and Albertini at the top down to the ordinary members, the party was permeated with teachers, many of whom came with a bias in favor of German culture. The pro-German academic orientation combined with the pro-German Socialist tradition to impel the party toward collaborationism, but of a less violent nature than some of its rivals. The leader of the Union de l'Enseignement, Pierre Vaillandet, a former Socialist deputy elected in Avignon during the Popular Front victory of 1936, was obliged, as was Déat, to defend himself against charges of having been a Freemason. The Union espoused higher wages for teachers and called for educational reforms to remove clerical influence from French schools and prepare French youth for a society both "national" and "socialist." The members shared with their colleagues in the Axis states a predilection for moralism and character training. In its monthly bulletin, L'Ecole de demain, the Union cited the injunction of Jaurès to teach what one is rather than what one knows. Zoretti, who specialized in education issues, began establishing a network of schools for workers. Dedicating himself to the reestablishment of technical schools similar to those he had helped create in the CGT, Zoretti wrote: "Workers' education is our own task, our preferred task." a phrase that expressed much of the spirit of the RNP.[34]

Although its collaborationist stance meant abandoning an independent labor structure during the war and embracing a counter-revolutionary corporatist doctrine, the RNP through its various subsidiary agencies manifested a genuine concern for the workers and it served as a pole of attraction for some of them in Paris and the more urban areas of the northern zone. With the traditional workers' parties banned by the Germans and with Vichy adopting policies that called into question gains made by the workers from the 1936 Matignon Accords, many workers were ripe for a new movement that might

[34]Guy Lemonnier, "La Réforme de l'Enseignement," report of the First National Council of the Union de l'Enseignement, April 18, 1943, published in L'Ecole de demain, no. 2 (August 1943). Much of the report was taken from the book France, forge ton destin by Zoretti. See also Pierre Vaillandet, "Précisions," L'Ecole de demain, no. 6 (December 1943) and "Sur les traitements," in the same newspaper, no. 7 (January 1944). Zoretti's technical school reform is outlined in his article "Une tâche essentielle," L'Ecole de demain, no. 8 (February 1944). On Déat as a journalist, see Brissaud, p. 88.

articulate their concerns and defend their interests. Accepting the RNP, however, meant supporting collaboration as well and this became increasingly painful, especially when the Germans began drafting labor for their factories. Whatever minimal benefits the RNP might achieve for some workers in their daily lives, the party would ultimately stand or fall on the issue of collaboration.

Although its rivals attempted a similar strategy, the RNP cultivated its subsidiary organizations more assiduously than the other collaborationist groups, perhaps because the RNP was less prone to street fighting and similar more striking diversions than, for example, the PPF and the Francistes. By 1944 the RNP possessed the elements of a totalitarian party with its affiliates on paper reaching into virtually all aspects of French community life. In addition to the Front Social du Travail, the Union de l'Enseignement, and the Centre Syndicaliste de Propagande which had by then been integrated into the party, the RNP had a youth movement, a peasant organization, and a plethora of technical committees. Its Centre Social Franco-Européen sponsored collaboration-oriented cultural events. As with all the collaborationist movements, the RNP's appeal was mainly urban and its Centre Paysan was less effective than some of its labor and cultural subsidiaries. The party's paramilitary arm, the Légion National Populaire, was reorganized by Paul Montagnon, who had led the battle against the Delonclists, but the LNP did not develop the fighting élan of its rival combat formations. Its activities after the purge of the Delonclists were mainly assuring order at party meetings and providing honor guards on special occasions.[35] In response to Laval's creation of the Milice early in 1943 in the southern zone, Déat decided upon the creation of an RNP militia, the issue that drove Château out of the party. Dubbed the Milice National Populaire, the new formation was small.

The territorial organization of the RNP was comparatively simple, consisting of local party sections grouped together in federations corresponding to the departments of France. Local party leaders dealt with the secretary-general, Albertini, who played the key role in party administration while Déat devoted his primary efforts to journalism and speech-making. In theory the RNP, like all the other

[35] *French Basic Handbook,* p. 147.

118

collaborationist factions, was run on the leadership principle although in practice Déat left much of the administration of the party to others. He did not dominate the RNP to the degree that Doriot, in contrast, overshadowed the PPF.[36]

RNP membership reached a peak of between twenty and thirty thousand in 1942. Albertini estimates twenty-five thousand members in 1943, although their numbers declined during the latter part of that year. Another RNP official, the head of the Paris youth affiliate, estimated the list of those who were sent the party organ, the *National Populaire,* at thirty thousand in 1942. Of these, however, some were nonmembers, so that the real membership figure was probably closer to twenty thousand. Since the *National Populaire* began publication only in June 1942, the list of subscribers should not have included any of the followers of Deloncle. Until November 1942 the RNP was not legally recognized in the southern zone. Even after the occupation of the south by the Wehrmacht allowed the extension of party activity there, the RNP remained primarily a product of Paris and the northern zone. Party strength in the various regions of the country often depended upon local factors such as the presence of active party organizers in the given area. A relatively strong organization was developed by Gabriel Lafaye in Bordeaux, the political fief of Marquet, the former Neo-Socialist associate of Déat. In addition to its strength in the northern mining areas, the RNP was strong in Rennes, the seat of the German-encouraged Breton separatist movements.[37]

Although the RNP leadership was largely professional and white collar, and most of its former Socialists had not themselves been factory workers, party rank and file contained a greater proportion of industrial workers. In a recent study of RNP membership in the departments Indre-et-Loire and the Loiret, Yves Durand and David Bohbot suggest that Déat was able to use his extensive experience in parliamentary campaigning to win over at least some of the workers there. The authors positively identified 119 in Indre-et-Loire and 258

---

[36] *RNP Bulletin des Cadres,* no. 1 (September 1943), supplemented in an interview with Georges Albertini, July 4, 1973.

[37] Henri Amouroux, *La Vie des Français sous l'occupation,* 2 vols. (Paris: Fayard, 1961), 2:386–387; Varennes, pp. 81ff.; and Albertini, interview, July 4, 1973.

in the Loiret as having belonged to the party. The membership lists to which Durand and Bohbot had access covered the entire occupation period, so that there was no way to tell how many members the party sections had at any given time. In both departments the RNP attracted more members than its rivals, the PPF, Francistes, and MSR. Describing the RNP membership figures as "limited but not negligible," the authors pointed out that in the Loiret, the RNP membership approached the level attained by the Communist party at the end of 1935, just prior to the rise of the Popular Front.[38]

Of the RNP membership studied by Durand and Bohbot in their two departments, over two-thirds joined the Loiret party between its establishment in February 1941 and November of the same year, and only six joined after July 1943. The authors point out that 1941 was the year in which Axis victory seemed most likely and also that many joined the RNP in the hope that by so doing they might effect the release of friends and relatives held as prisoners of war in Germany. Another factor was the support of Deloncle and his MSR faction, enjoyed by the RNP until November 1941. In some localities the departure of the MSR contingents virtually ended RNP activity. The party was largely adult, as opposed to youthful. In both departments only about a fifth of the RNP members were younger than thirty and in the Loiret almost one-fifth were sixty or above. RNP party membership in the two departments was found to be generally older than those of the PPF and Francistes but younger than the memberships of the MSR and Group Collaboration of Alphonse de Châteaubriant.[39]

The age findings for the two departments confirm the general view of the RNP as relatively "softer" in style and tactics than the PPF and Francistes. The Groupe Collaboration, a more culturally oriented movement appealing to more prosperous and established middle-class elements, might be expected to have an older population than the other collaborationist groups. The MSR, as rough and ready as any, was built up in large part from the Cagoule of the 1930's, which was reflected in its aging population in the two departments studied by Durand and Bohbot.

The social backgrounds of the RNP members in Indre-et-Loire and

[38]Durand and Bohbot, pp. 64–65.
[39]Ibid., 65.

the Loiret included a wide range of professions, with particularly strong representations of shopkeepers: 18.9 and 16.5 percent in the Loiret and Indre-et-Loire respectively. Other occupations showing up frequently included artisans, office workers, and in the Loiret, teachers and journalists. Workers formed the second largest block of party members with 14.3 percent in the Loiret and comprised the largest single occupational group, 18.5 percent in Indre-et-Loire. In both departments the work of Dumoulin, Lafaye, Mesnard, and the other labor leaders among the RNP leadership had born some fruit. A similar study of collaborationist groups in the city of Dijon showed the RNP strongest among the workers. Of the three leading collaborationist parties in Dijon, the *RNP, PPF,* and Pierre Costantini's Ligue Française, the RNP was best represented among the workers and salaried employees, whereas the PPF recruited mainly in the middle class and the Ligue Française attracted a scattering of support from nearly all the social milieux.[40]

In Indre-et-Loire the proportion of workers in the RNP was greater than their proportion in the department population whereas the corresponding proportion of *employés* in the party was smaller. In contrast, the relationships of workers and *employés* in the RNP and general population was reversed in the Loiret. RNP representation was stronger in the industrial towns in the Loiret. The patterns of membership of the RNP in the two Loire-area departments and of all the collaborationist factions in the Dijon region confirm the urban character of the Ultra parties. The number of peasants involved was minimal.[41]

Where the RNP was strong, the reasons for its strength varied. In some locales, such as the town of Montargis in the Loiret, Neo-Socialist interwar strength was carried over into support for the RNP during the occupation period. Almost all of the cadres of the RNP in Indre-et-Loire who had been active in interwar political life had been in leftist political movements or labor organizations. Of the twenty-seven RNP members who had engaged in political activity in the Loiret before the war, nineteen had come from the Left, yet some

[40]P. Gounand, "Les groupements de collaboration dans une ville française occupée: Dijon," *Revue d'histoire de la deuxième guerre mondiale,* 23 (July 1973), 52. See also Durand and Bohbot, pp. 66–68.

[41]Gounand, p. 50 and Durand and Bohbot, p. 69.

question might be raised as to how "left" they really had been. Most of the former Socialists had followed Déat into the Neo-Socialist movement. A smaller number of RNP militants came from the inter-war Right, in particular the PPF and Colonel de la Rocque's Parti Social Français.[42]

Many of the workers who joined the RNP believed with Déat that German support would help them against a Vichy they saw as dominated by the trusts. The publication of Vichy's Labor Charter in October 1941 brought immediate criticism from Déat, who correctly charged that the new corporate structure would serve only the employers, allowing them to maintain their unity while dissolving the workers' organizations. He also called for higher wages and repeatedly argued that wage freezes in France were the consequences of rapacious big business rather than German exactions.[43]

The stronger proportion of women in the RNP, in contrast to its collaborationist rivals, is striking. In Dijon 24 percent of the 128-member *Ligue Française* were women and women made up 14 percent of the 87-member PPF contingent. For the RNP, however, 65 of 117, or 55 percent, were women. The proportion of women in the RNP of Indre-et-Loire and the Loiret was smaller but still significant. Durand and Bohbot show that 25 percent of Indre-et-Loire's 263 RNP members and 27 percent of the Loiret's RNP contingent of 299 were women. In their analysis of the RNP strength in the Loire region, Durand and Bohbot used statements made by members during post-Liberation investigations together with party lists and police records from the occupation period to assess motivations for joining the party. In both departments a majority of men seem to have joined the RNP from political conviction, whereas the women joined in most instances from constraint of one sort or another. Combining their totals for the two departments, one finds that constraint or the influence of others was given as the reason for joining by 73 percent of the women but only 23 percent of the men.[44]

[42]Durand and Bohbot, pp. 72–74.

[43]Déat, "La Charte du Travail: survol du passage social," and "Renaissance du Syndicalisme," *L'Œuvre,* October 30 and November 19, 1941, respectively.

[44]For the Dijon figures, see Gounand, p. 51 and for the Indre-et-Loire and Loiret departments, Durand and Bohbot, p. 64. The breakdown in party membership resulting from "constraint" as opposed to "conviction" may be found in Durand and Bohbot, p. 74.

In many cases women joined as a result of pressure applied by husbands or fathers, often simply to add to the membership figures for the party. Young women frequently joined the collaborationist parties as an opening to a more active social life during the dreary days of the occupation, when early curfews were accompanied by prohibitions against public activities including dancing. The same motivations worked for men also, in addition to the desire to sport a uniform or colored shirt. It was not uncommon for young men and women who met in a collaborationist political party to marry. Invariably the women members of the collaborationist movements were grouped together in separate women's divisions, which engaged in charity and hospital work, providing an outlet for female activity without upsetting the male domination of the parties. Many women joined the collaboratonist movements, the RNP in particular, in the hope that doing so would enable them to obtain the release of a family member or friend from a German prison camp. The great hoopla of the RNP meetings and demonstrations may have led them to overestimate the party's influence with the Germans. Although Déat could hardly be classified as a feminist as the term is understood today—he made clear his opposition to the woman suffrage movement in France—he did oppose Vichy's plans to reduce educational opportunity for women and criticized those who wished to remove them from the professional world.[45]

Having been established to pressure for the return of Laval to power, the RNP continued to clamor for his return to the government all thoughout the period of Admiral Darlan's administration. Déat was cool toward the Darlan government in which he, like so many others, saw the occult hand of Synarchy. The legend of a secret plot in which capitalists and technocrats planned to control Europe and the world was nourished in the hothouse atmosphere of suspicion in Vichy. The mysterious death of Jean Coutrot, a businessman with international connections, and papers found in his possession seemed to indicate a plot with international ramifications. A belief spread that the technocrats of Darlan's government who were collaborating in economic matters with the Germans were preparing for eventual

[45]Déat, "Les femmes à l'école," *L'Œuvre*, October 8, 1940. Some of the women's motivations for having joined the RNP are discussed by Durand and Bohbot, p. 74; some were mentioned by Georges Albertini, in an interview, July 4, 1973.

world rule. Déat suspected almost all bankers, industrialists, and technocrats. In the aura of mystery that surrounded the supposed Synarchist plot, no one could be certain who was involved, but Déat suspected Interior Minister Pucheu, Finance Minister Yves Bouthillier, Minister of Industrial Production François Lehideux and his successor Jean Bichelonne, Communications Minister Jean Berthelot, and several others. Darlan, according to Déat, had brought the whole clique into power in France. In addition to those mentioned, Deloncle was widely believed to be involved because of his personal ties to Darlan.[46]

The return of Laval to power in April 1942 brought few of the rewards Déat had anticipated, either in his own personal advancement or in the restructuring of the French political order along national socialist lines. With fond memories of his brief cabinet stint as aviation minister in 1936, Déat looked forward to the prospect of another cabinet post in a new Laval ministry. His party had campaigned ceaselessly for Laval's return to office and his editorials in *L'Œuvre* had been directed toward the same end. However, he overestimated the strength of the personal bond he shared with Laval following the August 1941 assassination attempt at Versailles where both had been wounded.

In 1942, Laval made a pretense of visiting Déat and soliciting his advice on the composition of the new cabinet, but the RNP leader was not offered a post. Déat then began to pose as the heir apparent to the leadership of the government and gradually his relations with Laval worsened. While awaiting the succession, Déat and the RNP continued to defend Laval in public. For their pains they took much of the criticism from the other collaborationist groups that might instead have been directed at Laval. Laval was content to have Déat and the RNP as a foil with which to threaten more moderate elements in France and as a scapegoat for the more strident collaborationist attacks, especially those of the PPF. In return, he subsidized the RNP. In 1942 the PPF was a more potent threat than the

---

[46]For Déat's view of Synarchy, see "Attention aux technocrates," *L'Œuvre*, February 21–22, 1942. See also Varennes, pp. 139–141. On the subject of the Synarchy itself and its fundamentally mythological nature, see Richard F. Kuisel, "The Legend of the Vichy Synarchy," *French Historical Studies*, 6 (Spring 1970), 365–366.

RNP to Laval, who was glad to be able to utilize Déat against Doriot.[47]

As 1942 progressed, Déat found himself increasingly in the position of the suitor spurned in regard to Laval, just as the collaborationists in general stood in relation to Berlin. Although the RNP continued to defend Laval in public well into 1943, it was becoming obvious to Déat that Laval had no intention of remaking France into a national socialist state or of bringing the RNP or its leader into the government. The party was too weak to attempt a seizure of power on its own, a step more Deloncle's style than Déat's anyway. Nor were the Germans willing to help the RNP to power. Déat's response was to launch a new campaign for a single party. He announced the drive at the RNP national congress in July 1942, and followed with a series of newspaper articles in support of the idea.

Reaction of most of the other collaborationist factions was cautiously favorable at first. The Francistes approved the idea of common action but made clear their distaste for Doriot, whose Communist past they would not forgive. Their leader, Marcel Bucard, expressed willingness to cooperate with the other collaborationist groups under the aegis of Marshal Pétain, but rejected any organic union of the various parties. Afraid to lose control of his shock troops, which were reputed to be among the best and most daring of all the Ultras', Bucard opposed any merger of the parties. Déat's call for a single party was also supported by the now independent MSR, René Château's *La France Socialiste,* and two journalists prominent in the Paris collaboration, Jean Luchaire and Georges Suarez, the latter the successor to Henri Jeanson at *Aujourd'hui.* Déat felt that he now had

[47]In a conversation shortly before Déat was named minister of labor and national solidarity in March 1944, Laval told Marshal Pétain that he had been paying Déat as well as Bucard and other collaborationists in Paris. When Pétain inquired why, Laval told him that if he, Laval, did not pay the Ultras, the Germans would and Laval preferred to keep them more under his influence. No mention was made of the PPF by Laval and it is unlikely that any of his funds were directed that way. See Tracou, p. 188. Déat's purge of Jean Goy is discussed by Varennes, p. 82, as are his relations with Laval at the time of the latter's return to the government, pp. 130–131. Déat later wrote that it had been his wife who had contacted Grosse for help after his arrest on December 14, 1940. On German preference for Laval as opposed to Déat, see Grimm, Report to Foreign Ministry, July 27, 1943; T-120/6442H/E481249 and for Déat's relations to German personnel in Paris, see Brissaud, pp. 292–293.

enough support to attempt a new venture and announced on September 16, 1942 the creation of a unified collaborationist front, the Front Révolutionnaire National (FRN). The FRN was spelled out clearly as a common effort on the part of the already existing "national" parties in which each would retain its independent organization and membership. Only after the FRN had proved successful in common action would the constituent parties then discuss actual integration into one movement.[48]

The FRN was a clever scheme of Déat's to put pressure on Laval to move more vigorously toward the creation of a national socialist France. Even more important was its aim with respect to the PPF, which was threatening to topple Laval's government during October and November 1942. Doriot would either have to bring his party into the FRN and lose control over it as it merged progressively with its smaller rivals in a formation largely under Déat's domination, or run the risk of appearing to impede collaborationist unity by rejecting the FRN. While Déat continued to press for the FRN during the fall of 1942, Doriot remained silent. It soon became evident that a decisive response would come only during the PPF party congress scheduled for November. This was the much ballyhooed "congress of power," a monster manifestation staged by the PPF at a time when Doriot's star appeared to be in the ascendancy and his party within striking distance of seizing power.

Doriot saw nothing to be gained by his association with smaller groups, which he felt were doomed to certain failure and ultimate absorption by the PPF. At the party congress he rejected any PPF participation in the FRN. Although the FRN was able to stage some demonstrations early in 1943, it was killed by Doriot's rejection. Another of Déat's schemes for a single collaborationist movement shimmered into failure. The PPF responded by organizing several "vigilance committees" in Paris and elsewhere, ostensibly in preparation for a possible Allied invasion of France after the landings in North Africa. The vigilance committees, however, were also the PPF's attempt to forge a collaborationist unity at the lower levels of party organization in the hope that these committees would furnish a

[48]Déat, "Front Révolutionnaire National," *L'Œuvre*, September 16, 1942. A good survey of the reactions in the Paris press to Déat's idea of a *parti unique* is offered by Cotta, pp. 260–264.

means by which the larger PPF could absorb the militants of its rivals. While Déat sought unity from the top down, Doriot worked from the bottom up. Although the collaborationist factions did succeed in cooperating at times in various localities, the events of autumn 1942 show clearly the continuing fragmentation within the French radical Right. By the end of 1942 the PPF and RNP, the two leading parties of the collaboration, had both failed decisively. The differences in their memberships and political cadres combined with the mutual distrust and personal rivalries of their two leaders to preclude any concerted joint action.[49]

The RNP has been described as a rare example of a national socialist movement whose cadres had come from the political Left. The party drew its support in large measure in reaction to the existence of a government, oriented sharply to the Right, in Vichy. If the RNP was unique in occupied Europe, it was due to the existence of a French government, a major difference between France and other countries occupied by the Germans. A product of the firing of Laval in December 1940, the RNP remained basically oppositional after his return to power. It campaigned against Vichy's threats to undo the 1936 Matignon Accords, despite the presence of the labor representatives René Belin and Hubert Lagardelle in the government.

Despite the leftist origins of many of its members, the RNP cannot be called a party of the Left. Few party members and even fewer of the leaders moved directly from the Left into the RNP. Many, including Déat himself, had begun their political evolution toward the center in the interwar years and many had joined the Neo-Socialist movement. Dumoulin, Lafaye, and the others from the labor movement were dissidents who had broken with the Popular Front after 1936 and were receptive even before 1940 to a more centrist alternative. Neo-Socialists and trade unionists who followed Déat after 1940 had long before abandoned thoughts of revolution and fundamental social change. Theirs was a defensive mentality: anti-Popular Front in 1936 and anti-Vichy in 1941 when they were reduced to a futile defense of the Matignon Accords. Added to the trade unionists were

[49] *French Basic Handbook,* p. 146. See also Cotta, pp. 265–267. A vigilance committee in the Loiret included both PPF and RNP members and the local committee was fatally weakened by the rivalries of the two parties, as each sought to attract as many new members as possible; see Durand and Bohbot, pp. 60–61.

teachers defending the lay school system and their jobs against Vichyite clericalism and some Republican office holders in fear for their jobs. Rather than a revolutionary party, the RNP after 1941 became a pressure group and an increasingly weak one as time went on. In the words of a contemporary source, the RNP represented "the sober calculation of men of the world anxious to make the transition to the New Order without undue excesses."[50]

Since the war, former members of the RNP have argued that it was the only vehicle available for those who opposed Vichyite conservatism but wished to remain loyal to Marshal Pétain, the legal ruler of France. The RNP under Déat was the least virulent in tactics of the collaborationist parties. For a short time there seemed to be room in it for genuine pacifists such as Château and for those like Spinasse, who wished to retain as much as possible of the pluralistic Republican tradition. As the war progressed, however, and increasing German pressure upon the people and resources of occupied France sharpened the necessity for choice, Déat did not hesitate. His consistency led him straight down the German path and those who did not wish to accompany him were forced out of the party. What started out as a protest against the royalism, clericalism, and business-oriented corporatism of Vichy was forced by the logic of the occupation situation to look to the Germans for help. In so doing, it adopted positions on the major issues of the day virtually identical to those taken by the other movements that from the beginning of, and in some cases even prior to, the war had been more openly fascist.

Alone among the major collaborationist movements, the RNP had been established in direct opposition to the Vichy government by groups seeking to preserve their interests in the transition from the Third Republic. They embraced the collaborationism of the RNP in the hope that a fully fascist regime would eliminate the threats they saw in the monarchism, clericalism, and capitalism of Vichy. Many of those who defended Republican institutions in the RNP had been among the dissidents of the interwar years. From oppositional roles in the Third Republic they went to opposition under Vichy, a transition typified in the career of their leader Déat. Cast adrift by the par-

---

[50] *French Basic Handbook,* p. 146. For a discussion of the RNP as "an almost unique instance of a national-socialism that drew its inspiration and cadres from the Left," see Eugen Weber, *Varieties of Fascism,* p. 137.

liamentary elites in the thirties, they fared no better under Vichy. A constant theme in Deat's articles was that of lost opportunities.

The dissident groups who followed Déat under the occupation were outsiders during the interwar years who saw in the changed conditions of 1940 and 1941 a chance to take the center of the political stage. The development of the Vichy regime and its support by the Germans, however, once more pushed Déat and his followers to the fringes of the political arena. Déat denounced the parliament but defended the Republic while indulging in the most strident collaborationist rhetoric. The ambivalences within his movement were seen in its open support and private criticism of Laval in 1942 and 1943. By 1942 the weakness of the RNP was manifest. It was not RNP rhetoric that put Laval back into power, and the party received little aid from him thereafter. The RNP could do little to influence Vichy policy with regard to the workers. Its biggest coup was the appointment of Déat to the Labor Ministry in 1944, a post he owed more to the influence of his journalism than his party. He recognized this by continuing to write for *L'Œuvre* but virtually ignoring the RNP after his nomination to the government.

Because the RNP was the product of dissident groups, especially during the months of the Déat-Deloncle fusion, party members were more accustomed to playing oppositional roles than to compromising and preparing for political power. Right- and left-wing interwar dissidents could not long be contained under its umbrella in 1941. As "new" as it claimed to be, the RNP was still characterized by the brittle rigidity traditional in French political parties. Even before the split in 1941, however, the RNP was gravely weakened by internal ambiguities. Under Déat the RNP never mounted even the campaign for power put on by the PPF in late 1942. Although it continued to grow in some parts of France in 1942, the RNP had lost momentum. Its ambivalent attitude toward the Laval government muffled its voice while Déat schemed for a cabinet post. The fortunes of the party waned even before those of the Axis, and collaborationists with serious pretensions to political power in 1942 turned to Doriot and the PPF.

4 Collaborationism in Full Bloom: The Parti Populaire Français

I cannot believe in the victory of senile capitalism over a young, powerful, and fervent revolutionary force.

—Doriot discussing Nazi Germany, *Réalités*, 1942

The tall story of the week: we will have the choice only between Doriot and a Gauleiter. Absurdity. Doriot? The Germans are now letting him fall and Laval is delighted: But the semi-popularity of the President [Laval] here is due to the popular fear of Doriot.

—Maurice Martin du Gard, *La chronique de Vichy*, late 1942

The dismissal of Laval, which had brought about a major turning point in the history of the collaboration, was followed by a second watershed in mid-1941. The spring of 1941 had seen the emergence of the RNP and in June the invasion of the Soviet Union. Dissension in the RNP during the following autumn opened the way to Doriot's PPF, which in 1942 became the most important political movement of the collaboration. From the summer of 1940 the PPF had looked toward changes that would release in France the kind of popular energy that Fascism and National Socialism had unchained in Italy and Germany. More than any of his rivals, Doriot incarnated the fascist man of will and determination, a powerful speaker born of the people. He came closest to filling the role of *chef*. Even more than the RNP and MSR, the PPF was the movement of one man. Massive and powerfully built, Doriot would remove his jacket and necktie and roll up his shirtsleeves, better to harangue the crowds that had come to hear him. Whether as leader of the PPF or in his earlier Communist days, he was an elemental force. His speeches in Paris halls during the occupation attracted thousands of listeners, although as with the RNP rallies, many came out of curiosity. It was Doriot's death in German exile in February 1945, not the liberation of France six months earlier, that finally convinced the remnant of his following that their party was finished.[1]

During the fall of 1940, Doriot's reserve toward and even criticism of Laval had made him suspect in the eyes of Abetz. Although relations between Doriot and the German ambassador were correct, any threat to Laval implied a threat to Abetz as well and the PPF would never enjoy the kind of support that Abetz directed on occasion toward the RNP. Having declared himself a supporter of Marshal Pétain, Doriot remained more nuanced on the issue of collaboration, which he supported but not yet with the fervor he would show after the attack on Soviet Russia. The PPF was undoubtedly in a difficult position in 1940 and early 1941. Whereas the RNP and MSR started under the occupation with a burst of optimism and a clean slate, the party Doriot led in 1940 was but a shadow of the prewar PPF, which had been gravely weakened by his own support of appeasement at Munich and Danzig. The party network was severely hampered by the division of France in 1940 into zones, in neither of which did the authorities look kindly upon PPF. As the leader of a "revolutionary" party, however, Doriot needed to offer his followers a field of action more exciting and adventurous than the mere selling of newspapers. For the time being, anti-Jewish demonstrations such as those of August 1940 in Vichy and raids against rival Ultra parties on the order of the episode described in June 1941 by Deloncle had to suffice. An aggressive group of militants in search of a cause, the Doriotists were obliged to wait.

Like its leader, the PPF was characterized most strongly by its anti-Communism. Although all the parties of the collaboration were staunchly anti-Communist, there was a particularly sharp edge to PPF anti-Communism. In addition to Doriot, many of the party leaders, Henri Barbé and Victor Barthélemy among them, were former Communists. They turned against their ex-comrades with all the bitterness of disillusioned former believers. As long as the Ribbentrop-Molotov pact precluded too strong an anti-Communist line on the part of the Ultras, the PPF held its fire. Overnight,

---

[1]Jean Hérold-Paquis, *Des illusions . . . Désillusions! . . . Mémoires 15 août 1944 – 15 août 1945* (Paris: Bourgoin, 1948), pp. 110ff. For a comparison of the singular role of Doriot as leader with Déat, see *French Basic Handbook,* p. 146.

however, the party changed its tune upon learning of the German invasion of Soviet Russia. A party congress had started on June 21, 1941 at Villeurbanne, near Lyons. The next day, the German onslaught began in the East. Several party officials who heard the news burst into Doriot's hotel room to apprise him of the latest development. "Now," he is reported to have said, "it is another war. It is really our war." In his closing speech before the assembled party members Doriot vigorously denounced the Communists. Within hours after learning of the invasion, he sent a telegram, similar to Deloncle's, to Marshal Pétain requesting the establishment of a volunteer unit to fight against the Russians. The PPF was able to open up once more against its most implacable foe, the Communists.[2]

The creation of the Anti-Bolshevik Legion offered Doriot an opportunity and an escape. Like the other Ultra leaders, he volunteered for service with the legion, and, unlike any of them with the exception of Pierre Clémenti, leader of the small Parti Français National-Collectiviste, he actually went to the front. Déat was incapacitated by the wounds he received in Colette's assassination attempt, and two other leaders of the Anti-Bolshevik Legion, Deloncle and Pierre Costantini, avoided service in Russia. Between the time of the legion's creation and the end of the occupation Doriot spent more time at the Eastern front than he did in France. He hoped that his service at the front would give the PPF an edge on its rivals among the Ultras. His long absences, however, weakened the cohesion of the party. For Doriot the Eastern front became not only the hoped-for scene of Franco-German collaboration in action but also the escape from an unpromising political situation at home. PPF activity during the summer of 1941 was devoted largely to recruitment for the Anti-Bolshevik Legion. Typical of the relationships among the various Ultra factions was their maintenance of separate recruiting programs despite their joint support of the legion. A massive rally on July 18 at the Vélodrome d'hiver in Paris kicked off the recruitment drive, but then each faction went its separate way, all of them competing in

[2]This account is based upon the personal recollections of Victor Barthélemy, told to the author, July 9, 1974. I have not seen specific documentation to indicate whether Doriot's or Deloncle's request for the creation of the Anti-Bolshevik Legion came first to Pétain. Deloncle's connections to Darlan probably enabled him to assume the presidency of the legion's steering committee in preference to Doriot.

making wild claims about the numbers they would bring to the legion.[3]

On September 4, Doriot left Paris for military service with the legion in the East. With him went many of the more active members of the PPF, which weakened the party in relation to other Ultra groups less heavily committed to the anti-Bolshevik adventure. Doriot and many of those who joined him in the legion participated in the autumn 1941 German attack on Moscow. Placed in the front line by the German military command, the legion's soldiers came tantalizingly close to the Soviet capital before being driven back with heavy losses. It is one of the great ironies of the Second World War that French volunteers were with the Germans at the apex of their military success, near Moscow in 1941, and again at the depth of the German defeat, with French SS volunteers among the last defenders of Hitler's Berlin bunker in late April and early May 1945. It is also ironic that Doriot fought as a volunteer, for his early career in the Communist party had been inspired by a desire that the experience of the first war never again be repeated. He had been sixteen in 1914 and until 1917 had worked in the war factories of Saint-Denis. Then he was mobilized and experienced with so many others of his generation the carnage of the trenches. Back from the war, Doriot became deeply involved in the *Jeunesse Communiste,* with which he campaigned actively against the French repression of a Moroccan rebellion led in 1925 by Abd-el Krim. Eventually, Communist policy shifted and so began the long process of disillusionment that culminated in 1934 with Doriot expelled from the party after he had tried in defiance of Comintern policy to form a broadly based alliance of the antifascist Left. Gradually he took up the cause of nationalism and the PPF, created in 1936, evolved toward a fascist line, completed after 1940.

From his early days Doriot had retained his activist spirit and his desire to overturn the upper-middle-class establishment and stalemated society of bourgeois France. With some justification he blamed the Communists for expelling him in 1934 and then pirating his political line when they came out in support of the Popular Front. The Communists, he felt, having been sovietized, had lost intimacy

---

[3]Cotta, p. 272.

with the people and were incapable of making a real revolution. Like Déat he saw a revolutionary man emerge in the form of the victorious Wehrmacht soldier, whose élan and organization found a responsive chord in the PPF leader. Doriot's combative spirit was given free rein in the Anti-Bolshevik Legion, which he also expected would give him the opportunity to savor his revenge upon the Communists in Moscow. Like his rival Déat, he prized the camaraderie of the military or paramilitary life and he had long before given up his opposition to war. His military career with the Anti-Bolshevik Legion lacked the lustre of that of the Rexist leader Léon Degrelle, but Doriot rose within the legion ranks and became a lieutenant in the Waffen-SS. Like so many other dissidents from established French political parties of the interwar years, he wanted to see his own war-tempered generation take the lead in a new toughened society.

Although less a movement of war veterans than some of its rivals with stronger right-wing ties, the PPF shared with other extremist groups, including the Communist party, a spirit of generational revolt against a stalled society controlled by the pre-1914 generation. Like fascists throughout interwar and wartime Europe, the French Ultras felt hemmed in by their elders and impatiently demanded their turn at the levers of control. The PPF shared with other fascist movements a rhetoric of "dynamism," by which they meant strident attacks against what they called the "bourgeois" values of complacency and material comfort they associated with their elders. Their radical revolt was a moralistic one against "bourgeois conformism," not against the social order. Members of the PPF were simultaneously obsessed by the Communists' threat to the French social order and haunted by a desire to be more radical than they. They solved the dilemma by constant evocation of the Blanquist and Sorelian spirit of revolt while rejecting its revolutionary content. Appeals to militant and idealistic youth in quest of a mission masked the reality that the PPF and its Ultra rivals were mainly a new generation of outsiders, "little people," seeking power and influence rather than social change.

Eugen Weber points out that many people in twentieth-century France came to make their fortunes in Paris when they were young and later returned to the provinces to retire. The provinces were rendered more conservative while Paris, flooded with the often unemployed young, was radicalized but in the direction of the Right. Doriot provided the chance for political militancy, often shocking one's elders, while at the same time enhancing one's future place in the social order by expelling Communists, Freemasons, and Jews from positions of influence. PPF radicalism meant tactics, not social goals. This suited the unemployed and marginally employed young migrants to the capital when the range of opportunities was restricted further by the disaster of 1940 and the post-armistice privations. During the bleak and boring days of the occupation in France, the Anti-Bolshevik Legion also offered young men a chance for clamor and an attractiveness for women, all of which had no parallel in the ascetic and guerrilla life imposed upon members of the maquis.[4]

Just at the time of Doriot's departure for the East, the PPF press announced an agreement negotiated between him and Pierre Costantini, the head of the smaller Ligue Française, to coordinate their political activities. Costantini was best known for having personally "declared war" on England after the Mers-el-Kébir attack. His war had been conducted with political tracts and posters distributed all over Paris. A Corsican, Costantini had served with distinction as an aviator during the First World War and had been cited several times for valor. He shot down several enemy aircraft, was wounded and captured, and escaped. Between the wars he worked in a Ford motor factory, traveled, and in Switzerland wrote a book called *La grande pensée de Bonaparte*. To Costantini, Napoleon represented an earlier form of European unification transcending Franco-German enmity and undoubtedly he saw himself as following in a great Corsican tradition. He served during the 1939–1940 campaign as commander of the Naval Air Station at Coulommiers.

---

[4]For a discussion of the appeal of uniforms as opposed to what the Resistance could offer, see David Littlejohn, *The Patriotic Traitors: A History of Collaboration in German-Occupied Europe, 1940–45* (London: Heinemann, 1972), pp. 122–123. Doriot's personal inclinations toward the militarized life despite his earlier "pacifist" convictions were brought out in statements to the author made by Victor Barthélemy and Claude Jeantet, July 9 and 17, respectively, 1974. For a discussion of the evolution of Doriot and his experiences in World War I, see Gilbert D. Allardyce, "French Communism Comes of Age: Jacques Doriot, Henri Barbé, and the Disinheritance of the *Jeunesses Communistes*, 1923–1931," *Durham University Journal*, 66 (March 1974), 131. On the revolt against gerontocracy, see Eugen Weber, "France," in Hans Rogger and Eugen Weber, eds., *The European Right: A Historical Profile* (Berkeley and Los Angeles: University of California Press, 1966), pp. 121–122.

Shortly after the armistice Costantini embraced the cause of collaboration. Like Darlan, Deloncle, and so many other navy people, he was enraged at the English attack on the French fleet at Mers-el-Kébir, which intensified traditional French naval Anglophobia. Costantini's position was made clear in two tracts entitled "Je déclare la guerre à l'Angleterre" (I declare war against England) and, not surprisingly, "Assez" (Enough), the latter a typical Ultra diatribe against the Republic. Costantini hoped for support from former German pilot Julius von Westrick, with whom he had become friendly after shooting down his plane in World War I. Westrick came to France as a counselor in the German embassy and was later charged with liaison to the Anti-Bolshevik Legion. The Westrick connection was exploited by Costantini to help get his Ligue Française off the ground.[5]

The Ligue Française never developed the influence of the larger Ultra parties, although in some localities it established strong organizations. Costantini published a weekly newspaper, *L'Appel,* and competed for followers with some of the smaller Ultra groupings, notably the Parti Français National-Collectiviste of Pierre Clémenti. The Ligue's program was similar to those of the other Ultra movements but with more Bonapartist overtones. Ligue political tracts depicted Napoleon as a fighter for European unity and an anti-Semite. Costantini's association had its greatest success when it staged its only national congress during the occupation, attracting several thousand spectators to a two-day meeting, November 14–15, 1942, in Paris. Costantini also took a turn as head of the steering committee of the Anti-Bolshevik Legion, in whose establishment he had participated in July 1941.

Like other Ultra movements under the occupation, Costantini's possessed a plethora of subsidiary organizations including a militia and a youth movement, but these affiliates existed only on paper or were at most small. Ligue activity was centered mainly in coastal areas prone to Anglophobia: the Charente, Charente-Maritime, Gironde, and Côtes-du-Nord departments. Active organizations also existed in the Marne and Côte d'Or departments and in Paris. The movement was never extended into the southern zone. In most cases, as with

[5]On Westrick, see Galtier-Boissière, *Crapouillot,* 4 (1948), 269. An account of the PPF–Ligue Française joint action program, with clippings from *L'Appel,* may be found in Cotta, pp. 258–260.

other Ultra parties, local Ligue strength depended on the presence of strong and active leaders in a given area. Party membership does not appear to have climbed above two thousand, although precise figures for all of the occupied zone are unavailable. After the war Costantini, judged not responsible for his political activity, was institutionalized briefly. The alliance of the Ligue with the PPF had not appreciably increased the size or political influence of either.[6]

Doriot and Costantini agreed to joint action, not a merger of their movements. If Doriot expected the agreement to constitute the first step in the organization of a single party under his leadership, he was to be disappointed. Back in France again at the beginning of 1942, he engaged in a speaking tour, sharing the platform with Costantini. Allied to the Ligue Française at home and making contacts with German officials at the Eastern front, the PPF was gaining strength relative to the other Ultra parties in late 1941 and early 1942. On October 29, 1941, the party received "authorized" status from the German authorities, meaning that it could operate openly in the occupied zone. By contrast, the RNP had been awarded similar status on February 26, whereas Deloncle's MSR never received "authorized" status from the Germans. Costantini's Ligue received it in February 1942.[7]

The year 1942 was marked by a concerted PPF drive for power, thwarted ultimately by Hitler's preference for Laval. Having returned to France from the Eastern front, Doriot possessed a personal prestige in the pro-Axis community unmatched by any of his rivals. He anticipated aid from the contacts he had made within German military and police services. A clamorous PPF campaign opened at the beginning of the year and its tempo was stepped up progressively during the spring government crisis that led to Laval's return to power. The drive culminated with a five-day-long PPF congress dur-

---

[6]The history of Costantini's political endeavors is given in the *French Basic Handbook,* pp. 150–151. For Ligue doctrine, see Costantini, "L'heure de la France," in a folder of Ligue brochures in the BDIC, O pièce 22831. Of related interest are tracts entitled "Pierre Costantini, Chef de la Ligue Française, un homme nouveau à la tête d'un mouvement nouveau" and "Nos idées" available in the library of the Comité d'Histoire de la Deuxième Guerre Mondiale. For the November 1942 Ligue congress, see *Le Ligueur,* the party journal, no. 2 (November 1942).

[7]Der Militärbefehlshaber in Frankreich. Anlagen zum Lagebericht für die Monate Februar/März 1942, CDJC document CDXCV, 10.

ing November in Paris, the so-called "congrès du pouvoir," and quickly dissipated when Hitler made it clear to all concerned that Laval was his man in France.

Laval's victory over Doriot led directly to the formation of the Milice, a paramilitary force under Vichy's control, intended to recruit among the parties of the Ultras and divert their militants to Laval's side. Joseph Darnand became secretary-general of the Milice and he served under Laval. By 1944 Darnand was able to wrest effective control of the Milice from Laval, whom he continued nominally to serve, and create the only Ultra organization capable of rivaling the PPF during the last year of the occupation. The failure of Doriot in November 1942 opened the way for Darnand. What must have rankled Doriot and the PPF leadership was that the party's failure in France was accompanied by success in Tunisia, where its adherents took over the government. There they were able to help organize the pro-Axis elements among the French community in determined resistance to the Allied onslaught of late 1942 and early 1943. With local PPF help, a Phalange Africaine of several hundred local volunteers from the French community in Tunisia was formed to fight alongside the retreating Axis forces. To some within the PPF and perhaps to Doriot himself, the party's role in the Tunisian events appeared a dry run for a future takeover in France herself.[8]

Although the PPF was not much, if at all, larger than the RNP and the Milice and was considerably smaller than Châteaubriant's Groupe Collaboration, it was the only Ultra group with serious pretensions to power during the occupation. Unlike the RNP, the PPF never committed itself to Laval, of whom it was openly critical, and the Doriotists were even willing to be less gentle than their rivals to Pétain. Doriot was more stridently "revolutionary," in the parlance of the day, than Déat, who felt the need to spare Laval and defend his own parliamentary past. The Milice, for all its radical rhetoric in 1943 and 1944, was hampered by being an arm of the government and

[8]The role of the PPF in organizing resistance to the Allies in Tunisia is discussed in the *French Basic Handbook,* pp. 145–146; Charbonneau, 1:387ff.; Géo London, *L'amiral Estéva et le général Dentz devant la haute cour de justice* (Lyons: R. Bonnefon, 1945); Rudolf Rahn, the representative of Ribbentrop to Tunis, *Ruheloses Leben: Aufzeichnungen and Erinnerungen* (Düsseldorf: Diederichs Verlag, 1949), I; and more recently René Pellegrin, *La Phalange Africaine: la L.V.F. en Tunisie 1942–1943* (Paris: published by the author, 1973).

although Darnand feuded privately with Laval, he was unwilling to denounce his chief in public. The PPF was the only one of the major collaborationist movements totally committed to a political takeover and its leadership corps, trained in large part earlier by the Communists, contained the highest proportion of professional agitators, the strongest potential counterrevolutionary elite. In comparison to Doriot's movement, the RNP was a pressure group of sometimes conflicting interests and the Milice a ragtag organization of ruffians inspired by fascist ideals but without realistic political leadership or direction. Such comparisons, of course, are relative, for the PPF shared the weaknesses and internal contradictions of its rivals, but the Ultra who wanted to achieve more than merely a personal statement by his activism had no choice but to follow Doriot after 1941.

The story of the PPF attempt at power in 1942 has been well narrated by Dieter Wolf. At the end of 1941, Doriot secured permission to return from the Eastern front to France in order to help in recruitment for the Anti-Bolshevik Legion. He defended Germany passionately as a young revolutionary society in mortal combat against the "inhuman" capitalism of England and America and Communism of the USSR. To Doriot, National Socialism had succeeded in humanizing a technological society and giving each citizen a place and stake in it. Two civilizations with two different conceptions of man were at war. Vigorous, young, and united, Germany could not lose.[9]

In his recruiting for the Anti-Bolshevik Legion during January 1942, Doriot visited Cardinal Baudrillart, rector of the Catholic Institute in Paris, who supported the legion enthusiastically. The PPF chieftain also paid a call upon Marshal Pétain in Vichy. Pétain and his aides remembered Doriot as the man who had led the Communist opposition against the French military repression of the Abd-el Krim insurrection in 1925 in Morocco. Consequently, Doriot received a decidedly cool reception from the chief of state. Nor did he receive much more encouragement from Admiral Darlan. The Vichy leaders made it plain to Doriot that the Anti-Bolshevik Legion was a private venture on the part of the Ultra factions and had no government standing. On February 1, Doriot returned to Paris, where he delivered a speech at the Vélodrome d'hiver. Roughly 15,000 turned out to

[9]Doriot, *Réalités* (Paris: Les Editions de France, Collection "Les Temps Nouveaux," 1942), pp. 62–63.

hear him speak not only for the legion, but also call for support for the PPF. Doriot left for the front again three weeks later but a month after that he was back in France, campaigning once more for the legion in a series of speeches in major cities of the occupied zone. Ostensibly recruiting, Doriot was making himself a major public figure throughout the northern zone. Aware of the possible effects of his campaigning, the Vichy authorities refused to allow him to recruit for the legion in the unoccupied zone.[10]

Two events during the spring of 1942 seemed to enhance the political prospects of the PPF. On April 18, Laval returned to the government, replacing Admiral Darlan at its head. At almost the same time Hitler strengthened the SS and German police presence in the occupied zone of France by the appointment of a Höhere SS- und Polizeiführer im Bereich des Militärbefehlshaber in Frankreich (high leader of the SS and police in the jurisdiction of the military command in France). Reacting to a growing number of attacks against German personnel stationed in France, Hitler now placed all police matters relating to the security of Germans in the northern zone under the authority of the new post, filled by SS-Brigadeführer Karl Albrecht Oberg. In May, Oberg was officially installed in his Paris offices by Reinhard Heydrich. Heydrich also informed Vichy that he wanted men of the Ultra parties brought into the French police network in the north because the number of SD personnel in occupied France was relatively small. The strengthening of the SS and SD presence drastically altered the power relationships of the various German services in France. Eventually there, as throughout occupied Europe, SS and SD authority eclipsed that of rival German agencies. Abetz hardly counted by the time the occupation ended.

The reinforcement of the SS in Paris provided increased opportunities for the PPF, which had better contacts than the RNP among the SS. SS officers were also more likely than those of the Wehrmacht to take seriously Hitler's propaganda about Germany's crusade to unite a new Europe. Army officers tended to retain a stronger spirit of Prussian military traditionalism, inclined to see all French, Ultras included, as Germany's hereditary enemies. By 1942,

[10]Wolf, pp. 259–260.

Doriot had made contact with Roland Nosek, who headed the political section of the SS in Paris.[11]

Laval's return to the government followed the progressive discrediting of Darlan's cabinet in the eyes of the Germans. The government had opened a series of trials at Riom, where leaders of the Third Republic were to have been called to account for their alleged misdeeds. The Germans wanted to see these leaders blamed for having initiated the war but instead the trials focused upon responsibility for having lost the campaign of 1940. Léon Blum gave an eloquent defense of his role in the government and even Pétain, who had been defense minister in the 1934 Doumergue government, was implicated in the charge of having insufficiently prepared France for war. Dissatisfied with the direction the trials had taken, Hitler demanded they be indefinitely postponed. The trials did not endear the Darlan government to the Germans nor did a protracted series of negotiations relating to possible Franco-German military collaboration in North Africa. Darlan adamantly refused to let the Germans have access to the French fleet at Toulon.[12]

The weakening of the Darlan government had brought Laval once more to the fore. Despite their sharply differing personalities and political styles, Laval and Doriot were not averse to working together during the early months of 1942. Accustomed to dealing on a personal, often folksy level, Laval was never one to overlook potentially helpful allies. Doriot had been critical of him in 1940 but the PPF was an organized political force in 1942 and Laval had none of his own. In December 1941, Doriot and two of his aides, Victor Barthélemy and Jean Fossati, were received by Laval at Chateldon. The PPF negotiators asked for several posts, including the Interior Ministry for Doriot, in a new Laval cabinet. Not wishing to see Doriot in charge of the police, Laval cautiously rejected the proposal but left the door open to continued negotiations. These led in March 1942 to a pledge of PPF propaganda support for Laval in return for the prom-

[11]Victor Barthélemy interview, July 9, 1974, and Wolf, pp. 260–261.

[12]For the German loss of confidence in the Darlan cabinet, see Abetz, report of January 5, 1942, in which Hitler plainly stated his mistrust of the French government's will to collaborate, in *Mémorandum d'Abetz*, p. 130. See also ibid., pp. 141–142, on the Riom trials.

ise that any new government he headed would facilitate the functioning of the party in the unoccupied zone. [13]

Laval returned to the government in April, after which he became noticeably cooler toward the PPF and less willing to back its propaganda campaigns. The PPF once again turned upon him, now comparing him to Alexander Kerensky, the Russian leader whose short tenure in office had prepared the way for a more radical revolution. By May relations between the PPF and the new head of government had grown seriously strained, and it became difficult even to arrange meetings between Laval and party officials. Nonetheless, on June 6, Doriot again got to see Laval, this time to suggest that he (Doriot) undertake a speaking tour of the unoccupied zone and French North Africa. Laval rejected the idea, and once more, Doriot returned to Paris empty-handed. [14] The party press intensified its attacks on Laval, denouncing him in tones reminiscent of those Doriot had used during Laval's tenure in office in 1940. In 1942 there was more truth than there had been two years earlier to PPF accusations that Laval was impeding Franco-German collaboration despite his support in high German places. Doriot and his supporters renewed their charge of 1940 that Laval was a republican parliamentary politician, insufficiently willing to align France ideologically with the New Order.

Doriot had reasons to feel embittered at his treatment by Laval, although in view of the latter's reputation as a political dealer he should not have been surprised. When he no longer had any use for the PPF, Laval had lost interest in it, much as he had earlier in the RNP. In reality, the PPF had contributed no more than the RNP to his return to office, determined by forces over which collaborationists had no influence. Both Doriot and Déat came away empty-handed in the spring of 1942, reflecting Laval's political skill and the weakness of the Ultras. Although the Axis forces were at the height of their success during the spring and summer of 1942, the war situation had

[13]The account of the relations between Laval and Doriot is taken largely from a document dated October 21, 1942 and entitled "Bericht über die Beziehungen Laval-Doriot," CDJC document CDXCIV, 1. It is otherwise unidentified. From its content it could be one in a series of reports from occupied France by Professor Friedrich Grimm.
[14]"Bericht über die Beziehungen Laval-Doriot."

changed since 1940 with the entry of the Soviet Union and the United States, making longterm Axis victory more questionable. Laval still hoped that a compromise peace might be arranged between Germany and the Western powers with France emerging in the role of mediator. This meant soft-peddling the Montoire policy and avoiding too close an identification of himself with the collaborationists.

While Doriot was calling the Laval government "reactionary," Laval let his fears be known that Doriot was receiving SS help, which Oberg personally denied. The PPF now resumed its tactic of autumn, 1940, staking out the most extreme collaborationist ground for itself in an effort to outflank its rivals. Laval found himself the target of attacks from Ultras on one side and the growing Resistance on the other. Doriot's political line and his real and imagined contacts with the Germans appeared increasingly treasonous to the French who began to believe in and hope for Allied victory. Laval believed as late as July 1944 that he might still have a role to play in a transitional government following the liberation of France. Doriot, on the other hand, a fanatic, had burned all his bridges behind him by his decisive commitment to German victory and the Anti-Bolshevik Legion.

But by 1942, although retreat was no longer possible for Doriot, he was still waiting to reap the rewards of his pro-Axis commitment. He shared with his rivals in the Ultra camp an elitism which became more pronounced in the latter stages of the war. A growing sense of isolation was born of the awareness that the Ultras represented a small minority in France and that only a German victory would make it possible for them ever to achieve power there. They had to continue to believe in German victory or cease to be collaborationists, but this view appeared decreasingly realistic after 1942. As the war situation grew more desperate for the Germans, and the French were drawn progressively into participation, a civil war developed which allowed no room for *attentisme*. Laval, therefore, shared the fate of many of the Ultras against whom he had turned in 1942.[15]

The stalling of the German offensive against the Soviet Union in 1941 had led to the beginning of a shift from *Blitzkrieg* to a strategy of total war. Requirements of the military together with the needs of a

[15]Wolf, p. 262.

vastly expanding war machine in 1942 were placing great strains upon the German manpower supply. In 1942, Fritz Sauckel was named commissar-general for labor, and a systematic policy of utilizing the labor forces of the occupied Western countries for the German war machine was implemented. Sauckel began visiting France, asking the government to help round up large numbers of laborers for service in Germany. Suspended over the heads of the French officials was the implied threat that the Germans would do it themselves if the French did not. Laval resisted the idea and in stormy and tortuous sessions with Sauckel tried one ploy after another to delay and minimize the German exactions of French labor. First he proposed the *Relève,* a scheme by which one French prisoner of war in Germany would be released for every three skilled French workers who volunteered to work in the Reich. Despite an intensive propaganda campaign, supported by the Ultra groups, the *Relève* was unable to produce volunteers in nearly the numbers demanded by Sauckel.

Doriot took the view that even involuntary labor in Germany was necessary for the war effort. The French should not seek to shirk their share of the burden of liquidating Bolshevism. Doriot offered PPF help to Sauckel and Laval shrewdly took advantage of the offer to have the names of PPF members put on lists of volunteers bound for labor in Germany. This ploy had been tried earlier by Deloncle against Déat's faction in the RNP and from 1942 to 1944 Laval used it with some success to weaken all of the collaborationist movements.

The acceptance by Doriot and the other Ultras of the principle of involuntary labor service in Germany may have done more than any other one issue to alienate them from the vast majority of French popular opinion. Despite propaganda to the contrary, it was widely believed in France that labor conditions for foreigners in Germany were abysmal and that the chances of returning alive from such service were slim. The forced labor drafts did more than anything else to swell the numbers of French taking to the maquis. Sauckel was sardonically dubbed the "father of the French Resistance." Given their ideological proclivities, the Ultras had little choice but to accept the principle of forced labor but it was politically very costly to them. Doriot now denounced Laval for his reticence in meeting Sauckel's demands for labor and called for French adherence to the Anti-Comintern Pact and a French declaration of war against England and the United States following their landings in North Africa.[16]

Doriot used his leave from service in Russia to rebuild the PPF organization. In the unoccupied zone, the party operated openly under the pseudonym Mouvement Populaire Français, although its activities there were facilitated by the return of Laval to office. Figures for the PPF vary widely, with a high estimate of 300,000 party members at the end of 1942, provided by the former secretary-general of the party. More plausible is the evaluation of some 20,000 plus, made by the historian Henri Amouroux.[17]

Even in 1942 when the party was unquestionably at the peak of its strength for the occupation period, its territorial organization was uneven. Wolf found 50 to 60 of the local party sections regularly holding meetings in 1942 with an additional 150 to 200 similar groups meeting sporadically. As in all Ultra parties, authority in the PPF flowed from the top down. Beneath Doriot there functioned a Politbureau or executive committee including Barthélemy as secretary-general of the party; Simon Sabiani, the leader of the Marseilles organization; Marcel Marschall, PPF mayor of Saint-Denis; Henri Lèbre, director of *Cri du Peuple*; Roger Vauquelin, head of the Jeunesse Populaire Français, the party's youth movement; and several others. Below the level of the Politbureau were regional, departmental federation, and section organizations. In practice there were too few party members to give much substance to the regional and departmental organizations with the result that the scene of most party activity was the local section.

By 1943 the local sections had been organized in a manner to enable the party to operate clandestinely in the event of an Allied victory or a German move to outlaw the organization, which Laval

[16]Ibid., p. 263.
[17]See Amouroux, 2:386. The estimate of 300,000 PPF members comes from Victor Barthélemy in a statement to the author, July 9, 1974. German authorization of the PPF and other political parties in the northern zone can be found in Der Militärbefehlshaber in Frankreich, Anlage 32 zum Lagebericht, Februar/März 1942, and for the status of the Mouvement Populaire Français in the southern zone, see *French Basic Handbook*, p. 144. For a general discussion of the problems in assessing membership figures for the Ultra parties and some examples of attempts by their newspapers to exaggerate them, see Cotta, pp. 250–251. Laval's request and Ribbentrop's refusal to dissolve the PPF can be found in Ribbentrop (Sonderzug), 1614 to Abetz, December 26, 1942 (T-120/935/298684-7), cited in Paxton, p. 255.

had requested in vain at the end of 1942. On the section level, party activists were placed together in groups of four under the command of a fifth. Known as *mains* (hands), these groups were the basic local units which could be combined into larger formations under the *chef de section*. Section leaders were subordinated to the federal secretary. The goal of the PPF organization was to provide strong centralized control with flexibility and rapidity of mobilization. Small groups also impeded infiltration by hostile elements. Patterned after Communist party cells, the small units of the PPF were copied by the Milice, also organized for paramilitary action. Such tight structure contrasted with the looser organization of the RNP. After the Liberation, the PPF organization enabled it to engage in acts of sabotage, aided by party agents trained in and parachuted from Germany, against the new provisional government.[18]

Less totally centered in Paris than the RNP, the PPF had strong contingents in Marseilles, where Sabiani held sway, Nice, and North Africa. The party also attracted support from workers in some of the Paris suburbs, especially Doriot's prewar stronghold of Saint-Denis, whose mayor during the occupation period was Politbureau member Marschall. Although it recruited among factory workers, the PPF did not make quite the inroads that the RNP did among the French proletariat, nor did it attract as many teachers and others from the professional strata. Instead, the PPF was much more the party of the artisan class and it attempted to link its social views with the French tradition of Pierre-Joseph Proudhon and its militant activism with the revolutionary tactics of Auguste Blanqui. Party spokesmen extolled the Communards of 1871, contrasting the native French "socialism" of Proudhon and Maurice Barrès to what they denounced as "international" and "Jewish" socialism elaborated by Marx and Léon Blum. The revolutionary tradition of Georges Sorel, who also moved from radical Left to radical Right, was often evoked. Party doctrine was squarely in the tradition of the French radical Right middle classes, which in the words of Eugen Weber "could not admit a doctrine of class war that threatened their good conscience

[18]The discussion of the clandestine organization of the PPF comes largely from the *French Basic Handbook*, p. 144. See also Wolf, p. 264. The account of the secret organization of the PPF was also substantiated for the author in conversations with several former members of the party.

when it suggested that their interest did not necessarily coincide with that of the whole nation."[19]

The PPF even more clearly than the RNP reflected a radicalizing of the formerly moderate and nonpolitical lower middle classes, politicized by the crises of the interwar years and the disaster of 1940. They wanted to acquire what they perceived as proletarian cohesiveness and sense of historical mission while protecting their property and careers. A PPF propagandist wrote in 1943 that according to Sorel what the bourgeoisie needed was some of the energy of the proletariat.[20]

Although the PPF shared with most fascist movements a vagueness of doctrine, it evoked the Jacobin, Proudhonist, and Sorelian traditions with which it clothed its political militancy while carefully avoiding social revolution. By the late 1930's the party had added corporatism, looking back to La Tour du Pin in France, and anti-Semitism in the tradition of Drumont and Barrès. PPF anti-Semitism reflected the views of its middle- and lower-middle-class supporters, who wished to cover their interests in the cloak of national solidarity and identified the Jews with "international finance," especially in North Africa where the PPF was strong. The PPF and its collaborationist rivals could honestly contend that the roots of their political ideas were French. The vigor with which Doriot and his leadership corps embraced the tradition of revolutionary rhetoric in France, intensified by the socially conservative purposes to which it was put, gave the PPF an aura of activism lacking in its major rivals and helped make it the only Ultra movement with any serious pretension to power.

The popular constituency of the PPF, uneven as it was throughout France, nevertheless provided Doriot with a base from which he considered seizing government power during the summer and autumn of 1942. When General Henri Giraud escaped from captivity in Germany and returned to Vichy, the PPF press denounced the gov-

[19]Weber, "France," in Rogger and Weber, eds., *The European Right,* p. 107. See also Maurice-Ivan Sicard, "La Commune de Paris contre le Communisme," the printed text of a speech delivered by Sicard on March 25, 1942 at an anti-Bolshevik exposition in Paris, pp. 26–27 and 50–51.

[20]Maurice-Ivan Sicard, *Vive la France!* (Paris: Les Editions de France, 1943), p. 54.

ernment for refusing to arrest him and turn him over to the Germans. Sauckel was making new demands upon French labor. Ultras of all factions saw in these events a growing necessity for France to choose between Axis and Allies. Secretary-general Barthélemy declared that the PPF represented France's last hope and that it would soon take power. While Laval attempted unsuccessfully to repair the rifts in Franco-German relations, the party prepared for a mammoth congress, the "congress of power," to be held during the first week of November in Paris.[21]

Doriot did not possess sufficient German support to gain power in 1942. Abetz suspected that the newly installed SS and SD staff in Paris were behind the PPF—which would have put Oberg and his assistant Helmut Knochen in direct opposition to official policy in Berlin—but he had no hard evidence. Several French political figures, among them Jacques Benoist-Méchin, secretary of state for the Council of Ministers, and Admiral Charles-René Platon, were known to have wanted a Doriot government. Benoist-Méchin, who later wrote a widely read military history of the May–June 1940 campaign, and Platon had close ties to the PPF.

Any real possibility of a Doriot government, however, came to an end on September 21 when Ribbentrop sent Abetz a telegram telling him that Hitler had ordered scotched any rumors that a Doriot regime was contemplated for France. Hitler's statement effectively dashed PPF hopes and although it did no more than confirm previously existing policy, it was a major turning point in the history of the collaboration. It marked the beginning of a decline for the PPF, which had been deprived of its *raison d'être* and prepared the way for the creation of a different type of collaborationist movement, the Milice. By his statement Hitler reiterated his awareness that, fully committed in the various theaters of the war, he needed a tranquil France. To this end Laval seemed more promising than Doriot. Ideological solidarity took second place in Hitler's calculations. He would turn to Doriot only after France had been liberated and Pétain and Laval had persistently refused to exercise their government functions in enforced captivity in Sigmaringen. As with the Salò Republic in Italy in 1943 and the Arrow Cross regime of 1944 in Hungary, Hitler turned

[21]Barthélemy's statement appeared in *Cri du Peuple*, May 18, 1942, and is cited in Wolf, p. 265.

to the truly millenarian movements of the radical Right only after the failure of more conservative and traditionalist elements and only in defeat. When Doriot finally received his opportunity in the autumn of 1944, it no longer mattered.[22]

Hitler's checkmate of the PPF did not halt plans for the "congress of power" which the party organized in the hope that its strength and militancy might yet win it the support it lacked in Berlin. Laval had no intention of bringing the party into the government and no one in Berlin was going to force him to do so. Just as the political and military situation of the war had changed dramatically during the June 1941 party congress, the 1942 congress was upset by news of the Allied landings in French North Africa. The congress was held from November 4 through 8 and on the last day of the meetings the news of the landings reached France. This time the battlefield news came from closer to home than the Soviet Union, and more directly involved France.

In Paris the congress went on as scheduled. Careful preparations had been made and party delegates came from throughout France and North Africa to the Gaumont Palace where the sessions were conducted. Party figures indicated 6,000 delegates in attendance. A party study of the congress, cited by Wolf, spoke of 7,200 delegates gathered in Paris and divided them by political origin. As Wolf indicated in discussing the report, many of the delegates represented constituencies hardly larger than themselves and perhaps a few friends, especially those from outside the centers of party strength such as Saint-Denis, Marseilles, and Nice. The party show in Paris appeared far more impressive than grass-roots strength would indicate. Nonetheless, the figures for the political origins of the delegates are of interest in showing the backgrounds of the more active members.

The delegates included 1,556 former Communists, 588 former Socialists, 1,007 former backers of Colonel de la Rocque, and 420

[22]Wolf, p. 266. See also Martin du Gard, p. 293 and Alfred Fabre-Luce, *Journal de la France, 1939–1944* (Brussels: Cheval Ailé, 1946), pp. 495–499. A journalist, Fabre-Luce had been involved with a variety of rightist movements before the war and was an exceptionally keen observer of events in occupied France. See also "Bericht über die Beziehungen Laval-Doriot," October 21, 1942. For Abetz's suspicions of SS involvement in Doriot's plans see *Mémorandum d'Abetz*, p. 170.

former members of Action Française. Significantly, 3,011 delegates indicated no political affiliation prior to their membership in the PPF. There is little evidence to show that the former Communists, Socialists and Maurrasiens were successful in bringing many of their erstwhile party comrades into the PPF. If one uses Wolf's figure of 7,200 as the total attendance at the congress, the breakdown shows the political origins of 91.4 percent of the delegates. Of these, 41.8 percent, almost half, had declared no prior party affiliation. Among those having been involved in other political movements, 43.6 percent had been Communists and 16.5 percent Socialists, meaning that 60 percent of those politically active before joining the PPF had come from the Left. Twenty-eight percent had had their political origins in the various movements of de la Rocque and 11.8 percent in the Action Française, giving a total of 40 percent to the Right for those with earlier political activity.[23]

These figures cast some doubt upon the generalizations made by Jean Plumyène and Raymond Lasierra to the effect that the PPF was an extension of the Communist party and the RNP an extension of the Socialists under the altered circumstances of the occupation. In the main, their view is useful, considering the origins of the two movements themselves, but the scattered political backgrounds of the PPF delegates is a reminder of the complexities involved in such generalizations.[24]

Most striking, however, is the fact that almost half of the party

[23]The figures for the political origins of the delegates to the PPF November party congress are given by Wolf, p. 266, n. 1. Wolf has taken the data from a PPF report of the party congress; see ibid., p. 354, n. 952. In his statement of July 9, 1974 to the author, Victor Barthélemy furnished general figures on the political origins of the party membership which approximated those given by Wolf. Interestingly, Barthélemy also denied that the phrase "congrès du pouvoir" had actually emanated from PPF circles. He claimed that the party leadership was sufficiently realistic to recognize that the Germans would not allow them to take power. Whatever the private convictions of Barthélemy and his associates, however, the nature of the propaganda campaign accompanying the preparations for the congress and the public statements of the party leaders were open for all to see. The congress itself and the elaborate preparations necessary for its organization are described in a party pamphlet, "Unité—Force—Honneur 4ème Congrès National. Paris. 4-5-6-7-8 Novembre, 1942. Programme des Travaux. PPF," BDIC, O pièce 22036.

[24]For the view of the RNP and PPF as inverted analogues of the interwar Socialists and Communists, see Plumyène and Lasierra, p. 156.

delegates listed no previous political affiliation. This implies a high proportion of relatively young people, drawn from previously nonpolitical sectors of society. In addition, the people at the party congress were the leadership cadres of the movement with presumably more political experience than ordinary party members. In the absence of contradictory evidence, it seems that half or more of the PPF membership as a whole had engaged in no political activity before joining the Doriotists and that many, if not most, of these party militants were quite young, anti-establishment but also anti-Communist, and lured by the charismatic personality of Doriot. With the failure of the PPF to attain power in 1942 and the continuing strife among the various Ultra factions, some of these restless young souls passed into Darnand's paramilitary Milice and the more directly military formations of the collaboration, the Anti-Bolshevik Legion and the Waffen-SS.

During the November party congress PPF goals were defined as a totalitarian France, national, social (meaning reconciliation rather than conflict among social classes), imperial, European, and authoritarian. While calling for a totalitarian France, Doriot also defended a contradicting policy of federalism as a gesture toward Breton separatists who were being encouraged by the Germans and whose support he wanted. Wolf indicates that Doriot, himself the son of a Breton mother, met with Raymond Delaporte and Olier Mordrel, leaders of the separatist Parti National Breton (PNB). Doriot also came out strongly for freedom for Christians to practice their faith, an obvious bow toward the Church. He included in his platform racial anti-Semitism, in which he spoke of a Celtic French race that he hoped would ally with the Germans in an Aryan solidarity. One wonders whether the PPF chief ever reflected upon the irony of his "Aryan" parody of the Maurrasian "bloc Latine."[25]

The party congress was to close on November 8 with a final speech

---

[25]The Germans gave the PNB "tolerated" status; they were unwilling to support it more enthusiastically because of their belief that too visible a German backing of separatist movements might rebound politically against them. See Militär-befehlshaber in Frankreich. Anlage 32 zum Lagebericht für die Monate Februar/März 1942. On the subject of Doriot's relations with the Breton separatists see also Wolf, p. 267, n. 1. For his definition of the PPF program before the congress, see *Le Cri du Peuple*, November 5, 1942.

in the Vélodrome d'hiver by Doriot. By the closing day, however, the PPF leaders and all France had heard the news of the Allied landings and the Vichy French resistance in North Africa. Laval immediately ordered a ban on further PPF mass meetings and forebade Doriot to speak. Angry party militants using bullhorns demonstrated in the streets of Paris, where Doriot harangued a crowd, demanding that France enter the war against the Allies. The Allied forces rapidly overran much of French North Africa after Admiral Darlan had arranged a cease-fire in Algiers. German armed forces then crossed the demarcation line and occupied all of metropolitan France, except for the eight departments in the southeast administered by Italy. Vichy thereupon ordered the scuttling of the fleet at Toulon in order to prevent its falling into the hands of the Germans.

With an ever-weakened France being drawn increasingly into the vortex of the war, collaborators *de raison,* so called for collaborating out of a sense of "realism," in view of superior German strength after 1940, began now to change camps. Those left in the Axis camp were the passionate Ultras, who might well have been termed "collaborators *de coeur"* Yet these Ultras had seen their path to power blocked by the Germans themselves. Increasingly after 1942 they were trapped with no political escape route left. As the journalist Alfred Fabre-Luce stated at the time, the Ultras could only follow their German allies to defeat and destruction. The minoritarian Ultra community could only intensify its resistance to a fate which became clearer with each passing month and from which it had cut all avenues of escape. The futility of its position became plain within weeks as the PPF in Tunisia helped organize an anti-Allied resistance that fought bravely against an outcome that must have been clear to its members from the start.[26]

During the days that followed the November party congress, Doriot continued his attempt to enlist German support in his campaign to succeed Laval. SS-Standartenführer Walter Schellenberg, who headed the SS intelligence bureau, condemned Laval for failing to support the Axis fully immediately after the landings in North Africa and praised Doriot for his strong pro-Axis stand. Aware that the landings had intensified an already growing French Ger-

[26]Fabre-Luce, p. 496. See also Hamilton, p. 284.

manophobia, he began to wonder whether Laval, without a solid constituency of his own, could contain it.[27]

Doriot, meanwhile, approached anyone willing to help him in his quest for power: the Breton separatists, the Catholic church, and toward the end of November, even Marcel Déat. German policy, however, had not changed and Goebbels confided to his diary that Doriot was becoming too bold and might require forcible restraint. Once more Hitler made his views known when he invited Laval to visit him in December in Germany. When, during his visit, Laval met Ribbentrop and asked him to dissolve the PPF, the German foreign minister refused. The PPF was neither to be allowed to take power nor to be dissolved. Its role was defined by Hitler, Goebbels, and Ribbentrop as oppositional, a sword of Damocles suspended over Laval's head, available when the Germans might wish to pressure Vichy. By keeping Doriot available in the wings, the Germans also hoped to make Laval appear by contrast less distasteful to the French population. Doriot was now to be used by the Germans against Laval in the same way Laval had previously been used against the Darlan government.[28]

By the beginning of 1943 the steam had gone out of the PPF even if the party leaders did not admit it. Disaffection spread among the party faithful in Paris and its surrounding area. Most party members did not quit the movement; instead they withdrew into apathy and ceased attending party meetings. If morale was somewhat better in the provinces, this was due in part to the indefatigable efforts of Fernand Canobbio, who had held several PPF posts and later became a Politbureau member, and other party stalwarts. Canobbio in particular traveled throughout the country, exhorting the faithful. It must have been a disheartening task. A number of party leaders in

[27]The favorable SS evaluation of Doriot comes from Schellenberg, Reichssicherheitshauptamt VI, Report to Reichsführer-SS [Himmler], 27668/42g, November 17, 1942, CDJC document CCXXVII, 12.

[28]For information about Doriot's brief flirtation with the RNP and the Francistes, I am indebted to a ranking member of the MSR who kindly allowed me to see a number of unpublished materials in his possession, including a secret report on a meeting at which Doriot spoke, December 6, 1942. The account of Laval's meeting with Ribbentrop is based in large part on the account in Wolf, p. 269. For Goebbels' view of Doriot, see Joseph Goebbels, The Goebbels Diaries, 1942–1943, ed. and trans. Louis P. Lochner (New York: Doubleday, 1948), entry of December 7, 1942, p. 235.

Paris, among them Fossati, were disillusioned with Doriot and felt that he had allowed himself to be deceived by the Germans and the SS in particular. The disgruntled PPF leaders blamed the SS for encouraging Doriot to attack Laval, and then leaving him in the lurch. A vague anticollaboration sentiment was said to be spreading among disillusioned party members, who were further upset by an article in *Schwarze Korps,* the SS organ, which maintained that there were no French collaborators worthy of the Germans. Laval also used the opportunity provided by the PPF setbacks to move against the party. On November 25, 1942, on order of the prefect of the Loire, a number of PPF officials of the Loire federation were arrested and charged with having passed documents to the Germans, helping them catch political enemies in the southern zone immediately after the German army had entered it. Recognizing the futility of his political position in France, Doriot requested and received permission to rejoin the Anti-Bolshevik Legion on the Eastern front. Amid renewed anti-Communist demonstrations and widespread publicity, he left Paris on March 24. He was to remain away from France for most of the next year.[29]

While Doriot was making his unsuccessful bid for power in France, his party helped organize a futile last-ditch resistance to the Allies in Tunisia by seizing power in a coup which Doriot hoped would become the model for a future PPF strike in France. When the Allies landed in Algeria on November 8, it took a few days and several thousand Allied and Vichy French casualties to arrange an armistice with Admiral Darlan, visiting his sick son in Algiers. The delay gave the Axis powers time to land considerable forces in Tunisia. While Pétain gave public orders for resistance against the Allies, he let Darlan know that the accommodation reached with them in Algiers was acceptable. Interestingly, Jacques Lemaigre-Dubreuil, a French businessman who had helped work out the arrangment between Darlan and the Allies, was an ex-*Cagoulard.* On November 9, Axis forces had begun to land in Tunisia and two days later the southern zone of

---

[29]For the general account of conditions within the PPF in early 1943, I have consulted a secret intelligence report on the PPF made for the MSR, dated January 22, 1943, in the private collection cited in n. 28. The arrests in the Loire department were recalled after the war by Georges Potut, prefect of the Loire, deposition 285, May 27, 1955, in *France during the German Occupation,* 1:505.

France had been occupied by the Wehrmacht. The situation remained highly complicated as Pétain and Laval, the latter negotiating with Hitler at Berchtesgaden, refused German offers of full alliance and tried instead to keep channels open to America. The Vichy government's double game in respect to the North African landings did not deceive the Germans but it did cause great confusion for the French officials on the scene.

On the morning of November 11, German and Italian troops in Tunisia began to deploy in preparation to meet the Allied advance. Admiral Louis Derrien, the commandant of the French naval base at Bizerta, received a telegram from Vichy ordering him to allow the Germans to land more troops there but avoid all contact with them. General Bridoux, Vichy's secretary of state for war, sent a similar telegram at the same time to General Georges Barré, the commander of all French forces in Tunisia. Axis forces were to be allowed to land but without French authorization. Matters, however, reached a peak of confusion as the day wore on and Admiral Derrien received three different additional orders, first instructing his forces to prepare to fight against the Germans, then a second ordering him to a strict neutrality, and a third telling him to support the Axis. The French in Tunisia might wonder who the enemy was but the Germans used the period of confusion to implant their forces in sufficient strength to require a six-month military campaign by the Allies to dislodge them. Only in May 1943 were the last Axis troops finally expelled from Tunisia. On November 15 and 16, 1942, Admiral Platon, the secretary of state attached to Laval, was sent to Tunis with orders directing Admiral Jean-Pierre Estéva, Vichy's resident-general there, to collaborate with the Axis forces, which he and Derrien did. Barré's position was summed up by Maurice Martin du Gard, who wrote that in view of all the conflicting orders he had received, the general had decided to resist everyone: "He positioned his troops with one part facing the sea, against the Germans, the rest at the Algerian frontier to bar the road to the Anglo-Saxons. Then, when the Germans had installed themselves, he entrusted his wife and daughter to them, announced that he would fight against the Anglo-Saxons, and hurried off to join the Allies and Fighting France [de Gaulle]."[30]

[30]Martin du Gard, p. 344. For a discussion of the confusion in Tunisia that followed the Allied landings in North Africa, see Aron, *The Vichy Regime,* pp.

While Vichy pursued its intricate attempt to balance off Americans and Germans in North Africa, Doriot called upon France to sign the Anti-Comintern Pact and create a *légion imperiale* to defend the Empire against the Allies. In Tunisia his stand was echoed by the local PPF as well as Commandant Malcor, who headed Darnand's Service d'Ordre Légionnaire there. The SOL had been organized by the most politically active members of the Pétainist Légion des Combattants, supporters of the National Revolution whose organization ultimately evolved into the Milice. In Tunisia the SOL joined with the PPF to lead the French community toward a staunch pro-Axis stand. The cooperation of SOL, largely Pétainist and rightist in political origins, and the PPF in Tunisia has been described by a historian of the Ultra adventure there:

> These positions, taken by so disparate a group of men as those of the PPF, the SOL, and the remainder of the Legion, formed an extremely coherent unity which marked six months of the history of Tunisia. In the absence of their leaders and main cadres, away at the party congress at Paris, most of the PPF members spontaneously placed themselves at the orders of the SOL leaders. Their integration into that organization was accomplished without difficulty, as the revolutionary doctrine of the two organizations coincided perfectly, the spirit of struggle animating them was the same.
>
> Among the ranks of the SOL were a professor's son who was the provisional leader of the Tunisian Federation of the PPF, and also the militants "of 1936," C. and Z. On November 11, 1942, PPF members G., Barnavaux, Chaban, and A. (oldest son of a family of eight children) entered the SOL in turn. Two months later both groups [of volunteers] were counted among the first volunteers for the Phalange Africaine.[31]

401–416 and, from an American point of view, William L. Langer, *Our Vichy Gamble* (New York: Knopf, 1947), pp. 357–360. The political situation in Tunisia is discussed in considerable detail in Pellegrin, pp. 21–33.

[31]Pellegrin, p. 36. In Pellegrin's account, based mainly on the diaries and memoirs of those involved in the Tunisian events of November 1942–May 1943, he has respected the wish for anonymity for the Phalange Africaine veterans still alive. Hence his occasional use of initials rather than names. Contemporary French historians of pro-Axis military formations such as the Anti-Bolshevik Legion, the French units of the Waffen-SS, and the Phalange Africaine have frequently utilized initials and pseudonyms to protect the anonymity of their informants.

The PPF and SOL in Tunisia were galvanized into action by a visit of Georges Guilbaud, one of the leaders of the PPF, who had been given a message for Admiral Estéva by Marshal Pétain. Guilbaud had been the delegate of the Information Ministry to the three departments of France overseas and consequently was well acquainted with North Africa. Like so many others within the PPF, he had once been a Communist. Initially a railway worker, Guilbaud had obtained a university degree, had become expert in organizational and managerial techniques and prior to the war had helped run Communist newspapers and the Paris metal workers' union. A visit to the Soviet Union in 1938 had disillusioned him and he became convinced that Stalin was sacrificing international Communism for the sake of Soviet interests at the time of the Munich crisis. Guilbaud then turned against Communism and took a teaching post at the Alliance Française in Cairo. In Syria at the outbreak of the war, Guilbaud had been mobilized into the army and he remained in the Middle East during the 1939–1940 campaign in France. After the armistice he returned to France, where he joined the PPF. Guilbaud was twenty-eight years old when sent to Tunisia in November 1942. Perhaps more than anyone else, he was the incarnation of the ideal PPF activist: bright, talented, tough, and young; a professional political agitator. One of Guilbaud's associates in the CUAR described him as having "acquired a toughened experience of life and a profound knowledge of politics and men. A realist with sharp ideas, clear views, and a well-tempered will."[32]

Arriving in Tunis on November 23, Guilbaud brought a directive in which Estéva was ordered to resist any Allied incursion. Laval now ordered the creation of a *légion imperiale,* consisting of volunteers to help the Axis forces repel the Allies from North Africa. Fearing that the PPF might yet undercut his support in Berlin, he proposed the new legion as a tactic to stave off the PPF, placate the Germans, and, by keeping Vichy officially neutral, maintain open channels to the Allies. Robert Aron has pointed out that Laval's attempted double game was disastrous for France. She lost the Empire, the unoccupied zone, the fleet, and the American card. After November 1942, Vichy

[32]Claude Martin, "Une expérience révolutionnaire," pp. 84–86, an unpublished manuscript of 1943 cited in Pellegrin, p. 54.

sank progressively into diplomatic isolation and satellite status. Abetz, Laval's strongest German supporter, was called back to Berlin by Ribbentrop and told to take no more personal diplomatic initiatives in France.[33]

Having informed Estéva of his duty to support the Axis, Guilbaud then organized a Comité d'Unité d'Action Révolutionnaire (CUAR), to comprise representatives of all groups wishing to fight for the Axis in Tunisia. The new committee was soon bolstered by the return from the Paris party congress of the PPF delegates, including Federation Chief Jean Scherb.

Led by Guilbaud, the CUAR staged a coup which placed it in control of the administrative centers in Tunis on November 25. Shortly thereafter it took control of the *Tunis-Journal,* the only French-language daily newspaper in Tunis. The local police and government bureaucracy were purged and officials whose political views were questionable were replaced with pro-Axis personnel, mainly from PPF or SOL circles. The *Tunis-Journal* was now headed by Claude Martin, a member of the CUAR, and Radio Tunis was also taken over by the CUAR early in December. To administer social welfare, the CUAR created a branch of the Comité Ouvrier de Secours Immédiat, which sequestered wealth from local Jews to help non-Jewish war victims. Guilbaud's CUAR was able to render significant help to the Axis by identifying and arresting anti-Axis Frenchmen in Tunisia. It was also able to help pacify the civilian population, freeing the Axis forces to concentrate on military defense. The coup and subsequent purges carried out by the committee were fashioned in a manner described as brutal even by the German Foreign Ministry representative in Tunis.[34]

The CUAR domination of Tunisia illustrates in microcosm what

---

[33]Aron, *The Vichy Regime,* pp. 419–420. See also *French Basic Handbook,* p. 145. For the role of German pressure in Laval's grant of authority to Guilbaud, see the report from Rudolf Rahn, who claimed to have pressured Laval to send Guilbaud to Tunis, telegram 1567, December 21, 1942 from Woerman to the Foreign Ministry in Berlin. This telegram was reproduced as Document NG-3149, Office of Chief of Counsel for War Crimes, for the Nuremberg War Crimes Trial, and is available as CDJC document CXXV, 108.

[34]Rahn in Woermann, telegram 1567, December 21, 1942. Also Pellegrin, personal statement to the author, July 14, 1974, and pp. 57, 59, and 60–63; and the *French Basic Handbook,* pp. 145–146.

might have followed a PPF takeover in France. Within limitations imposed by the conditions of war, the CUAR was able to dominate and politicize all aspects of life in Tunisia. A school for political cadres was set up, its organizational structure and function patterned after the Communist school for cadres at Bobigny. A one-party fascist state, in which all was organized by the CUAR, was established in Tunisia under the benevolent eyes of Admiral Estéva and the Germans. In the *Tunis-Journal* Guilbaud and Martin called for a new moral climate in which the French colony would follow a more generous line toward the local Moslems and rally the total population of Tunisia to the Axis cause. To the CUAR, Admirals Derrien and Estéva represented the old order, the generation of 1914 in Tunisia, whereas Guilbaud and his men were of a new generation.[35]

The generational revolt of the radical Right against the French gerontocracy can be seen nowhere more clearly than in the Tunisian events, which represented the culmination of organized collaborationist success during the occupation. For almost six months a new generation of fascists, who had failed politically in France, ruled in Tunisia. The differences between backers of the PPF and SOL had disappeared. United in their desire for a French empire associated with the "New Europe," purged of Communists and Jews, the young militants of the CUAR were dislodged only by the Allied military victory in May 1943.

Besides its work in securing the home front for the Axis forces in Tunisia, the Guilbaud committee was also instrumental in recruiting for the Phalange Africaine, the corps of volunteers which evolved out of Laval's call for a *légion imperiale*. At first the Phalange Africaine had been envisioned as a corps of volunteers from throughout France, to parallel the Anti-Bolshevik Legion. One estimate gave a figure of 3,000 volunteers for the Phalange Africaine in all of France but the issue became theoretical for the French lacked the aircraft needed to transport these troops to Tunisia. The Germans could not or would not spare their planes, and the result was that only a handful of French officers were able to cross to North Africa. Consequently,

[35]Pellegrin, statement to the author, July 14, 1974, and p. 76. The statement of Claude Martin is from his "Une expérience révolutionnaire," pp. 114–115, cited in Pellegrin's book, p. 71. For the description of Guilbaud as a "born revolutionary," see Rahn, *Ruheloses Leben,* p. 207.

159

recruitment for the Phalange Africaine was limited to the French community in Tunisia. The officers who arrived in Tunisia included Commander Cristofini, a Corsican who had made a career in the colonial army and was named to head the Phalange. The choice was made by Colonel Edgar Puaud, the head of the Anti-Bolshevik Legion which in July 1942 had been granted legal standing and renamed Légion Tricolor by Vichy. Described by an associate as "unsubtle and a fanatical nonentity," Cristofini was later wounded during the campaign and succeeded by Major Jean-Emile Curnier, a career officer who had served with distinction during the First World War and had been active in Darnand's SOL in Nice. Other officers included Captains Daniel Peltier and Roger Euzière, both experienced in colonial service, Captain Henry Charbonneau, formerly of Deloncle's MSR, and Lieutenant-Colonel Sarton du Jonchay, charged with political liaison between the Phalange Africaine and Admiral Estéva. Both Charbonneau and Sarton du Jonchay were the sons of French army generals.[36]

The volunteers for the Phalange Africaine came largely from the French community in Tunis, although other towns in Tunisia were also represented. According to René Pellegrin, who has chronicled the Tunisian campaign, 330 volunteers came from the French Tunisian colony with an additional 150 Tunisian Arabs. Most of the *pied-noir* volunteers came from the local SOL or PPF. Among the volunteers, Pellegrin counts the librarian of the city of Tunis, three teachers with several of their relatives, two engineers, one hundred soldiers, both noncommissioned and career officers, and a hundred "anciens employés," workers or *colons* from collaborationist political circles. The Phalange also included the son of a ranking Tunisian official (*controlêur civil*) and several students from the philosophy class of the Carnot Lycée in Tunis. Two Jews also found their way into the Phalange Africaine—not all that unusual, as Jews occasionally tried to protect themselves during the war by hiding in collaborationist organizations.[37]

[36]Charbonneau, 1:388–389.

[37]Pellegrin, p. 79, n. 1. Here Pellegrin takes strong exception to Aron's description of the Phalangistes as "the scum of Tunis, syphilitics and disease-ridden of all kinds, whom he [Cristofini] attracted by offering them good meals and money" (Aron, *The Vichy Regime*, p. 450). Figures for the size of the Phalange Africaine range from

Reflecting years later upon his service in the Phalange Africaine, Charbonneau described the mood of the time:

> We know that for us there can be at the end of this story neither success nor glory and that everything has to turn out badly! The future appears disastrous. But that doesn't prevent good cheer. Christian [du Jonchay] has always loved mad escapades; Cristofini dreams of triumphal return to the Gulf of Juan; Curnier will carry the flag if someday we go back to France; the *spahis* [North African Arab troops] and I are not yet thirty years old. We love risk and life, the good life, but also honor, grandeur of spirit, and whatever sacrifice is necessary. So, it's in the hands of God![38]

Career military men viewed service in the Phalange Africaine as obedience to their supreme leader, Marshal Pétain. Italian claims to Tunisia were well known and the presence of a French force in the Axis camp was seen as a guarantee that in the event of Axis victory, Tunisia would remain French. Although the German defeat at Stalingrad portended ill for the Axis cause, General Rommel still had a large force under his command in North Africa and his reputation had been well established by early 1943. Anti-Semitism was especially strong in North Africa, where many in the lower-middle and white-collar classes identified the sizable local Jewish community with finance capitalism. The tradition of *colon* anti-Semitism included anti-Dreyfusard riots at the turn of the century in Algiers and was the base upon which the interwar PPF had built a strong popular following. Anti-Semitism had always been stronger among the PPF in North Africa than in metropolitan France and Doriot had been chided by his North African supporters for his moderation on this issue.[39]

Aron's estimate of 150 to Charbonneau's 450; see Pellegrin, p. 91. In 1942 there were roughly 100,000 Tunisians of French origin. If Charbonneau's figure is accurate the ratio of volunteers to French Tunisian population, if applied to France as a whole, would have produced 180,000 volunteers!

[38]Charbonneau, 1:394.

[39]Gilbert D. Allardyce, "Jacques Doriot et l'esprit fasciste en France," *Revue d'histoire de la deuxième guerre mondiale,* 25 (January 1975), 39–40, mentions the particularly strong anti-Semitism of the North African PPF organizations; Doriot's attempts to bridle it led Victor Arrhigi, the party director in North Africa, to resign from the party in 1939 in protest. Metropolitan France, with a population in 1939 of

The Phalange Africaine saw action during the spring of 1943 in the Tunis area. On January 23, Cristofini received an eye wound while attending a German antitank exercise at the front, and was evacuated to Sicily and replaced by Curnier. (Cristofini was later returned to France and made his way back to his native Corsica. He was arrested after the liberation of Corsica and executed by a military tribunal of the Gaullist committee in May 1944 in Algiers.) Early in April 1943 the Phalange Africaine was sent to the front. The volunteers were caught in the middle of an Allied advance and were too few to stem the tide. One of their officers was awarded the German Iron Cross medal, second class, for bravery in combat.[40] After the final defeat of the Axis forces in May, the Phalange Africaine was disbanded. The PPF now began to parachute agents as spies and saboteurs behind the lines in "enemy-held" North African territory, a foretaste of their reaction after France itself was liberated. Although the Doriotist rearguard actions failed both in North Africa in 1943 and in France the next year, they gave testimony to the vigor and boldness of the party that had emerged in 1942 as the most daring of the factions in the Ultra camp.[41]

The brief PPF takeover organized by Guilbaud in Tunisia stands in marked contrast to the failure of the party in metropolitan France. In Tunisia the PPF was able to cooperate with other collaborationist forces, notably the SOL, to organize anti-Allied resistance. In France, by contrast, the PPF remained on terms of most bitter rivalry with other Ultra groups, including after 1943 the SOL's successor, the Milice. Collaborationist unity was easier to achieve in Tunisia because the French community was small and isolated in regard to the local Italians and Moslems. The unity achieved by Guilbaud and the CUAR occurred against the backdrop of war in progress, whereas similar conditions did not exist in metropolitan France until the

---

roughly 40 million, had about 240,000 Jews, or .06 percent of the population. Tunisia, with a total population of 2.6 million, had approximately 60,000 Jews, a proportion of 2.3 percent. The Tunisians of French origin, of course, were only a small proportion of the total, and of the French Tunisians many were Jews. In this perspective the relatively high proportion of Jews as opposed to non-Jewish French Tunisians becomes clear.

[40]Charbonneau, 1:397–399 and Pellegrin, pp. 93 and 132.

[41]On the subject of PPF parachutists being dropped in liberated North Africa, see Pellegrin, p. 164.

Normandy landings. Finally, in Tunisia, the local collaborationist groups were cut off from their national leaders, whose unending personal feuds impeded united action. Local instances of cooperation occurred throughout France but the rivalries among the leaders helped deepen and perpetuate divisions among the rank-and-file.

The fragmentation of French political life meant that thousands who accepted the wartime beliefs of the PPF nonetheless joined other political movements. Doriot and his entourage of former Communists brought to the PPF a militancy, toughness, and organizational skill that was one of the party's major strengths, differentiating it from its rivals. The strength of the PPF, however, was also its weakness. Too many on the radical Right, whose support was essential for any mass fascist movement in France, saw Doriot as an opportunist, despite the fact that his break with the Communists had long predated the war. The only leader produced by the collaborationists with the skill and charisma to be a fascist chief, Doriot killed by his strident sectarianism any possible chances for Ultra unity. Instead of trying to unite the diminishing collaborationist clientele after 1942, he insisted that the other parties join the PPF on his terms. His tactics, reminiscent of the post-1928 Communist attacks against Socialists as "Social Fascists," perpetuated the fragmentation of the Ultra camp. The PPF became a reflection of the organizational and activist strengths but also the divisive weakness of its leader.

The composition of the PPF, like that of the RNP, oriented it away from political compromise. Those of its members with prior political experience were dissidents from other movements, reinforcing the French tradition of brittle, narrowly ideological political parties. The phenomenon of the inveterate joiner quitting one party after another, common in the interwar years, persisted under the occupation. Many who joined the PPF came in search of total truth in response to Doriot's interwar phrase, "we have the answer." These members of the lower middle classes, merchants and salaried personnel, comprised the popular base of most fascist movements. They joined disillusioned ex-Communists in search of a new truth, an ideology to provide for them the kinds of answers offered by Communism, liberalism, and even Christianity to their believers. The PPF promised a new vision along with bold leadership and a well-organized party prepared to defend the interests of its supporters. The moralism

163

that the PPF and the other French Ultras used to shield their basic social conservatism made joining these movements an act of faith, similar to engaging in a crusade. Such attitudes made compromise difficult. The PPF also attracted many political neophytes, especially during the occupation years. Often on the fringes of urban society or unemployed, these recruits lacked experience in the art of political compromise. Financial and industrial tycoons who sometimes supported the PPF also made donations to other movements in order to hedge their bets. They had no reason to foster collaborationist unity.

The failure of the PPF in 1942 was assured by Doriot's leadership, which exacerbated longstanding and deep-seated fissures in the French collaborationist political community when the limited appeal of Germanophilia required unity. Doriot's personal frustration by the appearance of so many rivals during the occupation is eminently comprehensible. Having been excluded from effective action in the Left by the Communists in 1934, he now faced two new rivals after having completed his shift to fascism. The RNP and Milice had both entered territory Doriot claimed as his by right of hard-fought political struggle in the interwar years. First claim has no standing in political life and Doriot was unable to develop an effective strategy to eliminate his rivals. The tactic of awaiting their attrition failed because time was running against the Axis. Their growing problems worked against all the Ultra parties, the PPF included.

Superimposed upon the political fragmentation in France was German policy, which allowed success for the PPF in Tunisia but denied it in France. Hitler's policy was consistent. In both cases he wanted tranquillity on the home front while Germany fought her war. In Tunisia the PPF worked through Guilbaud's CUAR for the domestic quiet the Germans needed at the time of the Allied attack. In France, however, the best guarantee of tranquillity in the eyes of Hitler and his top aides was Laval, and the PPF could serve only as a disruptive force. Consequently, the Germans gave the French Ultras free rein in Tunisia and kept them effectively in check in metropolitan France.

The PPF success in Tunisia whetted Doriot's desire for power in France itself and strengthened his conviction that his party was the only vigorous force capable of propelling France into the New European Order. Determined to await the weakening of his rival Ultra factions, Doriot expected their members to fall, like ripe fruit from a tree, into the ranks of the PPF.[42] In the end his policy worked. By 1944 the rivals had in fact been weakened and the PPF had emerged as the major Ultra faction in the eyes of most German observers. But when the PPF attained leadership, whether in Tunisia or among the French exiles in Germany after the liberation of France, it was too late for the party to do much except drop parachutists behind the Allied lines.

[42] *French Basic Handbook*, p. 146.

5 The Milice Française: A New Movement in a Dying World

I am not one of those who will tell you: "Monsieur le Premier Président, I played a double game." I marched. I simply marched. I am proud of what I did. I was mistaken but I acted in good faith. I believe that I, too, served.

—Darnand at his trial, October 1945

The beginning of 1943 found the government of Pierre Laval in a strengthened position with respect to the collaborationist movements based in Paris. The RNP, unable to recover the momentum of its early days, was no closer to power than before. The great wave of the PPF campaign for power had broken in November 1942 against the rock of Hitler's opposition. Berlin had no reason to favor Doriot as long as Pétain and Laval were willing to do much of the Germans' bidding in efforts to avoid direct German administration of France— the fate of Poland or "polonization" as the French called it. The Vichy government made increasing concessions to growing German pressure. It reached positions on key issues such as treatment of Jews in France, manpower for work in the Reich, and repression of a growing domestic resistance that approximated the stands taken by the collaborationists. With Vichy approaching the position of the extremists, Hitler was content to continue supporting Laval's government. Doriot was still available as a threat to force Laval's compliance should it be necessary.[1]

Nonetheless, Laval had been alarmed by the Doriotist campaign of late 1942. As well as fearing Doriot, Laval mistrusted Pétain, who might at any time attempt a repeat of the scenario of December 13, 1940. He decided to create his own single party, an elite of the southern zone forming a kind of praetorian guard for his personal security. Such a movement might provide him with a firmer base of popular support and would also help drain away members from

[1]Hoffmann, "Collaborationism," pp. 386–387.

166

Doriot's PPF and the other troublesome collaborationist parties based in the northern zone.

The new movement was to be a combination totalitarian political party and private police force, which might also be used against the growing power of the Resistance. To lead the new organization, Laval turned to Joseph Darnand, a war hero and a military man with little reputation for political savvy. When Laval visited Hitler shortly after the Allies had landed in North Africa, he asked the German leader for permission to create just such a political movement, subject to his own control in Vichy. Previously existing political formations would be allowed to continue their activities as long as these were "positive," specifically working for the goals of the Axis and making no polemical attacks upon the Vichy government or its leader. Thus was born the Milice Française, known simply as the Milice, created by Pierre Laval. [2]

The Milice was the second of the major collaborationist movements in which Laval had a hand. He had also been involved in the creation of the RNP and it is significant that neither possessed quite the single-minded purpose of taking power that animated the PPF, the one major group in which Laval played no role. It is a measure of Laval's political domination that he was able to help channel two of the three major collaborationist formations away from attempts at direct seizures of power. Established as an arm of the Vichy government, the Milice could hardly contemplate seizing power from its own masters. The organization suffered from ambiguities in purpose for Laval wanted it to maintain public order while Darnand and his friends, more concerned to build a new fascist elite, recruited many disorderly types who subverted Laval's intentions. The Milice unquestionably contributed to the disorder it was supposed to suppress.

Joseph Darnand was first and foremost a soldier. A hero of both world wars who relished the camp life, he was to impart his love of this style of life to his followers in the Milice. Tried by the Gaullist government after the war, Darnand depicted himself as a "simple soldier" and after being found guilty of "intelligence with the enemy" and condemned to death, he saved his last words for the faithful of

---

[2]Abetz, Anlage zur Anschrift, December 23, 1942, "Vorschläge Lavals nach seinem Empfang im Führerhauptquartier," T-77/884/5632988.

the Milice. He was the great white knight of the collaboration who inculcated in his followers the ideals of service, self-sacrifice, and simplicity, in short the romantic cult of medieval chivalry which characterized virtually all fascist movements in interwar and wartime Europe. The Milice was to be a twentieth-century incarnation of the crusading orders of the Middle Ages. Darnand was a straightforward soldier, direct and often blunt, with a strong sense of honor and integrity conceived of in the military tradition, analagous to the German officers who refused to act against Hitler for fear of violating their military oath. Neither a political theorist nor an orator, he possessed at most a mediocre level of political sophistication. He was not, however, a simple man. With considerable organizational skills, he had run a successful trucking enterprise between the wars at Nice and, although as head of the government Laval was titular head of the Milice, it was Darnand who organized it and made it into the fighting force that battled the maquis in full-scale civil war during the spring and early summer of 1944.

Above all, Darnand was an activist. His physical courage was uncontested. He had participated in the raid that uncovered the secret of the impending German offensive of July 1918 and also in the raid on Forbach, one of the few French military offensive actions during the *drôle de guerre* of 1939–1940. Darnand had a very low tolerance for words and gestures unsupported by acts. He was a twentieth-century *homme engagé*. A member of Action Française during the 1920's, Darnand gravitated toward its most militant wing, the Camelots du Roi, and in 1928 was named head of the veterans' organizaton within Action Française. Soon afterward, the Papal condemnation of Maurras' organization and the aging of its leadership corps led to a progressive enervation of the movement, and the 1930's found Darnand shifting from one radical Right political organization to another in a vain attempt to find one whose proclivity for action and potential for success were strong enough to satisfy him. His political peregrinations brought him into contact with Deloncle's *Cagoule* and then with Doriot's PPF. By 1944, Darnand had built the Milice into what American intelligence called the most formidable profascist political organization in Vichy France.[3]

[3] United States Office of Strategic Services. Research and Analysis Branch. R and

Darnand's fanatical activism covered a feeling of personal insecurity perceived by his close friend, the Dominican father R. -L. Bruckberger, who fought alongside him in 1939–1940. Although Bruckberger turned to Gaullism almost immediately after the armistice, he never abandoned his old friend and comrade. After the war he was to try unsuccessfully to use his excellent Resistance credentials to have the life of Darnand spared. When he failed in the attempt, Bruckberger shared Darnand's last hours with him and accompanied him to the execution site. The *"jusqu'au boutisme"* (to the [bitter] end) which characterized the leader of the Milice masked Darnand's own awareness that in political life he was facing men with wider intellectual horizons and deeper subtlety than his own. The particular circumstances of 1943 and 1944, in which the Germans were engaged in a total war effort against an increasingly powerful coalition, provided Darnand with an opportunity to play out his activism to the end, supported by the occupation authorities. Hard pressed on all fronts and needing a "bulldog," in Gustav Noske's term of a generation earlier, to maintain order in France, the Germans turned to Darnand. He was willing to be their man.

Darnand's entire political career had been spent in the camp of the extreme Right. He shared with many in France a fierce anti-Communism and also showed a tendency toward authoritarianism, reinforced by his experience at the front during the First World War. His heroism in 1918 had been rewarded with a personal decoration by Pétain to whom his loyalty was thereafter lifelong. The attention paid him by Pétain reinforced the tendency of the young Darnand to direct his loyalty more toward persons than abstract ideals. Unlike Doriot and Déat, Darnand did not openly endorse collaboration until Pétain had taken the lead in October 1940 at Montoire. His veneration of Pétain was undoubtedly more genuine and deeply rooted than were the feelings of his rivals toward the old marshal. Having once received the order for collaboration, Darnand would carry it through to the end.

Born in 1897 in Coligny in the department Ain, at the edge of the plain of Bresse in the foothills of the Burgundian Alps, Darnand was

---

A No. 1694, "French Pro-Fascist Groups," an American intelligence report paralleling the *French Basic Handbook* and dated August 30, 1944, pp. 12–13. The OSS report is available in the Hoover Institution Library at Stanford University.

one of seven children, his father a railway worker. At the age of ten he was sent to board and study at the diocesan seminary at Belley, but he was unable to complete his schooling there because of insufficient family funds. He was obliged to return to Coligny, where he became a cabinetmaker's apprentice, the situation in which the outbreak of war in 1914 found him. With the enlistment of his master in the army, the young Darnand was left with nothing to do. Caught up in the war fever that gripped so many young men across the Continent in 1914, he attempted to enlist. At first rejected on the grounds that he was too lean, he was finally accepted into the French army in 1916, progressed rapidly through training, received his first war wounds and military decorations in the trenches, and then volunteered for service with a squadron assigned to particularly dangerous missions.

On one such mission, July 14, 1918 in the Champagne section of the front, Darnand was sent in a reconnaissance attempt to gain information on what the French general staff expected to be a forthcoming German offensive. With a small force, he penetrated the German lines and returned with twenty-seven prisoners and information detailing the precise time and location of the impending offensive, which the French were then able to blunt. French forces were subsequently able to regain the offensive which they retained until the Germans were forced in October to request an armistice. Darnand emerged a major war hero, called later by Poincaré an "artisan of victory," an accolade shared only with Foch and Clemenceau. Following the end of the war, Darnand reenlisted with the hope of promotion into the officer corps, but that hope was soon frustrated. It is possible that the officers feared the derring-do of a man such as Darnand, but he attributed his rejection to social prejudice against his humble origins. Deeply embittered, Darnand left the military in 1921. His anger over his treatment by the army was a major contributing cause of his subsequent turn against the Republic and his repudiation of everything connected to it. In personal resentment lies much of the cause of his conversion to the counterrevolutionary Right.[4]

[4]Brissaud, pp. 113-114, and Jacques Delperrie de Bayac, *Histoire de la Milice* (Paris: Fayard, 1969), p. 12.

During the interwar years, Darnand's trucking firm provided a network for him to keep abreast of political developments throughout southeastern France. The ex-war hero worked hard and was a dutiful boss, demanding much from those who worked for him but never asking anything he was not prepared to do himself. He was taciturn, almost shy, and did not readily verbalize his thoughts to others, traits he shared with Marcel Déat. Darnand communicated with others through personal example, whether on the battlefield or the highways of southeastern France. Although married and a father, he seems to have been unable to draw from his family life the affection and companionship he needed. For this he turned to his old cronies, the war veterans associated with him in the veterans' organization of Action Française, and the other right-wing movements with which he was later affiliated. Darnand would spend long evenings with his friends, drinking and puffing on his ever-present pipe, sharing reminiscences about the old days in the trenches. His ties to his friends were strong and his sense of loyalty to them almost unlimited. In 1944 he would excuse excesses committed in his name by Miliciens who happened to have been old friends.[5]

Darnand left Action Française in 1928 because he believed it given more to rhetoric than to deeds. Eight years later he found his way to the *Cagoule* of Deloncle and Jean Filiol, also dissidents from Action Française. Deloncle's organization was busy establishing secret cells and stockpiling arms in hidden places throughout France in 1936, and Darnand emerged as one of its principal figures in the Nice area, where his trucking connections proved most useful. When Popular Front Interior Minister Dormoy moved against the *Cagoulard* conspiracy in November 1937, Darnand was arrested but quickly released for lack of incriminating evidence. Back in Nice he reestablished his various political connections and awaited events. When war broke out again in 1939, he was to have another opportunity for heroic action.[6]

Volunteering for military service, Darnand reentered the army as a

---

[5]Compte rendu stenographique de la Procès de Joseph Darnand, in *Les Procès de Collaboration. Fernand de Brinon. Joseph Darnand. Jean Luchaire* (Paris: Albin Michel, 1948), p. 245, and Delperrie de Bayac, pp. 14–15. The trial account is cited in subsequent footnotes as *Procès Darnand*.

[6]Delperrie de Bayac, pp. 26–27 and 29–30.

lieutenant second class. He asked to be allowed to form a free-corps fighting unit to undertake dangerous missions, as he had done in 1918. He was uneasy about the war. He questioned the spiritual and material level of French preparedness for it and was dubious about fighting for the Republic. Unlike other former *Cagoulards*, however, Darnand went into battle resolved to do his duty.[7] He knew no other way. In February 1940 his corps of thirty men was assigned to surveillance duty in Forbach, a small town on the Maginot line. The French had previously evacuated Forbach, and Darnand's men reoccupied it one night under cover of darkness. The following morning the Germans returned in superior numbers and a battle ensued in which Darnand's superior officer and close friend Félix Agnély was killed. Darnand managed to lead the survivors back to safety behind the French lines but the thought of his friend's body lying unattended on the battlefield disturbed him deeply. The next night he led a small group of volunteers back to the scene of the skirmish, where they searched the area through snow and darkness until they had retrieved Agnély's body, which they then brought back to the French lines. The exploit of Darnand and his men, courageous under any circumstances, stood out as heroic during the generalized boredom of the *drôle de guerre*. Darnand was again cited for valor and his name was feted throughout France. A picture of the war hero standing ramrod stiff in salute graced the cover of the magazine *Match*.

During the debacle of June 1940, Darnand was taken prisoner by the Germans but escaped from a detention center in Pithiviers in the northern zone. He returned to Nice in the autumn of 1940, giving his wholehearted support to the new regime of Marshal Pétain. When the marshal decreed the formation of the Légion Française des Combattants as a kind of elite to help carry through the National Revolution and in so doing shortcut single party pretenders such as Déat and Doriot, Darnand was ready. In view of his outstanding military record and his loyalty to the marshal, he was asked to head the Nice

[7]For a discussion of Deloncle's orders to his *Cagoulard* followers not to prosecute the war too vigorously in 1939, see "Grand Chef de la Cagoule et du MSR Jacques Corrèze se défend âprement," *Libération*, October 7, 1948. The position of the *Cagoulards* before and after 1940 is discussed more fully in my article, "The Condottieri of the Collaboration: Mouvement Social Révolutionnaire," *Journal of Contemporary History*, 10 (April 1975), 263–265.

unit of the Légion. As of 1940 he had demonstrated no signs of Germanophilia. He brought into the unit many of his old friends and collaborators from the extreme Right of prewar days.

Under Darnand's leadership, the Nice contingent stood out as a staunchly *Maréchaliste* group. The Légion as a whole, not to be confused with the Anti-Bolshevik Legion created by the Paris collaborationists to fight in Russia, quickly evolved into little more than a fraternal or social organization. Gradually Darnand and those closest to him began to shift toward a collaborationist position. Father Bruckberger later blamed Marshal Pétain for having too strongly influenced Darnand, whom he viewed as a man of limited intelligence. Undoubtedly the public stand taken by Pétain at Montoire and his prestige were factors, as were several personal visits he made to Darnand in Nice. Apart from Pétain's influence, collaboration opened up broad new vistas for Darnand, ever in quest of political activity. It gave him a chance to participate in the construction of the new authoritarian French state much more in conformity than the Republic with his own political preferences. The fall of the Republic also gave Darnand an opportunity to turn the tables on those he blamed for thwarting his military career twenty years earlier, discredited by the defeat of 1940. The proud bearing and glamour of the German soldiers in the full flush of their military victories also impressed Darnand, especially after 1942 when he came into more frequent contact with them.

By 1940, Darnand was clearly in the radical Right and the prospect of integrating a fascist France into Hitler's New Order appealed to a man of authoritarian disposition and military spirit such as he. Practical considerations also played a role. In Nice the threat of Italian occupation was real and to many seemed more imminent than any direct German threat to French territorial integrity. Close collaboration with Hitler might be counted upon to help keep Mussolini at bay. Darnand, however, could never overcome the feeling of resentment of the outsider against an establishmentarian clique that he felt had unjustly kept him from his proper role in the French military. He would find his niche as leader of the Milice, a paramilitary organization of outsiders with no political antecedents in the Third Republic. As a frustrated social climber who turned against a system that kept him on the outside, Darnand typified thousands if not millions of

173

those who joined fascist movements in interwar and wartime Europe. He did not seek an overturn of the system. He wished for merely a change in personnel. Pétain may have pointed the way but Darnand had his own reasons for following "jusqu'au bout."

Darnand's evolution from Germanophobia to collaboration began early in 1941. As late as that January he had appeared willing to cooperate with Colonel Groussard in an anti-German military intelligence network for the government in Vichy. By May of the same year, however, Darnand was professing his belief in collaboration. He told Bruckberger that France had been wrong to fight Germany in 1939 and that Agnély's death had been in vain. The German attack on the Soviet Union in June reinforced Darnand's evolution toward collaboration. A fervent anti-Communist, Darnand would later assert that France and Germany were fighting the same enemy, the Communists. His view of the Resistance, widely shared among the French middle classes, was jaundiced by the presence of the Communists as a major force in it. Darnand's anti-Communism did not reach the obsessive lengths of Doriot's, which was personal as well as ideological. The PPF leader's visceral wrath against the Communists was paralleled by Darnand's anger at the military. Nonetheless, the events of June 1941 played a significant role in determining Darnand's course. Anti-Communism, veneration of Pétain, personal resentments against the Republic, and Darnand's longstanding predilection for authoritarian rule and the life of the military camp all led him toward collaboration. [8]

Not surprisingly, a man of Darnand's temperament quickly found the Légion Française des Combattants insufficiently active in carrying out the National Revolution. The very ambivalence of the Légion should have suggested to him that Pétain himself was not totally committed to the idea of collaboration, but Darnand looked only at the marshal's public statements, especially those made at Montoire, which pointed toward a closer Franco-German collaboration. Repeatedly Darnand justified his political activities by claiming to follow the lead of the marshal. In July 1944, with Allied forces closing in on

[8]The reminiscences of Father Bruckberger were published as *Si grande peine: Chronique des années (1940–1948)* (Paris: Bernard Grasset, 1967); see p. 93. For Darnand's willingness to cooperate with Groussard in January 1941, see Georges A. Groussard, *Service secret, 1940–1945* (Paris: La Table Ronde, 1964), p. 463.

Paris, Pétain was to disillusion Darnand by rebuking him for excesses committed by the Milice. At his trial Darnand recalled bitterly that he had received continual encouragement in his evolution toward collaboration from the marshal, only to be jettisoned when the Allies were at the gates. In the words of Jean Galtier-Boissière, the anti-Vichy editor of the "nonconformist" magazine *Crapouillot* after the war: "In all parties, the militants who dirty their hands are always fools. Despite his rise, Darnand remained one of these men on the bottom whom one directs readily to dirty business, then disavows if things turn out badly."[9]

Whatever doubts Darnand might have harbored concerning the wisdom and morality of his course were dissipated by the feeling of loyalty to Pétain, of service to France, and by the busyness which enabled him to lose sight of larger issues in the daily routine of administering his section of the Légion and its successor organizations. Amid his entourage of *copains,* Darnand overcame his relatively weak capacity for self-doubt and calm reflection. As president of the Alpes-Maritimes section of the Légion, he helped organize one of its largest and most militant contingents and quickly became an important force. During the autumn of 1940 he helped Groussard and Commandant Georges Loustanau-Lacau create a secret military shock force to be used in the event of an attempt by Italy to seize French territory in the Alpes-Maritimes area.[10]

From the Légion in Alpes-Maritimes grew the Service d'Ordre Légionnaire, the SOL, an organization built by Darnand with his friends Pierre Gallet, Marcel Gombert, and Jean Bassompierre. The SOL was envisioned as an elite within the elite, the most militant members of the veterans' legion who would serve as the cutting edge of the vaguely defined National Revolution. By the end of 1941 the SOL had spread throughout the unoccupied zone and it ultimately became the germ of the collaborationist Milice. Joining Darnand in the SOL was Noël de Tissot, a zealot in the cause of the New Order, who would perish in 1944 in the uniform of the Waffen-SS at the Russian front. The SOL received official recognition in January 1942

[9]Galtier-Boissière, *Crapouillot*, 5 (1948) 352–353. For Pétain's repudiation of Milice excesses in 1944, see *Procès Darnand*, p. 333.

[10]Delperrie de Bayac, p. 78.

when Pétain called Darnand to Vichy and placed him in charge of the entire SOL operation for the unoccupied zone.

In 1942 the SOL comprised a force of paramilitary militants determined to build what they dreamed of as a new France, stronger and authoritarian but not necessarily fascist. Committed to Pétain, the SOL had yet to define its position with respect to the Germans. Significantly, the occupation authorities denied permission to the Légion and the SOL to expand into the northern zone. German suspicion was a result in part of pressure from their collaborationist allies in Paris who regarded Darnand's organization as a potentially powerful new rival, but was also a consequence of a basic mistrust of Darnand and the two organizations in which he was involved. Darnand was aware that many in the SOL would be unwilling to follow him to open collaboration. Many of the recruits to the SOL brought with them an unaltered Germanophobia from Action Française and were unwilling to embrace the less intellectually refined fascism of Darnand, who had to move cautiously so as not to lose his followers in 1942.

Darnand's appointment to head the SOL was a major step up for him but it still did not provide him the freedom and authority he sought. The SOL remained part of the Légion and, accordingly, Darnand was subject to the authority of the Légion leader Raymond Lachal. SOL doctrine was vague but its ceremonial was elaborate, combining a romanticized chivalric sentiment with the then current fascist practice. Recruits took oaths of membership on their knees, and in their hymns they swore to die, singing, if necessary for the new France. The movement claimed thirty thousand members in October 1942 although at the time only six thousand had taken the oath. A number of early members of the SOL were secretly members of the PPF, attempting to subvert it from within. Doriot and his party wanted no rivals on the stage of the collaboration. These infiltrators were progressively eliminated but the differences in tactics between the boy-scoutism of the early SOL and the more refined *agitprop* techniques of the PPF clearly reveal the divergent origins of the two political movements.[11]

[11] *French Basic Handbook*, p. 172. For discussion of the relationship of chivalry and boy-scout ideals to the Milice, see Eugen Weber, "France," in Rogger and Weber, eds., *The European Right*, p. 101.

In July 1942, Darnand visited Poland, where he met members of the Anti-Bolshevik Legion, and his experiences there convinced him further that the Soviet Union represented a more serious threat to France and all of Europe than did Nazi Germany. Upon his return home he discussed SOL participation in the effort against Bolshevism. A number of his closest aides, including Bassompierre, Jean Boudet-Gheusi, and Charles Barbe volunteered for service in the German uniforms of the Anti-Bolshevik Legion. The SOL committed itself further to collaboration when in the months after November 1942, SOL volunteers joined Georges Guilbaud and the PPF in Tunisia in organizing resistance against the Allied forces fighting there. The German military staff still did not trust Darnand and his supporters and warned against allowing them to bear arms.[12]

By the end of 1942, Darnand was a rising political star in occupied France. His outstanding service record and proud military bearing made him an attractive figure even to Madeleine Jacob, a hostile journalist who covered his postwar trial. Darnand's political activities had been conducted exclusively in the unoccupied zone, which meant that he had had little contact with the Germans. Thus he lacked some of the stigma attached to the northern zone collaborationists in the eyes of the French public. The SOL, however, provided too limiting a scope for Darnand, who began to forge contacts with northern zone collaborationists and the Germans. He seemed ideally suited in Laval's view to lead the new Milice. Here was a popular war hero whom Laval expected to be able to manipulate and at the same time use to defuse the collaborationist movements, especially Doriot's PPF, in Paris. From the outset, however, Darnand and Laval had differing conceptions of the role of the Milice, which was created officially in January 1943.

[12]Woermann, telegram from Foreign Ministry in Berlin to German embassy in Rome, January 3, 1943, T-120/6445H/E481930. For the role of the SOL in the anti-Allied resistance of French colonists in Tunisia, see Pellegrin, pp. 47ff. and 91ff., and for Darnand's orders to the SOL to oppose the Allies, *Procès Darnand*, p. 299. Discussions of the impact of the German attack on the USSR in pushing Darnand toward collaboration are found in Charbonneau, 1:357 and Jean Bassompierre, *Frères ennemies*, which appeared in Charles-Ambroise Colin, *Sacrifice de Bassompierre* (Paris: Amiot-Dumont, 1948), p. 133. For Darnand's brief thought of turning against the Germans in the summer of 1943, see Brissaud, p. 136 and Delperrie de Bayac, pp. 202–203.

Darnand was named secretary-general of the new organization, to serve directly under the head of the government, Laval. Laval wanted the Milice to buttress his own political strength and attend to his personal security but Darnand looked to the new formation as a heroic elite that would push through the National Revolution as conceived by himself, Noël de Tissot, and their friends. By early 1943 this meant collaboration with the "New Europe," exclusive of Jews, Freemasons, Communists, and all other enemies of the counter-revolution militant. In his fight against Laval for control of the Milice, Darnand sought allies among the Germans. The growth of the Resistance served him in inducing the hard-pressed Germans to turn for help to increasingly extremist elements among their supporters in France. A paramilitary French collaborationist organization such as the Milice would have been unthinkable during the days of 1940 and 1941 when German dominion in France was unchallengeable. The situation had changed greatly by 1943 and even more so by the time the Milice pursued open civil war against the Resistance in 1944. Mesmerized by the totality of the 1940 German victory, Darnand could not envision German defeat and plunged ahead. Even Laval, it must be recalled, still contemplated a compromise peace in the West in 1944.[13]

To gain effective control of the Milice, Darnand faced formidable obstacles. German mistrust of the organization was strong, intensified where possible by the northern zone collaborationist movements. One German observer reported late in 1942 that just as Darnand had set up a secret force to fight the Italians in 1940 in Nice, he might attempt to turn his SOL against the Germans. The Wehrmacht occupation authorities, particularly distrustful of Darnand and his friends, made clear their view that the Milice was to serve only as a supplementary police force to protect the Vichy government, for which it needed no arms. General von Rundstedt was willing to allow small standing units of the Milice where needed to help protect the members of the Vichy government, but denied their request to be armed with captured war materiel and the confiscated weapons of the French Armistice Army, disbanded after the occupation of the southern zone. Thwarted years earlier by the tra-

[13]For discussion of the situation in 1943 and 1944, see Paxton, pp. 327–328.

ditionalists of the French army, Darnand in 1943 encountered an analogous resistance to his projects from the anti-French traditionalists of the German Wehrmacht. He was more successful with the SS establishment in France, many of whom, like himself, had been outsiders to the traditional elites of their own country.[14]

The history of the Milice in France falls into two periods, with the start of 1944 as the dividing line. On January 1, 1944, Darnand was brought into the government as Secretary-general for the Maintenance of Order. Thereafter the activities of the Milice and Darnand's own personal authority were both vastly expanded. During 1943, however, he had to struggle against the authority of Laval and to win this fight he needed to gain the confidence of at least some of the German services operating in France. Tension between Darnand and Laval surfaced on a number of occasions. At a banquet on March 16, 1943 that both men attended, Darnand made a speech in which he indicated that at long last the head of the government had a party, the Milice, behind him. Laval's tart reply was that his goal was the achievement of a national union of patriotic Frenchmen and not a Lavalist political party. He already feared that Milice excesses in the maintenance of "order" were contributing to the tension and violence in the country. Angered by Laval's reply, Darnand left the Hotel Majestic, where the banquet was being staged, in the account of a German witness, "with lips pressed together tightly." At a cabinet meeting two months later, Darnand was called in by Laval to defend the Milice against charges of excesses made earlier in the day by a number of police prefects from the southern zone. Miliciens, they had told Laval, were trying to exert undue influence in the local administration. The grievance was settled amicably between Laval and Darnand but the struggle for power remained basically unchanged. A confidant of the Germans in Lyons reported in August 1943 that once again Darnand and Laval were on bad terms with each other.[15]

[14]Friedrich Grimm, Bericht, December 1942 T-120/6442H/E481195; and Oberleutnant Witzleben, Arbeitsstab Frankreich, Gruppe Heer, August 11, 1943, "Ständige Einheit der französischen Miliz, Vermerk," T-77/1492/5595227-8.

[15]Kontrollinspektion der Deutsche Waffenstillstandskommission [DWStK], Kontrollabteilung, Az. 12, no. 2030/43g, "Meldungen," Bourges, August 19, 1943, T-77/842/5585851. For the March incident see "Miliz und Propaganda der Regierung,"

At issue between the two men was also the question of arming the Milice. This became especially important during the spring of 1943 when members of the organization began to fall victim to attacks from the Resistance. Although the Milice was not yet armed and did not engage in hunts for Resistance members until 1944, its men were suspected of passing intelligence about Resistance activities to the Germans. On April 24, 1943, Paul de Gassovski, the adjunct departmental head of the Bouches-du-Rhône Milice, was assassinated. Other attacks followed. When Darnand asked Laval for arms he was told variously to ask the Germans or was put off with delaying actions. In July 1943, two Miliciens in Saône-et-Loire received packages which exploded when opened. Although Vichy supplied the Milice with funds, requests for arms continued to go unheeded. Leaders of the Milice complained that the lack of weapons increased their vulnerability to attacks from the Resistance, especially the Communists, and substantially impeded recruiting for the organization.[16]

Angered at Vichy's failure to provide the arms Darnand felt were needed to protect his men, the Milice leader for a brief time overcame his anti-Gaullist scruples and contemplated switching sides. He contacted Groussard, then working with the Resistance in Switzerland, but Groussard indicated that he would accept Darnand only as a subordinate, a condition the latter refused.[17] An attempt by Darnand to contact the Free French in London went unanswered. He turned back to the Germans. During the summer of 1943 the Germans had decided to create a French unit of the Waffen-SS, and the Milice offered a potentially good source for recruits. Darnand's personal prestige was also considered helpful in making enlistment in the Waffen-SS acceptable to a wider segment of the French population than might otherwise have been possible. An arrangement was reached whereby in return for Darnand's joining the Waffen-SS with

March 31, 1943, CDJC document CDXCIV, 1. The May incident is discussed in Krug von Nidda, telegram no, 1267, Diplogerma Paris, May 15, 1943, T-120/2318/485184, and Martin du Gard, p. 400.

[16]Kontrollinspektion der DWStK, Kontrollabteilung, Az. 20, no. 1500/43g, "Monatsbericht Nr. 3," Bourges, July 3, 1943, T-77/842/5585998. See also Kontrollinspektion der DWStK, Kontrollabteilung, Az. 12, no. 1634/43g, "Meldungen," Bourges, July 7, 1943, T-77/842/5585975.

[17]Groussard, Service secret, pp. 459–460 and 464–465.

some top aides and his opening the Milice to SS recruiters, he received arms for his men. SS authorities allowed Darnand to set up training camps for thirty Miliciens in each of twenty-one departments in the southern zone. A force of six hundred was thereby established and provided with light arms confiscated by the Germans from the Armistice Army. Sturmbannführer Best, who had helped start the Corsican Milice, was put in charge of the political and military formation of the entire Milice organization. In addition to the force of six hundred, which was expanded in the late summer and fall of 1943, Milice leaders were also allowed to bear arms. [18]

Placing his Miliciens in the Waffen-SS offered Darnand a chance to match or perhaps surpass the influence of Doriot, whose PPF supporters had come to dominate the Anti-Bolshevik Legion. After conferring with his closest aides in the Milice, Darnand in August took the oath of personal fidelity to Hitler and became a *Sturmbannführer* (a rank equivalent to commandant in the French army and major in the German and American armies) in the Waffen-SS. In one spectacular gesture he had surpassed even the collaborationist leaders in Paris in his identification with the German cause.

Darnand was nonetheless never sent to fight on the Eastern front. A number of his close friends in the Milice did go, and one of them, Pierre Cance, became the leader of the French Waffen-SS battalion. Oberg, the head of the SS and German police in Paris, opposed sending Darnand to the East on the grounds that foreign propaganda would then depict him as having sold out to the Germans. Arguing that the French unit was too small to be led by a *Sturmbannführer,* Oberg suggested that Darnand first prove his loyalty to the Axis cause by his work in France. Oberg's negative recommendation on Darnand's request to go to the Eastern front caused a quarrel within the ranks of the SS, but ultimately Himmler decided in Oberg's favor and

[18]For the deal by which the Milice obtained arms, see Krug von Nidda, telegram no. 1704, from Vichy to Paris, June 28, 1943, T-120/3797/E042725; and Kontrollinspektion der DWStK, Kontrollabteilung, Az. 20, no. 2570/43g, "Monatsbericht Nr. 6," Bourges, October 7, 1943, T-77/842/5585829. Armistice Commission suggestions about arming the Milice appear in DWStK, Wiesbaden, "Besprechungsnotiz," November 23, 1943; and Wehrmacht reservations are recorded in Blumentritt, Oberbefehlshaber West, note to Militärbefehlshaber in Frankreich, October 28, 1943, T-77/1492/5595214–6 and 5595217, respectively.

Darnand remained in France. He was plainly of more use to the Germans in his own country.[19]

In France Darnand spent the first part of 1943 getting the Milice organized. At first the Germans allowed it to operate only in the southern zone. Only after Darnand had been named Secretary-general for the Maintenance of Order in January 1944 did they permit it to be extended into the northern zone. Most of Darnand's close aides came from the extreme Right of the interwar years, although there were exceptions such as Francis Bout de l'An, a professor of history and geography who in 1932 had been president of the Ligue d'Action Universitaire Républicaine et Socialiste. Bout de l'An became director of propaganda in the Milice. François Gaucher, a former Socialist who had followed Marcel Déat into the Neo-Socialist movement and later joined the PPF, ended up as head of the Milice in the northern zone after January 1944. Most, however, had right-wing political origins. Gombert, who headed the Milice's security service, had been involved in the *Cagoule* before the war, as had Henry Charbonneau, who edited *Combats,* the organization's weekly newspaper. Joseph Lécussan, head of the Milice at Lyons, had previously worked at the Commissariat General des Questions Juives, Vichy's ministry for Jewish affairs, under Darquier de Pellepoix. A former navy man, Lécussan had also been associated with the *Cagoule*. Bassompierre, a driving force in the creation of the SOL, had been a member of Pierre Taittinger's Jeunesses Patriotes prior to the war.[20]

Of the three major collaborationist movements, the Milice possessed the least clear prewar political antecedents. The organization itself was totally new, one of the few new contributions made by Vichy to the history of French political institutions. Its political attitudes and much of its personnel came from the extreme Right, with Action Française and the Jeunesses Patriotes supplying many of the recruits. Bout de l'An and Gaucher joined as individuals without

[19]Karl Albrecht Oberg, letter to Himmler and Gottlob Berger, May 5, 1944, and Berger's opposing view expressed in a letter to Dr. Brandt, a member of Hitler's personal staff, May 29, 1944; CDJC document CDXXXV, 41.

[20]For brief discussions of Bassompierre, Lécussan, and Bout de l'An, see Delperrie de Bayac, pp. 29, 26, 110 and 173. For the prewar political careers of Gaucher and Lécussan, see *Combats,* April 15 and August 21, respectively, 1943.

followings. The Milice, like the PPF and RNP, represented a revolt against a gerontocracy which dominated the interwar Right as well as the parliamentary system as a whole. Many, like Darnand, had left Action Française in protest against the inaction of Maurras and some had joined Deloncle's *Cagoulards.* Some who joined Pétain's veterans' legion in 1940 again felt the frustration of inaction imposed, as they saw it, by an older generation that refused to move aside. Through the SOL and the Milice they were given a chance to make their mark. The elaborate ceremonial of the SOL and Milice, combining scouting, Catholic, and fascist ritual, reflected the youthful composition of the two organizations. The growth of the Milice and similar organizations was undoubtedly inhibited by an aging population, the demographic effects of the First World War which sharply cut the number of French youth during the Second.

The Milice was organized into regional federations, each one headed by a leader who served as liaison between the department and the central office in Vichy and between the local Milice and the regional police prefect. Milice officials were nominated by Darnand and subject to confirmation by Laval, but as time went on, Laval's effective influence in the organization's internal matters waned. Subordinate to the regional head was the departmental leader who in 1943 had extensive authority. When Darnand was named Secretary-general for the Maintenance of Order the Milice's internal structure was tightened. Department leaders were placed entirely under the jurisdiction of the regional chieftains, who could appoint and dismiss them at will. Within each department the Milice was structured in a hierarchical manner down to the smallest unit, the *main,* which comprised four men and a leader to provide the greatest possible flexibility in action. In some cases these groupings existed on paper only. The highest estimate of the size of the Milice was approximately 30,000, a figure which also included its elite Francs-Gardes, the paramilitary arm of the organization expanded from the original 600 armed men of June 1943.[21]

The Francs-Gardes were split into two components: standing and reserve. The standing Francs-Gardes were professionals paid from

---

[21]Milice organization is discussed in the *French Basic Handbook,* p. 174, and "French Pro-Fascist Groups," pp. 12–13.

3,500 to 4,000 francs per month to live in barracks and undergo intensive political and military training. Reservists received the same training but lived at home and carried on their normal civilian routines. They were, therefore, less readily available for military action. All Francs-Gardes received two weeks of special training at the Ecole des Cadres at Uriage or at a similar center established by the Milice at Calabres. The Francs-Gardes were divided into cohorts, the units for each region, which were further subdivided into groups of one hundred (*centaines*), thirty (*trentaines*), and ten (*dizaines*). They were all given training in sports as well as military and political affairs.[22]

The efficiency of the various local organizations varied widely. During the spring of 1944, the cohort of the Lyons region was said to be weak and poorly armed whereas that of Limoges was relatively well armed and took part in combat against the Resistance, as did the Milice unit in Haute-Savoie. The Francs-Gardes were the best disciplined of the Miliciens. By early 1944 the organization as a whole was concentrating much of its energy on the recruiting of Franc-Garde volunteers, together with attempts to raise the resources needed to support them. By 1944 the Milice had also developed a youth movement, the Avant-Garde Milicienne, directed by Jean-Marcel Renault, who earlier had led the southern zone Jeunesse de France et d'Outre-Mer (Youth of France and Overseas), a small *Maréchaliste* organization which he now integrated into the Milice.[23]

The size and quality of the Milice's membership is difficult to determine with precision, although the figure of 30,000 maximum, given above, has been widely accepted. It ranked in size, therefore, with the PPF and the RNP, forming the third, chronologically, of the three major movements of the collaboration. As with the others, the

[22]For the Francs-Gardes, see Kontrollinspektion der DWStK, Kontrollabteilung, Az. 20, no. 200/44g, "Monatsbericht Nr. 10," Bourges, February 8, 1944, T-77/842/5585775; and Der Höhere SS und Polizeiführer im Bereich des Militärbefehlshabers in Frankreich, Jgb. no. 1968/44g, Paris, June 17, 1944, to Verteiler Kontrollbericht DWStK, T-77/838/5578658-9. The training of the Miliciens at Uriage is elaborated in the series *Documentation des Cadres de la Milice Française* (Uriage: Ecole des Cadres de la Milice Française, 1944). Among the subjects discussed in articles in the series is the use of captured weapons in what more recently has come to be called "counterinsurgency" warfare.

[23] *French Basic Handbook,* p. 175.

strength of the Milice varied in different localities, but unlike them, it was strongest in the southern zone and never achieved much success in the north after it was allowed to expand there in the beginning of 1944. Like the other movements of the collaboration, the Milice represented a small proportion of the French population but enough to be significant in some sections of the country.

Monique Luirard, who has studied the Milice in the department of the Loire, found that at most the organization could claim from 250 to 500 members in the department and that it drew most of its strength from the urban areas there. While more provincial than its rivals in the northern zone, the Milice was still an urban organization. It attracted workers, *employés,* artisans, small-time functionaries—in short, elements similar to those which comprised the PPF. Few employers joined the Milice and, unlike the RNP with its contingent of teachers, Darnand's much less intellectually oriented movement attracted few from the liberal professions. Luirard found many of the most rough-and-ready members of the Milice to have come from the marginal elements of urban society in the Loire department. Some were criminals, ready to enrich themselves under the guise of legality the organization provided. Unlike the Resistance, the Milice could offer uniforms and at least the possibility of the public bearing of arms. To many of those on the fringes of society in the cities it gave an enhanced status available to them from no other source.[24]

During the latter months of 1943, the Milice suffered from a period of relative inactivity during which many of its more moderate elements, including some of those from the SOL, left while the more militant partisans of the New Order pressed for more vigorous action. In tracing the history of the Milice in the Loire region, Luirard found that as 1943 turned into 1944, the departmental leadership became more radical under the influence of the adjunct department chief, Raymond Le Guilloux, a former merchant from Mâcon. Having received small arms from the Germans early in 1944, the Loire Milice was able to join the German police and the French forces of order in campaigns against the maquis. These operations often involved seizures of the treasuries and goods of the Resistance, usually under-

[24]Monique Luirard, "La Milice Française dans la Loire," *Revue d'histoire de la deuxième guerre mondiale,* 23 (July 1973), 79–81.

taken when the Milice was able to act with little risk. Luirard reports cases of theft and rape committed by Miliciens who also participated in the extortion of protection money from vulnerable Jews in the Loire area. In a variety of ways, the Milice sought to help the Germans; the local organization provided aid, for example, when the Germany army unit stationed in its area was forced to move by a flood of the Allier River. When at the time of the Allied invasion in June 1944, Darnand ordered the Milice mobilized, few in the Loire area responded to the call and most tried instead to lose themselves in the anonymity of their private lives. [25]

Using the figures pertaining to Miliciens who were tried after the Liberation by the civil court (Chambre civique) in the Loire, Luirard found their average age to have been thirty-two, with 38.6 percent having been born between 1920 and 1928 and an additional 25.4 percent born between 1910 and 1919. She estimates that 500 would have been a high figure for the number of Miliciens in the Loire and that at the time of Darnand's nomination as Secretary-general for the Maintenance of Order, the figure was 230. Fifteen percent were women, a proportion of women lower than was common in the RNP. Of these Miliciens, somewhere from 90 to 100 were actively participating in meetings and other functions of the organization. [26]

Figures supplied by the German Armistice Commission service in southern France support those of Luirard, although they are slightly higher. According to German sources, the Milice in the Loire as of June 30, 1943 numbered 225 with an additional 475 in the Franc-Garde for a total of 700. The German Armistice Commission officials did not provide the sources of their figures, but they show the Milice relatively evenly distributed with roughly several hundred members in the various departments in the regions of Clermont-Ferrand, Limoges, Lyons, Marseilles, Montpellier, and Toulouse. The figures given for the Franc-Garde in relation to the Milice as a whole seem high in relation to most other sources but the total figures are roughly consistent with most estimates. For the regions of the south-

---

[25] Ibid., pp. 86–88, 90–91, and 96. On the help rendered to the Germans by the Allier Milice, see Neubronn, Der Deutsche General des Oberbefehlshabers West in Vichy, letter to Bridoux, Staatssekretär für die Verteidigung, Vichy, October 28, 1943, T-77/833/5571799.

[26] Luirard, p. 101.

ern zone, the figures given for the Milice are 30,412, of whom 12,945 were said to be in the Franc-Garde. These figures, provided in Appendix A, excluded the departments under Italian administration in June 1943.

A handful of departments were listed with a thousand or more Miliciens. These included the departments of Rhône in the Lyons region, Hérault and Pyrénnées Orientales in Montpellier, and Haute-Garonne and Lot-et-Garonne in the Toulouse area. The Marseilles area was strongly represented with a figure of 1,400 for the Vaucluse and over 10,000 listed for the Bouches-du-Rhône, making the latter the department with by far the largest Milice contingent of those canvassed in the report. An earlier German survey showed lower figures during the spring of 1943 for the departments of southern France, but once again, particularly strong organizations existed in the Marseilles area and in the Haute-Garonne department in the Toulouse region.

The German figures do not permit an exact geographic analysis of Milice strength, but they do show the urban nature of its support. Miliciens came from the large cities such as Marseilles, Lyons, and Toulouse and their suburbs. Sources of popular support for the Milice closely resembled those of the northern zone collaborationist parties. Marseilles, which also supported a large PPF organization, was exceptionally heavily represented in the Milice. A city known for its high proportion of toughs and marginal elements, Marseilles provided fertile ground for fascist movements in occupied France. Many of the leaders of the local Milice organizations were former officers in the disbanded Armistice Army. In general, the German officials complained that recruiting for the Milice was going unsatisfactorily during the middle of 1943 and added that some of the departments had actually suffered losses in Milice strength as against earlier in the year.[27]

The doctrine of the Milice differed little from the ideas expounded by the northern zone collaborationist movements. It was summarized

[27]The German figures are taken from Kontrollinspektion der DWStK, Kontrollabteilung, Az. 20, no. 1500/43g, "Monatsbericht Nr. 3," Bourges, July 8, 1943, T-77/842/5585997–9; and "Monatsbericht Nr. 4," Bourges, August 11, 1943, T-77/842/5585902–4. For the complete figures provided by the latter report, see Appendix A.

in the "Twenty-One Points" taken over from the SOL. These points called for faith, enthusiasm, a spirit of community, hierarchy, authority, and discipline, the values usually associated with radical Right movements during the interwar and wartime period in Europe. The Twenty-One Points supported corporatism, the primacy of labor over money, and national and racial "purity," and explicitly condemned Gaullism, Communism, Freemasonry, and Judaism. Point twenty-one supported "Christian civilization," giving the Milice a difference in tone if not in doctrine from the northern zone collaborationist parties. All collaborationist movements paid at least lip service to the ideal of Catholic France. Doriot, despite his Communist past, even conducted meetings with French church leaders in attempts to secure their support and Déat was especially careful to point out that his attacks on clerical influence in politics were not to be construed as anti-Catholic. The Catholicism of the Milice, however, was more deeply rooted in the movement than were the expressions of the PPF and RNP. Although not as pronounced as in the imagery of the Rumanian Legion of the Archangel Michael, the ideal of the Christian crusader was very much a part of the Milice's intellectual baggage.

As an organization, the Milice had begun in the Alpes-Maritimes and had then been extended throughout the southern zone, arriving in Paris only after it had already fully developed its doctrines and institutions in the more traditionalist and less worldly small towns and cities of the south. It always remained much more a movement of the provinces without the heavy domination of Paris that characterized its northern zone rivals. It retained a boy-scout kind of innocence and naïveté, less influenced by the sophistication of Paris. In its simplicity, the Milice resembled the Francistes more than either PPF or RNP and Darnand was temperamentally closer to Bucard than to either Doriot or Déat. The temperamental differences in the leadership of the movements reflected a sophistication, if not cynicism, gained by the PPF and RNP leaders in their interwar evolution from Left to Right. Both Darnand and Bucard were politically less seasoned and this was apparent in their movements.

Darnand himself had been raised in a staunchly Catholic home and had begun his education in a church school. Although the Catholicism of the Milice was but one component in an amalgam that included Nietzschean romanticism and German and French racialism, it stands out as an element taken very seriously in the organization. The most eloquent spokesman for the Milicien crusading knight ideal, indeed for the Axis cause in France as well, was Philippe Henriot, who had come to the Milice with a deep-seated conviction that Christian civilization was engaged in a life-and-death struggle against Bolshevism. Together with Darnand, Henriot was imposed upon the Vichy government by German pressure at the end of 1943. During the civil strife preceding the Liberation, he emerged as the leading spokesman for the forces of Vichy and collaboration. His voice, heard throughout France in daily radio editorials, became known as one of the most eloquent of the entire war period. From Bordeaux, Henriot had long been active in Catholic political circles and his passionate commitment to a defense of what he felt was endangered Catholicism led him ultimately to the Milice and the ideal of collaborationism. Personified by men such as Darnand and Henriot, the Milice emerged in 1943 as a representation of provincial fascism, more traditionalist, simpler and perhaps more naïve, rougher than the more self-conscious intellectualized fascisms of writers such as Drieu la Rochelle and Robert Brasillach, or even of the leadership corps of the PPF and Déat's RNP.[28]

In 1943, Darnand faced two major problems in carving out an independent sphere of action for his organization. It received a regular budget from Vichy but this was controlled by Laval, who was thereby in a position to exert constraint upon the activities of the Milice. Darnand's second problem was to secure the arms necessary for greater independence and for defense against attacks from the Resistance. With his followers chafing under the restrictions imposed by the lack of weapons, he faced a potential threat to his leadership. The Milice was invariably short of funds because the goals set by its leaders extended far beyond those envisioned by Laval and consequently government funding of Darnand's men rarely met their desires.

One account had the Milice receiving 200 million francs a year, an amount insufficient to support the France-Gardes, the newspaper

[28]For fuller discussion of Henriot and his political impact, see below, Chap. 10, n. 26–28.

Combats, the Ecole des Cadres, and the other subsidiary organizations. In his study of the Milice, Jacques Delperrie de Bayac gives its original budget of February 1943 as 20 million francs. In June, however, the Milice requested 102 million francs to pay for the creation of a center for 1,381 Francs-Gardes but the project had to be postponed because it ran into opposition from the Wehrmacht command. According to Delperrie de Bayac, the Milice requested a total of 188 million francs in 1943 of which it received 80 million. Similar insufficiencies in government funding were reported on the local level. In the department of Haute-Vienne the local Milice received a monthly allotment of 40,000 francs but exhausted these funds rapidly and complained of getting no further help from the government. As their activities intensified and campaigns against the maquis were launched, Milice leaders maintained continual pressure upon the Finance Ministry for more funds. In 1944 they requested 2,859 million francs of which only 440 million were obtained. With the Allied landings in June 1944 and the official mobilization of the Milice by Darnand, the organization began to supplement its funds with extra-legal requisitions.[29]

In addition to its government funds, the Milice attracted private financial support from anti-Communists and friends such as the head of a chemicals plant in Nice who, according to German sources, supplied two to three hundred thousand francs monthly to help support the SOL and later the Milice. Not interested in ideology, this benefactor sought merely to improve business connections through ties with Darnand.

Securing funds was a problem matched only by the difficulty in obtaining arms. Darnand never won over the military officers of the Wehrmacht. In the second half of 1943 the German Armistice Commission in Wiesbaden began to argue that the Milice leadership had proven its fidelity to collaboration and that it made little sense to deny arms to the one organization in France prepared to fight civil unrest

---

[29]See Delperrie de Bayac, p. 189. On German reaction to the Milice's project of establishing a permanent camp for 1,381 Francs-Gardes, see von Witzleben, "Ständige Einheit der französischen Miliz, Vermerk," August 11, 1943. The government funding of the Milice in Haute-Vienne is discussed in Kontrollinspektion der DWStK, Kontrollabteilung, Az. 12, no. 1634–43g, "Meldungen," Bourges, July 20, 1943, T-77/842/5585977.

and Allied invasion. Members of the Armistice Commission had been approached for arms by local Milice leaders including Lécussan of Lyons and Tessier of Drôme and Ardèche. Laval presented an obstacle for Darnand because as titular leader of the Milice, he was the proper authority to request arms from the Germans, but he made no move to do so. The initiative in the requests for weapons came from Darnand and his subordinates, not Laval.[30]

By the end of 1943, however, the Milice was receiving arms through the efforts of the Armistice Commission and, more important, the SS. The Wehrmacht insisted that no French force be armed unless under the direct supervision of a German service, so the SS took the Milice under its wing and claimed official jurisdiction over its weapons. In the deal that solidified Darnand's support for the German cause, the Milice received SD arms and supplied officers for the new French unit of the Waffen-SS. As a whole, the Milice was placed under the jurisdiction of the Armistice Commission, while the SS attended to the training of its shock troops. The Milice was on its way toward becoming the feared fighting force associated with its 1944 campaigns against the maquis. It continued to receive arms, usually from seized French and captured enemy and Resistance stocks. Trucks for the Milice in the spring of 1944 came from the supply of the Chantiers de la Jeunesse, a Vichyite youth organization disbanded that year by the Germans.[31]

The German wish to toughen the Vichy government in its struggle against the Resistance and prevent a possible shift of Pétain and Laval toward neutrality led to the Milice's extension into the northern zone. German pressure in December 1943 pushed Darnand and Henriot into the government. Henriot became Secretary of State for Information and Darnand was named Secretary-general for the Maintenance of Order, a new position combining all French forces of order under his control. The Milice in January 1944 was extended into the

[30]Chef des Generalstabes, DWStK, Wiesbaden, October 25, 1943, note to Oberbefehlshaber West, Paris, T-77/1492/5595218-22. See also Rudolf Schleier, telegram, August 26, 1943, to Zweigstelle Vichy, T-120/3546/E022157. On Faucamberge, who helped fund the Milice, see the unsigned "Abschrift," Paris, April 12, 1943, and Struve, Tgb. No. 1264/43, May 11, 1943, T-120/2318/485291-3 and 485294-5, respectively.

[31]For the discussion of trucks, see DWStK, Aussenstelle Paris, "Aktenvermerk," Paris, April 24, 1944, T-77/838/5578665.

northern zone, where it began to compete directly with the PPF and the RNP for recruits from a continually draining pool. Relations between the Milice and the northern zone parties were complex. Both PPF and RNP had attempted at various times to infiltrate the newer organization, and the relations between Darnand and Doriot were extremely bad. The PPF regarded the Milice as a band of amateurish provincial upstarts and the Miliciens never forgot the Communist political origins of Doriot and many of his aides. Doriot would accept no compromise with Darnand, whom he consistently belittled.

The RNP was less hostile to the Milice, and Déat on occasion welcomed the new movement, suggesting that RNP party members also join it. Politically weaker than Doriot in 1943, Déat intended to widen his options by putting his movement in a position either to subvert or to join the Milice, depending on the circumstances. Darnand was more favorably inclined toward Déat in 1943 than he was toward the PPF chieftain, probably because he correctly guessed that Déat was heading for a government post and also because he feared Déat less. In the northern zone, Darnand spoke openly of an alliance between the Milice and the RNP, clearly a case of the two weaker parties combining against the strongest in a power balance. Although Déat and Darnand occasionally appeared together on rostrums and spoke of joint action, the Milice leader and Doriot were to remain implacable foes until the end.[32]

The willingness of Darnand and Déat to consider joint action was more than merely tactical. By late 1943 both men were coveting places in the government, which they ultimately received. Doriot was more purely concerned with replacing the government, Pétain excepted. Darnand's political independence was limited by his subordination to Laval. As late as 1943 Déat was publicly supporting Laval, although his private comments were quite different. Only Doriot was fully free to seek a total transformation of the government. He set his sights higher than Déat and Darnand, who were more content to settle for posts in Laval's cabinet. Whereas all three movements spoke of governmental change and a "new order" for France, the PPF was

[32]Oberst Reichel. "Stimmungsbericht," Vichy, January 8, 1944, T-501/DGV 70-23588/328. On the subject of the infiltration of Resistance agents into the Milice, see Neubronn, "Aufzeichnung," Vichy, May 29, 1943, T-77/833/5572419.

clearer in its concept of its mission. Strident propaganda to the contrary, the RNP and Milice remained more limited and less clear in their goals as a result of the commitments of the former to Laval and the governmental status of the latter. In German exile in Sigmaringen after the Liberation, Darnand and Déat would ally in the rump Governmental Commission to bar the door to Doriot.

The spirit of the Milice was reminiscent of the German freebooters of the early 1920's described by Ernst von Salomon in his book *Die Geächteten* (The Outlaws). Both Milice and Freikorps arose ostensibly as forces for "order" against Communism in defeated countries where revolution appeared possible. Fundamentally opposed to parliamentary liberalism, whether of the infant Weimar Republic or the legacies of the Third Republic, they both in the words of one historian "answered the pressing psychological need of the confused and the insecure."[33] How else could Miliciens so thoroughly identify French nationalism with the cause of Nazi Germany of 1944? Middle class and peasant in its social composition, the Freikorps attracted those who felt betrayed in 1918, just as many Miliciens felt betrayed by the Republic in 1940 and by Vichy in the subsequent years. The *Freikorps* "gave them a chance to forget their own inefficacy by identifying themselves with a movement which promised them everything which they lacked as individuals: the opportunity for dramatic action and power. They welcomed this chance to barter personal freedom for a new security and a new pride in participating in power."[34]

The product of a France in crisis during the latter stages of the occupation, the Milice bought security for its members by trading off the interests of France. It was the final schismatic paroxysm in the development of the interwar and wartime radical Right. The break Darnand made with all he thought conventional was described in an article he wrote for the newspaper of the French unit of the Waffen-SS. Entitled "Nous avons rompu" [We have broken (with the past)], the article declared: "We have broken forever, and France must ultimately break, with a decadent past, with principles, institutions, culture; with the men who led us to the disaster [of 1940]. We have broken with much that we hold most dear in order not to betray

[33]Robert G. L. Waite, *Vanguard of Nazism: The Free Corps Movement in Postwar Germany, 1918–1923* (New York: Norton, 1969 [originally published, 1952]), p. 43.
[34]Ibid.

our faith; certain of us have even had to leave families, scorned by a blind world, and no longer have any family but the fraternity of combat."[35]

Darnand and his close aides and supporters were in many cases the incarnations of characters sketched by fascist writers in France. The Milice leader could well have been the *homo fascista,* the new twentieth-century combative and chivalric youthful hero vaunted by Robert Brasillach in 1941 or the toughened fascist man described twenty years later by Maurice Bardèche. To Bardèche the fascist possessed "courage, discipline, the spirit of sacrifice, energy: virtues one demands of combat soldiers, pioneers, squads in danger . . . qualities strictly speaking military and, let it be said, animal."[36] Darnand was not a leader with the political skill of Mussolini, Hitler, or even José Antonio Primo de Rivera, or Doriot. He was the fascist soldier personified, the ideal of the Milice. In practice the movement more often resembled a band of desperadoes making use of political circumstances for enrichment and careers.

During the first half of 1944 the Milice represented one side in the culminating stage of the Franco-French civil war, to be sketched in a subsequent chapter. The evolution of Darnand and the Milice toward full collaborationism was visible in a comment made in May 1944 by Friedrich Grimm, who two years earlier had suspected the SOL as the potential nucleus of an anti-German secret army. Grimm estimated the Francs-Gardes to number approximately three thousand and he described them as "political fanatics . . . ready to fight on the side of the Germans against the English and Americans." Grimm's recommendation that the Miliciens be armed was a direct reversal of his earlier evaluation and attests to Darnand's success in gaining the confidence of the occupation authorities.[37]

[35]Darnand, "Nous avons rompu," *Devenir,* February 1944.

[36]Maurice Bardèche, *Qu'est-ce que le fascisme?* (Paris: Les Sept Couleurs, 1961), pp. 191–192 and Brasillach, p. 235. See also Robert J. Soucy, "The Nature of Fascism in France," pp. 49–51.

[37]See Grimm, Bericht, May 16, 1944, T-120/6442H/E481307–8, which should be compared with his report of December 1942, cited in n. 14 above. See also Helmut Knochen, SS-Standartenführer und Oberst der Polizei, letter to General von Stülpnagel, Militärbefehlshaber in Frankreich, May 27, 1944, CDJC document LXXV, 192, in which Knochen terms Darnand's behavior *"politisch absolut einwandfrei"* (politically absolutely irreproachable), and suggests that men be chosen from among Darnand's entourage to staff the prefectures of France.

The Milice was to sow deep discord in a France Darnand had wished to see united. Ultimately, the disorderly elements within it prevailed over its mission as a force for order. Its spirit was captured by one of Darnand's close aides who wrote of the Miliciens' love of battle.[38] The combativeness of the Milice, reflected in its paramilitary organization, led it to help unleash a bloodbath which has blackened its name since. Even more outside the mainstream of French political life than were the RNP and PPF, the Milice was the last desperate movement in the proliferation of French collaborationism. Created by Laval when the war had begun to turn against the Axis, the Milice lacked even the faint hopes of power held by the RNP in 1941 and the PPF a year later. A repressive paramilitary force more than a political party, it attracted the uncritical types readily exploited by a seasoned politician such as Laval. As Darnand argued at his trial, however, his superiors in Vichy must share in the responsibility for the excesses and crimes committed in their name by his men.

The Milice incorporated the contradictions that existed within virtually all fascist movements, in particular a spirit of youthful revolt and opposition to the bureaucratic methods of modern government in conflict with the authoritarianism and quest for order of the Vichy government. With no other outlets for its activism, under the slogan of anti-Communism it turned against the Resistance in 1944. Determined to find their place on the political stage, Darnand and his men made use of the crisis situation of the last year of the occupation to turn Maurrasian rhetoric into bloody reality. The "socialism" of the Milice, developed mainly by Bout de l'An and Gaucher, came from the same reservoir of radical rightist thought that informed the other movements of the collaboration. The provincial lower middle classes were mobilized rhetorically against big business, whose financial aid was accepted willingly by Darnand, just as by Doriot and Déat. The Milice was the culmination of the radical Right in action.[39]

[38]Pierre Cance, "C'est la lutte," *Combats*, June 12, 1943.

[39]The spiritual legacy passed from conservatives to the radical Right in France is discussed by Soucy, "The Nature of Fascism in France," pp. 36–38.

6 The *Enfant Terrible* of the Collaboration: Eugène Deloncle and the Mouvement Social Révolutionnaire

To tell it straight, this man [Deloncle] was a born adventurer. Anything monotonous, anything bourgeois stifled him. Undoubtedly he would have made a splendid soldier given the opportunity to fight to the end.

—Georges Groussard, *Chemins secrets*

The RNP, PPF, and Milice were by no means the only movements produced by the collaborationist community. Three lesser, but still significant, groups, all with fascist characteristics, joined the tangled political rivalries of the Ultras in occupied France. Like the three major movements, they came to prominence in a roughly chronological sequence, in which they will be considered here. First was the MSR, which Deloncle had established in September 1940. A swashbuckling and violent organization, the successor to the *Cagoule,* the MSR during the spring 1941 was subordinated by Deloncle to the RNP. Next came the Francistes, an openly fascist interwar movement resurrected by its leader Bucard early in 1941. The third organization considered is the Groupe Collaboration, headed by the writer Alphonse de Châteaubriant, which was oriented more toward cultural than political collaboration, and claimed a membership of at least one hundred thousand when it peaked in 1943. Although larger than any other collaborationist party, the Groupe never threatened to strike for political power. The presence of these lesser organizations, each with prewar roots, contributed significantly to the weakening of organized collaboration in France.

When Eugène Deloncle and his followers were expelled by Déat from the RNP in November 1941, they resumed an independent political existence. The MSR had been recruited in large measure among former members of the *Cagoule,* but the memberships of the interwar and wartime organizations were not identical. Whereas the *Cagoule* had been staunchly anti-German in addition to anti-Communist prior to the war, the MSR called for Franco-German collaboration. In addition, the *Cagoule* had had an entirely secret existence, whereas the MSR, according to Deloncle, was to be open and visible. In reality much MSR activity was also carried on behind closed doors, and the movement continued in the conspiratorial tradition of its predecessor. The fragmentation so characteristic of French dissident politics could be seen in the three-way split of ex-*Cagoulards* among de Gaulle, Pétain, and Deloncle in 1940. Had Deloncle marched on Vichy with the Légion National Populaire, he would have encountered former *Cagoulards* led by Méténier in Vichy's Groupes de Protection on the other side. [1]

The failure of the fusion with Déat was the first in a series of setbacks for Deloncle which led eventually to his loss of control over the MSR itself and the reorientation of the party away from collaboration. The MSR, which had the potential for a bright future in late 1940, could not function in Paris without German support. At the postwar trial of one of Deloncle's lieutenants in the movement, the German embassy was said to have supported Deloncle to the tune of 300,000 francs per month. The source for this statement was Rudolf Schleier, deputy to Ambassador Abetz. Schleier's statement is unverifiable and it is more likely that Deloncle was helped by Thomas and the SS in creating the MSR. Deloncle's secretiveness makes his activities difficult to trace but later events suggest that he was more likely to look for support to the SS than to the embassy. Another contemporary source, from Corvignolles circles, suggests that Deloncle had made contact with General von Stülpnagel, the Wehrmacht commander in Paris, and that the MSR was being helped by the Propagandastaffel office, attached to the Wehrmacht in Paris. The presence of direct German financial aid was denied by a number of members of the MSR, a denial characteristic of most surviving members of collaborationist parties. It is difficult, however, to envision an organi-

[1]Désert, pp. 60–61. Désert was a police agent who investigated the *Cagoule*. On the subject of the royalism and tactics of the *Cagoule,* I am indebted to a former member of Action Française, the Camelots du Roi, and the MSR for an interview, which took place on July 10, 1974.

zation such as the MSR functioning in occupied Paris without some kind of German aid. Yet the official German attitude toward the Deloncle movement remained cautious. The MSR was "tolerated" rather than "authorized" in an unpublished decree, May 26, 1941.[2]

Events showed soon enough the wisdom of those who distrusted Deloncle, who quickly became a divisive force among the French collaborationists and the German services posted in Paris. In 1941, Deloncle was leader of the MSR, member of the five-man RNP directorate, and the first president of the steering committee of the Anti-Bolshevik Legion. He lost all three positions in less than a year. His prior activity as *Cagoule* chief and his well-known predilection for action rather than words lent him a certain prestige among those who blamed the Republic for the defeat of 1940. He appeared to some as a thoroughgoing revolutionary without the sort of leftist past that Déat and Doriot had.

The MSR shared with the Milice a pedigree of the radical Right. Most of Deloncle's closest aides had been with him in the *Cagoule* and many had entered political life through Action Française. Like the Milice, Deloncle's movement comprised many activists who had turned against Maurras after February 1934, and the *Cagoule* and MSR constituted a part of the radical Right revolt against the stalemate society. Men such as Deloncle and Schueller, the director of L'Oréal perfumes in Paris, wished to bring a more dynamic brand of capitalism to France and appeared willing to resort to terrorism to establish the right-wing dictatorship they believed necessary for their purposes. Many of the MSR recruits had been active in the Camelots du Roi, the action arm of Maurras' movement, as was also true of many later Miliciens. Because the MSR was restricted to the north-

[2]For Deloncle and Thomas, see Michel, *Année 40*, p. 172. The statement on embassy aid is from J.-H. Morin, "Michel Harispe, principal inculpé du MSR," *Libération*, October 5, 1948. See also Bourdrel, p. 260. Colonel Georges Groussard, whose activity in the Corvignolles and subsequently in the Resistance parallels that of Loustaunau-Lacau, wrote of Deloncle's contacts with the Wehrmacht; see Groussard, *Chemins secrets*, p. 111, as well as his subsequent *Service secret*, p. 94. In a statement made to me on July 20, 1973, Georges Soulès, a ranking member of the MSR after 1941, denied ever seeing German funds. Another MSR member indicated that he joined the movement only after being assured that it was not supported by German money (interview, July 22, 1974). For the unpublished decree conferring "tolerated" status upon the MSR, see Der Militärbefehlshaber in Frankreich. Anlage 32 zum Lagebericht für die Monate Februär/März 1942, CDJC document CDXCV, 10.

ern zone and had ceased to exist when the Milice was allowed to recruit there, the two movements never competed for membership. Several leading Miliciens including Darnand and Henry Charbonneau, the editor of the Milice newspaper *Combats,* had followed Deloncle, although Darnand had not been involved with the MSR. Deloncle's movement became a blend of Saint-Simonian technocratic modernism, Blanquist conspiratorial terrorism, and Maurrasian right-wing authoritarianism, although by 1940 Deloncle had long since abandoned royalism. Its momentary potential for popular appeal was killed by German mistrust and the political ineptness of its leaders.

The MSR attracted dissidents from Action Française who, like Deloncle, had repudiated the Germanophobia of Maurras and Jacques Bainville. Others in the MSR came from Colonel de la Rocque's Parti Social Français, the PPF, and the Frontistes, the antiwar splinter movement led during the 1930's by Gaston Bergery. Dissidents from de la Rocque's movement criticized the colonel as insufficiently anticapitalist, anti-Semitic, and antiparliamentarian. Some from the PPF questioned the sincerity of Doriot's ideological convictions. The movement also attracted some old revolutionary Socialists, who in the tradition of Georges Sorel, had opposed the reformism of Léon Blum. Some former Communist workers, disenchanted with Moscow, but still militant in spirit, also found their way to the MSR. Another source of recruits for the MSR, as well as for other collaborationist groups, was the French prisoner-of-war population being held in Germany. A former member of the Trotskyist Gauche Révolutionnaire faction of the Socialist party, Georges Soulès helped organize a Cercle Pétain, a clandestine political group among the French prisoners in his Oflag (prison camp for officers). (Cercles Pétain were established in a number of prison camps.) Released by the Germans in March 1941, Soulès returned to Paris where he worked with the MSR.[3]

[3]Interview with Georges Soulès, July 20, 1973. For a full discussion of the MSR, its composition and history, see the German memorandum of May 23, 1942, "Note sur le Mouvement Social Révolutionnaire." This memorandum, originally found among the archives gathered for the Nuremberg war crimes trials, is available as document XIXa, 15 in the CDJC. For Soulès specifically, see the account of his speech to the first party congress of the RNP, occurring while the MSR was still a

The MSR, which appeared for a brief time capable of becoming a potent French political force, was described in one contemporary account as the kernel of a rising fascism in occupied France:

> The MSR's base of militants appeared as the first synthesis in France of Nationalist and Socialist tendencies, up until its creation mutually opposed. Undoubtedly this base, drawn from the people, presently contains the best French revolutionaries—the most solid in physical combat and the most politically educated due to the diversity of their origins, the quality of their past experiences, and their profound present awareness of the prejudices which kept them divided from each other.[4]

The size of the MSR is difficult to pinpoint but it does not appear to have approached the figure of 175,000 given for the prewar *Cagoule* at the peak of its influence. Twelve thousand MSR members in the Paris region in May 1942 were supplemented by an additional six to eight thousand in the provinces. Like the other collaborationist movements, the MSR was urban. Of the twelve thousand members in the Paris area, four thousand were said to be militants, ready for mobilization at any time. The remaining eight thousand had not reached as high a level in their political training. In a familiar tactic, an additional hundred thousand were claimed as members on the grounds of their membership in professional associations whose leaders were in the party. Like the RNP, the MSR was banned by Vichy in the unoccupied zone and obliged to confine its development to the German-occupied northern zone during the first two years of the occupation. In their study of the Loire region, Durand and Bohbot found the average age of the MSR members there older than those of most of the other collaborationist groups. The PPF and the Francistes were the youngest groups, the RNP members somewhat older, and the MSR the oldest, except for the Groupe Collaboration. Their findings, together with the other accounts of MSR membership characteristics, indicate that the organization had a higher proportion of recruits who had been politically active before the war, largely in

---

part of that movement, published in *Rassemblement,* June 22, 1941, and Charbonneau, 1:342–343.

[4]The quotation is from "Note sur le MSR." The translation is my own and appears in my article "The Condottieri of the Collaboration," p. 266.

the *Cagoule*. It also suggests why the MSR members might have been described as among the "most politically educated" in France.[5]

The violent character of the MSR was amply demonstrated when party members dynamited several synagogues in Paris during the night of October 2–3, 1941. The incident shows not only the nature of MSR tactics but also the means by which Deloncle was attempting to gain credibility with the Germans at the time of his split with Déat. It also highlighted the deep-seated divisions among the various German services in Paris. Without informing the Wehrmacht command, Deloncle approached SS-Obersturmführer Hans Sommer with the proposal that in retaliation for the assassination attempt of August 27 against Laval and Déat, MSR men were prepared to blow up several synagogues in Paris. According to Sommer's account of the incident, Deloncle informed him that the Jews had been behind the assassination attempt, ironic in light of the suspicions of Deloncle himself harbored by the two victims. The MSR chieftain offered some of his men for the job but he needed explosives, which Sommer was asked to produce. Apparently securing the approval of Max Thomas and Helmut Knochen, his superiors in Paris, Sommer obtained the explosives in Berlin and supplied them to Deloncle's men. Deloncle assumed full responsibility for the action. Carried out during the night of October 2–3, the attack damaged or destroyed some half dozen synagogues. The MSR men described their night's work to Sommer on the morning of October 3. Some indiscretions on Sommer's part in the presence of German army officers at a Paris nightclub led to Wehrmacht Commander Otto von Stülpnagel's being informed of the role of the MSR and the SS in the incident. As head of the army command in Paris, Stülpnagel reacted angrily to the affair, an infringement upon his authority, and a major crisis within German circles in Paris ensued.[6]

[5]The figures are all taken from "Note sur le MSR." Charbonneau, 1:341–342, estimated some six thousand MSR members in Paris with an additional six thousand in the remainder of the occupied zone in 1941. For the age comparison of the MSR members with those of other collaborationist groups in the Loire region, see Durand and Bohbot, p. 65.

[6]Hans Sommer, SS-Obersturmführer, Declarations on the bombings of Paris synagogues, "Anlage 2 zu T464/g K dos.," October 6, 1941; CDJC document I, 22. See also "Michel Harispe, principal inculpé du MSR," trial account in *Libération*, October 5, 1948. More recent accounts of the Paris "crystal night" include Pierre

Stülpnagel heatedly demanded the recall of Thomas and Knochen. Having intervened once before to prevent Deloncle from joining his followers in the Anti-Bolshevik Legion at the Russian front, Stülpnagel maintained a deep mistrust of Deloncle and his men. This time, however, the general was only partially successful. Thomas was moved out of Paris but Knochen remained, supported by Heydrich, who claimed total competence in dealing with the Jews of occupied Europe. Abetz also supported Knochen against the Wehrmacht commander. When the French government prosecuted Knochen after the war, it learned that Deloncle had contacted the SD as early as March 1941 in an effort to gain its support for his aspirations to high government position in Vichy. Told to prove his newfound loyalty to the Germans, Deloncle had produced the scheme to blow up the synagogues long before the August 27 assassination attempt against Laval and Déat. He had been introduced to Knochen by Sommer, and the plot had also received the blessing of Heydrich, who told Knochen not to inform the Wehrmacht command. Although Deloncle by early 1941 had decided to play the SS card, the MSR also received assistance from other German sources in France. The Gestapo was represented in Paris by Theodor Dannecker, who provided financial support for the Institute d'Etude des Questions Juives, whose officials were openly critical of Déat's insufficiently virulent anti-Semitism. This organization engaged in propaganda and lent support to other friendly groups, whose members frequently joined the Institute. Its relations with the MSR were excellent.[7]

The more secretive presence of the SS conformed better to Deloncle's own conspiratorial style and, like the MSR chief, its members

---

Bourget, *Histoires secrètes de l'occupation de Paris* (Paris: Hachette, 1970), 1:323–345; Jean Cathelin and Gabrielle Gray, *Crimes et trafics de la Gestapo française*, 2 vols. (Paris: Historama, 1972), 2:179; Jäckel, p. 227; and my own account in "The Condottieri of the Collaboration," pp. 272–273.

[7]For the relationship of the MSR and the other collaborationist groups to the Institute d'Etude des Questions Juives, see the report "L'Institute d'Etude des Questions Juives," document XCVI, 80; pp. 59 and 63; in the CDJC. The role of the SS in the synagogue bombings is taken up in Heydrich, Chef der Sicherheitspolizei und des SD, 1434/41 g RS, Berlin, November 6, 1941, to Oberkommando des Heers, Herrn General Quartiermeister Wagner, CDJC document I, 28; Abetz, note for Ambassador Ritter, February 2, 1942, CDJC document CXX, 18; and "Procès Oberg-Knochen," a stenographic trial account in eleven fascicles, September 1954, I, 7; III, 177; and VII, 5–7; document CCCLXIV, 1 in the CDJC.

were men of action. The entire German establishment in Paris, however, was embarrassed by the affair of the synagogues, which did Deloncle no good. By late 1941 his prestige and that of the MSR were in decline. Deloncle had failed in his bid to control the RNP. He had been blocked by Stülpnagel from effective participation with the Anti-Bolshevik Legion at the Russian front. The MSR was beginning to lose members to the RNP and especially to the PPF, parties with more capable leadership, more refined doctrines, and greater chances for political success.

The assassination of Marx Dormoy, popularly attributed to Deloncle's men, also tarnished the MSR image. MSR daring and adventurism increasingly appeared as frivolous intrigue. Deloncle had led his movement into a political wilderness. He had relied upon the SS which, when it did gain more power in 1942, favored the more successful and promising PPF of Doriot. By 1942, Deloncle was beginning to develop doubts about Germany's ability to win the war, displaying a sense of realism uncommon in collaborationist circles. After that May, however, his views no longer mattered as far as the MSR was concerned, for a new upheaval within its ranks turned him out of the party.

With the expulsion of the MSR faction from the RNP, the MSR leadership itself split into three rival factions. During the summer of 1941, Deloncle had been named to direct the steering committee of the Anti-Bolshevik Legion, and he and his aide Jacques Corrèze were becoming increasingly preoccupied with the affairs of the legion and the war against the Soviet Union. Corrèze, a former interior decorator, had been imprisoned for *Cagoulard* activities before the war. He had come to Paris, where he lived with Deloncle in the sixteenth *arrondissement,* a stronghold of the radical Right.[8]

A second MSR faction, led by Jean Filiol and Charbonneau, turned sharply against Deloncle's leadership in early 1942. Both men had

[8]"Curriculum vitae: Jacques Corrèze," CDJC document XXIX, 53. See also "Grand chef de la Cagoule. . . ," *Libération,* October 7, 1948. On the assassination of Dormoy, see "La Cagoule au pouvoir, Marx Dormoy assassiné," clandestine tract of the Comité d'Action Socialiste, August 1941; BDIC document 4° Δ 177/Rés. 3. This document admits the possibility that PPF elements might also have killed Dormoy who as interior minister had removed Doriot from his post of mayor of Saint-Denis. Doriot had been heard to threaten Dormoy in July 1940.

found their way to the MSR from Action Française. Filiol had been in the Camelots du Roi, the youth movement of the Action Française, had organized its unit in the sixteenth district of Paris, and had helped Deloncle organize the *Cagoule*. During the brief association of the MSR with the RNP, Filiol had been adjunct head of the Légion National Populaire and with Deloncle had helped organize party raids on Jewish-owned apartments and businesses in Paris. By late 1941, Filiol and Charbonneau had grown tired of what they considered Deloncle's unproductive leadership and had also become angered at his high-handed manner of running the movement. They felt that he lacked the confidence of the Wehrmacht post at Paris, which they feared would doom the MSR to perpetual political impotence. The affair of the synagogues was haunting Deloncle.[9]

The third faction emerging within the MSR was intellectually the most talented and interesting. It included romantic young activists such as Georges Soulès, also of the sixteenth district of Paris, and André Mahé, both of whom had been attracted by what they had perceived as the revolutionary activism of Deloncle and the MSR. These young men and others, mainly journalists and literary men, some of whom forged significant careers in the world of letters after the war, had seen Deloncle briefly as a heroic figure who would lead France into the New Order of Nazi Europe. In a book written in 1942, Soulès and Mahé tried to build a doctrine of their conception of the National Revolution. Basing their ideas on a mixture of Barrès, Sorel, Nietzsche, and Alfred Rosenberg, the two writers attempted to provide the MSR with the doctrinal luster that it, in contrast to Déat's RNP, lacked.

The book called for a new elite to rejuvenate France, give her a corporate society built upon "natural" communities, and integrate her into the New Europe. Arguing that liberalism and Marxism were of a piece, the writers called for a new racial myth to liberate the energies of the French in the way that Hitlerism had for the Germans. Demanding "mystique first", Soulès and Mahé expressed most of the values of German National Socialism, as seen by Rosenberg.

---

[9]Charbonneau, 1:349. See also Deloncle, Order no. 22 to Corrèze and Jacques Fauran, March 25, 1941, CDJC document CCCLXX, 110a; and Désert, pp. 70–71.

There was, however, a greater emphasis placed upon elites, more specific to French fascism, and Social Darwinist violence in history was downplayed. The book's conclusion reveals the romantic attraction held by the German model and the quest for political engagement that captivated the two young writers. "Our generation," they wrote, "is confronting its own destiny and can bind only itself, and it clearly feels the absolute necessity to participate in the revolutionary struggle for the victory of the values of *race, soil,* and *mission.* But in the accomplishment of its revolutionary task and even its victory, our generation opens anew and leaves free to following generations all the paths of the spirit."[10]

By early 1942 the Soulès-Mahé faction had come to the conclusion that Deloncle was not the man to lead them into the New Europe. Offended by what Soulès later called Deloncle's "Florentine methods" of dealing with his subordinates, the "literary" faction joined Filiol and Charbonneau in opposition to the party leader. Filiol had personal grievances involving Madame Deloncle, which had almost led to a duel between him and her husband. Personal feelings between Filiol and Corrèze were also bad. The two anti-Deloncle factions succeeded in isolating the Deloncle-Corrèze element, and on May 14, 1942 forcibly seized control of the party headquarters in Paris. After a violent confrontation the Delonclists were driven out with no intervention by French police or German occupation authorities. Vanor, a Deloncle supporter tried to enlist SS assistance. As during the purge of Deloncle by Déat the preceding year, the SS was either unwilling or unable to intervene. By May 1942 the SS authorities might well have decided that Deloncle was no longer worth a major confrontation with the Wehrmacht and embassy staffs.

[10]Georges Soulès and André Mahé, *La fin du nihilisme* (Paris: Fernand Sorlot, 1943), pp. 20, 61–62, 221, and passim. The quotation is taken from p. 250. The attraction of fascism and the MSR in particular to certain journalist and literary circles was discussed in my interview with Soulès, July 20, 1973. See also Soulès' statements in Marie-Thérèse de Brosses, *Entretiens avec Raymond Abellio* (Paris: Pierre Belfond, 1966), pp. 33ff. Abellio is the *nom de plume* under which Soulès became prominent in the literary world after the war. In 1946 he won the Sainte-Beuve prize for his novel *Heureux les pacifiques.* A brief but useful account of the history of the MSR, provided by André Mahé shortly after the war, may be found in Galtier-Boissière, *Crapouillot,* 4 (1948), 267. Under the *nom de plume* Alain Sergent, Mahé later wrote a novel, *Je suivis ce mauvais garçon,* inspired in part by his political activities during the war.

Laval was content to see Deloncle go and the MSR insurgents used personal contacts to secure the acquiescence of the French police and Interior Ministry. When Deloncle, Corrèze, Vanor, and their supporters tried to retake the party offices later during the day of May 14, they were driven off. In all, the insurgents needed fifty men to occupy the party installations. On May 19, Deloncle publicly announced his resignation from the MSR and his permanent cessation of all political activity on the grounds of ill health.[11]

More effective at plotting secret maneuveres as head of the *Cagoule,* Deloncle had gone beyond his depth in attempting to create a more open mass party. His movement was unable to attract a popular following, and the hostility of its collaborationist rivals combined with German suspicions to produce in the MSR a clandestine pattern of activity much like that of the *Cagoule.* Under Deloncle's leadership, the political program of the MSR differed little from those of the other collaborationist movements, except in perhaps being more vague. The ideas presented by Soulès and Mahé were those of individuals and did not constitute any sort of official party doctrine. An early MSR tract demanded an authoritarian regime, a regeneration of the French "race," destruction of Freemasonry, and a return to the soil. It also asked for a revival of the artisan class, the destruction of "speculative" capitalism, and collaboration with "Europe." The list of signatories, the members of the party leadership cadre, apart from Deloncle, included two industrialists, an architect, an engineer, a technician, a designer (Corrèze), a general (Paul Lavigne-Delville), a journalist, a lawyer, a salesman, a confectioner, a metallurgy worker, two *employés,* an insurance man, and a worker's assistant (*ouvrier ajusteur*).[12]

One of the industrialists listed on the tract was Schueller, who lent out his offices as meeting places for the MSR leaders. Having met Deloncle during the 1930's when both had opposed the Popular Front

---

[11]Interview with Georges Soulès, July 20, 1973. Soulès' forthcoming memoirs can be expected to provide further interesting details and insights concerning the various factions within the MSR. See also de Brosses, p. 31. Galtier-Boissière inaccurately gives the date of Deloncle's ouster as March 1942; *Crapouillot,* 4:267. See also "Grand chef de la Cagoule...," *Libération,* October 7, 1948 and "Note sur le MSR," p. 4.

[12]"MSR—Résurrection," a tract, BDIC: Q pièce 4469. This tract appears to have been printed late in 1940.

government, Schueller saw in his movement a chance to modernize the stalled society. A prolific writer both during and after the war, Schueller propounded what he called a "proportional wage," a scheme by which French workers would be paid on a piecework basis. A consistent critic of what he believed to be ossified production methods in France, he also called for a more adventurous managerial elite, willing to take the business risks necessary to modernize the French economy. The perfume tycoon Schueller seems to have felt a kindred spirit in the naval engineer Deloncle. Both were adventurous and daring in furthering their causes, and both viewed political life through the eyes of technicians. After 1940, Schueller contended that the increased production resulting from his proportional wage would by itself enable France to rebuild her economic structure and restore a measure of prosperity to her people. His bold new managerial elite, its methods in contrast to the conservative business practices traditional in France, would take its place in the rejuvenated state of the MSR. To this end he supported the MSR financially and when Deloncle brought his followers into the RNP, Schueller became the economic theoretician of that party. He followed Deloncle out of the RNP in November 1941. By March 1942, however, Schueller had left Deloncle. He told a member of the Trade Division of the German Foreign Ministry that he still favored collaboration and saw in Hitler the hope of a new Europe but that Deloncle's leadership had failed completely. The loss of Schueller's support weakened Deloncle in his confrontation with the MSR insurgents.[13]

Despite his public statement of May 19, 1942, Deloncle did not withdraw from political activity. He had too many personal contacts in French political circles and it would have gone against his nature to have given up the game. A number of his supporters joined the PPF after his ouster from the MSR and Deloncle himself was seen at

[13]Dr. Gerstner, Handelspol. Abteilung, Paris, "Aufzeichnung," March 18, 1942; T-120/2724/D532744-5. For Schueller's ideas, see his series of articles, "L'organisation professionelle," "Pour un nouveau salariat,'Le salaire 'au temps' remplacé par le salaire 'au produit,'" and "La révolution du patronat," in *Lectures 40*, a bi-weekly magazine edited by Fontenoy, no. 3, October 10, 1940, 96–100; no. 6, November 25, 1940, 202–208; and no. 9, January 10, 1941, 280–285, respectively. Schueller's major work published during the occupation was *La révolution de l'économie* (Paris: Robert Denoël, 1941). For Schueller, see also Charbonneau, I, 344 and Coston, pp. 966–967.

the November 1942 PPF party congress. He was no more successful, however, in getting together with Doriot in November 1942 in Paris than he had been two years earlier at Vichy. There was no room for two leaders in the PPF, as Deloncle quickly saw.[14]

In late 1942, Deloncle began to question the ability of the Germans to win the war. Deloncle was usually well informed, with access to information about the progress of the war which his rivals lacked. His prudent silence when Déat publicly discounted the possibility of German-Soviet war was a case in point. A close similarity existed between Deloncle's appraisal of the foreign situation and that of Darlan, who may have advised him to take the presidency of the steering committee of the Anti-Bolshevik Legion. Darlan's doubts concerning the ultimate outcome of the war were revealed to the world by his cooperation with the Allies when they landed in North Africa in November 1942. Deloncle, who may have secretly worked for Darlan, is said to have made contacts with Allied agents perhaps as early as the previous summer. In July 1942 he also initiated contacts with elements in the German military espionage network, the Abwehr, who were in touch with the anti-Hitler conspiracies of Abwehr leader Admiral Wilhelm Canaris. Deloncle's turn against Hitler was also an opportunity to seek revenge upon his French enemies and the German officials who had failed to support him in his battles for control of the RNP and the MSR.[15]

As a result of his earlier political activities and his many personal contacts, Deloncle was able to travel freely to Spain, a rare privilege for French citizens during the occupation. There were extensive *Cagoule* ties in Spain from the days of the Civil War and arms had been obtained there in 1936 and 1937. In addition, Spain had served as a refuge for fleeing *Cagoulards* when Dormoy had moved against them late in 1937. There were also former Cagoulards among the Resistance. Filiol was known by the Germans to have friends in Spain

[14]For Deloncle's flirtation with the PPF, see Saint-Paulien, *Histoire de la collaboration,* p. 227, and the statement of Soulès in de Brosses, p. 33.

[15]Bernard Voiron, "Deloncle Chef de la Cagoule fut abattu en janvier 1944 par la police allemande," *Europe-Amérique,* no. 175, October 31, 1948, 26 and Charbonneau, 1:350. Deloncle's relations with Darlan are discussed in Tournoux, *L'histoire secrète,* pp. 147 and 155ff.

attempting to contact supporters of General Giraud in 1943. Among the former *Cagoulards* at Vichy, Henri Martin, a specialist in intelligence gathering, was said to have had contacts with the British intelligence service. Jacques Lemaigre-Dubreuil, the French financier who had served as intermediary for the Franco-German Armistice Commission at Wiesbaden, also had had past connections with the *Cagoule*. Lemaigre-Dubreuil was instrumental in negotiating local French cooperation with the Allies prior to their landings in North Africa. He and the former MSR militant Michel Harispe later sought to utilize contacts in Madrid for peace feelers to the Russians and the Americans. [16]

Up to his ears in a swirl of intrigue, Deloncle could hardly have avoided arousing the suspicions of the German SD, especially in regard to his trips to Spain, which were widely known in Paris collaborationist circles. He was arrested by the Germans late in 1942 but released after a brief detention. Deloncle's activities, always shrouded in mystery, are particularly difficult to trace for 1943. He is said to have been issued a false passport by the Canaris plotters, who allegedly sent him to Madrid to sound out Sir Samuel Hoare about a compromise peace in the West upon the removal of Hitler. Whether he met Hoare or any other Allied representatives remains to be established. Back in Paris, Deloncle was surprised by a visit early in the morning of January 7, 1944 of a squad of Gestapo agents to his apartment. Presumably they had come to arrest him, although this is not totally clear. In any event, Deloncle took no chances and opened fire. He was killed in the ensuing fusilade. His physical courage

---

[16]The activities of Lemaigre-Dubreuil and Harispe are discussed in Bargan, telegram to the German foreign minister, July 11, 1944, T-120/4120/E071209. See also Abetz, telegram to the Foreign Ministry, July 7, 1944, T-120/4120/E071207 and for Lemaigre-Dubreuil's role in the Allied landings in North Africa, Langer, pp. 229ff. The curious Martin is discussed in the memoirs of Roger Worms, *nom de plume*: Roger Stéphane, *Chaque homme est lié au monde* (Paris: Sagittaire, 1946), p. 199, and his connection with the British intelligence service is mentioned in a note by Fernand de Brinon, "Note sur la politique française debut 1942," destined apparently for German eyes, T-120/4637/E208996. On Filiol and Spain, see the undated telegram, probably of May 1943, of Krug von Nidda, the German representative in Vichy, T-120/2318/485238. Krug's note misspells Filiol's name, but there can be little doubt of the identity. It also refers to its source as Darnand, whose name was likewise misspelled.

uncontested, Deloncle died at the hands of those with whom he had tried to collaborate. [17]

Ironically, the rump MSR followed a political course parallel to that of the deposed Deloncle. The new "literary" faction included Soulès; Mahé, a former member of the Communist youth; Jehan de Castellane, a journalist formerly of the Action Française movement; and a well-known Parisian gynecologist and former *Cagoulard*, Dr. Landrieu. They moved the MSR away from collaborationism and secured uncontested control of the party in November 1942, when Filiol was arrested by order of Laval. A secret committee now emerged into the open, where it was joined by some new figures who had never been involved in collaborationist politics. Aware of the increasingly harsh German policies in occupied France, the new group moved closer to Laval after his return to the government. On behalf of Laval they were given financial support by Finance Minister Pierre Cathala and began to use this aid in attempts to subvert the remaining collaborationist parties, none too difficult a task in view of the fragmented Ultra camp. The new MSR developed its own intelligence network which kept tabs on Deloncle's subsequent activities. More important from Laval's point of view, it kept a close eye on the activities of the PPF. When Déat launched his Front Révolutionnaire National to unify the collaborationist camp and entrap Doriot at the same time, Soulès, now working for Laval, joined as the MSR representative. By the end of 1942, the MSR as it had existed since 1940 was virtually dead. [18]

The Soulès-Mahé faction was strengthened in late 1942 by a new group, the "Unitaires," formerly men of Vichy rather than the Ultras. This group took control of what was left of the party after the expulsion of Deloncle and allowed it to die a quiet death.

[17]The account of Deloncle's death is taken from the postwar testimony of Corrèze, who was present at the time of the Gestapo incursion, "Grand chef de la Cagoule....," It was substantiated in an interview with Soulès, July 3, 1974.

[18]The account of the shift in MSR orientation following the victory of the "literary" faction is based largely upon my interviews with Soulès, July 3, 1974, and other ex-MSR members. The continued activities of Deloncle, in particular those intended to counter the new MSR leadership in 1943, are followed in the informal "intelligence" reports included in the private papers cited in n. 28, p. 153. For Filiol's activities after 1942, see Tournoux, pp. 144–145 and Delperrie de Bayac, pp. 123, 276, and passim.

They began to publish a clandestine tract, *Force Libre*, in which they called for an independent France with political institutions uniquely French. "As patriots," it said "we demand French sovereignty in the face of the Germans today, the Anglo-Saxons tomorrow, the Russians afterward." Recognizing that the Germans had lost the war, the Unitaires asked all those disillusioned with collaboration, Vichy, and the Free French to unite in an effort to create a truly free and independent France. Laval may have used Unitaire contacts in attempts to contact London indirectly in 1943.[19]

A new party, the Mouvement Révolutionnaire Français, was created in December 1943 by the Soulès-Mahé faction. More Lavalist than collaborationist, it gained little popular support. In the France of 1943 and 1944 there was no longer room for a middle position between collaboration and resistance. Leaders such as Soulès were obliged to hide first from Darnand's Milice, then from the Gaullist government. The immediate future was with the extremists of both sides and the death of the MSR coincided with the growth of the Milice. In September 1942 the entire MSR membership in the Nord and Pas-de-Calais departments went over to Doriot's PPF, and at the end of that year nine regional or departmental MSR leaders defected to Costantini's Ligue Française. Some members of the collaborationist groups who in 1943 wished to disassociate themselves from their earlier pro-Axis stands were said to have joined what was left of the MSR, which recruited some PPF militants in Bordeaux. By the time of the Liberation, however, the truly committed collaborationists in the MSR had found their way to other groups, most often the PPF. American intelligence regarded the MSR as a thing of the past.[20]

---

[19]The account of Unitaire contacts with London is based on information provided in interviews with Soulès, July 3, 1974, and others. I have found no references to such contacts in Allied, German, or other French documentation. François Piétri, Vichy's ambassador to Spain, was in frequent touch with Hoare, who represented Britain in Madrid, but this contact was suspended by Hoare in March 1943. See Piétri's testimony in Claude Gounelle, *Le dossier Laval* (Paris: Plon, 1969), p. 423.

[20]OSS, "French Pro-Fascist Groups," August 30, 1944, p. 31. See also "Ce que nous sommes, ce que nous voulons!" *Force Libre,* clandestine, June 1944. The information concerning shifts of members in and out of the MSR in its waning months comes from the *French Basic Handbook,* p. 150.

The political failure of the MSR under the conditions of the occupation is in some ways even more striking than the failures of its rivals. Many of the necessary ingredients for success existed in the MSR during late 1940 and early 1941. The party possessed disciplined and daring shock troops, and undeniable talent and boldness in its leadership corps. It had at least some access to business support, and personal contacts with the SS seemed promising. On the other hand, relations with the occupying authorities were damaged in maladroit adventures such as the Paris synagogues incident. Deloncle's megalomaniacal leadership offended subordinates attracted by the dynamic image he projected. One MSR member reported Deloncle claiming in 1943 that but for the malevolent influence of Alibert he would have been named interior minister three years earlier in Vichy. This delusion was compounded by the claim that Alibert had owed his position to him. Deloncle added that as a member of the government he would have made a "total revolution" and that Vichy feared him for that reason.[21] The MSR chieftain also allowed amorous interests to create ill will between himself and some of his closer supporters. Moreover, while a talented organizer and by all accounts a man of exceptional intelligence (in the many meanings of that word), Deloncle was not an inspiring speaker. He was unable to rouse the members of the RNP, for example, when he delivered a major address to them at their party congress of June 1941. There was none of the style of Hitler, Mussolini, or even Doriot in Deloncle. His failure was total and merited.

In a sense there were two MSRs, since the movement assumed a new character after the purge of Deloncle. Both MSRs, however, were closed and secretive, specializing in the intrigue that was Deloncle's hallmark. Unlike the RNP, the MSR developed few subsidiary organizations, nor did it stage major public demonstrations as the other collaborationist factions did. Its best organized activities were the paramilitary raids made against property owned by Jews and other enemies of the movement, including rivals within the collaborationist camp. These activities ceased with the movement's

[21]The story is taken from an intelligence report signed "Tacite," dated July 5, 1943, and currently in the private collection cited in n. 28, p. 153.

change in orientation after the ouster of Deloncle, but by that time all scope for effective independent political action was gone and the remaining MSR faction was limited to auxiliary intelligence activities for Laval. By the end of 1942 the MSR no longer existed as a party of the collaboration. Doriot, Déat, and company had one less rival.

7 An Older New Movement: The Francistes

The picture of the gangster in the blue shirt with all his tin-ware [Bucard's medals] presently covers the walls of Paris: "Follow the leader who has never been wrong!"
—Jean Galtier-Boissière, Mon journal pendant l'occupation, July 15, 1944

During the first four days of July 1943, amid extensive fanfare and publicity, three thousand uniformed Francistes gathered in Paris to celebrate the tenth anniversary of the founding of their party. Created in 1933 by the much decorated World War I hero Marcel Bucard, the Franciste organization openly claimed to be France's only truly fascist movement during the 1930's. In 1936, together with other paramilitary leagues, it was dissolved by the Popular Front government but the movement continued clandestinely until it was revived by Bucard under the occupation. Like the PPF, the Francistes did not have to start from scratch in 1940. To them, their rivals, Doriotists included, were all opportunist parvenus. Throughout the occupation period the Francistes emphasized their fascist credentials, praising Bucard for having foreseen the disaster of 1940. In words reminiscent of Mussolini, they called him the leader "who was never wrong."[1]

Marcel Bucard was a genuine hero of the First World War. Born in 1895 to a prosperous peasant family in Saint-Clair-sur-Epte in Normandy, Bucard received his education in a Catholic seminary. His meditative disposition and frail state of health, resulting from a bout with typhoid fever, made a good student of him. He seemed destined for the priesthood, but like so many others, he found his plans interrupted by the war in 1914. Sharing in the patriotism of his generation, the young Bucard enlisted for military service and at age nineteen in April 1915 was sent to the front. Cited ten times for extraor-

---

[1] The theme of continuity appears in virtually all Franciste propaganda of the occupation period. See, for example, the party brochure "Un combat de 10 ans," a special supplement to the weekly *Franciste*, September 1943.

dinary valor, by age twenty-two he had risen from soldier to the rank of captain. Two years later he was awarded an officership in the Légion d'honneur. He was one of the youngest men to be so distinguished in France. Wounded three times during the war, Bucard returned to his unit after each injury. His wounds, however, included head injuries requiring two trephinations in 1942, which later raised questions about his mental powers.[2]

Bucard came out of the war determined to protect the interests of the veterans. Thoroughly militarized by his experience, he opted for a career in right-wing politics and journalism and under the tutelage of André Tardieu, he ran in the May 1924 parliamentary elections. He selected the Seine-et-Oise constituency, where he cut an attractive figure resplendent in uniform, but, although popular among veterans, he lost the election and turned bitterly against the Republic. For the next nine years Bucard participated in the politics of the radical Right, first in Georges Valois' Faisceau and later with the newspaper *L'Ami du Peuple,* published by the perfume magnate François Coty. As a speaker for the Fédération Nationale Catholique of General Edouard de Castelnau, one of the heroes of the First World War, Bucard defended the Catholic church, especially before war veterans. Married in 1928, Bucard combined what one historian called a "bourgeois" style of living with continuing political prominence in the veterans' organizations of the far Right, including the Croix de Feu of Colonel de la Rocque.[3]

The Franciste movement was launched by Bucard on September 29, 1933, when Doriot was still a Communist, Déat in transition from Socialism to Neo-Socialism, and Deloncle's *Cagoule* three years in the future. It was openly proclaimed the successor to Valois' Fais-

---

[2]At his postwar trial, Bucard's defense counsel attempted to use the trephinations to indicate diminished responsibility. See *Quatre Procès de trahison devant la cour de justice de Paris. Paquis. Bucard. Luchaire. Brasillach. Réquisitions et plaidoiries* (Paris: Editions de Paris, 1947), pp. 65–67. For the chronology of Bucard's early life, see the tract "Ce qu'est la Jeunesse Franciste," p. 8; BDIC pièce 901.

[3]Arnaud Jacomet, "Les chefs du Francisme: Marcel Bucard et Paul Guiraud," *Revue d'histoire de la deuxième guerre mondiale,* 25 (January 1975), 48. Jacomet has also devoted considerable study to the history of the Francistes up to the Second World War. See Jacomet, "Marcel Bucard et le mouvement franciste 1933–1940," *Maîtrise,* University of Paris X, 1970. See also Weber, *Varieties of Fascism,* pp. 133–134.

ceau and the only truly fascist movement in France, the latter a claim it continued to make throughout its history. The Francistes drew upon the same sources in French political thought as their collaborationist rivals but worried less about doctrinal niceties. Bucard denied that his movement was right-wing and argued that it represented a reconciliation of Left and Right, but it shared the nationalism, authoritarianism, cult of leadership, and social conservatism of the radical Right. Bucard also accepted aid from big business men such as Coty between the wars, although his record on this under the occupation is less clear.

Francisme's uniqueness lay in its imitativeness, which drew scorn from its Ultra rivals who questioned how a movement with pretensions to fascism and nationalism could so openly ape foreign models. The military élan of Bucard's troops, however, inspired their respect. Like their rivals on the radical Right, the Francistes represented a younger generation in revolt against their elders' control of the stalled society, but more than any other, Bucard's movement was a veterans' group. Impatient veterans who followed Bucard mistakenly thought that the transformation of Republican France into an authoritarian state would somehow eliminate politics from French life. Previously nonpolitical, these veterans epitomized the fascist trait of intolerance of ambiguity, and their militancy gave the Francistes a combative mystique that attracted a small number of dedicated young fighters, including some factory workers, between 1933 and 1944. More than any of their rivals, the Francistes in their cult of action resembled the early Italian Blackshirts and the Nazi SA.

The name "Franciste" had been used in 1933 prior to the formation of Bucard's movement by Henry Coston—a self-proclaimed disciple of the anti-Semitic doctrines of Edouard Drumont—and Jacques Ploncard d'Assac, for a small nationalist movement. Bucard's Francistes, however, were neither anti-Masonic nor anti-Semitic at the outset. Never able to rally the popular support that Doriot and the PPF enjoyed in 1936 and 1937, the Francistes were relatively strong in Alsace and Lorraine, where Bucard was aided by anti-German sentiment and opposition to the government's extension of French anticlerical legislation to the newly regained territories.

The élan of the Francistes gave Bucard's movement a prominence out of proportion to its numbers throughout its entire history. The members quickly came to blows with leftist militants, and a sharp war of words developed between *L'Humanité* and the weekly *Franciste*. They also participated in the international fascist congress held in December 1934 at Montreux. With the dissolution of the leagues in June 1936, the organization maintained a semi-clandestine existence and had to struggle to retain its members, some of whom were attracted to Doriot's new PPF. Bucard rejected all cooperation with Doriot or de la Rocque, while his newspaper began to denounce Jewish influence in France and demanded the outlawing of the Communist party. By 1938, *Le Franciste* was forced to suspend publication. Bucard responded by trying to renew Franciste political activity through the transformation of the movement into a legally recognized political party, dubbed the Parti Unitaire Français d'Action Socialiste et Nationale, (French Unitary National and Socialist Action party).[4]

Recalled to military service in August 1939, Bucard faced the outbreak of the Second World War in uniform. Franciste political activity was suspended with the coming of the war. As a captain in the army, Bucard was involved in heavy fighting near Belfort. When French forces there began to collapse in 1940, he and some others escaped the oncoming Germans by fleeing into Switzerland, where several thousand French soldiers were interned after the armistice. They were released at the end of 1940, and Bucard returned to Paris where he reconstituted the Franciste movement. Officials in the German Foreign Ministry felt that he might be useful to them in Paris and feared the Swiss would release him to the unoccupied zone where Vichy would prevent his further political activity. While still in Switzerland, Bucard was secretly informed that the Germans were trying to secure his release to the occupied zone and that once in Paris he was to contact Abetz for further aid.[5]

---

[4]For Franciste activity in the 1930's, particularly in regard to the Montreux congress, see Michael Arthur Ledeen, *Universal Fascism: The Theory and Practice of the Fascist International* (New York: Howard Fertig, 1972), pp. 114 and 120–125; and, in general, the chronology of Franciste activity in Jacomet, "Marcel Bucard et le mouvement franciste," pp. 197–207. See also "Un combat de 10 ans," p. 24.

[5]Picot, "Aufzeichnung," for Luther and Schwarzmann in the German Foreign Ministry, December 4, 1940, T-120/4120/E070953; and SS-Brigadeführer [signature illegible], to Ambassador Luther, chief of Abteilung Deutschland of the German Foreign Ministry, December 7, 1940, T-120/4120/E070954. There was an exten-

217

Despite German fears of official Vichy hostility to Bucard, he was received by Pétain, and Bucard interpreted this as support for a renewal of Franciste activity. Encouraged by what he heard in Vichy, he was strengthened in his resolve by the subsidies he received from Petain's government for his Francistes. The authorities at Vichy welcomed Bucard as a competitor with the other collaborationist leaders and his military allure won him some points there as well. He, on the other hand, was deeply impressed with the reverence in which Pétain was held and he was personally moved by their meeting. Bucard's veneration of Pétain resembled Darnand's, and he returned to Paris to prepare for the next stage of the National Revolution, in which a fascist France would emerge. [6]

Bucard was joined at the helm of the newly reconstituted Francistes by party theoretician Paul Guiraud and the leader of the party's shock troops, Dr. Rainsart. Guiraud, an *agrégé de philosophie* at Strasbourg who had joined the Francistes in 1935, was the most intellectual of the movement's leaders. He was able to exert a strong personal influence upon Bucard, especially because the latter's war injuries necessitated major surgery in 1942 and January 1943. It was Guiraud who advised Bucard to revive the Franciste movement during the German occupation and he continually counseled Bucard to more extreme pro-Axis positions during the latter stages of the war. Called by a historian of the Francistes the "âme damnée" (cursed soul) of Bucard, Guiraud attempted to use Bucard as a heroic if increasingly impotent symbol of leadership while scheming to assure real power and a possible succession for himself. Guiraud's arrogance

---

sive correspondence at this time among representatives of the various German services concerning the possibility of illegally freeing Bucard from his Swiss detention and returning him to Paris. A decision was made to await an imminent formal liberation of all the French detainees by the Swiss.

[6] For German aid to Bucard after. 1940, see Röhrig, "Aufzeichnung über das Gesprache mit dem SD-Hauptstrumführer Dr. Kuntze, Bucard betreffend," Paris, October 28, 1943 [Nuremberg Document NG 3669], CDJC document CXXVa, 83. For Vichy's encouragement and aid to the Francistes see *Procès Bucard*, pp. 57–58, and Tracou, p. 188, and on Bucard's visit to Pétain, Galtier-Boissière, *Journal*, entry of August 5, 1941, p. 70. The Franciste position on the need to carry the National Revolution through to a fascist conclusion and integrate France into the "New Europe" is expressed in Paul Guiraud, "Idées premières de la prochaine révolution française," an undated tract which was published shortly after Bucard's return to France.

together with Bucard's physical infirmities and weakness of character drove Rainsart and some of the more militant Francistes out of the party and into Darnand's Milice. (Bucard had wept at the funeral of Maurice Maurer, the propaganda chief of the party, who had been killed in an accident. Aspiring *duces* were best advised not to show their tears in public!)[7]

Although estimates of the party's size vary, it was considerably smaller than the PPF or the RNP at any given time. Estimates in 1943 ran between ten and fifty thousand members in all of France. As the higher figures come from Franciste sources, the lowest figure seems most accurate. The membership of the party was divided with roughly half in each zone of France. Preexisting contingents in the unoccupied zone gave the Francistes a base despite Vichy's ban on political parties there. They skirted the ban by operating in the southern zone under the name "Comité de Diffusion du *Franciste*," ostensibly working to publicize their newspaper, as the Doriotists were doing at the same time. The organizational structure of the Francistes resembled those of the other collaborationist parties, in which all power, theoretically at least, flowed downward from the leader, who was assisted by a central council in Paris. A chain of command extended downward through regional and departmental delegates, although in many areas, especially in the southern zone, the organization existed on paper only. Like their rivals in the collaborationist camp, the Francistes were strongest in urban areas, with hardly any following at all in the countryside. Interwar Franciste strength could be found in the northern regions of Flanders, Artois, Picardy, Upper Normandy, the Tours area, Paris, and Alsace and Lorraine, and in the cities of Bordeaux, Nice, and Marseilles. This pattern remained relatively constant after the armistice with some increased strength in Brittany, encouraged by German propaganda there.[8]

[7]The account of Guiraud's role in Franciste affairs during the occupation is taken from Jacomet, "Les chefs du francisme," p. 62.

[8]For the geographic distribution of the prewar Francistes, see Jacomet, "Marcel Bucard et le mouvement franciste," p. 78. Jacomet's information was supplemented by my interview with an aide to the leader of the Jeunesses Francistes, July 22, 1974. For the organizational structure of the Francistes and their numbers, see the data in the *French Basic Handbook*, pp. 148–149; OSS, "French Pro-Fascist Groups," p. 29; the "Anlage 32 zum Lagebericht für die Monate Februär/März 1942," p. 4; all

Like the larger parties of the collaboration, the Francistes attempted to create affiliated organizations. The most successful of the Franciste organizations was the youth movement, the Jeunesses Francistes. Headed during the occupation period by Claude Planson, one of Bucard's earliest recruits to the Francistes, the JF later sent a significant proportion of its members to the French contingent in the Waffen-SS. Mustering a few thousand young people, it was built around the motto "Honneur—Héroisme—Esprit de Sacrifice." As in the other collaborationist youth movements, the Jeunesses Francistes included divisions for girls and provided a rare vehicle for socialization among the young people of both sexes in occupied France. Marriages among the young party members were not infrequent. Although the Franciste youth organization resembled the other collaborationist youth movements in occupied France, it became unique in December 1942 when accorded legal recognition by the Vichy Secretariat of Youth. A move by Vichy to increase dissension among the collaborationist groups, the recognition was given wide publicity by the Francistes who saw in it their future ascendency. Recognition of the Jeunesses Francistes, though not the party as a whole, brought with it added government financial support. [9]

Although the members of the Franciste youth were recruited from the same social circles as the members of the parent organization and were often the offspring of the regular party members, an important difference in tone became evident during the occupation. Francistes who had been active in the movement before the war tended to be more strongly Italophile than Germanophile, whereas the reverse was true of the younger members. The original proclivities of the movement and of Bucard himself had been more toward Italian Fascism than German National Socialism, although the group had agitated for Franco-German reconciliation during the late 1930's. The Francistes had tended to think in international terms almost from their inception as suggested by their participation in the international fascist

providing information supplemented during my interview of July 13, 1974 with Jean Dufresne, who represented the Francistes in dealings with the Germans during the occupation in Paris.

[9]Interview with Dufresne, July 13, 1974. The subject of the Jeunesses Francistes is discussed in the tract "Ce qu'est la Jeunesse Franciste," pp. 4, 15, and passim.

congress of 1934. After 1940 international fascism implied a German orientation and the impressive German military machine attracted the romantic younger Francistes who had not experienced the Italophile tendency of the earlier days. Whereas many of the younger Francistes were among the most militant collaborationists, the party feared that the German victory of 1940 might open its ranks to opportunists. There is some indication that the party leadership was careful to differentiate, discreetly rather than publicly, between those who joined before and after the armistice. Like the German National Socialists, more confident in members who had joined during the *Kampfzeit* before 1933, the Franciste leadership was unwilling to confer sensitive party posts on those who had not suffered with the movement in its early days.[10]

The Francistes were relatively late in organizing a paramilitary legion because the entire party was paramilitary. In the spring of 1943 a Légion Franciste was created to include party members between ages eighteen and fifty. In late 1942 and early 1943 there was growing talk of union among the collaborationist factions and a legion gave the Francistes an additional bargaining counter, especially in view of the establishment of the Milice. Increasing frequency of attacks by the Resistance and the enhanced possibility of obtaining weapons from the occupation authorities also figured in the creation of the Légion Franciste.[11]

More notorious than the Légion Franciste was the Main bleu (Blue Hand, blue being the party's color), Bucard's personal bodyguard, kept at about one hundred strong. Recruited from the toughest elements of Paris and other towns, the Main bleu included North Africans, attracted by Franciste pledges of full equality for all within a rejuvenated French empire. Subject only to Bucard's command, the Main bleu was used to carry out personal reprisals and other acts of violence against enemies during the occupation. Bucard exercised little control over the behavior of the Main bleu recruits and their activities gave rise to rumors about their sexual conduct, in which he was said to be involved.

Such stories cannot be verified for they were spread by enemies of

[10]Interview with Dufresne, July 13, 1974. See also the *French Basic Handbook,* p. 149.

[11]The Légion Franciste is discussed in the *French Basic Handbook,* p. 149.

221

the Francistes and were emphatically denied by the Francistes themselves. Whatever their truth, however, the stories harmed the Franciste cause. Potential recruits were turned away by the rumors concerning the Franciste leader. Unable to establish the accuracy of the stories, the Germans adopted a more cautious policy than they otherwise might have in aiding the Francistes. Bucard ended up in the ironic situation of being questioned by some on moral grounds and by others who suggested that his quiet "bourgeois" life with his wife and four children disqualified him from being a true fascist chieftain. The tension between traditional European middle-class family values and the rebellious youthful nonconformism in all fascist movements was manifested in the controversies that swirled around the Franciste leader. [12]

Like their collaborationist rivals, the Francistes attracted most of their members from the middle and lower middle classes and included some industrial workers as well. Some former Communists, Socialists, and trade unionists were added to the petty tradesmen, artisans, and *employés* in their ranks. A large proportion of those who joined during the occupation had engaged in no prior political activity. The Main bleu attracted fringe and marginal elements of urban society, largely from Paris, and a contingent of Black Africans from the empire complemented Franciste ranks. During the first years of the party's development, some Jews were active in Francisme, but they left after 1936 and were entirely out of the movement by the time of the war. Many Francistes during the occupation were veterans of either the First World War or the 1939–1940 campaign. In contrast, there were fewer students in the Franciste ranks than in Action Française or Pierre Taittinger's interwar Jeunesses Patriotes.

Many young people choosing the Francistes over other collaborationist movements after 1940 did so because of a military orientation in their own family backgrounds. Franciste leaders came

[12]Interview with Dufresne, July 13, 1974. For the view of a German observer, see Röhrig, "Aufzeichnung über das Gesprache mit dem SS-Hauptsturmführer Dr. Kuntze, Bucard betreffend," which makes the point that in more than three years of observation under the German occupation, the SD had been unable to confirm or deny the rumors circulating about Bucard's private life. Its failure was attributed to the intense loyalty and reticence of the men around Bucard. For a brief discussion of the opposite problem, the questioning by some Francistes of Bucard's too proper family life, see Jacomet, "Les chefs du francisme," p. 52.

largely from the broad spectrum of the middle classes. Bucard, although of peasant stock, came from a family that had been able to send him to a seminary. Guiraud's father was editor of the Catholic newspaper *La Croix,* and he himself had a degree in philosophy. Godefroy Dupont, another party theorist, had been a *technicien* and Maurice Maurer, at whose funeral Bucard had publicly wept, was the holder of a degree in letters. Maurer had been influential in pushing the party in an anti-Semitic direction. He had served briefly as editor of the *Libre Parole,* the organ of the anti-Semitic rival Francistes of the early days, led by Coston and Ploncard d'Assac. Planson, the head of the Franciste youth during the occupation, had joined the movement while still a student. The head of the female youth, Monique Antoinet, a school teacher, served until August 1943, when she became engaged to another Franciste.[13]

Despite the uniqueness of Francisme's fascist pedigree, its doctrines differed little from those of its collaborationist rivals after 1940. It too argued for a strong and authoritarian state, with one leader, corporatism, and a vague "socialism." It denounced Jews, Freemasons, Communists, and all political vestiges of the Third Republic. In foreign policy the Francistes, who had particular reason to resent the German absorption of Alsace and Lorraine after 1940 in view of their interwar strength there, proclaimed support for a collaboration in which France and Germany were equals. Wide publicity was given to Bucard's phrase, "We have no taste for slavery." Here again, the Francistes resembled their rivals; all proclaimed the necessity for France to be treated as an equal but none spoke of the fate of Alsace and Lorraine after 1940.[14]

The Francistes' desire for a fascist international differed little from the position of their collaborationist rivals, but their tone was somewhat more "European" in the parlance of the day. It was no coincidence that several months after the defeat of 1940, Guiraud published a short book dealing with Corneliu Zelea Codreanu and the Iron Guard, the Rumanian fascist movement. Franciste Roman

[13]Interview with Dufresne and other Francistes, July 1974. See also *French Basic Handbook,* p. 149.

[14]Paul Guiraud, *Codréanu et la Garde de Fer* (Rio de Janeiro: Colectia Dacia, 1967 [a reprint of the 1940 edition]), "Avant-propos" and "Introduction," in which Franciste political positions of 1940 were spelled out.

Catholicism to some extent paralleled the staunch Orthodox identification of Codreanu's Iron Guard. Both Bucard and Guiraud had firm backgrounds in the church and although the Francistes were not openly clerical in the manner of the Iron Guard, they referred more often than their collaborationist rivals, with the possible exception of Darnand's Milice, to French Catholic tradition. Bucard and Guiraud had far less ground to make up in their approaches to the church and the faithful in France than did Déat or Doriot and there was, accordingly, more traditionalist Catholic sentiment among the Francistes than in the RNP or PPF.[15]

During the early years of the occupation, Franciste activities were mainly concerned with reestablishing the party network where possible and spreading propaganda. The sale on street corners of the weekly *Franciste* occupied much of the time and energy of the party faithful. Although the members avoided major confrontations with their rivals of the collaborationist community, small skirmishes occasionally occurred, more often than not involving party workers distributing newspapers. Like the other collaborationist leaders, Bucard faced a difficult problem providing an outlet for the energies of his more restless followers. Summer camps and training sessions for the youth helped in this regard, as did anti-Semitic exhibitions organized by the party in 1941 and 1942 in Nice. Such exhibitions, which featured crude stylized displays depicting physical "traits" of Jews and Freemasons, were sponsored by several groups including Vichy's Commissariat Général des Questions Juives, the special department established by the government to deal with "Jewish questions." Yet as late as October 1940, Friedrich Grimm in one of his first reports from occupied France suggested to the Foreign Ministry in Berlin that the Francistes were receiving money from the Jewish electrical tycoon Ernest Mercier. Grimm, whose own political origins had been in the German Left, looked askance at the Francistes, which he considered

[15]For the Franciste stand on collaboration, see Guiraud, "Conditions préalables à toute collaboration," BDIC S pièce 10589, a reprint of a speech delivered October 26, 1941, p. 10. The general outlines of Franciste doctrine during the occupation period were elaborated in Guiraud, "Idées premières de la prochaine révolution française," BDIC O pièce 21703; Godefroy Dupont, *Introduction au Francisme* (Paris: Le Coq de France, 1941); and Bucard, "Si la guerre finissait demain. . . ," published version of his speech at the close of the ninth annual Franciste party congress, September 27, 1942, BDIC O pièce 22881/1.

a party of the Right. In 1935, Bucard had crossed swords journalistically with Julius Streicher, editor of the rabidly anti-Semitic *Der Stürmer* in Germany. Streicher had "accused" Bucard of having created an organization working on behalf of the Jews, and the Franciste leader had pointedly advised Streicher to mind his own business. Grimm's attribution of Jewish money behind the Francistes in 1940 is unsubstantiated elsewhere, but it illustrates the suspicion in which some Germans held Bucard. [16]

Like the other French collaborationist groups, the Francistes soon learned that not all German services were equally sympathetic to them. While favoring Franco-German reconciliation, Bucard had been less Germanophile during the interwar years than his aides Rainsart and Guiraud. The Germans were aware of Franciste activity in prewar Alsace and Lorraine, and although Bucard did not openly oppose their annexation of these two provinces in 1940, they could not be certain of his pliancy on this issue. The Franciste official in charge of relations with the Germans in Paris found the attitude in the embassy cold and uncooperative. Francistes found more rapport with the SS representation; by temperament and political commitment both groups were the Ultras of the Ultras within the radical Right spectrum. Relationships between the Francistes and the Wehrmacht staff were sometimes strained when the Propagandastaffel sought to censor material in *Le Franciste,* and there were occasional threats from the Propagandastaffel that the supply of newsprint would be cut off. In such instances, especially after 1942, the Francistes usually appealed to the SS. [17]

The suspicions that Grimm and other Germans held of the Francistes were shared by many French otherwise favorable to the idea of

---

[16]Grimm, Report to Foreign Ministry, October 30, 1940, T-120/K1634/K402989. For reference to the Bucard-Streicher editorial duel of 1935, see Jacomet, "Marcel Bucard et le mouvement franciste," p. 112, n. 7. The anti-Semitic exposition put on by the Francistes in Nice received official attention from both French and German governments; see respectively Paul Marion, Secretary of State for Information, letter to Paul Creyssel, director of Propaganda Service, August 18, 1942, CDJC document CIX, 84; and Fritz von Valtier, undated "Arbeitsbericht," T-120/2543/D520793. Von Valtier's report is from 1942.

[17]Interview with Dufresne, July 13, 1974. For German suspicions concerning Bucard's attitude toward their policies in Alsace and Lorraine, see Röhrig, "Aufzeichnung über das Gesprache mit dem SS-Hauptsturmführer Dr. Kuntze, Bucard betreffend."

collaborationism. The importance of the Francistes in the Byzantine political life of the collaborationist community was determined not by the size of the movement but by its reputation for militancy and boldness. Under the influence of its high proportion of war veterans, a paramilitary spirit pervaded the entire organization. Aware of this, Bucard rejected all thought of union with the other collaborationist parties. Franciste reaction to Déat's attempt to set up his Front Révolutionnaire Nationale was cautious. Although he did not dare oppose cooperation in public, Bucard stated that the Francistes would retain their own base, independent of the other parties. He saw no reason to merge his shock troops into a larger organization and lose his only important source of influence. In late 1942 the Francistes adopted the slogan "unity of action," which allowed for cooperation with other parties but no organic unification. The resentment that Bucard and his colleagues felt at the sight of their movement, an authentic fascist party vintage 1933, outstripped by parvenus and "renegades" from the Left such as Doriot and Déat can readily be imagined. [18]

Franciste activity reached a crescendo with the party congress held in Paris early in July 1943, commemorating the tenth anniversary of the party. Soon afterword, the limited influence of the movement evaporated. The publicity campaign leading to the July party congress was launched amid high hopes by the Francistes. Their youth movement had shortly before been accorded legal standing by the Vichy government. Déat's unified front had failed and responsibility for the failure lay more with Doriot than with the Francistes. The collaborationist parties of the northern zone were now in process of forming militias, partially to ward off the growing number of attacks by the Resistance, partly to meet the threat of Darnand's Milice. It seemed a propitious moment for the Francistes to launch a major propaganda drive under their "unity of action" slogan and perhaps obtain for the first time a more substantial popular following. Bucard

[18]Bucard writing in *Le Franciste*, September 19, 1942, quoted in Cotta, p. 264. For the military organization of the Francistes during the occupation, see the *French Basic Handbook*, p. 149. A favorable evaluation of the valor of the Franciste shock troops, together with the statement that the movement lacked the popular support held by the PPF, may be found in Grimm, "Bericht über meine Reise nach Paris vom 12.–26. July 1943," July 27, 1943, T-120/6442/E481242.

had reason to believe that his unity plan might succeed where Déat's had failed, especially as some within the PPF seemed receptive.

At their party congress the Francistes put on an impressive show. Several thousand uniformed blue-shirted faithful filled the Vélodrome d'hiver in Paris and a number of their detachments took part in an impressive march down the Champs Elysées. It was a high-water mark from which the fortunes of the movement declined rapidly. Part of the fault lay with the party strategists, who had announced amid great publicity that Bucard's closing speech at the congress would be based on the theme "l'homme à abattre"—"the man to strike down." The Francistes gathered at the congress waited eagerly to learn the identity of the man to be beaten down: many must have expected Laval to be named. Despite Vichy's funding of the party. Laval had instructed the government apparatus to impede Franciste preparations for the congress in Paris, and the party encountered resistance from the local bureaucracy. The identity of "l'homme à abattre" was kept secret until the last day of the congress when Bucard revealed that the "man" was in reality the black market. The Francistes and other collaborationists were agreed that a rigorous suppression of the black market was a necessity, but the way in which Bucard made his pronunciamento had the effect of letting air out of a balloon. A movement such as Francisme, so dependent upon the reputation and allure of its leader, could ill afford a gaffe such as Bucard's "l'homme à abattre."[19]

The summer of 1943 also brought failure to the Francistes' unity-in-action plan. As in the case of Déat's abortive revolutionary front, the rock against which the wave of Bucard's plan for collaborationist unity broke was Jacques Doriot. The Franciste call for common action had at first found a positive reception in the PPF directory but was subsequently rejected by Doriot when he returned from the war in the East. Having promised the success of his plan to the Francistes at their party congress, Bucard suffered another setback to his per-

---

[19]Pierre Nicolle, *Cinquante mois d'armistice: Vichy, 2 juillet 1940–26 août 1944, journal d'un témoin,* 2 vols. (Paris: André Bonne, 1947), 2:209. See also Saint-Paulien, *Histoire de la collaboration,* pp. 216 and 408, and Jacomet, "Les chefs du francisme," p. 63. For discussion of the administrative impediments Vichy placed in the way of the Francistes and the PPF, see Schleier, telegram, July 27, 1943, T-120/4120/E071127.

sonal prestige. Even more serious shocks came to the Francistes from the evolution of the war. In July, Mussolini was voted out of office by the Fascist Grand Council. The end of Fascism in Italy was a blow to all French collaborationist movements, but especially to the Francistes, who had always looked to Italy for emotional and intellectual inspiration and who had received financial support from Mussolini before the war. By the end of the summer of 1943, Franciste prospects had dwindled from marginal at best to virtually hopeless. The hard-core collaborationists were being led by force of circumstances into the PPF and Darnand's Milice.[20]

By late 1943 and early 1944 the Francistes had become a lame-duck political movement. Their tendency toward precipitous acts became more pronounced with the growing frustration of political failure and irresponsibility. At the Café Floréal on the Boulevard Bonne-Nouvelle in Paris, a patron was stabbed on July 27, 1943 after refusing to buy a proffered copy of Le Franciste. A commotion resulted and a student was killed by a Franciste who seems to have escaped prosecution because of German influence on his behalf. Contingents of Francistes sometimes accompanied Miliciens and German police in tracking down members of the maquis in the Nièvre, although on other occasions Francistes and Miliciens clashed with members of the PPF and Francistes heckled Darnand during an Anti-Bolshevik Legion rally in June 1943 in Paris. Guiraud had charged the Milice with weakness because of its support of the Laval government. Perhaps Guiraud had forgotten that the Milice was an organ of the Vichy government, technically under the supervision of Laval.[21]

Early in July 1944, with Allied forces fast approaching Paris, Bucard was imprisoned after some of his bodyguards engaged in a shootout with French police who had come to arrest him on the charge of attempting to "appropriate" the contents of an apartment belonging to a Jewish jeweler. The police chased Bucard and several

[20]For a fuller discussion of the impact of Bucard's joint action proposal on the PPF, see below, Chap. 10.

[21]For descriptions of Franciste clashes with the Milice and the PPF, see Combats, the weekly newspaper of the Milice. "A chacun sa verité: Unité d'action en action" and "A chacun sa verité: Point final à une sotte querelle," June 19 and July 3, 1943, respectively. The incident of Café Floréal and the joint Franciste-Milice ventures against the Resistance were brought out by the prosecution during Bucard's trial; Procès Bucard, pp. 47–49; see also Crapouillot, 4 (1948), 269.

of his guards in their car until they reached the Franciste headquarters, where a volley of shots preceded the arrest. Claiming that Bucard was totally innocent, the Francistes angrily charged that he had been the victim of a plot, possibly by the government. Abetz ostentatiously visited him in the Santé prison, where he had been incarcerated, and several days thereafter was able to have him released. Bucard's brief stay in prison was his last significant political activity, if such it was, in occupied France. He was released in time to join the exodus of collaborationists in August, on their way to political exile in Germany.[22]

The energy that characterized the Franciste movement had been dissipated in fruitless quarrels because of the lack of opportunities for effective political action. Instead of attracting many Frenchmen, the purity of the Franciste fascist origins gave the movement too imitative an appearance. Most collaborationists joined the larger movements, less obviously inspired by foreign models. The Francistes might have been more successful as the paramilitary arm of another party with more competent political leadership and greater mass appeal. Buccard's allure was limited to a small segment of veterans and others with military traditions. More a soldier than a political leader, Bucard was not the man to build a mass following, and he failed to exercise control over the men close to him. The reputation of the Main bleu may have helped attract several hundred young displaced toughs, but it scared off those within the ranks of the more conservative middle classes, whose support was essential for a mass movement of the radical Right. Lacking a clearly defined social clientele, unable to escape the reputation of irresponsible ruffians, the Francistes were condemned to political marginality even within the limited ranks of the collaborationist camp.

[22]The account of Bucard's arrest is from Galtier-Boissière, *Journal,* pp. 244–245, and Bucard's liberation by the Germans, p. 247. See also Amédée Buissière, the police prefect in Paris at the time, in his deposition of October 8, 1951 in *France during the German Occupation,* 1:554. The Franciste version of the incident was elucidated in a letter to party militants written by André Cacheux, a member of the Bureau de la Fédération des Anciens Combattants Francistes, the Franciste veterans' organization, July 18, 1944. I am indebted to Jean Dufresne, who allowed me to see this unpublished letter from his personal archives.

8 Parlor Collaborators:
The Groupe Collaboration

Hitler has never lied to us, say the National Socialists, he has kept his promises.
Why should one suppose that he would lie only in external questions?
Has he not said: "I will hold to what I sign"?

Châteaubriant, *La gerbe des forces,* 1937

One of the paradoxes of the political situation in occupied France
was that the largest collaborationist movement never approached the
political importance of the RNP, PPF, or Milice. The Groupe Collaboration, founded in September 1940 by the essayist Alphonse de
Châteaubriant, was not in the strictest sense of the word a political
party. Committed to the promotion of Franco-German collaboration
in the sphere of culture, the Groupe Collaboration held public discussions of collaborationist themes, showed films produced in Axis
countries, and sponsored lectures by visiting Germans, including
many by Professor Grimm during his visits to France. Because it was
not considered a political party, the Groupe Collaboration was
allowed to pursue its activities in both zones of France, although local
government officials sometimes made things difficult for it. The
movement continued to grow during 1943, when all other collaborationist groups, with the exception of Darnand's Milice, were
losing strength.

Although the Groupe Collaboration was not considered a political
party and managed to maintain fairly good relations with the other
collaborationist movements, it did act in a political sense. By 1943 it
was asking the Germans for arms with which to defend its members
from attacks by the Resistance. The Groupe also sponsored a youth
movement, the Jeunesse de l'Europe Nouvelle (JEN), as militant as
the youth affiliates of the collaborationist parties and engaging in the
same types of activities. Many members of the Groupe Collaboration
were also affiliated with one or another of the collaborationist political parties. By 1943 the Groupe Collaboration claimed a membership

230

of over one hundred thousand, with some estimates running as high as two hundred thousand.[1]

Alphonse de Châteaubriant was descended from an old noble family in western France. Born in 1877, he was considerably older than the other leaders in the collaborationist camp. Having been deeply affected by his experience at the front during World War I, Châteaubriant returned after the war to a quiet life of writing on his country estate. There he searched for the causes of the events that had taken so heavy a toll on his and the succeeding generation. He found the soul of France in her Christian past. France and the West, he believed, had been undone by a progressive unfolding of materialism unchained in 1789 and climaxed by the Bolshevik Revolution. In the tradition of Joseph de Maistre and Louis de Bonald, Châteaubriant looked to the spiritual values of medieval Christendom for the salvation of twentieth-century France. In 1912 he had won the Prix Goncourt for his novel *Monsieur des Lourdines*. After the war he turned to nature. True spirituality, he wrote, was found in nature rather than the church and it was in the solitary communion with nature that man met God. Châteaubriant visited Germany in 1936 and returned deeply impressed. He found the Germans:

> Tanned, a dagger at the hip, eyes straight, militarily straight, body at attention, such are the men of the National Socialist Party, the guardians of the thought, of the Idea, the obscure servants of the new German principle brought forth by Hitler, and the living pillars of all German organization born of this thought. All the same, these men, beneath their tanned skins, all the same, like wolves, like foxes, like all species of nature which wear feathers or fur around the spark of their instinct.[2]

[1] In June 1942, Abetz estimated the membership of the Groupe Collaboration as 38,000, of whom 26,000 were in the northern zone. See Abetz, "Notiz für III; Betrifft: Groupe Collaboration," June 19, 1942, T-120/2346/487456-7. At the beginning of 1943, the vice president of the Groupe Collaboration gave a figure of 100,000; the following year British intelligence suggested 200,000. See, respectively, Schleier, "Aufzeichnung für Herrn Botschafter Abetz, Betrifft: Besprechung mit Jean Weiland, Generalsekretär der Groupe Collaboration am 19.1.1943 um 17:30," January 19, 1943, T-120/3814H/E043100, and *French Basic Handbook*, p. 152. For Groupe Collaboration requests for German arms, see Schleier, Bericht, Paris an Zweigstelle Vichy, no. 2263, August 26, 1943, T-120/3546/E022157.

[2] Alphonse de Châteaubriant, *La gerbe des forces* (Paris: Bernard Grasset, 1937), p. 29.

National Socialism, according to Châteaubriant, had revived the energies of the German people after the defeat of 1918 and the subsequent disasters of inflation and depression. Most important to Châteaubriant was his belief that National Socialism offered to the peoples of the West a last chance to organize a society based upon communitarian ideals in which man was once again in harmony with the spiritual forces of nature. He was not the only French apostle of nature to be attracted by National Socialism. The writer Jean Giono flirted with it and some of Giono's younger disciples later found their way into the French unit of the Waffen-SS.

Totally ignoring the neopaganism that was an important part of the Nazi movement, Châteaubriant viewed the new German phenomenon as entirely within the tradition of nineteen centuries of Christian spiritualism. In the words of Paul Sérant, he allowed himself to become convinced by symbolism rather than discursive reasoning. His interest in nature and belief in the educative role of natural elites were combined in a panegyric to Hitler and National Socialism entitled *La gerbe des forces,* which appeared in France in 1937, the year after his visit to Germany. In the book, Châteaubriant cited Hitler's repeated professions of friendship for France as proof that Nazi Germany posed France no threat. The appearance of *La gerbe des forces* caused a scandal in France but it established its author as one of the leaders in the pro-German camp during the interwar years and gave his name a credibility in German circles that was to prove helpful after the 1940 armistice. [3]

In the days following the armistice, when Abetz wished to create a pro-German press in France, he turned to Châteaubriant. Abetz's staff created a newspaper which it called *La Gerbe* and confided its directorship to Châteaubriant. A weekly, the paper was oriented toward literary circles and its staff included several figures prominent in them. Bernard Faÿ, who was to cross swords with Déat on the issue of Freemasonry, wrote for it as did Abel Bonnard, a collaborationist who in 1942 became Vichy's education minister, and Jacques Boulenger, an anti-English journalist; and after 1941 Camille Fégy served as editor-in-chief. The business manager in

---

[3]Despite a growing interest in the French collaboration in recent years, Châteaubriant has received surprisingly little study. See Sérant, pp. 115–122 and passim.

1940 was Marc Augier, who had been active in the French youth hostel movement prior to the war and later became the editor of *Le Combattant Européen*, the newspaper of the Anti-Bolshevik Legion. An early assessment of *La Gerbe's* readership included 35,000 members of Augier's youth movement, the Centre Laïc des Auberges de la Jeunesse (a lay splinter group of the Catholic youth hostel movement founded by Marc Sangnier in 1930) and an unspecified number of peasants in Jacques Leroy-Ladurie's Union des Syndicats Agricoles. Although the embassy staff and the Propagandastaffel aided as many pro-German publications and organizations as possible during the summer of 1940, *La Gerbe* was the only newspaper actually created by the German officials in France during the weeks immediately following the armistice.[4]

The Groupe Collaboration was formed on September 24, 1940 as a direct response by Châteaubriant and his associates to what they saw as a need to press for collaboration in all fields. From the start, the Groupe's leaders stressed that their movement was not a political party with a desire to challenge any of the established parties for supremacy in occupied France. Members of other parties were often invited to attend the various lectures, discussions, and film showings staged by the Groupe. Châteaubriant's organization built upon a longstanding tradition of Franco-German reconciliation of centrist and moderate political figures including Gambetta, Jaurès, Briand, and Laval in France. It also laid claim to the political legacy of financial and industrial capitalist collaboration with Germany represented by former premier Joseph Caillaux. Although new in 1940, the Groupe Collaboration had origins in interwar days. Many of its

[4]This assertion was made by Rudolf Rahn, a counselor in the German embassy during the summer of 1940; Tribunal Général de Governement Militaire pour la Zone Française d'Occupation en Allemagne, Interrogatoire de Botschafter Rahn, February 28, 1947, CDJC document XCVI, 93. Rahn and other Germans were questioned by French officials investigating war crimes in their zone of Germany after the war. For the discussion of the readership of *La Gerbe,* see Abetz, still Vertreter des Auswärtigen Amts bei dem Militärbefehlshaber in Frankreich, Paris, July 15, 1940, report to German Foreign Ministry, in *Akten zur deutschen Auswärtigen Politik*, D, X, p. 178. For the staff of *La Gerbe* in 1940, see Picot, Anlage 45 zum Schreiben des Chefs der Sicherheitspolizei und des SD vom 4 d. M., December 30, 1940, An der Herrn Reichsaussenminister, T-120/475/229317. This report was a German translation of a paper prepared for the French Armistice Commission delegation at Wiesbaden and obtained by agents of the German SD.

more influential members, including Châteaubriant himself, had been active in the prewar Comité France-Allemagne, the Franco-German reconciliation committee established in 1935. The Comité France-Allemagne was headed at the outset by Georges Scapini, a veteran blinded in the 1914–1918 war, who under Vichy became a French representative for prisoners of war to Berlin. It had numbered in its ranks Fernand de Brinon and Jacques Schweizer, the latter the future leader of the Groupe Collaboration's youth affiliate, the JEN. Among the Germans prominent in the prewar organization were Fritz Bran, a Foreign Ministry official who later supported the JEN, and Abetz. The Comité France-Allemagne engaged in cultural activities, sponsoring youth tours to Germany and many of the types of events later promoted by the Groupe Collaboration.

Among the honorary patrons of Châteaubriant's Groupe were the physicist Georges Claude, who invented liquid air; Abel Bonnard and Abel Hermant from the world of letters; and Cardinal Baudrillart, along with Bonnard and Hermant a member of the Académie Française.[5] Routine matters for the Groupe Collaboration were managed by Jean Weiland, its director-general. Châteaubriant was generally content to write his articles for *La Gerbe* and other newspapers and frequent the social circle of salon parties and lectures. In the spring of 1943 the organization, which had already been operating legally for some time in the southern zone, was allowed by the Vichy government to establish a branch office in the provisional capital, subordinated to the movement's main headquarters in Paris. With local organizations throughout France, the Groupe Collaboration was less centralized than were the Ultra political parties. As more local organizations were set up in 1943, the lines of command became thinner, allowing more autonomy for the local groups.[6]

Of all the collaborationist movements in occupied France, the Groupe, as the names of the members of its committee of patrons suggest, carried the most social and intellectual prestige. The

---

[5] *French Basic Handbook,* pp. 151–152, has a brief discussion of the origins and organizational structure of the Groupe Collaboration. For the history and activities of the Comité France-Allemagne, see Jacques Schweizer, "Le Dialogue Franco-Allemand," speech of May 17, 1941, reprinted in Schweizer, *De France-Allemagne à France Europe* (Paris: JEN, 1943), pp. 10–17.

[6] *French Basic Handbook,* pp. 151–152.

Groupe's membership was drawn from urban middle and upper middle classes, with large numbers of professionals and white-collar people. They tended to be older and better educated than the members of the other collaborationist groups. At the outset the Groupe Collaboration was oriented toward propaganda activities in which prosperous and established "bourgeois" types might participate without soiling their hands, effectuating a manner of collaboration quite different from that of a Darnand. It was a polite collaborationism, centered largely in the salons and parlors of the affluent.

As the war continued, the attacks of the Resistance failed to differentiate between "polite" and "dirty-handed" collaboration, and the Groupe was forced into a more militant position in which it increasingly assumed the characteristics of a political party. These pressures were intensified by its youth affiliate, the JEN, which took a tougher collaborationist stand and pressed the parent organization to do the same. The Groupe Collaboration was also steered toward more political action by members of the other parties, notably the PPF, who infiltrated its ranks. Early in 1943, Weiland felt compelled to remove the southern zone Groupe Collaboration leader partly for having failed to give a proper accounting of the movement's funds but also for having introduced too many PPF members into the Groupe. The offending official had built up several local Groupe Collaboration sections exclusively of PPF personnel, and Weiland objected to his movement's being based too heavily on one political party. Weiland also found leaks of information to the Resistance. The case was a microcosm of the difficulties of the collaborationist factions in general: corruption, rivalry, and subversion by the Resistance and competing collaborationist groups.[7]

The most openly political segment of the Groupe Collaboration was the JEN, its only affiliated subsidiary formation. JEN activities were hardly distinguishable from those of the youth auxiliaries of the other collaborationist movements. The creation of the JEN was a lengthy process, beginning in May 1941 with a speech delivered by Jacques

---

[7]Schleier, Paris, January 19, 1943, letter to Diehl, German Foreign Ministry, Berlin, T-120/3814H/E043103-5. A growing fear of Resistance attacks was expressed during the summer of 1943 by members of the Groupe Collaboration in Lyons. See Kontrollinspektion der DWStK, Kontrollabteilung Az. 12, no. 2030/43g, "Meldungen," Bourges, August 19, 1943, T-77/842/5585851.

Schweizer in Paris and culminating in its establishment in both zones in June 1942. A small number of young men, including Schweizer and Marc Augier, launched the JEN and Schweizer quickly was recognized as its leader. A lawyer by profession and a supporter of Franco-German reconciliation prior to the war, Schweizer had attended several Nuremberg party congresses and had become acquainted with Abetz. He had also been a member of the Jeunesses Patriotes. Others in the JEN had also come from the Jeunesses Patriotes, but many of its members were too young to have engaged in political activity before the war.[8]

The social composition of the JEN resembled that of its parent organization. Many of its members were students. Few had seen action in the campaign of 1939–1940: the JEN was no more oriented toward war veterans than its parent organization, which engaged proportionately fewer veterans of World War I than the Milice or the Francistes. Like the other youth movements of the collaboration, the JEN adopted a runic symbol and its members wore uniforms. Because it remained aloof from the rivalries and mutual recriminations among the other youth groups, it was able to retain good relations with all of them. It developed no ties with the Vichyite youth organizations, the Chantiers de la Jeunesse and the Compagnons de France, which existed in the southern zone and gradually turned anti-German. At the peak of its influence in 1943, the JEN claimed about four thousand members in all of France, of whom about five hundred were in Paris. From the JEN some, including Augier, joined the Anti-Bolshevik Legion. Others found their way into the NSKK (National Sozialistische Kraftfahrzeugkorps, National Socialist Trucking Corps), a motorized transport section of the German armed forces opened to French volunteers in 1942. The Waffen-SS attracted still others and a number of JEN members volunteered to join the French labor force working in Germany. Speaking at a regional JEN congress held in January 1944 at Vichy, Schweizer declared that to his organization the National Revolution meant a "European" France and National Socialism.[9]

[8] Much of the information concerning the JEN was furnished me during an interview with Jacques Schweizer, June 28, 1974.

[9] See Schweizer's speeches, "Les Jeunes de l'Europe Nouvelle et la Révolution Nationale," at the second JEN National Congress, Paris, June 14, 1943 and "Vers l'Union de la Jeunesse Française," at the JEN Regional Congress, Vichy, January 9,

Although the JEN ideologically resembled the other collaborationist youth movements, its tactics were more moderate. Schweizer made clear JEN opposition to Jews and Freemasons but he also told his supporters that their actions were to be open and educative rather than hidden and marked by intrigue. He criticized the secret chalking of slogans on walls and the denunciations of Jews listening clandestinely to Radio London. JEN activity, together with that of its parent organization, was to remain on the high-minded level of propaganda. With the other leaders of the collaboration, the JEN chieftain called for an involved youth, a *jeunesse engagée*: "Youth is not a stage of life in which one prepares for future action. Avoid those who preach patience and resignation to you. Do not listen to those who speak to you of experience: we have already paid for relying on that [the 1940 disaster is meant]. . . . Think European."[10]

By 1944 the JEN had acquired the rudimentary organs of a totalitarian movement: protection squads to serve as guards at Groupe Collaboration and JEN meetings, Cadets de JEN for children aged eleven to fourteen, an affiliate that never really developed, and a women's auxiliary. The story of a young woman of seventeen who joined the JEN *section féminine* was representative. A university student, she had been idled by the wartime shutdown of the universities in Paris. With most conventional social outlets closed by rigorous occupation strictures, she and other young people turned to the collaborationist groups as a vehicle for social activity. This young woman came from a Parisian merchant family and her father was a Pétainist in 1942 when she joined the JEN. There she attended weekly meetings and saw films, in addition to helping to nurse the wounded veterans of the Anti-Bolshevik Legion returning from the Russian front. For a young person of relatively comfortable circumstances, the JEN offered an opportunity for social life in a collaborationist direction that was neither as risky nor as scandalous as some of the other Ultra youth movements.[11]

1944; reprinted in Schweizer, *La Jeunesse Française est une Jeunesse Européene* (Paris: JEN, 1944), pp. 20 and 32, respectively. A list of JEN activities for March and April 1943, a fairly representative period, is provided in the confidential JEN organ *Les Jeunes de l'Europe Nouvelle*, no. 6 (April 1943), BDIC Q pièce 4282.

[10]Schweizer, "Vers l'Union de la Jeunesse Européene," speech of November 8, 1942, in *De France-Allemagne*, p. 27. See also ibid., p. 8.

[11]Author's interview with Odette Paineau, July 25, 1974. On the JEN affiliates, see *Les Jeunes de l'Europe Nouvelle*, no. 10 (January 1944), BDIC Q pièce 4282.

Despite JEN pressure for more narrowly political activities, the Groupe Collaboration maintained the primacy of its literary interests and a certain tension always remained. By 1943 and early 1944, the JEN often acted independently of the more timorous Groupe. Even in its more restricted activities, the parent organization ran into resistance from local government officials, despite having received official blessings from Vichy when Abel Bonnard became education minister.

Leaders of the Groupe complained repeatedly to the Germans of harassment by Vichy officials. Laval made promises of support but refused even to meet with the Groupe's delegate to the southern zone. Other difficulties encountered by the Groupe Collaboration included a preliminary rejection of a request to be allowed to establish an office in Vichy. The turndown came from the office of Admiral Platon, known to be a partisan of the PPF. Despite its pretensions to nonpolitical status, the Groupe Collaboration was obviously not spared the effects of the various rivalries within the collaborationist camp. Krug von Nidda, the German counsel in Vichy, was involved when Vichy impeded lectures by Claude and other Groupe speakers. A result of the government harassment was the erosion of the support for Laval within the Groupe. Most of the members continued to support him, but an active minority headed by General Delegates de Flotte and Carrette turned against him. Both men had been named to their posts by Weiland, who remained a supporter of Laval. Vichy's policy of harassment succeeded in engendering a major rift within the Groupe Collaboration, although the minority faction remained in the organization.[12]

In addition to its difficulties with the Vichy authorities and its occasional problems with other collaborationist factions, the Groupe Collaboration also encountered trouble with the Germans. In June 1942 the indefatigable Georges Claude was once more the center of a dispute. He was to make a public speech in Dijon but was opposed by the director of the German Institute there, who feared that the Germanophobic sentiment of the local population would turn the talk into a fiasco. It went on as scheduled and Claude vindicated himself by filling Dijon's largest auditorium with a friendly crowd. Ambas-

[12]Krug von Nidda, Zweigstelle der deutschen Botschaft in Vichy, letter to German embassy, Paris, February 4, 1943, T-120/2335/486972-3.

sador Abetz added his voice to those of the Groupe in asking for more positive gestures by the Germans in the interest of collaboration. In Lyons and Marseilles, the leaders of the Groupe were criticized by German officials who contended that they lacked the respect of the French people and were therefore unsuited to represent the ideal of collaboration. Members of the Groupe in Vichy provided the Germans with inaccurate descriptions of leading French political and business personalities, inadvertently endangering the cause of collaboration. A subsequent German complaint demonstrates the way in which all collaborationist groups were regarded by the occupation authorities. Their value was in direct proportion to the quantity and reliability of the intelligence that they could furnish on people and conditions in France.[13]

Despite occasional disputes with the Germans, however, the Groupe found general support from the embassy in Paris, facilitated by Abetz. A series of letters exchanged in 1943 between Weiland and Schleier reflected the increased activity of the Groupe and its growing need for funds. Schleier had raised the German subsidy for the first quarter of 1943 from 300,000 to 450,000 francs and Weiland requested that the payment for the period beginning July be raised to 500,000 francs. The additional money was paid, authorized by Schleier. Apparently the subsidy for the last quarter of 1943 was again set at 300,000 francs, for once more Weiland wrote to Schleier, requesting this time 450,000 francs for the first quarter of 1944. According to Weiland, the Paris office alone employed fifteen officials costing the movement 150,000 francs per month. Much of this expense, he told Schleier, could be covered by contributions from members, but the Groupe needed German financial aid to extend its propaganda activities outside Paris. In late 1943 and early 1944, when most of the other collaborationist movements were trying desperately to retain their membership, dwindling because of the altered course of the war, the Groupe Collaboration was contemplating expansion of its membership and its activities. The funds secured from

---

[13]Dr. Kuntz, Handelspolitisch Abteilung, German Foreign Ministry, "Aufzeichnung für Herrn Gesandten Rahn," Paris, October 27, 1942, T-120/3814H/E032096. For the events surrounding Claude's lecture in Dijon, see Abetz, "Notiz für III," the Cultural Affairs Bureau of the Foreign Ministry, Paris, June 19, 1942, T-120/2346/487456-7.

Schleier and raised by its own efforts were supplemented with financial backing from Vichy after Laval's return to the government, when Education Minister Bonnard was able to channel money from his ministry to the Groupe. The ambiguities in Vichy's policies toward the collaborationists were shown nowhere more clearly than in its treatment of Châteaubriant's movement.[14]

Increased German aid and permission to establish an office in Vichy strengthened the Groupe Collaboration in 1943. The news of the German defeat at Stalingrad also helped the organization as more middle-class Frenchmen began to feel threatened by Communism at home and abroad. Grimm was told by the head of the Groupe in Bordeaux that a decline in membership after the Allied landings in North Africa had been reversed with the German defeat at Stalingrad. The new recruits, described by Grimm as "middle class," brought the Bordeaux contingent up to two thousand. According to Grimm, the French had a clear perception of the danger presented by the Soviet Union but were more difficult to rouse against the Americans. He was especially pleased with his receptions in Angoulême, Royan, and Bordeaux.[15]

In the southern zone, relative to the other collaborationist factions the Group held its own. Figures for the Bouches-du-Rhône department in 1942 showed approximately 600 in the Groupe Collaboration, 100 Francistes, and 1,700 in the PPF. By March 31, 1943, these figures had shifted to 800, 150, and 1,240, respectively, showing increases in the Groupe Collaboration and Francistes by a third and a half respectively. The PPF, in contrast, lost more than a quarter of its members during this period, which saw the demoralization that followed the failure of the party to take power in November 1942. In Montpellier the figures for the Groupe Collaboration were put at roughly 150, whereas the Francistes attracted 25 and the PPF 250. Corresponding figures for Nice and Toulouse were 400, 50, 4,000

[14]Interview with Schweizer, June 28, 1974. For the Weiland-Schleier correspondence on the subject of German financial support, see Weiland, letter to Schleier, June 28, 1943; Schleier, "Answeisung für die Kasse," September 27, 1943; and Weiland, Letter to Schleier, December 21, 1943; T-120/2335/487006, 3814H/E043132, respectively, and the letter of December, microfilmed in two places: T-120/2335/486971 and T-120/3814H/E043098.

[15]For Bordeaux and the northern zone, Grimm, Bericht, March 3, 1943, T-120/6442H/E481208.

and 200, 50, 400 respectively, showing the well-known strength of the PPF in Nice. In each case, the Groupe Collaboration fell somewhere between the PPF and the much smaller Francistes. The numbers are difficult to assess in that members of the Groupe sometimes also joined the (more properly speaking) political parties. They do reveal substantial collaborationist activity in the metropolitan areas of the southern zone, despite German complaints that they were too small. [16]

Of all the Ultra factions during the occupation years, the Groupe Collaboration was least characterized by a youthful revolt against gerontocracy, which explains the tension between it and its youth affiliate. Less openly fascist than the other Ultra movements at the outset, the Groupe, like many of the men of Vichy, mainly sought German protection for the existing French social order and was little concerned with flags, uniforms, and single parties. The increase in its strength in 1943, when most collaborationist factions were losing members, was a white-collar flight from the growing imminence of a Resistance victory. By 1943, however, the growing polarization of French political life obliged the Groupe Collaboration to identify itself ever more closely with the Germans, whose National Socialist ideals and practices it was increasingly constrained to adopt.

Growing Resistance activity, including violence against members of the Groupe Collaboration, led in 1943 to the creation of a protection squad and requests were made to the Germans for arms. The members of the protection squads were drawn from the JEN and were to serve as guards at all offices and meetings for the personal security of the members of the parent organization. The squads were estimated in 1944 to number no more than 400 men, some of whom were armed, and they functioned only in the southern zone. Even after having occupied all of France in 1942, the Germans maintained very careful scrutiny over the distribution of arms to the French in the northern zone and allowed Vichy a freer hand in the south. Attacks against members of the Groupe Collaboration resulted largely from suspicions in the Resistance that members of the Groupe were serving the Germans as informers. By the time of the Liberation,

[16]For the discussion of the Groupe Collaboration in the southern zone, see Spiegel, Deutsches Generalkonsulat Marseille, Bericht Nr. 167, April 8, 1943, T-120/3551/E022817-8.

most of the older, more cautious members of the Groupe were trying to regain the anonymity they hoped would enable them to survive the postwar period. Many of the younger more militant members of the JEN and the protection squads continued the battle along with other collaborationist groups, notably the PPF, Milice, and Francistes, or joined German military and paramilitary formations.[17]

Because the Groupe Collaboration did not function exactly as a political party and never developed the tightly structured organization of movements such as the PPF, it was never a threat in terms of assuming power in France. The JEN by itself posed no serious threat, but in alliance with the other collaborationist organizations it was able to make its presence felt. The impact of the Groupe Collaboration, however, was made in lobbying and propaganda. By their participation, well-known literary men such as Châteaubriant and Bonnard and scientists such as Claude lent prestige to the cause of collaboration. The Groupe compromised many older and well-established middle-class French who might have refrained from involvement with the less refined collaborationist parties. It also opened channels of information to the Germans that they might not otherwise have had. The arrest of collaborators in North Africa in the spring of 1943 by the Gaullists made the members of the Groupe painfully aware of the fate awaiting them in the event of Allied victory. Having placed their lives on the line, they felt entitled to better treatment than they got from Vichy in 1943 and 1944. Like the other collaborationists they argued that a true National Revolution could be made only with new personnel in the government and although they refrained from openly attacking Laval, their inference was clear. The political position of the Groupe Collaboration, despite its pretensions to nonpolitical status, was summed up in a memorandum prepared in 1943: "German National Socialist doctrine, contrary to the opinions of persons reputed to be informed, seems in the

[17]On the subject of the protection squads, see Robert Despeux, "Groupe de protection," Les Jeunes de l'Europe Nouvelle, no. 6 (April 1943); and OSS, "French Pro-Fascist Groups," p. 33. For Groupe Collaboration requests for arms and German reactions to such requests, see respectively Ernest Fornairon, secretary-general of the Groupe Collaboration, letter to Von Bose, German embassy, November 3, 1943, T-120/2335/487004 and Schleier, telegram no. 2263, August 26, 1943, from German embassy, Paris, to consular office, Vichy, T-120/3546/E022157.

present circumstances to be the right kind of political system, and the revolutionary French elements belonging to the Groupe Collaboration think that it holds the solution."[18]

More than any of its rivals, the Groupe Collaboration was inspired by a positive interest in Germany. What it sought in Germany, however, were answers to French problems. Economically comfortable and dilettantish in their politics, the members of the Groupe hoped that German domination would more effectively protect them from Communism than the parliamentary Republic had been able to. Few within the Groupe Collaboration paid much attention to the mystical eulogies of Hitler poured forth from the pen of Châteaubriant. The members of the Groupe wanted the excitement yet also the security that fascism seemed to offer. Groupe activities provided a social outlet for businessmen and professionals in the same way that the JEN and other Ultra youth organizations did for the middle-class young. More an association of fellow travelers than an independent political movement, the Groupe nonetheless contributed to the demoralization produced by the collaborationist camp in France. It satisfied the voyeurs rather than the participants in the wartime French fascist experience.

[18]"Note sur les moyens politiques propres à assurer la rénovation de la France en vue de lui permettre de contribuer à l'édification de la Nouvelle Europe," no author, no date, but written most certainly during the first half of 1943, T-120/3814H/ E043108-13.

9 Military Collaborators:
The French in German Uniforms

The freedom allowed the various French parties in propaganda, in recruiting legionaries, and in organizing the Legion, and the activity of the party leaders within the legion have proven harmful. Recruits join . . . solidly committed to support their party leaders and spread their views. Splits within the legion have followed immediately from this.
                    —Jean Mayol de Lupé, Chaplain of the Anti-Bolshevik Legion

I am enough of a child to want a National Socialist France.
                    —Philippe Merlin, French volunteer in the Waffen-SS

The increasing futility of their political activities in France, especially after the failure of the PPF bid for power in 1942, led many of the more activist French collaborationists to express their political faith as soldiers in German uniforms on the Eastern front. Most of them fought at the Russian front or against local partisans behind it. Some enlisted as individuals in the German army and navy. These included Alsatians and Lorrainers whose home departments had been annexed to the Reich after 1940. Others volunteered for the German NSKK or the antiaircraft defense units organized by the Vichy government.

The most significant military formations with respect to the political development of the collaborationist camp in France were the Anti-Bolshevik Legion and the French units of the Waffen-SS organized after 1943. Together they recruited about ten thousand Frenchmen, many of whom were killed along the Eastern front during the Soviet offensives of 1944 and 1945. Some of the last defenders of the remains of the Reich chancellery after even the suicide of Hitler were French SS fighters.

A variety of factors induced young Frenchmen to risk their lives in combat against the Soviet Union. Fear of the Bolshevization of Europe in the event of a Soviet victory was paramount. Some volunteers in the Waffen-SS saw participation in the German war effort as the best way to forge real Franco-German collaboration. Many were militants frustrated by the unending internecine strife within the collaborationist camp and their inability to achieve significant political success at home. Doriot and Pierre Clémenti were the two collaborationist party leaders who hoped that their service in the Anti-Bolshevik Legion would win them German support against their rivals at home and Laval in Vichy. The Waffen-SS attracted some who were enchanted with Nietzschean heroism and adolescent types who wanted to prove they could equal the best of the German troops they had seen parade in victory in 1940. Still others were lured by the exotic-sounding names of the battlefields they read about in the French press. In the dreary life of occupied France, with curfews and growing shortages of food and other necessities, the German crusade in the East offered an escape with one's basic physical needs assured. Career military men demobilized after the defeat of 1940 or the dissolution of the Armistice Army in 1942 sometimes enlisted in the Anti-Bolshevik Legion. Some of the first volunteers in the legion during the summer of 1941 expected their projected military service would comprise little more than a victory parade through the streets of Moscow or Leningrad. Their successors after 1942 and those who joined the Waffen-SS in 1943 knew better.

The creation of the Anti-Bolshevik Legion followed the German invasion of the Soviet Union by several weeks. Although the early legion was a joint venture of many collaborationist groups, the parties recruited for it separately and tension in it was ever present. During its first year the legion was wracked with dissension as the various Ultra organizations fought to control it and turn it into a party armed force, possibly to be thrown into the balance against Vichy. The launching of the legion was undertaken by Déat, Bucard, and Costantini, in addition to Doriot and Deloncle, and was warmly supported by Ambassador Abetz. Abetz suggested to Berlin a French volunteer force of 30,000 to include several pilots in an air wing, which pleased the former flying ace Costantini, who wanted to form an air corps within the legion. Abetz had everything to gain by the establishment of a large legion, which served his own ambitions for increased influence in Berlin. Hitler's opinion of the French as warriors, however, was notoriously low and his generals had no interest in sharing anticipated victory parades in Russia with foreigners. They were especially loathe to accept help from the recently defeated French, for whom they shared their Führer's contempt and mistrust. Abetz was instructed to see that the new legion be limited to 15,000 volunteers.[1]

The summer and early autumn of 1941 were devoted to intensive recruiting campaigns by the various Ultra factions, each of which promised wildly exaggerated numbers of party members for volunteer service in Russia. The central committee was headed by Deloncle, perhaps because of the influence of Admiral Darlan. A subordinate committee was formed to supervise recruitment in the southern zone and was headed by Simon Sabiani, the PPF potentate at Marseilles. The composition of the two committees reflected the uncomfortable alliance of the Ultras; especially uneasy were the Doriotists, who jockeyed for influence with the supporters of Déat and Deloncle. A third committee, entitled "Comité d'Honneur," grouped together several luminaries of the French academic and literary world who served as patrons of the legion to enhance its respectability. They included de Brinon, Cardinal Baudrillart, Abel Bonnard, Abel Hermant, and Maurice Donnay of the French Academy, as well as Georges Claude, Auguste Lumière, Horace de Carbuccia, Jean Luchaire, and Châteaubriant from the scientific and journalistic community.

The prestige lent by the committee of honorary members was needed because, despite an intensive propaganda campaign appealing to anti-Communist and Christian crusading traditions in France, recruiting was difficult. With German military patrols coursing through the streets of Paris and three-fifths of France, the beginnings of mass arrests and execution of hostages, and the annexation of Alsace and Lorraine, it was difficult for the collaborationists to

---

[1]Abetz, telegram to Foreign Ministry, July 6, 1941, in *Akten zur deutschen Auswärtigen Politik*, D, XIII, pp. 81–82 and 82, n. 8. See also Abetz, "Notiz für Herrn Botschafter Ritter," Foreign Ministry, July 26, 1942, T-120/926/297241-2. Hitler's putting Germany first and using "Europe" as a smokescreen is discussed by Jäckel, p. 181. The origins of the Anti-Bolshevik Legion were studied by Owen Anthony Davey, "The Origins of the *Légion des Volontaires Français contre le Bolchévisme*," *Journal of Contemporary History*, 6 (October 1971), 29–45, and also in Jacques Delarue, *Trafics et crimes sous l'occupation* (Paris: Livre de Poche, 1972 [originally Fayard, 1968]), pp. 147ff., and Bourget, 1:291–322. Bourget's chapter, entitled "Les mercenaires de la L.V.F.," oversimplifies the motivations of many of the volunteers.

persuade many of their compatriots that the Soviets represented a greater menace than the Germans to France. On July 18, a mass recruiting rally was staged by the Ultra parties at the Vélodrome d'hiver in Paris. It attracted approximately 8,000 of the committed and the curious who listened to one collaborationist leader after another preach the necessity of a French presence in the "European" crusade against the Soviets. The scene there was described in a report by a police observer, published in Pierre Bourget's *Histoires secrètes de l'occupation de Paris:*

> The Vélodrome d'hiver was far from full. The crowd could be estimated at about eight thousand persons, a fourth of whom were women.
>
> The ground floor, containing about four thousand persons, was reserved for the associations which had organized the meeting, as follows:
> —Costantini's Ligue française;
> —Clémenti's Parti National Collectiviste Français;
> —E. Deloncle's MSR and M. Déat's RNP united for the occasion [*sic*: The PPF is not listed as an organizer].
>
> Costantini appeared to have collected a few dozen partisans, Clémenti four hundred, the PPF five hundred to six hundred. The rest belonged to the MSR or the RNP.
>
> The upper floors were filled mainly with simple sympathizers or the curious. Many did not even applaud any of the speakers.
>
> The speeches delivered were all conceived on the same model, which involved pointing out the grandeur of the present hour and the need for France, if she wished to figure honorably in the Europe of tomorrow, to take part now with Germany in her struggle against Bolshevism.
>
> Clementi's speech, because of the obscurity of the speaker, was sparsely applauded.
>
> Costantini gained more success by attacking the Jews and asking for executions.
>
> He finally announced that he would join the legion's air corps.
>
> M. Déat produced a great impression on the audience.
>
> He roused applause at the same time for the Marshal, who had given his approval to the formation of the new legion, and for Chancellor Hitler, who equally gave it his support.
>
> After having asked for the reawakening of the spirit of sacrifice in France, he ended by stating his belief that if the government did not take the necessary steps, he and his supporters would know how to replace it on their own.

M. Déat was applauded vigorously but his name was not acclaimed, which seems to indicate that he does not enjoy any great personal prestige among his supporters.

Doriot showed himself by far the better speaker.

He also referred to the Marshal but without any threat.

It should be borne in mind that he has declared himself united with the other associations only for the limited end of forming the new legion.

He showed the evils of Bolshevism and mocked those petty bourgiois, industrialists, even members of the clergy, who, despite all, wished for the victory of Stalin.

One single experience of twenty-four hours of the Soviet regime would make them change their opinion, he said.

With a mediocre speech Eugène Deloncle finished the series of orations.

After recalling his twenty-three months of captivity [for his prewar *Cagoulard* activities], which gave him the right to be at the head of the struggle against Bolshevism, he endeavored to be technical. He read several passages from the legion's statutes, demanded from the government the means of power to prevent this legion from being a laughingstock, and announced the sending to Vichy of Generals Lavigne-Delville and Hassler, who will negotiate with the government the technical questions concerning recruitment and the formation of the legion.

His speech was equally vigorously applauded by the audience. The partisans of the MSR and in particular the militia men cried, "Deloncle," rising and raising their arms. The meeting closed with some sort of music. Some youngsters called out, "the *Marseillaise!*" but no one listened to them and the crowd dispersed. [To play the *Marseillaise* at a public meeting under the occupation, special German authorization was needed in the northern zone].[2]

Despite the publicity campaign, the legion attracted no more than 3,000 by October 1941. Shops and apartments belonging to Jews in France were requisitioned for use as recruiting centers, and the legion's central office in Paris was established in the former offices of Intourist, the Soviet travel agency. Recruits were to be between ages eighteen and forty with an upper limit of fifty for officers. Volunteers

[2]Renseignements Généraux, report, August 21, 1941, quoted in Bourget, 1:301–303. See also Davey, pp. 33–34.

leaving civilian jobs were assured that they would find their jobs still available upon completion of their service, and the unemployed were especially encouraged to volunteer. Jews were not allowed in the legion. Pay and rank were equivalent to the regular French army and volunteers were promised that they would wear French uniforms. The Germans later insisted that they wear German *feldgrau* with the name "France" lettered on a tricolored badge on the right sleeve.

Finding volunteers was not the only problem faced by the collaborationists; they also needed a qualified military man to head the new legion. On July 8, Déat's newspaper. *L'Œuvre,* announced that it was to be commanded by General Hassler, an Alsatian to whom the post had been offered. When the article appeared Hassler had not yet accepted. He resented being publicly coerced into taking a post about which he was dubious anyway. Denouncing German annexation of his native Alsace, Hassler recalled that members of his family were being held in German prisoner-of-war camps. He rejected the offer. The leadership of the new legion went instead to Colonel Roger Henri Labonne, a career officer whose military activity had consisted of desk jobs, the last as military attaché in Turkey. Labonne, described later as "incapable" by de Brinon, was quickly replaced by another military career man, Colonel Edgar Puaud.[3]

A sequence of events during the late summer and early autumn of 1941 boded ill for the legion's future. On August 27 the first contingent of volunteers was inducted at the Borgnis-Desbordes barracks, an old installation in Versailles allotted to the legion by the Germans. French and German dignitaries present included Laval and Déat who were wounded in the assassination attempt by Paul Colette precipitating the break between Déat and Deloncle. The split within the RNP weakened the cohesion of the Anti-Bolshevik Legion and opened a power vacuum there, filled by supporters of Doriot. On the day after the assassination attempt, 1,679 volunteers were examined by German doctors for fitness to serve in the Wehrmacht, in which

[3] De Brinon's statement is taken from his memoirs published posthumously in *Europe-Amérique,* November 24, 1948, and quoted in Galtier-Boissière, *Crapouillot,* 4 (1948), 271, n. 1. See also Milton Dank, *The French against the French: Collaboration and Resistance* (Philadelphia and New York: Lippincott, 1974), p. 191. For Déat's attempt to push Hassler into the command of the legion and the refusal of the latter to accept it, see Delarue, pp. 149–152. Figures for the early enlistments are discussed at length in Davey, p. 37.

the legion was to become a unit. Eight hundred were rejected for medical reasons and approximately 70 percent of these for bad teeth. This was one of the ways in which Hitler's instruction to keep the legion small was implemented.[4]

At the same time, the volunteers learned that they were to fight in German rather than French uniforms, the rationale being that as long as France was not at war with the Soviet Union, soldiers caught in French uniforms by the Russians could be shot as irregulars. This issue evoked substantial disagreement between Germans and French, many of whom would fight only in the uniform of their own country. The Germans, however, held firm. Difficulties notwithstanding, a contingent of 800 men, Doriot included, left Paris on September 4 for training in Germany. The backers of the legion had promised 30,000 men but had delivered only 1,500. These volunteers were grouped into one regiment with two battalions and they were given neither artillery nor other heavy weapons. The German military command in France forbade any public ceremonies or demonstrations accompanying the departure of the legionaries. At the end of September, a projected third battalion was still short by 600 men.[5]

The military adventure of the Anti-Bolshevik Legion in Eastern Europe has been told several times, notably by Marc Augier, who had helped create the Jeunesse de l'Europe Nouvelle, the youth affiliate of Châteaubriant's Groupe Collaboration. Augier later volunteered for service with the legion and became editor of its newspaper, *Le Combattant Européen*. He emerged as one of the most ardent and articulate defenders of the legion's volunteers. The legionaries were assigned by the Germans to the training camp at Deba, roughly two hundred kilometers south of Warsaw in what was then the area of the General Government, the German administration of conquered Poland. With few exceptions, the Wehrmacht command regarded the French volunteers with a mixture of hatred and contempt in the best Prussian tradition of Ludendorff combined with the condescension of Hitler. Friction over the uniform issue developed, and many of the

---

[4]Davey, pp. 40–41.
[5]Colonel Gutscher, Wehrwirtschafts- und Rüstungsstab, "Besprechung beim Chef des Kommando-Stabes am 24.6.1941," and "Besprechung beim Chef des Generalstabes beim Militär-Befehlshaber am 23.9.41," CDJC document CCXXVII, 50.

French volunteers refused to take the oath of lifelong personal allegiance to Hitler required of all members of the Wehrmacht. A special dispensation was given to the French, who were allowed to take an oath binding them to Hitler only in their capacity as soldiers at the front and only for the duration of their service there. Some of the French volunteers who refused to take even the modified oath were demobilized and sent home, some were imprisoned, but most ended up going through the formality. Dissension in the camp was rife, especially between the partisans of Doriot and Deloncle. Labonne was unable to control the situation; rather, he seems to have aggravated it. During an October 1941 visit by de Brinon to the training camp at Deba, a quarrel erupted between Labonne and one of his officers, who ended up leaving the legion and returning to Paris.[6]

By early autumn, 1941, the Anti-Bolshevik Legion had been incorporated into the Wehrmacht as the 638th Infantry Regiment. It was placed in the seventh Bavarian division, which had been Hitler's division during World War I. At the end of October the first two battalions of the Anti-Bolshevik Legion, integrated into the German army, left the Deba training camp for Moscow. Through the ice and snow of November 1941 the legionaries moved by rail, truck, and finally on foot northeastward past Smolensk until they reached Djukovo, little more than sixty kilometers west of Moscow. There they found the front. The legion joined the German drive stalled before Moscow and suffered serious losses when the Russians counter-attacked in the beginning of December and pushed the Germans back. It was returned to Poland and early in 1942 assigned duty combating partisan guerrilla bands behind the German lines.

The French volunteers, many of whom had had antiguerrilla combat experience in North Africa, were better suited to antipartisan warfare than were the Germans, whose training in the Wehrmacht

[6]Legationsrat Dr. Carltheo Zeitschel, Aufzeichnung für Herrn Botschafter Abetz Über die Reise des Botschafters de Brinon vom 14.10 bis 29.10.41, Besuch bei der Légion des Volontaires Français in Deba," November 3, 1941, CDJC document VI, 134. On the installation and training of the French volunteers and their relations with the Germans at Deba, see Saint-Loup [Marc Augier], *Les volontaires* (Paris: Presses de la Cité, 1963), pp. 32–36, and also the memoir of another legionary, Eric Labat, *Les places étaient chères* (Paris: La Table Ronde, 1969 [original publication, 1951]), pp. 38–39 and 46–47.

prepared them more for conventional battle. In general, the French seemed more flexible in their dealings with the local inhabitants, who occasionally helped them gather military intelligence on the partisan bands in their area. Instead of destroying the *isbas,* the wood houses of the local villagers and peasants, as the Germans invariably did, the French legionaries often moved in and shared them with their inhabitants. Anti-Slav ethnic prejudice was less prominent among the French than among the Germans in the Wehrmacht. Nonetheless, antipartisan warfare was costly in energy and lives, especially during the cold winters. After participating in the assault before Moscow, the French faced the Red Army directly in only one other major engagement. During the Soviet advance in the summer of 1944, the Red Army caught up to the legion at Bobr, near the Beresina River. There the legion again took heavy casualties as it fought to delay the Soviet advance to provide time for the main German force to regroup west of the Beresina.[7]

The introduction of the Legion into combat at Djukovo and the subsequent campaigns against the partisans did nothing to quell its internal factionalism, which caused the Germans to condemn its "lack of discipline" while applauding its courage during the early months of its activity. Doriot's presence in the legion in the fall of 1941, the emergence in 1942 of his PPF as the leading collaborationist movement in France, and the weakening of Deloncle and the MSR, gave the Doriotists a preponderant influence in it. After his return to the government in April 1942, Laval had good reason to fear that the legion might be turned into a private army by Doriot for use in an attempted coup. On leave from his duties in the East, Doriot delivered a series of recruitment speeches for the legion, publicizing the PPF and helping cement the identification of the legion with the Doriotist movement in the public mind.

---

[7]Augier's eye-witness account of the attack on Djukovo is given in the book published under his own name, *Les partisans* (Paris: Denoël, 1943), pp. 53–56. In both that book and *Les volontaires* he also discusses extensively the life of the volunteers in Russia and their relations with the local inhabitants. The influence of North African experiences upon the antipartisan battle tactics of the legionaries is discussed in the anonymous memoir of another former legionary, *Vae Victis ou deux ans dans la L.V.F.,* with a preface by Colonel Rémy of the Resistance (Paris: La Jeune Parque, 1948), p. 47. The various eye-witness accounts were supplemented in interviews accorded me July 4, 1974 and July 19, 1976 by Marc Augier.

To forestall Doriotist use of the legion and as a gesture of goodwill toward the Germans, Laval announced on the first anniversary of the German invasion of Soviet Russia the conversion of the Anti-Bolshevik Legion from private to official status. Renamed the "Légion Tricolore," in July, the unit was now to be an organ of the French state. Benoist-Méchin was named to head its central committee and recruiting stations were expanded into the southern zone. The name change also indicated that the legion might be used anywhere, not only against the Russians. A second training camp was established in the southern zone and the central committee was enlarged with the addition of Darnand, but the influence of Doriot went undiminished. In January 1943 the Légion Tricolore was again renamed, this time "Légion des Volontaires Français," without specific mention of Bolshevism, a recognition of the failure to give the unit wider appeal. Darnand found no real place for himself within it and took charge instead of recruiting in France for the Phalange Africaine.[8]

The appropriation of the legion by the government helped the volunteers by improving their image and some of their veterans' benefits, but even then government officials and local police impeded its propaganda and recruitment efforts in France. An arrest in April 1943 of a legionary in Ales, in the department Gard, provoked a strong protest from the German military command in Vichy, which denied any right to the French police to arrest someone in German uniform. The man in question had a prior police record for stealing.[9]

[8]Abetz, "Notiz für Herrn Botschafter Ritter," July 26, 1942, T-120/926/297244-8. For the development of the legion through its Légion Tricolore phase and back again to LVF, as well as the reasons for keeping the Phalange Africaine separate from it, see *French Basic Handbook,* p. 178. Doriot's use of recruitment speeches for the legion was duly noted by the German propaganda staff, Propagandastaffel Paris der Propaganda-Abteilung Frankreich, Gruppe Presse, "Vertrauliche Information zur Lage in Frankreich," Nr. 306, February 2, 1942, T-77/1027/2499794.

[9]The legionary's account of his arrest and subsequent treatment by the French police is given in a written deposition included in a note from the Kommandant des Heeresgebietes Südfrankreich, Abt. Ic., Lyons, to the Deutsche General des Ob. West, Vichy, July 19, 1943, and the official French account, quite at variance with that of the accused, General C. Caldairou, Chef de Cabinet of Bridoux, letter to the representative of the Oberbefehlshaber West in Vichy, September 13, 1943, T-77/833/5571879-82 and 5571864-6, respectively. On the subject of police and administrative harassment of recruiting even after the organization became the Légion Tricolore, see Deutsche Waffenstillstandskommission Gruppe Wehrmacht, Ic, "Lage unbesetztes Gebiet (Auswertung von Berichten der Kontroll-Inspektionen)," Wiesbaden, July 31, 1942, nr. 1596/42 geh.; T-77/1027/2499985.

More damaging to the legion than the harassment it took from French officials was the attitude of Hitler, who on September 17, 1942 vetoed any expansion of it. He decreed that the legion might accept new recruits only to replace those lost in battle to bring its strength up to regiment size. The French, in addition, were not to be told of the decree but were to be put off in a dilatory manner. The legion was also to be kept away from the front. In an ironic sense the recruitment process for the legion was indeed a process of selection. To be allowed to sacrifice one's life on the frozen steppes of Russia, a volunteer had to overcome both French and German bureaucracies![10]

Hitler's directive to slow the development of the legion had immediate repercussions in a very nervous Vichy. Benoist-Méchin was caught in a crossfire between anti-German elements in the French army and the veterans' organization, the Légion Française des Combattants, on the one hand and the Germans on the other. Trying to figure out why the Germans were so reserved in their attitude toward a volunteer force which supported them fully on the international scene, Benoist-Méchin concluded that they were dissatisfied with Laval's domestic policy. France, he believed, needed to bring her government closer ideologically to the Axis powers and, accordingly in the autumn of 1942 he turned to Doriot. Jittery about Doriot and the possible involvement of Benoist-Méchin in PPF plans for taking power, Laval had Benoist-Méchin replaced by de Brinon, whose commitment to collaboration was total and whose personal qualities included a deep-seated aversion to Doriot. De Brinon remained at the head of the legion's central committee for the duration of its existence.[11]

The ideal of the legion was the crusading warrior in the medieval mold, although the image of the Christian crusader coexisted in uneasy tension with that of the Nietzschean neopaganism and racism of Nazi Germany. Legion spokesmen frequently evoked memories of the Grande Armée of Napoleon, whose attempts to conquer Europe were often pictured as predecessors of twentieth-century European unity

[10]Warlimont, Der Chef des Oberkommandos der Wehrmacht, note to General Stab des Heeres/O. Qu. IV, September 19, 1942, T-120/926/297170-1.

[11]For a discussion of the effect of Hitler's order on the collaborationist political intrigues, see Abetz, telegram to the German Foreign Ministry, Berlin, no. 4367, September 30, 1942, T-120/926/297156-8.

by collaborationists. The legion's newspaper, *Le Combattant Euro-péen,* carried an article entitled "Dream of a Legionary," which ran:

> I dream of the Europe of tomorrow: "Luminous spring dawn, risen, magnificent and serene, from a long and bloody winter!"
> Don't you anticipate this dawn, sooner or later?
> What matter! Does not our noble sacrifice, freely consented to, have as its stake peace and the regeneration of a triumphant Europe? A long era of happiness will be born from the conflict joined in the East.
> A glorious past is at stake. France is taking an active part in an-nihilating the savage hordes of the base Caucasian. What matter the dangers! We are indifferent to death itself. "Conquer or die! Is that not the true motto of the warrior!"
> Our glorious conquerors of yesterday, brothers in arms today, tomor-row reconciled forever, have traced for us the road to follow: the protec-tion of our threatened peoples and our ancient civilization. We have deliberately followed them in this most sacred task. [12]

Jean Fontenoy, attached to the legion as head of its propaganda company in December 1941, described the volunteers as half idealists and half adventurers. Postwar accounts of the Anti-Bolshevik Legion have usually focused upon its mercenaries and adventurers to the exclusion of the idealists. The legion and later the French Waffen-SS contained a number of romantic volunteers from the Centre Laïc des Auberges de Jeunesse (CLAJ), the secular offshoot of the Catholic youth hostel movement. During the 1930's CLAJ had attracted large numbers of urban middle-class young, in quest of camaraderie and adventure in rural byways. Some of these camping visionaries in France, as in Germany, eventually wound up in jackboots. French examples included Marc Augier and Philippe Merlin. Augier joined the Anti-Bolshevik Legion and Merlin ended up in the Waffen-SS. [13]

---

[12]Légionnaire Haudey, "Rêve du Légionnaire," *Le Combattant Européen,* October 15, 1943.

[13]The CLAJ youth who ended up in the legion and the Waffen-SS had analogues in Germany; see Peter H. Merkl, *Political Violence under the Swastika: 581 Early Nazis* (Princeton: Princeton University Press, 1975), p. 231. Merkl discusses young Germans who went from what he calls the "Peter Pan stage" to become storm troopers. One can agree with Merkl, who wistfully wishes some of these carefree and fanciful young people had never had to grow up. Fontenoy's comment about the makeup of the legion at the end of 1941 was reported in an "Abschrift" included in a

Young people from CLAJ had been drawn in the years before the war to the idyllic pastoral stories of Jean Giono. In his accounts of rural folkways, Giono, a pacifist, provided a focal point for urban middle-class youth in quest of spiritual values, which they believed lay in the countryside. Although CLAJ was nonpolitical, its members shared a general if somewhat vague pacifism and a critical view of what many of them considered the materialistic conformity of their elders. They were mainly interested in camaraderie, the outdoor life, and becoming acquainted with French rural ways. Giono represented these ideals to them. Although he was not active in fascist movements and attempted in the main to eschew politics, his critiques of urban life, the bourgeoisie, and materialism, and his emphasis on intuition as opposed to rationalism were seen even before the war as potential fascism. Giono's neoprimitivism, drawn from the tradition of Rousseau, reappeared in fascism and attracted the young Augier and Merlin.[14]

The son of a cement plant owner, Augier was born in 1908 in Bordeaux. He became a journalist and from 1935 until 1940 edited the Centre Laïc's newspaper, in which he described his own mountaineering treks into the Swiss Alps and winter ski trips to Norway. Chosen to represent his organization at a world youth congress in 1938, Augier reacted negatively to what he perceived as a Communist attempt to turn the meeting into an antifascist event. He emerged as a militant anti-Communist. As a pacifist, he opposed war with Germany but he was convinced that the Communists could be stopped only with force. Upon his demobilization after the armistice in 1940, he joined in establishing the Jeunesse de l'Europe Nouvelle.

Augier saw in Nazi Germany the camaraderie and spirit of outdoor life he had prized in the hostel movement, but the JEN did not offer sufficient opportunity to fight Communism. After the invasion of

---

report from the Ausbildungsstab Französische Legion, Süd-Demba [Deba training camp], January 2, 1942, to Oberkommando der Wehrmacht. Abteilung Wehrmacht-Propaganda IV, T-77/1027/2499770.

[14] The possible relationship between fascism in general and the ideas of Jean Giono was considered in Henri Pollès, *L'opéra politique* (Paris: Gallimard, 1937), pp. 30–33, 48, 145 and 155; and in a review of this book by André Billy, "Naturisme et 'Fascisme' de Giono," *L'Œuvre*, August 29, 1937. *L'Œuvre* in 1937 had not yet come under the political influence of Déat, although the then Neo-Socialist leader contributed articles to it.

Soviet Russia he joined the Anti-Bolshevik Legion. Although the expacifist had turned warrior, Augier remained temperamentally and intellectually a romantic crusader, a Don Quixote in search of an ideal. Writing in *Le Combattant Européen* in 1943, he discussed the German-Soviet war: "What is it about? Two conceptions of man are face to face. On one hand, *homo ratio,* the man of pure reason going from Voltaire to the historical materialism of Marx, on the other a kind of *homo deo*, which I can define in no better way than to say he is the man of the disinterested life, the man who ignores himself for the profit of his fellow, that is to say, in modern parlance, social man."[15]

Augier praised the new military spirit among the youth of all the countries engaged in the war and viewed the "crusade in the East" as the opportunity for French youth to efface the stain of the 1940 defeat. He gloried in the fact that he could walk down a street in Berlin and be saluted by uniformed Germans. Another former member of the youth hostel movement, a young artisan from Lyons, volunteered for service in the legion after the German defeat at Stalingrad increased the danger he saw in Communism for France. After the dissolution of the legion in 1944 he joined the Charlemagne division of the Waffen-SS, as did Augier who became its political officer. Roughly 20 percent of the personnel of his unit were said to have been members of CLAJ. The spirit of Robert Brasillach's "homo fascista" was evoked with the prewar writings of Giono and the mystique of the hostel movement, carried by the small minority of its members who joined the Anti-Bolshevik Legion.[16]

In his postwar history of the legion, Augier differentiates between

---

[15]Augier, "Ce siècle avait deux ans... ," *Le Combattant Européen,* June 1943. Prior to his joining the legion, Augier had suggested that the JEN take the lead in a grand project involving 80,000 French workers in the construction of a railway through French Africa, from the Mediterranean to Dakar. See Augier, "Les jeunes devant l'aventure européene" (Paris: Les Conférences du Groupe "Collaboration," October 1941), pp. 14–17. The evolution of Augier's political views was described in his book *Les partisans,* pp. 13–17 and 21–22, and amplified in interviews, July 4, 1974 and July 19, 1976. His opposition to war against Germany even during the 1939–1940 campaign was evidenced in his article, "Nous sommes 'le parti de la vie'," *Le Cri des Auberges de Jeunesse,* 7 (February–March 1940).

[16]On the subject of former CLAJ members in the *section chasse* of the third legion battalion, I am indebted to one such veteran, Léon Colas, who accorded me interviews on August 28, 1973 and July 3, 1974.

the neopagan ideologues in the unit and those who saw themselves in the more traditional role of Christian crusaders. He describes exchanges between a former Delonclist, Le Fauconnier, a graduate of the Ecole Normale Supérieure, deeply committed to the warrior, elitist, and racial ideas of Hitler's Germany, and the more traditionalist Catholic personalities in the legion. Le Fauconnier had volunteered to fight in the legion "to find again the taste of the aurochs, like the Russians, to climb back to the sources of the true Hellade, those of the blond barbarians who came from the north," as he told Brasillach. In search of Nietzsche's blond beast, Le Fauconnier quit the legion, which he found too Christian. He applied for admission into the Waffen-SS and was ultimately accepted into the SS-Division Brandenburg. His view stood in tension with the more widespread image of the legion as a modern-day Christian crusade against Eastern barbarism.[17]

The Christian image was articulated by Count Jean Mayol de Lupé, the legion's chaplain. A longstanding monarchist who was also said to have had the "Horst Wessel Lied" sung in his house even before the war, Mayol de Lupé volunteered at the age of sixty-seven to serve as chaplain to the organization. He gained the respect of many of the legionaries by sharing with them all the privations and hardships of war. To Mayol, Hitler was the last hope of believing Christians against materialistic Communism, yet he also condemned as dangerous for the legion Le Fauconnier, who took seriously Nazi racism and its neopagan attack on Christianity. The tense relationship between Mayol and Le Fauconnier symbolized the tension between two related yet different ideals in the legion and the European radical Right in general.[18]

The composition of the legion was heterogeneous throughout its four-year history but it attracted support from some of the most respectable elements of French society. A German observer late in

[17]On Le Fauconnier, see Saint-Loup, *Les volontaires*, pp. 14, 20, 244, and 315–316. In ibid., pp. 299–300 there is a discussion of Mayol de Lupé and his influence in getting Le Fauconnier transferred to the Brandenburg division.

[18]For background on Mayol, see "Souvenirs de jeunesse de Jean Mayol de Lupé," *Le Combattant Européen*, June 1, 1944, and on his pro-German activities in 1938, see SS-Standartenführer Hewel, Vienna, letter to Chef der Sicherheitshauptamt SS-Gruppenführer Heydrich, April 26, 1938, T-120/1746H/403584.

1941 found its Marseilles recruiting office to be supported by well-known local personalities from the military, high finance, and the clergy. The governmental legitimization of the legion in 1942 and the German defeat at Stalingrad, which became generally known early in 1943, led to a higher proportion of serious-minded recruits. Some who joined in mid-1941, expecting a quick victory over Soviet Russia and a triumphal parade through the streets of Moscow, left. Others who were found to have criminal records were sent home by the Wehrmacht authorities. After being taken over by Vichy, the legion was more likely to attract nationalist traditionalists such as Jean Bassompierre, who had helped Darnand form the SOL, the seed of the Milice. A friend of Darlan, Bassompierre conducted public meetings in which he recruited for the legion in the southern zone during the spring and summer of 1942. Less the romantic crusader than Augier or Le Fauconnier, Bassompierre was more representative of the traditional soldier following his leaders, Pétain and Darnand, into battle. A Maurrasian, Bassompierre was willing to recognize and honor what he considered true patriotism when he found it among members of the Resistance, which drew upon him the criticism of Mayol de Lupé. While Augier and Le Fauconnier looked across the borders of France to a new German-dominated international order, to Bassompierre *la patrie* was the highest good and he admitted to Mayol de Lupé having elevated France above God in his heart. Involved in the bloody repression of a prison riot shortly before the Liberation in 1944, Bassompierre was executed four years later as a collaborator despite having had a brother killed fighting the Germans in 1945. Father Bruckberger, who had tried earlier in vain to save Darnand, was equally unsuccessful in the case of Bassompierre.[19]

---

[19]See Bassompierre, *Frères ennemis*, pp. 132–134 for his account of his reasons for joining the legion, p. 146 for his praise of the French who had died at Bir-Hakeim, and pp. 224–225 for his postwar reflections on his patriotism. On p. 173 Bassompierre refers to his brother killed in 1945, whose memory inspired him to entitle his memoir "*Frères ennemis.*" See also Saint-Loup, *Les volontaires*, pp. 304–306, and Bruckberger, pp. 217–218. A German appraisal of Bassompierre's efforts to recruit for the legion is given in Deutsche Waffenstillstandskommission, Gruppe Wehrmacht Ic/Nr. 2024/42 geheim, Wiesbaden, September 15, 1942, "Lage unbesetztes Gebiet im August 1942 (Auswertung von Berichten der Kontroll-Inspektionen), T-77/1027/6500049. For the discussion of the support among the middle classes and clergy of Marseilles for the legion, see the unsigned report

Not all who volunteered for service in the legion were as committed ideologically as were Augier, Le Fauconnier, Mayol de Lupé, and Bassompierre. In the organization's early days, many of its recruits were members of the collaborationist parties who had been pressured by their leaders into joining. Colonel Labonne told Fontenoy that he intended to join the PPF himself because he expected all future military honors within the legion would be awarded on the basis of political influence and the Doriotists appeared to be gaining the upper hand late in 1941. The original intention of the legion's creators had been to accept only recruits with prior military experience but the paucity of their numbers obliged them to take those without experience as well. Consequently, some of the recruits had to be instructed in the basics of handling weapons. Fontenoy observed that few volunteers appeared eager to learn anything about German National Socialism. Among the recruits he found a Jew who had joined in the apparent hope of escaping persecution in France. Another volunteer was an officer who was believed to have been involved in financial swindles.[20]

On the other hand, Mayol de Lupé complained of the nefarious influence in the legion of party men such as Fontenoy himself and Vanor of the MSR. The chaplain told a German staff officer that Berlin was placing too much value on the likes of Fontenoy, Doriot, Déat, and Costantini, all of whom, he maintained, were being supplied by the Germans with funds. He suggested a thoroughgoing change in the legion's officer corps. Another German observer early in 1942 also made the point that the influence of the party leaders, Doriot in particular, was too strong within the legion. He suggested that recruitment be taken out of the hands of the political parties, which had entered "volunteers" under false pretenses and with fraudulent papers in order to increase their own influence in the legion. What was needed, instead, was a more purely military recruiting system with the role of the parties limited to one of propaganda.[21]

Colonel Labonne also weakened the legion by trying to magnify his

---

"Generelle Eindrücke aus dem unbesetzten Gebiete," T-120/K1634/K402834. This report was microfilmed only in part and therefore it is not dated, although it appears to have been written while Darlan headed the government and is included in a series of army reports to the Foreign Ministry for September and October 1941.

[20]Fontenoy, report, T-77/1027/2499770-1.

own role in order to appear as a kind of General de Gaulle in reverse. He was accused of being too subservient to Doriot. With leaders such as Labonne most of the legionaries lost confidence in their officers and discipline slackened. Many of the legionaries while in training in Poland were said to be engaged in illegal trafficking with the Poles, and some accumulated substantial wealth there. Thefts were also common. Two companies had been infiltrated by Gaullists and Communists, unknown to the company commanders, who made little effort to become acquainted with their men. Anti-German propaganda within the legion was facilitated by the generally low level of their material supplies from the Wehrmacht and the indifference of many of their officers. The efforts of Vichy to make a more effective fighting force out of the legion were supported by the German embassy, which was also at pains to assure Berlin that the organization would not thereby become too powerful. [22]

The negative evaluations by Mayol de Lupé and the German observers were shared by de Brinon, who accused Vanor of trafficking in legion property and questioned the capability of Labonne. Extensive efforts were made to recruit among the demobilized men and officers of the Armistice Army, dissolved in November 1942. Despite appeals by well-known military personalities such as Colonel du Jonchay of the Phalange Africaine and intensive propaganda campaigns in newspapers and on wall posters, volunteers were few. Abetz apparently felt pressed to make good on his earlier exaggerated forecasts of legion strength. A report of early 1942 showed recruitment proceeding more satisfactorily in the southern than in the northern zone, ironic as the collaborationist parties drew most of their support north of the demarcation line. [23]

[21]Aktennotiz über die Rücksprache des Sonderführers Bisschopinck mit Msgr. Majol [sic] de Lupé am 16.1.42," also a staff report, Rittmeister, "Bericht über die Legion," December 31, 1941; T-77/1027/2499804 and 2499805, respectively.

[22]Rittmeister, "Bericht über die Legion," T-77/1027/2499806-9. See also Abetz, Notiz für Herrn Botschafter Ritter, July 26, 1942, T-120/926/297243.

[23]For German accounts of difficulties in recruiting for the legion, see Grimm, Bericht, August 14, 1942, T-120/6442H/E481172; for the southern zone in particular, see Deutsche Waffenstillstandskommission, Gruppe Wehrmacht Ic, nr. 550/42 geh., Wiesbaden, April 1, 1942, "Lage franz. Mutterland (Auswertung von Berichten der Kontroll-Inspektionen)," T-77/1027/2499843-4; and for the effects of du Jonchay, "Besuch des Capitaine Schnitzler, Adjutant des Colonel du Jonchay bei General von Neubronn am 12.7.43, 11.00 Uhr," T-77/833/557255. For de Brinon's

Many recruits came from marginal social background; some were so poor and covered with vermin that they were rejected as unfit for service. A recruit accepted later wrote an anonymous postwar memoir in which he described himself as "no idealist." A Parisian of middle-class origins, he was impressed by the series of German military victories in the summer of 1941 and was attracted by a recruiting poster he saw in the Paris *métro*. Even after enlisting and beginning their training at Versailles, several recruits ran away and were never found. Because the legion was a private organization at first, it had no authority to track down deserters, nor were the police or regular military authorities inclined to cooperate.[24]

The legion also contained known criminals, such as one who, according to the anonymous author of *Deux ans dans la L.V.F.*, had killed a person in civilian life but preferred service in the legion to life in Lyons prison. On occasion, legionaries went A.W.O.L. and lived for extended periods with the peasants in the territories where they were stationed. Others left to join other units of the Wehrmacht. Captain Dewitte, a company leader, was described as a man who would have fit in well with Wallenstein and the German freebooters of the Thirty Years War or the earlier Saracen invaders of Europe. Dewitte, who subsequently joined the Milice, was executed by a postwar tribunal in Lyons. Prisoners of war sometimes sought to buy their freedom from German internment by volunteering for service in the legion. In 1942 the Vichy government decided that all volunteers from the Armistice Army who joined the legion would retain their army rank and all other privileges they had earned and conversely that all honors and privileges earned in service in the legion would be recognized by the French army. A year later, Laval announced that all volunteers for the legion would be exempted from the obligatory labor service, although some of the recruits in 1943 were forced to work three months for the German *Organisation Todt* as part of their training.

---

evaluation of the legion, see his *Mémoires* (Paris: L.L.C., 1949), p. 90. This should be compared with his glowing account of the legion to the Germans after his visit of 1943 to its training camp. See Abschrift, Auswärtiges Amt, nr. 4485, Schleier, telegram to A.A., July 6, 1943, T-77/1027/6500156-8.

[24] *Deux ans dans la L.V.F.*, pp. 8–10. Another adventurer in the Anti-Bolshevik Legion was Lieutenant Lapart, a member of the RNP Boulogne-Billancourt section, who wrote a short article, "Ce que j'ai vu en Russie," published in 1942 by the RNP; CDJC Library 8085.

Recruitment drives organized among French workers in labor camps in Germany failed abjectly. As with the collaborationist parties generally, the Anti-Bolshevik Legion's appeal was to a small minority only in occupied France. When reports began to circulate describing the horrid conditions of battle in the Soviet Union, it was hardly surprising that relatively few volunteered for the experience.[25]

Legionaries were allowed to wear French khaki while at home on leave but the requirement that they wear German uniforms while in service at the front rankled many such as Bassompierre. The appearance of French soldiers in German uniforms in France often provoked hostile demonstrations. Volunteers were recruited for all types of military duty but in practice they were assigned only to artillery and infantry, decreasing the legion's attractiveness for recruits. The organization's general unpopularity in France intensified the difficulties for those who did enlist. In 1942 a recruitment center's windows were smashed in Clermont-Ferrand and another center was blown up in Perpignan. The transformation of the Anti-Bolshevik Legion into the Légion Tricolore did not end the harassment of its recruiters by local police and government officials, and the establishment of centers to recruit Frenchmen for labor in Germany cut into the group's possible clientele.[26]

At first the reaction of official Vichy was to support the legion as little as possible without offending the Germans. To allow volunteers to join in 1941, Vichy decreed its members exempt from the law prohibiting French nationals from serving with foreign armies. Al-

[25]Exemptions from the labor service and the unsuccessful appeals to French workers in Toulouse and Montpellier are discussed, respectively, in the *French Basic Handbook*, p. 180, and Kontrollinspektion der Deutsche Waffenstillstandskommission, Kontrollabteilung Az. 20, nr. 2300/43g., Bourges, September 9, 1943, Monatsbericht nr. 5, T-77/842/5585848. For French prisoners of war seeking to join the legion, a policy was adopted based on the precedent used for Belgian prisoners of war joining the Légion Wallonie. See Kommandant Frank, M. Stammlager XIII C, Lager Hammelburg, October 12, 1942, note to OKW/WPr (IV k), T-77/1027/6500051. Comments on adventurers and criminals in the legion were made in *Deux ans dans la L. V. F.*, pp. 29 and 57; on Dewitte, pp. 105–106.

[26]Deutsche Waffenstillstandskommission, Gruppe Wehrmacht Ic, nr. 793/42 geh., Wiesbaden, May 2, 1942, "Lage franz. Mutterland," and DWStK, Gruppe Wehrmacht Ic, nr. 1596/42 geh., Wiesbaden, July 31, 1942; T-77/1027/2499945 and 2499985, respectively.

though Marshal Pétain was aloof, indeed brusque, when visited by Deloncle and Doriot, both of whom separately sought his support for the legion, he did issue a strong statement of encouragement to the organization in November 1941. Responding to a message of loyalty from Labonne, transmitted by de Brinon, Pétain replied that in fighting Bolshevism the legion was defending the honor of the French military tradition and simultaneously building the basis of collaboration with Germany. One historian of the early legion has suggested that Petain's message was given at the instigation of de Brinon.[27] In later years, legionaries and their apologists pointed to the statement as an indication that the legion represented all that was best in the military annals of France and had the blessing of France's chief of state. Pétain's message also helped pave the way for its transformation into the government-sponsored Légion Tricolore in June 1942. By 1943 as many as one-fourth of the legion's recruits were working in France, organized into a Service d'Etudes et de Documentation, which gathered intelligence in the northern zone in the same way that the Milice's Service de Renseignements functioned in the southern zone for Vichy. The SED is said to have worked closely with the German police and it was supported by a budget of 90 million francs for the second half of 1943. It appears that the Germans paid for legion expenses in Eastern Europe whereas the Vichy government funded it in France. Expenses in France included pensions and aid to the families of legionaries, support for the legion's training centers there, and salaries for legionaries and related staff, including SED, posted in France. According to British intelligence, the legion spent more to fund the SED during the second half of 1943 than it did on a widely publicized campaign to recruit an additional 5,000 volunteers from the ranks of the disbanded Armistice Army. Both Vichy and the Germans found the legion volunteers more useful to them in France than at the Eastern front.[28]

In Russia, the legion continued its war against the partisans until July 1944, when two events combined to bring the organization's

[27]For a discussion of Pétain's "legitimizing" message of November 1941 and de Brinon's role in drafting it, see Davey, pp. 44–45.

[28] *French Basic Handbook,* pp. 179–180. The law of February 11, 1943 and excerpts of other statutes pertaining to the legion were published in the article "Légionnaires, connaissez vos droits!" *Le Combattant Europé*en, November 15, 1943.

history to a close. First, it was caught in the Soviet offensive of the summer of 1944. Engaging the Red Army at Bobr, the legion suffered heavy losses and was forced to withdraw with the rest of the German forces. The army plot that culminated in the July 20 assassination attempt against Hitler induced him, already distrustful of his own military, to reorganize the German armed forces enhancing the role of the Waffen-SS. By 1944 the Waffen-SS was approaching the figure of one million men, of whom more than half were not German. The legion would have required reorganization in any event, following the battle of Bobr. In July 1944, following the Allied landing in France, some of the collaborationists, led by Déat, wanted the legion used against the Western powers. Laval scotched this idea and the legion instead was moved to Greifenburg in East Prussia, to be incorporated into a new division of the Waffen-SS, the Charlemagne, then in formation. The stormy life of the Légion des Volontaires Français had come to an end.[29]

The LVF had already begun to suffer recruitment losses from the competition of the Waffen-SS. In July 1943 the decision had been made to open the elite Waffen-SS to a French brigade, to be called the "Sturmbrigade Frankreich, Sturmbrigade-SS, No. 7." The decision in Berlin to admit a French unit into the ranks of the Waffen-SS was slow in coming due to opposition in some German circles to allowing non-Germanic units into the racially restricted formation. The Waffen-SS had been recruiting Frenchmen from collaborationist organizations and among the French workers in Germany as early as 1942 but on an individual basis only. Such volunteers had been assigned to various Waffen-SS formations. The idea of an SS unit composed solely of French volunteers met more resistance within German official circles. Himmler hesitated but his aide Gottlob Berger argued for inclusion of the French on the grounds that Léon Degrelle and his Rexist followers from Belgium had proven that "Latins" could be good warriors and that Frenchmen were already in the Waffen-SS serving as individuals. The Soviet offensive in the East and the fall of Mussolini and defection of Italy from the Axis helped remove any hesitations Himmler may have had concerning the creation of non-

---

[29]Laval's opposition to use of the legion in France after Normandy was expressed during a cabinet meeting, July 12, 1944. See Tracou, p. 355.

Nordic units of the Waffen-SS. Non-German Nordic formations had been created as early as 1940.

Once the German approval had been given for the creation of a French SS unit, Laval dragged his heels. He finally yielded after the application of German pressure but was able to extract as concessions that service in the Waffen-SS would be purely voluntary and that the French unit would not be used in France or employed against French dissidents, backers of de Gaulle or Giraud. On July 22, 1943, Laval signed a three-point decree establishing a French unit of the Waffen-SS. The decree allowed French volunteers to serve in it and receive the same pay and benefits as members of the LVF.[30]

Like their compatriots in the legion, the French volunteers in the Waffen-SS were a heterogeneous group but there were some significant differences. The Germans had a more direct role in the recruitment of Waffen-SS volunteers and they were better able to exclude Jews and Communists from the formation. During the latter stages of the war and in the years since, Nazis and their apologists have sought to depict the Waffen-SS as an international European army fighting against an "Asiatic Bolshevik menace" represented by the Soviet Union. In reality, as George Stein, a historian of the Waffen-SS, has shown, most Eastern European recruits came to the organization as a result of nationalist enmities, as in the case of Baltic volunteers fighting for national survival against the USSR. The volunteers from Western Europe more closely approached the image propagated by the Waffen-SS, but many of these developed their collaborationist and anti-Communist ideologies only after training in the intensive Waffen-SS educational centers and after experiencing combat in the East. According to Stein, 450 young Dutch volunteers were found to have been motivated by desire for adventure and better food, the prestige of the SS uniform in occupied Europe, boredom, a wish to escape obligatory labor service, and a variety of personal reasons including, on occasion, the desire to avoid prosecution for petty crimes. Berger, in charge of the foreign recruitment program for the

[30]Jean Mabire, *La Brigade Frankreich: La tragique aventure des SS français* (Paris: Fayard, 1973), p. 45. For Laval's reluctance to go ahead with a French SS unit and the German pressure placed upon him, see Schleier, telegrams from Paris to embassy office in Vichy, July 20, 1943 and July 28, 1943; T-120/3551H/E022824-5, respectively.

Waffen-SS, also recognized that relatively few of the volunteers came with specifically political motives and that many had criminal pasts. Police records, however, did not unduly trouble Berger, who noted a similar phenomenon in the SS and SA prior to 1933 in Germany.[31] The motivations of the recruits to the Waffen-SS were thus similar to those of the legion volunteers. Particularly important in France were the young men who wished to prove their manhood by emulating the elite of the German armed forces.

The Charlemagne division, formed in July 1944 from the remnants of the other French military collaboration units, had a greater number of people under coercion than did the Sturmbrigade, but the element of compulsion was also present in securing recruits for the earlier unit. German recruiters in 1943 looked to the demobilized officers and men of the Armistice Army for volunteers but they did little better than the recruiters for the LVF in this constituency. The brusque treatment of the French Armistice Army units by the Wehrmacht when it occupied the southern zone killed any potential desire for collaboration on the part of most French senior officers, although junior officers of the Sturmbrigade were French. Some volunteers came to the Waffen-SS from the First Regiment of France, the tiny ersatz army created by Vichy after the dissolution of the Armistice Army. The head of the First Regiment, Colonel Berlon, was asked to permit defections from his force to the Waffen-SS "in view of the great common goal, the victory over Bolshevism." In return, the Germans promised to refrain from launching recruitment campaigns aimed specifically at the First Regiment.[32]

To bolster the size of their Waffen-SS contingents from the occupied countries of Western Europe, the Germans also recruited among the foreign workers laboring in Germany during the latter

[31]Stein, pp. 138–139 and 140–142. For Hitler's "Germany first" attitude, see Jäckel, p. 181 and, for his low evaluation of the French SS, pp. 301–302.

[32]Major Dr. Meier-Faust, "Niederschrift über die Besprechung am 17.12.1943 im Hotel Claridge," T-77/834/5573704-5. German attempts to recruit volunteers from among demobilized members of the Armistice Army and their attempts to improve propaganda techniques are described, respectively, in Hagen, V.O.A. beim Deutschen General des OB West in Vichy, "Notiz über eine Besprechung mit Cpt. Ehrard am 13.8.43," T-501/roll 120/DGV 70/23591, and Fritz Bran, of the Foreign Ministry, "Bericht über die Sitzung des engeren Kreises am 20.8.43," T-120/3456/E022161.

stages of the war. The Vichy government had approved recruitment efforts for other units among the French workers in the Reich. Helmut Knochen, the aide of Oberg who headed the SS in Paris, prepared a report which examined the success of the recruiting efforts among the French workers in Germany. Approximately 3,000 letters sent home to relatives and friends by these workers were opened and read during the period from July 1 to July 19, 1943. They were written mainly by people working in the Rhineland and Ruhr areas. Knochen noted that most of the letters were critical of Laval and collaboration. A group of French workers in Essen were told that 300,000 of their compatriots had been signed up for service in the Waffen-SS. The reality, however, was more visible in a letter from Dessau, which claimed that six men only had been recruited and of the six, two had been recruited forcibly. Elsewhere, others were promised vacations if they joined the Waffen-SS. Some signed up while intoxicated and still others were offered food, money, and women. [33]

Although most of the foreign workers were recruited for service at the Eastern front, some were also sought to serve as police in their homelands. Enlistments were to run from four to twelve years. Those who served the full twelve years were promised homesteads in occupied Russia and administrative posts, although not in France. The Germans had no desire to create a new French elite of any kind, even SS. Former French prisoners of war who had been released to work in Germany were also asked to join the Waffen-SS. The few workers who did volunteer often met with ostracism or worse from their fellow French, as was the case with a worker in Bochum. Instead of going to Russia, the man wound up in a local hospital. [34]

The few pro-German French, according to Knochen, were of middle-class origin. A worker in Dortmund argued that a Soviet victory would affect France as well as Germany and would lead to the destruction of his family. Another worker in Dortmund indicated that volunteers for the Waffen-SS were usually found among those who had been among the first to volunteer for labor in Germany,

[33]Knochen,, "Abschrift. Abt. C/II. Bericht über die Auswirkung der Werbung zum Eintritt in die Waffen-SS unter den ausländischen Arbeitern der besetzten Westgebiete," Frankfurt am Main, July 21, 1943, T-175/70/2586749-50.
[34]Ibid., T-175/70/2586751-2.

presumably the most ideologically committed to the New Order. Other workers wrote of being attracted by the perquisites offered by the Germans and still others in their letters described a kind of preordained fatalism, which they pictured as drawing them toward the Waffen-SS. To some, the legitimacy bestowed upon the Waffen-SS by Vichy was a factor. They argued that they were duty-bound to obey the French government and by volunteering assure France a place in the New Europe. They were of course unaware of the hesitancy with which Laval had accepted the French Waffen-SS, nor were the German guards and recruiters likely to enlighten them in this regard. A few letters referred to hatred of England, engendered by Royal Air Force raids on the Ruhr, which threatened the French workers as well as the Germans there. Of all the letters opened and read by Knochen and his staff, the number judged as "positive," or pro-German, was estimated as one to one and one-half percent.[35]

In addenda to the report were excerpts from a number of the letters that had been intercepted and read. One French worker in Bielefeld put the entire matter succinctly in a letter to an acquaintance in the Paris suburb of Saint-Ouen. He wrote that things must have been going quite badly for the Germans to be obliged to turn for help to the defeated peoples. A worker in Mülheim wrote that 150 French workers were signed up there through the threat of force. German recruiters were most interested in signing the younger men, who were obviously intended for combat duty. A French worker who joined the Waffen-SS typified the attitude of many when he wrote:

> Shall I remain an unknown among the mass of men who are forced to labor and suffer more or less from hunger? . . . Or shall I be a man who lives with the New Europe and naturally leads a dangerous life? Whether one dies now or later, one has to die some day. And if I should return [to France, presumably], all will be fine and I will not have to worry about the future.
>
> "And in the event of defeat?" you will say. I have also thought about that. We SS people will always enjoy high regard. I have talked about this war with an SS man. I cannot go into details here, but you should know that this war was necessary for humanity, as the sun is necessary

for our life, as all that occurs is necessary, necessary for the passage of time, and we must subordinate ourselves to the laws of the world....

From the day I signed, all has gone on schedule, payment of 8,700 francs in a month. Security and care for you [are provided by the Waffen-SS]. I am feared by all, even by German soldiers, for I belong to the Führer's guard. I repeat, if things become very difficult, I personally hold in hand a trump that no one else in the world possesses.[36]

After showing promising signs in the first month after the creation of the Sturmbrigade, recruitment for the Waffen-SS in France slowed. Roughly 1,500 were claimed on August 6, 1943, but by October the flow of volunteers had diminished significantly. As a result, the height requirement was lowered and those who had been rejected previously as too short were encouraged to reapply. The youthful nature of the recruits was confirmed in a report on the enlistees of November 1943. No total figures were provided but of those who volunteered that month 54 percent were ages seventeen to twenty and 33 percent were between twenty and thirty, for a total of 87 percent aged thirty or younger. Only 9 percent fell into the thirty to forty category and 4 percent were between forty and sixty. For religion, 78 percent were listed as Catholic, 11 percent as Evangelical, with 10 percent "gottgläubig" ("believers," presumably in Christianity, although not defined in terms of denomination), and a scattering of others.[37]

Listed according to occupation, 38 percent were artisans, 20 percent employees and assistants, 6 percent in the various free professions, and 4 percent career soldiers. Only 7 percent came from agricultural pursuits, but significantly, 25 percent of the recruits were listed as students. The relatively low number of peasants is in keep-

[36]Ibid., "Anlage," T-175/70/2586753-7. The letters were written originally in French but appear in German translation in the report. This letter was written by a Frenchman working in Berlin to his wife or mother in Paris, June 28, 1943. Additional excerpts of letters are furnished in an "Abschrift" to this report, 2586758-61.

[37]The percentages for the recruits of November 1943 are taken from Walter Zwickler, Der SS-Führer i. Rasse- u. Siedlungswesen beim Höh. SS- u. Pol. Füh. Frankreich, Monatsbericht, to Hildegrandt, Chef des Rasse- u. Siedlungshauptamtes-SS, Berlin, December 8, 1943, CDJC document CXXXVIII, 26. Zwickler was in charge of the Paris office that checked among other things the racial background of the French Waffen-SS recruits. On problems of recruiting, see also the French Basic Handbook, p. 183.

ing with the collaborationist movements' urban character. The low proportion of career military men differentiated the French SS from the LVF, which drew more upon French military tradition and personnel. In contrast, the Sturmbrigade recruited a high proportion of students, who may have been in part seeking an escape from the restrictions of life in occupied France. Although the Resistance was another option for such students, many of them came from middle-class backgrounds and had strong scruples against the illegal political activity of the maquis. Anti-Communism often turned them away from the Resistance. The impact of family and home played a major role for those who opted for the collaboration in general and the Waffen-SS in particular. The French SS is shown to have been a younger, more fanatical movement than the Anti-Bolshevik Legion, more similar to the early SA and SS than to established social and military elites in either country. It was the Waffen-SS which tended to attract the true fascist fanatics, as the case of Le Fauconnier would indicate.[38]

Of interest is also the breakdown of political affiliations for the November 1943 recruits to the Waffen-SS. Twenty percent came from the PPF, 10 percent from the Milice, 9 percent from the Francistes, and only 4 percent from Déat's RNP. Thirty-eight percent had belonged to no political movement, a reflection of the youth of many of the recruits, and 19 percent were listed as having belonged to Anton Mussert's Dutch Nationaal-Socialistische Beweging and various other factions. The proportions show once more the relative strength of the PPF with respect to its rivals in the collaborationist camp in late 1943. Déat's RNP, true to its reputation as one of the "softer" collaborationist parties, furnished only a small contingent to the Waffen-SS. Significant groups came from the Milice, still largely in formation in November 1943, and the Francistes. Darnand had joined the Waffen-SS himself in an effort to gain German arms and Bucard had never been terribly enthusiastic about the LVF, too heavily Doriotist for his liking. The creation of the French Waffen-SS gave Doriot's rivals an opportunity to try to outflank him and the legion in their unending quest for German support. It also provided a chance for the most fanatical of the collaborationists to act out their

[38]German stormtroopers often came from military families; see Merkl, p. 241. The occupational breakdown of the Waffen-SS recruits is from Zwickler (see n. 37).

political creed. The particularly combative Francistes made a mark in the French Waffen-SS out of all proportion to their numbers in France.[39]

In his history of the Waffen-SS, George Stein has found ample evidence to indicate that its leaders, starting with Hitler at the top, never deviated from their basic conception of a German-dominated Europe ruled from Berlin. Statements made during the war by Himmler and Berger, the latter often mistakenly considered an exponent of the "European" idea, confirmed that the purpose of the Waffen-SS, whatever its composition, was to serve Germany. The idea of service in a common European army, whose victory would lead to a united Europe in which all nationalities would be honorably represented was but another example of Nazi myth-making to cover the need for manpower as the war situation deteriorated. Speaking to a group of non-German volunteers, Himmler said that he did not expect them to renounce their own countries or become Germans from opportunism. They were told instead to subordinate their national ideals to those of the Germanic Reich. By the end of the war, according to Stein, the Waffen-SS had become an army of Europeans but it never became a European army.[40]

The manipulative myth of a European Waffen-SS was taken seriously by a number of young middle-class Frenchmen in quest of a political crusade. Some of the earliest volunteers came from the Jeunes du Maréchal, a small group of secondary-school and university students recruited in the cities of the northern zone. The members of Jeunes du Maréchal had wished to become an elite among the youth of France in service to Marshal Pétain. Anti-English and anti-Communist, many of them admired the Hitler-Jugend. Their leader, Jean Balestre, was a young firebrand in his twenties, who wished to give the Jeunes du Maréchal a fascist-style paramilitary character. Balestre and one of his aides, Philippe Merlin, established the semi-monthly magazine *Jeune Force de France* early in 1943. Thoroughly collaborationist in every respect, *Jeune Force de France* attempted to become the magazine for a new generation of National

[39]Zwickler.
[40]Stein, pp. 145–148.

272

Socialist French youth. Many of its contributors came from Déat's RNP and Merlin served as editor-in-chief. Merlin held a doctorate in jurisprudence and, like Marc Augier, had been active before the war in the Centre Laïc des Auberges de Jeunesse, the youth hostel movement. He had been very much a disciple of Jean Giono. The same romanticism that had led him to the rural outdoor life prescribed by Giono later led him to National Socialism and the Waffen-SS. Continuing their laic orientation after the armistice, Merlin and several other former CLAJ members gravitated toward the RNP although it is unclear whether Merlin actually joined Déat's party.[41]

Merlin wanted to play more of a political role in the Waffen-SS than was desired by the Germans, who above all needed soldiers in the field. Once in the Waffen-SS, Merlin complained that the Germans did not take the French volunteers seriously enough and he began to question the reality of Germany's "European" commitment. He was not satisfied with the level of the spirit of service, sacrifice, and virility that he found in the real Waffen-SS. According to French SS lore Merlin went to Berlin to air his grievances personally before Himmler and came away deeply disappointed in the SS leader. Not long after his return, Merlin committed suicide. In remembrance of the ancient Vikings, he had willed that his body be cremated, with the ashes scattered over the North Sea. (Merlin's suicide parallels the better-known case of Drieu la Rochelle, another romantic adventurer in prolonged adolescence who in an autobiographical sketch published posthumously had discussed his fear of growing old, or perhaps growing up. A fugitive in liberated France, Drieu committed suicide in 1945). Although it is possible that Merlin did see Himmler, there is no record of their meeting. If he saw any ranking SS official, it may have been Berger.[42]

[41]Balestre and the Jeunes du Maréchal are discussed in Mabire, pp. 33–35, and Merlin on pp. 63–64 and 122–124. I am also indebted to Jean Mabire for an interview he accorded me, July 18, 1974. My sources for information on Merlin included interviews with Augier and several other veterans of the French Waffen-SS. See also the memoirs of an associate of Merlin in the Waffen-SS, Serge Mit, *Carcasse à vendre* (Paris: Dominique Wapler, 1950), pp. 32–34 and 40–45.

[42]The atmosphere in the Waffen-SS was such that after Merlin's suicide, some of his former comrades suspected him of having been an anti-German agent about to be caught. There were striking parallels between the case of Merlin and that of Drieu la

Merlin stands as an extreme example of the self-destructive nature of the adolescent romanticism that existed in all fascist movements and became more pronounced in the French collaborationist parties, removed from power in occupied France. As the cause of the Axis grew more doubtful, the sense of apocalyptic doom characteristic of radical Right counterrevolutionary movements intensified in the camp of the French collaborationists and among their militants in the German armed forces. Young rebels such as Merlin set up goals whose mystique of sacrifice, camaraderie, and virility were so far removed from reality that they could not possibly be attained and the inevitable disillusion was devastating when it came. Merlin and similar *exaltés,* whether in France or among the followers of José Antonio Primo de Rivera in Spain, Codreanu in Rumania, Massimo Rocca in Italy, or the early SA and SS in Germany, were doomed to political sterility.

The suicides of Merlin and Drieu la Rochelle attest to their realization of the contradictions between their own compulsions toward constant rebellion and the need for order of the modern state, especially one based on the authoritarian Right. Merlin failed to make political life itself a mystique, the cover for the psychological tensions produced by modernization. Like so many other middle-class fascists in interwar and wartime Europe, he sought escape from the ambiguities and loneliness of modern urban life in the retreat to an atavistic heroic, virile, tribal community. Even the Waffen-SS had been insufficiently pure for him. Writing in *Jeune Force de France,* in 1943 Merlin recalled his days as a follower of Giono seven years earlier. His words were retrospective and prophetic: "But we were sick: we needed the absolute. We were in search of certainty, in quest of a Bible. Everything had deceived us. Everything had failed us. We could no longer hang on to anything. We were perpetually at the point of suicide, but suicide brought nothing. So, we waited . . . we searched . . . for something that had to come." In his quest for certainty Merlin looked to Giono, but became progressively disillusioned as Giono moved toward fame and fortune, becoming a

Rochelle, who expressed his fascination with youth and aversion to growing old in his *Récit secret* (Paris: Gallimard, 1951), p. 11. For a psychoanalytic examination of Drieu, see Robert Soucy, "Psycho-Sexual Aspects of the Fascism of Drieu la Rochelle," *Journal of Psychohistory,* 6 (Summer 1976), 71–92.

focus of adulation from Parisian literary society. As later with the Waffen-SS, Merlin would not compromise. He turned away from Giono and his followers, a man and a movement now defiled in his eyes.[43]

Merlin was joined in the Waffen-SS by a friend who at age twenty in 1943 enlisted in the Sturmbrigade and then fought in the Charlemagne division. Attracted by the Germany of Wagner, the Nuremberg party congresses, and the Hitler-Jugend, this young man described himself as a "literary romantic." Balestre, another friend of Merlin's, also joined the Waffen-SS, praising its elitism and spirit of sacrifice, and attempting to connect it to the French military tradition. An unnamed volunteer, influenced by the writings of Drieu la Rochelle, wrote of the "restoration" of the value of the human body on which would then be based new spiritual values. This rather unclearly defined "revolution of the spirit" was representative of most French collaborationist thought. The Sturmbrigade also attracted several of the leaders of the Milice, dispatched there by Darnand to maintain a Milice presence. These included Noël de Tissot, a former science professor, who became a convinced National Socialist and one of the doctrinaires of the Milice and later the Sturmbrigade, depicting the French volunteers as a revolutionary elite. De Tissot was to die in Russia in 1944.[44]

---

[43]Philippe Merlin, "Adieu à Jean Giono," *Jeune Force de France,* January 27, 1943. See also the recollections of Giono and the CLAJ written by Guy Lemonnier, a ranking member of the RNP, "Les Ajistes au tournant de la vie," *Jeune Force de France,* December 1, 1943. Unlike Merlin, Lemonnier did not join the Waffen-SS but rather wrote on education and political ideologies for a number of RNP publications.

[44]Mit, pp. 72–73. See also Claude Delpla, "Correspondance d'un L.V.F. et SS. Français," *Bulletin de la Société Ariégeoise Sciences, Lettres et Arts, Textes et Documents,* 23 (1967), 191–195. A Waffen-SS volunteer discussed the influence of Drieu la Rochelle on his ideas in "D'un volontaire," *Devenir,* no. 2 (March 1944). See also Noël de Tissot, "Elite révolutionnaire," *Devenir,* no. 5 (July 1944), and on de Tissot, as well as Pierre Cance, another ranking Milicien who joined the Waffen-SS, see Jean Sylvestre, "Pages d'héroisme," *La France,* October 30, 1944. *La France* was a daily newspaper published by the émigré collaborationists starting in October 1944 at Sigmaringen. For the background of de Tissot, see Delperrie de Bayac, p. 74. Merlin's friend Balestre expressed his viewpoint in "Les soldats du Führer," *Devenir,* no. 2 (March 1944). Anti-Communism, an Action Française background and an infatuation with the Nuremberg party rallies and the Nazi style in general led the young Christian de la Mazière into the Waffen-SS. From a military family, de la Mazière

In August 1944 the Sturmbrigade saw action on the flank of the Horst Wessel division, attempting to slow and then stop a Red Army in advance in the area of Sanok and the Wisloka River as the summer Soviet offensive carried into southern Poland. The French in the Waffen-SS fought well but they lacked the men and material needed to stop the Russians. They took heavy casualties in the fighting and were evacuated westward, along with the rest of the retreating German forces.[45]

Survivors of the Sturmbrigade were joined with the LVF veterans in September 1944 to form the new Charlemagne division. By that time, remnants of the collaborationist parties, including Darnand and about 4,000 of his Miliciens, had taken refuge in Germany from the Allied tide that had swept across France by the end of August. Miliciens were now recruited into the Charlemagne division. One thousand two hundred of them were to be inducted into the Waffen-SS, with most of the others being used as laborers in German factories. Not all the Miliciens inducted were willing to serve in the Charlemagne division and some had to be cajoled or otherwise pressured. The element of coercion in regard to the French, however, was generally less than for Eastern Europeans in the Waffen-SS for, as George Stein has indicated, more Western Europeans took Nazi "Europeanism" seriously. By September 1944, with virtually all of France liberated, the volunteers in the LVF and the French Waffen-SS had no home to which they might return. Their bridges burned behind them, their identification of their own interest with those of the declining Reich had become a matter of necessity.[46]

German plans were to make of the Charlemagne contingent a division and it was officially listed as SS-Division no. 33, but it never recruited enough men for effective division size. With 7,000 members at most, it fought at brigade strength. The figure of 7,000 is

achieved notoriety with the witness he bore to his enlistment in Marcel Ophuls' film *Le chagrin et la pitié*. See de la Mazière, *Le rêveur casqué* (Paris: Robert Laffont, 1972), pp. 21–22.

[45]The Sturmbrigade's combat operations are discussed extensively in Saint-Loup [Marc Augier], *Les hérétiques* (Paris: Presses de la Cité, 1965); see especially pp. 32 and 69 for maps of the battlefield operations.

[46]Stein, p. 164. The utilization of Miliciens for the Charlemagne division is discussed in Reichel, Referat Inland IIc, Report to Gruppenleiter Inl. II, Berlin, October 2, 1944, T-120/3316/E007658.

given by a veteran of the Charlemagne division who later wrote its history. He also put at 5,000 the number of men in the Sturmbrigade, a figure unduly high in view of the number of volunteers found unfit for one reason or another and sent home from the training camp. The Charlemagne division, composed of the disparate elements of the French collaboration, was difficult to organize. PPF veterans of the Anti-Bolshevik Legion clashed with Darnand's Miliciens. French career officers, also veterans of the legion, often had trouble adjusting to the more Germanic spirit of the SS. French soldiers of the Waffen-SS, seeing themselves as the elite warriors of the Axis forces, showed open contempt for the legion officers, whom they viewed as the defeated military men of 1940. Waffen-SS officers were usually younger and more ready to share the dangers and privations of life at the front with their troops, and many of the French volunteers in the Sturmbrigade preferred their senior officers, who were German, to the French of the legion. In return, the French officers of the legion sometimes looked upon the French Waffen-SS officers and men as brash upstarts. Only the leveling effect of the war, as the fronts moved closer to Berlin, stilled the jealousies and bickerings among the French soldiers of the Third Reich.[47]

Early in 1945, the Charlemagne division was sent into combat in Pomerania, where it suffered severe losses trying to stop the Soviet drive toward Berlin. By the spring, many of the men were fighting simply for their military honor. Some still believed that miraculous new weapons would turn the tide of battle for Hitler's Germany, fighting desperately now against superior Allied forces on both east and west. During the last battles, Colonel Edgar Puaud, who had replaced Labonne at the head of the legion, disappeared. With his men, Puaud had been assigned to the Charlemagne division. Some

[47]For the expression of the confidence felt in the integrity of German as opposed to senior French officers on the part of a member of the French Waffen-SS, see the excerpt from a letter written by a volunteer identified only as Daniel V., February 27, 1944, in Delpla, p. 193. A similar respect for the younger German officers of the Waffen-SS was evidenced in an interview granted me by Léon Colas, August 28, 1973. The figures for the size of the Sturmbrigade and the Charlemagne division are taken from pp. 45 and 50, respectively, in an unpublished history of the military units of the French collaboration by Robert Soulat, who was kind enough to grant me an interview, July 21, 1974, and to allow me to consult his manuscript, written in 1949.

speculated that he deserted to the Russians, others that he died in battle or in a Russian prison camp. Bassompierre of the Milice, while fighting in Pomerania, was taken prisoner by the Russians who returned him to France, where he was executed after the war. By late April 1945 several dozen survivors of the Charlemagne division reached Berlin, where they joined in the final defense of Hitler and his bunker. Several were awarded Iron Crosses even as the Soviet army moved into Berlin and fighting erupted in the streets of the German capital.[48]

Even after the death of Hitler, French Waffen-SS troops continued to defend the remains of the Reich chancellery. There was no real alternative. German SS troops might be received back into German civilian life as men who had done their patriotic duty in wartime but the French would be seen as traitors. Caught between the Red Army and the new Gaullist government ready to try them in France, they had little choice but to go on fighting and seek escape through what was to become known later as the Odessa route. Finally, on May 2, the remnants of the Charlemagne division were called together by Boudet-Gheusi, an officer of the Milice and the LVF before joining the Waffen-SS. He advised the several dozen remaining French soldiers that the Charlemagne division no longer existed and counseled them to seek anonymity among the tens of thousands of homeless prisoners and refugees amid the debris of Hitler's Reich. Among the casualties of the Berlin fighting was Jean Fontenoy, either killed in battle or a suicide. For Fontenoy the adventure that had begun in 1940 in the frozen battlefields of the Russo-Finnish was ended five years later in the rubble of the German capital.[49]

[48]Most SS veterans in their accounts of the battle of Berlin give a figure of several hundred French fighters at the end. I have used the smaller estimate given by Ory, *Les collaborateurs,* p. 267. On the disappearance and fate of Puaud, see Soulat, p. 74 and Saint-Loup, *Les hérétiques,* pp. 300 and 520. Bassompierre and his battalion are discussed in Soulat, pp. 79–80.

[49]Soulat, p. 95 describes the final dismissal of the Charlemagne division by Boudet-Gheusi. The battles of the Charlemagne division are described in full detail in *Les hérétiques,* and the last battle, of Berlin, by Saint-Paulien [Maurice-Ivan Sicard], *Les maudits,* 2 vols. (Paris: Livre de Poche, 1973 [original edition: Plon, 1958]), 1: *La bataille de Berlin.*

10 Swimming against the Tide: The Collaborationist Movements in 1943 and 1944

Déat ... was angry with the Germans. Laval finds it pleasant that Déat is in the thick of it: it is certainly his turn! He wanted to be a minister, now he is. He believed that the occupation authorities would take into account the militant support he has continually given them in *L'Œuvre* and that his activity at the Labor Ministry would be facilitated thereby. Nothing like it has happened.

—Maurice Martin du Gard, *La chronique de Vichy*, May 4, 1944

For four years I received your compliments and good wishes. You encouraged me. And today because the Americans are at the gates of Paris you begin to tell me that I will be the blot on the history of France? You might have said so earlier.

—Darnand to Pétain, August 6, 1944

Many of the volunteers who faced the Russians quickly became aware of the increased manpower and firepower mustered by the Soviet Union during Red Army offensives in 1943 and especially in 1944. The impression of increased Allied strength evidenced in North Africa was reinforced early in 1943 as news of the German defeat at Stalingrad became generally known. In July 1943 the fall of Mussolini further intensified the conviction among many moderates and fence straddlers that the German cause was headed toward irreversible defeat.

Even then, however, there were many in France who could not forget the totality of the 1940 defeat and were unable to imagine the Germans in their turn suffering a similar catastrophe. A compromise peace between Germany and one or more of her adversaries, freeing her to fight the others, seemed possible to some who cited the 1939 Nazi-Soviet pact as precedent. Laval's policy after his return to power was based on his expectation that Germany would achieve a compromise peace with the Western powers, mediated perhaps by France, with all German resources subsequently freed for the struggle against the Soviet Union. Robert Paxton has pointed out that many who supported the Axis cause or at least Vichy did so in fear of the social upheavals they expected from a forcible liberation of France in which the Communists participated.[1]

The occupation of the southern zone by the German army made it more difficult for the French there to adopt a "wait-and-see" *attentiste* stance or to follow Maurras' counsel of "France alone." Increased German demands on French material resources, especially manpower, made neutrality increasingly difficult. The single greatest source of recruits to the maquis was the obligatory labor service program, which caused young men by the thousands during the latter stages of the war to opt for the Resistance rather than risk exploitation and what many felt certain death in a German labor camp. As Resistance activity was intensified, the German response grew more brutal. The shooting of innocent hostages in retaliation against guerrilla raids whose perpetrators could not be found rallied many of the French to the anti-German cause. The effect was to isolate the collaborationists further from the majority of French public opinion.

Sensing their isolation, many Ultras grew even more defiantly strident in their support of the New Order and denunciations of their enemies. A growing desperation began to haunt those who had been most compromised, whose earlier political activities gave them no choice but to play the game out to the end. By 1943 most collaborationists were no longer calling for a unique French form of fascism. Instead they concentrated their arguments on defending a Hitlerian Europe in which France was to have a small and subordinate place. Ideological solidarity had totally overcome national interest, completing the process begun by the interwar "pacifists." Drieu la Rochelle, who had broken with Doriot over the latter's support of Munich only to return to the PPF during the occupation, once more in 1943 began to raise doubts about the collaborationist course. The Ultras of necessity were more than ever in 1943 "Europeans," whose most militant wing made up the contingents of volunteers for the Waffen-SS. Their problem was that Hitler and his chief aides remained German.[2]

---

[1]Paxton, pp. 285–288.
[2]Fabre-Luce, pp. 496–497. See also Hamilton, pp. 284–285.

The most striking result of the events of late 1942 in the collaborationist camp was the decline of Doriot's PPF. Its drive for power in the autumn of 1942 had failed and the growing realization that Laval was the Germans' man in France took much of the wind out of the sails of the Doriotists. Defections began to outnumber new recruits and many who did not formally leave the movement simply ceased their activity within it. PPF militants vented their frustrations crying "death to Laval" at party rallies. In January 1943 a wave of resignations hit the Paris area party. Disillusionment reached into the uppermost echelons of the PPF leadership, where Fossati expressed bitterness against the Germans and the SS in particular, who were accused of having encouraged the party, only to leave it empty-handed later. With little left to do in France, Doriot returned to active duty with the LVF in March. Reports circulated not long thereafter of a meeting between the PPF leader and Hitler on the Eastern front, where Hitler allegedly told Doriot that present requirements necessitated keeping Laval at the helm in France and advised him to bide his time. Doriot would make the National Revolution, but only after final German victory in the war.[3]

By spring, 1943, the PPF had begun to moderate its criticisms of Laval. Party spokesmen argued that Laval would not remain in office even after a German victory. Fossati especially emphasized the independence of the party and maintained that the PPF alone possessed the energy and organization to govern France in the New Europe. In an apparent effort to broaden PPF popular appeal, Fossati turned briefly to General Giraud, a genuine war hero recently escaped from German captivity and known for his patriotism. He was believed more sympathetic than de Gaulle to Vichy. Fossati's move succeeded only in arousing the suspicion of other collaborationists who suggested ties between Fossati and the Banque Worms. It appeared to signal a cooling of PPF ardor for the Germans. Party strength, despite the efforts of Fossati and others, continued to ebb during the summer and autumn of 1943. Laval did what he could to accelerate the process by

[3]The problems confronting the PPF early in 1943 are described in the secret intelligence reports in the collection of private papers cited in n. 28, p. 153. One such report, dated May 15, 1943, discusses the Doriot-Hitler meeting. See also n. 29, p. 154.

sending members of the PPF and RNP as volunteer laborers to Germany.[4]

A police report covering thirty-one departments of the northern zone shows a pervasive weakening of the PPF between August and November 1943. As the party declined, the intensity of its attacks on its enemies often increased. In the Aisne department, it reputedly denounced the Vichy government in terms even more crude than those of the Communists. A perceptible diminution of PPF activity was noted in Belfort, and in several other regions party members did virtually nothing beyond chalking slogans on the walls of buildings and destroying busts of Marianne and other Republican symbols. Such petty and wanton acts often angered the majority of the local citizenry, further isolating the PPF from the mainstream of French public opinion in late 1943. In Côtes du Nord, a formerly strong local organization ceased all political activity. Large numbers of resignations were registered in the party's youth organization in the Gironde when its leader there left for work in Germany. The Orléans section in the Loiret was in danger of being closed for lack of funds after its failure to obtain any from the party's central office in Paris.[5]

The frustration felt in PPF circles gave rise to a split within the party in the Marne department where the secretary of the Epernay section favored unity with other Ultra parties. When overruled by the federation secretary, the Epernay leader left the PPF and took with him half the members of his section, killing the party there. A group of party members from the Orne department attended the August 1943 party rally in Paris but returned dispirited, even after having heard Doriot speak. Tired of speeches, some called for more concrete action but found little to do in the France of 1943. Depressed, they

---

[4]On Laval's depletion of the Ultra parties by sending their members to work in Germany, see Abwehr III F3 Nr. 61028/43g III F3, Paris, February 5, 1943, intelligence report to Referat IIIC, Militärbefehlshaber, CDJC document CDXCIV, 1. For discussion of the PPF's reaction to learning that it would succeed Laval in power—but not yet—I made use of a report of June 8, 1943 on the PPF in the collection cited in n. 28, p. 153.

[5]Documents édités par le Comité-Directeur du Front National afin de mettre à la disposition des militants de la Résistance des études et matériaux de documentation qui peuvent les intéresser: "Le PPF de Jacques Doriot: Extraits de 39 rapports des préfets de 31 départements de la Zone Nord, entre le début d'août et le début de novembre 1943," BDIC 4° P677 Rés.

left the party.[6] In the department Seine-et-Oise, the PPF, RNP, and Francistes established rival militias, with the Doriotists calling theirs the "Garde Française." As of October 1943 there were no prospects for unity or even concerted action on the part of the three militias. The German authorities also turned down a request for arms by the Seine-et-Oise Garde Française. In Vienne the administrative secretary of the PPF defected to the RNP, which did nothing to improve relations between the two rival collaborationist parties. In sum, the reports from the thirty-one departments paint a picture of a party still active but in severe disarray and losing members everywhere. The level of impatience and frustration shown by PPF militants exceeded that of Déat's supporters, less prone to violence and less stimulated by talk of an immediate seizure of power. RNP members generally refrained from the desecrations of walls and streets and destruction of Republican monuments that characterized the activities of the Doriotists in 1943. "To the degree that it becomes more violent," concluded the report, "the PPF becomes less numerous and is reduced more to a handful of ranters, adventurers, and toughs. This development has occurred and been accentuated in the last six months."[7]

Doriot's absence in the East deprived the party of much of its verve, though party affairs were administered by the political bureau. There was also a secret organization within the PPF which Doriot, remembering Communist clandestine activities, had organized in 1941. Members of cells were acquainted with one another by first name only and some were not even associated publicly with the party. Several party leaders formed a secret committee to supervise the clandestine organization of the PPF, preparing the party for underground activities in the event of a German ban or a successful Allied invasion and occupation of France. To counter attacks from the Resistance in 1943, the PPF organized its paramilitary Garde Française, which bore the same name as Charles Lefebvre's by then defunct paramilitary wing of Clémenti's Parti Français National-Collectiviste, the perpetrator of the attacks on Jewish-owned property along the Champs-Elysées in August 1940. PPF leaders may also

[6]Ibid.
[7]Ibid.

have envisioned the Garde Française as a weapon against Joseph Darnand's Milice, expanding in 1943 in the southern zone, or against Déat, who was still attempting to unite all northern zone collaborationist factions under his leadership in Paris. Although the German authorities refused arms to the Garde Française as an organization, they allowed some of its members to carry weapons. One estimate credited the Garde with 2,000 men in Paris and an additional 3,000 in the rest of France in August 1944.[8]

In 1943 and 1944 the PPF engaged in a bitter struggle with the Resistance. Doriot told Ribbentrop at the end of August 1944 that his party had lost 700 members, killed by the Resistance. He also complained of the Germans' having failed to arm his Garde Française properly despite the secret PPF apparatus gathering intelligence for the Abwehr, from which it received financial support. In his study of the PPF, Dieter Wolf amassed substantial evidence to indicate that, contrary to some postwar assertions, Doriot's association with the Abwehr was based less on venality than on his desire to help fight the Communists in France. Toward the end of 1943 the party established "Groupes d'action pour la justice sociale," according to Wolf a combination of political fanaticism and common criminality.[9]

Suggested by Sauckel, the *Groupes* were to help German authorities recruit French workers for labor in Germany. In this way the PPF helped Sauckel round up refractory French workers, something the Vichy police were hesitant to do. By the spring, 1944 the *Groupes* in many cases had assumed a relative independence from central PPF leadership, not always able to control them. In several French cities, notably Lyons, bands of *Groupe* rowdies were responsible for arrests, looting, and several murders. With the booty brought into the PPF coffers, it would have been impossible for Doriot to have been unaware of the activities of the PPF *Groupes*.

---

[8]OSS, "French Pro-Fascist Groups," pp. 22–23. On the subject of arms for members of the PPF, see Kontrollinspektion der DWStK Kontrollabteilung Az. 20, Nr. 1770/43g, Sonderbericht Nr. 8, Bourges, July 29, 1943, T-77/842/5585920, and on the refusal to arm the Garde Française as a body, Oberg, letter to DWStK, Aussenstelle Paris, May 18, 1944, T-77/838/5579074. The clandestine PPF organization is discussed in "La vérité sur la mort de Doriot," *Europe-Amérique*, November 1, 1945, pp. 22–23 and the unofficial intelligence report of May 8, 1943, the latter in the private collection, ch. 4, n. 28.

[9]Wolf, pp. 273–277.

Their members were not always exclusively PPF, although Laval later claimed that Sauckel had approached Doriot with the idea of their creation as early as August 1943. Collaborationists who supported the PPF *Groupes* argued that they promoted social justice by hunting down escapees from the compulsory labor service, thereby assuring that the burden would be shared equally by all. Members of the RNP sometimes joined the *Groupes* and when Déat was made minister of labor, he was also approached to lend his support to the enterprise but declined under the prodding of some of his subordinates in the Labor Office. The *Groupes* in reality were vigilante organizations which used the threat of deportation to commit many excesses and exact protection money from threatened individuals as well as wreak personal revenge for old scores. They were one of the more sinister formations of the French collaborationists during the occupation.[10]

While the PPF fought strenuously to maintain its strength, other Ultra groups suffered even sharper setbacks in the levels of their activity. By 1943 the MSR had virtually disappeared as a political force and the tiny groups such as the Parti Français National-Collectiviste were suffering defections to the larger and better-organized PPF and Milice. The Ligue Française of Pierre Costantini had already allied with the PPF, and Doriot now waited for all the other Ultra movements to follow the precedent. Despite military reverses, the Germans were still in control of most of Europe and their forces were deep inside the Soviet Union. The Allied advance into Italy had been held up south of Rome, and the Germans had rescued Mussolini and reinstalled him in power in northern Italy. Periodically, rumors of an impending Doriot government surfaced in Paris, especially when the PPF leader returned on leave from his service with the LVF, but Laval had the situation well in hand and retained the needed backing in Berlin.[11]

---

[10]Emile Boyez, deposition, March 26, 1949, in *France during the German Occupation*, 3:1240 and Pierre Laval, "Mémoire en résponse à l'acte d'accusation," in Gounelle, p. 409.

[11]Rumors of an impending Doriot government appear in Martin du Gard, p. 365. For information on this subject I am also indebted to a former high ranking Doriotist for an interview, which took place on July 17, 1974. Doriot's tactic of waiting for the smaller collaborationist groups to drop like ripe fruit into the

The rivalry between the parties of Doriot and Déat continued unabated through 1943. For the leader of the RNP, as for Doriot, 1942 had brought a number of disillusionments. The return of Laval to power had brought no corresponding gains to the RNP or Déat. By early 1943 he was accusing Laval of being too *attentiste* and insufficiently "revolutionary." Déat's single-party campaign of the previous summer and his Front Révolutionnaire National venture had both failed. Seeking to thwart the single-party movement, which continued to represent a threat to his own position, Laval suggested that the collaborationist movements form militias, in view of the increasing danger to collaborationist party members from the Resistance. When Déat suggested a united militia for the FRN, the Francistes demurred, insisting instead that each party retain control over its own militia. Bucard did not wish to lose his one source of strength in relation to the other Ultra faction leaders.[12]

The next move toward unity came from the Francistes. At their party congress of July 1943, Paul Guiraud suggested a program of joint action by the militias of the three major movements of the northern zone: the PPF, RNP, and Francistes. Unity would be achieved through common action, according to Guiraud, as had been the case in Tunisia. The Franciste proposal got no further than Déat's FRN, but it provoked a major quarrel within the ranks of the PPF. With Doriot away in Russia, Jean Fossati accepted Guiraud's proposal, which was announced in the middle of July by the PPF. Doriot returned angrily from Russia at the end of the month and at a

---

PPF basket is described in the *French Basic Handbook,* p. 143, and OSS, French Pro-Fascist Groups," p. 18.

[12]Déat was quite willing to express his displeasure with Laval's government to the Germans. See Grimm, Bericht, July 27, 1943, to Foreign Ministry, T- 120/ 6442H/ E481249, which reports that the RNP leader had described Laval's government to Grimm as "unbearable" and asked for immediate German intervention to change it. In August Déat was again asking for German permission to form a single party. He had apparently gained the support of Ernst Achenbach of the embassy, who was suggesting that Déat be made a minister. Complaints were being made that Laval was an *attentiste* who was keeping real collaborationists away from effective power. See Ritter, telegram, Westfalen, August 12, 1943, to German embassy, Paris, addendum, T-120/4120/E071144. The Doriot-Déat rivalry flared up in the July 5 issue of *Le Cri du Peuple,* which denounced rivals of the PPF as "manikins who wish to mimic revolutionaries"; see Martin du Gard, p. 353. Martin du Gard noted, "Laval is delighted. As long as Doriot attacks Déat, he will be content."

rally on August 8 he publicly and vitriolicly repudiated Fossati, who was deprived of all party posts and reduced in rank to the level of a simple party member. The loss of French North Africa to the Allies had particularly upset Fossati, who was from Algiers and had been instrumental in organizing the PPF there before the war. After his open break with Doriot he traveled to Spain, where he contacted American agents and might even have run into Deloncle, another disillusioned excollaborationist fishing in troubled waters there.[13]

Remaining true to his policy of waiting for the weaker Ultra movements to fall to him, Doriot rejected the Franciste proposal for joint action, despite German pressure on him to accept. There were German complaints that Doriot was too independent, and the PPF was even threatened with dissolution. Doriot, however, remained adamant in the position that collaborationist unity was to be achieved on his own terms or not at all.[14]

The PPF and the RNP continued to vilify each other in their respective newspapers, and although Doriot was no closer to power at the end of 1943 than he had been a year earlier, Déat's fortunes were improving. By the middle of 1943, some of the more adventurous RNP militants were joining the Milice, a few found their way into the PPF, with the less strongly committed attempting simply to cover their tracks in the anonymity of private life. Déat's personal star, however, seemed in the ascendancy within the Ultra camp even as his party declined. By force of his journalism, Déat had carved a major place for himself in the world of collaborationist politics, out of all proportion to the relative strength of the RNP in 1943. The overthrow of Mussolini in July combined with the continuing caution of Laval, as viewed through collaborationist eyes, led in September to the drawing up of an anti-Vichy "Plan de redressement national français," which was sent to several leading French and German officials.

The tract was written by five leading French collaborationists: Déat, Darnand, Luchaire, who by 1943 was head of the Press Corporation in Paris, Guilbaud, the organizer of the pro-Axis coup in

---

[13]For the postwar account of Fossati's role in PPF negotiations during the summer of 1943, see Maurice Garçon, *Procès sombres* (Paris: Fayard, 1950), pp. 196–197, the account substantiated in an interview with Victor Barthélemy, July 9, 1974.

[14]*French Basic Handbook*, p. 143.

Tunisia, and Noël de Tissot, Darnand's aide in the Milice and a volunteer in the Waffen-SS. Laval was not consulted. Requesting German intervention to oust Laval, the authors of the plan sought to replace his government with one committed to total collaboration with Germany and a national socialist transformation of France. The promoters of the plan read Mussolini's fall as a consequence of weakness, concluding that Fascism had been insufficiently monolithic in Italy and had allowed its enemies to organize and overthrow it. By focusing exclusively on the intrigue that led to Mussolini's ouster, the collaborationist leaders ignored the basic flaws in Mussolini's regime which had discredited him in Italy and brought on invasion by Allied forces in 1943. The plan expressed confidence that nothing similar would occur in Germany and asked only that the Germans prevent Laval and his government from following the course of Badoglio in Italy. A compromise between Déat and Darnand, the plan drew upon the ideas of the RNP and called for a single party but the people to whom it looked to lead France into the New Order were Darnand's Miliciens. Doriot, at the Eastern front, was not consulted.[15]

While the Ultras were putting together their *Plan de redressment,* they were also complaining directly to the Germans about Laval. Milice leaders in Lyons and Nice accused him of hindering rather than supporting their efforts on behalf of collaboration. PPF members in the Arriège department claimed that the schoolteachers and police there were all Gaullists. The vice president of the Cercle Européen, a collaborationist association of businessmen closely tied to Déat in Paris, quit his post in July 1943 as a result of the deteriorating Ultra position and death threats received from the Resistance. A PPF informant indicated that Doriot had directed his followers to refrain from joining the LVF because they were going to be needed to help suppress the growing disorder in France. The Groupe Collaboration suffered losses in Toulouse and Châteauroux and, in August,

[15]The history of the plan is detailed by Brissaud, pp. 82–85. Its full text is reprinted in Brissaud, pp. 541–561. A German discussion of it along with excerpts from it is presented in Schleier, telegram to Foreign Ministry, October 4, 1943, T-120/4120H/E071186-90. Déat's views on the toughness of German National Socialism as opposed to Italian Fascism were expressed in his article "Fascisme et National-Socialisme," *L'OEuvre,* August 17, 1943. The article is a prime example of Déat's capacity for self-delusion in the way in which he put an optimistic light on the fall of Mussolini.

news of the ouster of Mussolini led to a large number of resignations from the Milice. Darnand's quarrels with Laval were also reported to the Germans. Recruitment for the LVF was adversely affected in several southern zone departments following the news of Mussolini's overthrow. Among the members of the Groupe Collaboration in Lyons a growing fear of retribution was noted. [16]

The worsening situation of the collaborationist parties might not have unduly troubled the German leaders, but matters were brought to a head in the government crisis of November 13, 1943, when Marshal Pétain made known his intention to recall the National Assembly, which had not met since July 1940. The move was intended to reinforce the legitimacy of the marshal's government against threats from the Gaullists or Communists in the event of an Allied invasion of France. It also threatened to undercut Laval's position as head of the government and heir apparent to Pétain's position. The marshal planned to read a message over Radio Vichy announcing the convocation of the National Assembly but the local German authorities learned of his plans and the radio talk was barred. Angry exchanges between Pétain and Laval followed along with bitter letters from Hitler and Ribbentrop charging Vichy with duplicity and making it very plain that Laval was to continue in office and that the marshal was to remain on as a figure-head only. In his history of the events of the last year of the Vichy regime, André Brissaud called the series of events that followed the crisis the total abdication of Marshal Pétain. [17]

To insure the pro-German course of the government and stiffen its defense of order against the attacks of the Resistance, the Germans in December insisted that several prominent Ultras be brought into Laval's government. Abetz informed Pétain and Laval that Déat, Darnand, and Philippe Henriot were to receive cabinet posts. Oberg was especially anxious to see Darnand in charge of the police. Laval wanted none of the three Ultra leaders in his government and, when

[16]See the reports of the Kontrollinspektion der DWStK, Kontrollabteilung, Bourges, "Meldungen," Nrs. 1634/43g, July 20, 1943; 1839/43g, August 4, 1943; and 2030/43g, August 19, 1943; respectively T-77/842/5585975-78, 5585912-15, and 5585851.

[17]For a thorough account of the government crisis of November–December 1943 and the consequent "abdication" of Pétain together with the German pressure to bring the Ultra leaders into the cabinet, see Brissaud, pp. 164ff.

finally forced to accept them, attempted to hamstring them by placing moderates in the subordinate posts of their ministries. Pétain was more favorably inclined toward Darnand in view of his splendid war record, but he was cool toward Henriot and totally opposed to Déat. The pace of events, however, had passed the point where Pétain or even Laval might effectively shape them. A massive rally was staged on December 19 at the Vélodrome d'hiver in Paris where Darnand, Henriot, Déat, and several other prominent collaborationist leaders took turns denouncing Bolshevism and the "inactivity" of Vichy in combating it. France was being called once more to choose, to become engaged. Even before the invasion in Normandy the war was coming home to France.[18]

The appointment of Darnand, Henriot, and later Déat to the government completed the transformation of the Vichy regime into a thoroughgoing fascist state. Vichy's right-wing authoritarianism, socially conservative corporatism, and anti-Semitism all approximated fascism but until the beginning of 1944 the government lacked the turbulent activism of the Ultra groups. Its progression toward fascism, marked most clearly in the creation of the Milice, was enhanced by a continuing loss of popular support, requiring increasingly drastic measures to maintain power. Déat argued repeatedly in 1943 that France and all of Europe were in transition from a moderate "Girondin" to a more extreme "Montagnard" revolutionary stage. The collaborationists, political and social outsiders, were ready to carry the program of the more traditional and genteel Vichy Right to its logical conclusion. In 1944 that meant vigorous repression of the Resistance and total collaboration with Germany. As with the Girondins and Montagnards, the difference between the Vichyites and the Ultras was in part one of temperament. The Ultras, like the Montagnards of 1793, were willing to go *jusqu'au bout* when more moderate factions hesitated. Both Montagnards of 1793 and collaborationists of 1943 combined political radicalism with social conservatism which respected the property rights of the peasant and middle classes.[19]

[18]The pressure placed upon Laval by Abetz and, more important, Oberg was discussed by Captain Brunet of Vichy's Information Ministry in a report to the Militärbefehlshaber, December 27, 1943; CDJC document CDXCIV, 1.

[19]For Déat's references to Girondins and Montagnards, see "Guerre politique ou

Extremists though they were, the collaborationists were not the Jacobins of wartime France. The ends for which they attempted to borrow Jacobin élan were radically different from those of the revolutionaries of 1793, who spoke for revolutionary France against a counterrevolutionary Europe. The Ultras in contrast, an isolated minority in France, achieved their limited measure of power in 1944 only through the intervention of a hostile occupying power which wanted them to help maintain order. The more "legitimate" Right at Vichy, represented by Pétain and Laval in 1943 and 1944, recoiled from the consequences of their own actions and resisted the imposition of the Ultra leaders by the Germans. Neither resigned, however, when Darnand, Henriot, and Déat were brought into the government. Darnand was named Secretary-general for the Maintenance of Order, giving him control of virtually all domestic French forces of law and order. Henriot joined the government as Secretary-general for Information. In his negotiations with the Germans, particularly Oberg, whose power by late 1943 had far eclipsed that of Abetz, Laval succeeded in postponing the issue of Déat's entrance into his government.

A balance emerged within the collaborationist camp with Déat and Darnand establishing a minimal rapport in an effort to exclude Doriot, who was also *persona non grata* to the marshal. Some of Déat's followers in the RNP joined the Milice in late 1943, and Déat and Darnand appeared together in public at the December 19 rally. Doriot, at the Eastern front, was still being held out as a trump card by the Germans. Also by the end of 1943 the Milice had emerged as a fighting force which Oberg wanted to use against the Resistance. Unable to oppose German pressure for Darnand and unwilling to resign, Laval named two politically moderate police prefects to serve under him as undersecretary of state and director-general of the

---

guerre militaire?" and "L'épreuve décisive," in *L'Œuvre*, June 7 and July 31–August 1, 1943, respectively. See also Hoffmann, "Collaborationism," pp. 385 and 389–390. In a lecture comparing the French Revolution to National Socialism, Déat characterized Jacobins and Nazis both as a "fanatic elite." See Déat, "Révolution Française et Révolution Allemande, 1793–1943," the published text of a lecture given December 18, 1943, p. 8. The view of an inherently fascist Vichy government following its inner logic with the addition of the three Ultra leaders in 1944 is offered by Roger Bourderon, "Le régime de Vichy était-il fasciste? Essai d'approche de la question," *Revue d'histoire de la deuxième guerre mondiale*, 23 (July 1973), 40.

police. Pétain refused to sign the decrees nominating the three Ultra leaders but as Laval had already arrogated to himself the authority to name members of the government, the gesture was futile.[20]

A rude shock awaited Darnand when he arrived to take possession of his new offices in Vichy during the first days of 1944. His predecessor, René Bousquet, had had the rooms stripped bare of files and all other accoutrements. Darnand and his Miliciens found the offices empty, symbolic perhaps of future of the government that the new secretary-general was joining. The old Right only grudgingly made way for the new at Vichy. Taking possession of what they could, Darnand and his men staged an impressive ceremony at a dinner with speakers including Henriot, still a Milicien. A German guest commented: "The multi-hour meal ended with the singing of several songs from the Milice's period of struggle. All in all it may be said absolutely that a new and fresh spirit reigned at this gathering, which was reminiscent of our days after finally taking power" [1933 in Germany is meant].[21]

An immediate consequence of Darnand's entry into the government was German authorization to extend the Milice into the northern zone, where it became a direct competitor of the collaborationist parties centered there. Its relations with the PPF remained strained but it got along better with the weaker RNP. Déat encouraged members of the RNP to join the Milice in the hope either of capturing it from within or, failing that, combining with Darnand against Doriot. The northern Milice attracted a higher proportion of RNP and formerly leftist members of smaller Ultra movements than the older southern zone counterpart, which remained more homogeneous in its political composition. Jean Bassompierre and François Gaucher, two Milice leaders who had been sent to fight in the LVF, were recalled from the Eastern front by Darnand to organize the Milice in Paris. Max Knipping, one of Darnand's closest aides, was named General Delegate for the Maintenance of Order in the northern zone.[22]

[20]Martin du Gard, entry of December 29, 1943, p. 418, and Nicolle, 2: 256–257 and 421.

[21]Oberst Reichel, "Stimmungsbericht," Vichy, January 8, 1944, T-501/DGV 70-23588/326. See also depositions by Amédée Buissière, a police prefect, October 8, 1951, and by René Bousquet himself, 1945, in France during the German Occupation, 1:547 and 3:1477, respectively.

[22]For the discussion of the Milice in the northern zone, I am indebted to one of its

As Secretary-general for the Maintenance of Order, Darnand controlled the entire police organization in France. Although the Milice retained its separate identity and structure, many of its officers were put in charge of police agencies. A sort of parallel bureaucratic structure of police and Milice resembled the duality of state and party in Nazi Germany and other one-party states. Mixed groups of Miliciens and police were sent in forays to seek out members of the maquis and illegal dodgers of the compulsory labor service. Access to arms was facilitated and in many parts of France Miliciens now wore pistols and other firearms in public. In the Lyons area they began to launch counterinsurgency drives in January 1944.[23]

As Darnand organized the forces of order for the war against the Resistance, he received a new judicial power without precedent in modern French legal history. A law announced in the *Journal Officiel* of January 20, 1944 gave him authority to create special courts martial to try on the spot those caught in acts of assassination or other violent crimes against the state. He was empowered to name a court martial of three non-office holders, and the accused was allowed neither counsel nor time to prepare a case. If the accused was found to have been in "flagrant violation" of laws against murder and assassination, he was executed immediately. If not, he was referred to the public prosecutor. There was no appeal. Collective groups could be judged as well as individuals. No records were kept of the court martial proceedings and the "judges" were usually members of the Milice or the GMR (Groupes Mobiles de Réserve, special tactical police forces) from out of town, brought in at night for the purpose. The fact that only the accused, who were invariably shot immediately afterward, got a close look at their judges made it virtually impossible to identify them after the war. The courts martial functioned throughout France and were created in part to alleviate the burden of regular judges whose lives were threatened by Resistance reprisals for

Paris organizers for an interview, August 22, 1974. The view of the northern zone Miliciens as shirkers prone to pillage and theft was offered by Nicolle, 2:342.

[23]Kontrollinspektion der DWStK, Kontrollabeteilung, Az. 20, Nr. 30/44g. Monatsbericht Nr. 9, Bourges, January 8, 1944, T-77/842/5585807. For a German view of the reorganization of the French police and the increased toughness they hoped for from Darnand, see Scheer, Der Befehlshaber der Ordnungspolizei im Bereich des Militärbefehlshabers in Frankreich, Paris, January 29, 1944, "Kontrollbericht," T-77/838/5578700-02.

condemnations of captured *maquisards*. Together with the PPF-sponsored *Groupes d'action pour la justice sociale*, the Milicien-dominated courts martial were among the more sinister aspects of the spring, 1944, confrontation between the Ultras and the Resistance.[24]

Bloody incidents became commonplace as members of the Milice were shot down in ambushes by the Resistance and Darnand's forces retaliated with ever larger forays against the maquis. The cycle of violence and reprisal has been described in many places, notably by André Brissaud and more recently by the American writer Milton Dank. In January 1944 several hundred *maquisards* were encamped on the plain of Glières in the mountains northeast of Annecy in Haute-Savoie. Having decided to eliminate the Resistance pocket there, the Germans bombed the area from the air on March 26 and enlisted the aid of Darnand's police and Milice in a ground attack against the Resistance positions. A unit of the Milice's Franc-Garde, its armed wing, joined with the Groupes Mobiles de Réserve in assaulting the *maquisard* bastion, which was taken after a bloody battle. More than 600 Germans were killed at Glières but the end result was a major loss for the Resistance, one of whose strongholds had been wiped out. Glières was the largest single battle between Darnand's forces and the Resistance, but others were fought in Limousin and elsewhere, particularly in southern France where the Milice was older and better organized than in the north. In March 1944, Darnand took personal command of a unit of the Milice which flushed out a contingent of *maquisards* near Lyons. By June 6, when Allied forces landed in Normandy, France was already in the throes of full-scale civil violence.[25]

[24]The courts martial are discussed in Brissaud, pp. 270–271, and Dank, pp. 256–257.

[25]The involvement of the Milice in Haute-Savoie and Lyons is discussed in Kontrollinspektion der DWStK, Kontrollabteilung, Az. 20, Nr. 320/44, Monatsbericht Nr. 11, Bourges, March 8, 1944, T-77/842/5585760; the operations in Haute-Savoie were also described by Nicolle, 2:355, who noted that Darnand had gone to help supervise them. Nicolle (2:353) also pointed to *Cagoulard* origins of some of the Miliciens. Milice campaigns in the Jura were reported by Darnand himself in Kontrollinspektion der DWStK, Kontrollabteilung, Az. 20, Nr. 440/44g, Monatsbericht Nr. 12, Bourges, April 6, 1944, T-77/842/5585743. For Oberg's praise of Darnand's police work and his complaints that the French government was impeding the work of the Milice leader, see Oberg, Kontrollbericht, Paris, April 5, 1944, T-77/838/5578672. An account of the Glières battle through the eyes of a former Milicien

Like Darnand, Philippe Henriot could trace his political origins to the interwar Right. A brilliant speaker, possibly the best France produced during the occupation period, Henriot impressed the Germans with his speech at the collaborationist rally of December 19, 1943 in Paris. Almost 20,000 heard him and Oberg decided to include Henriot in the list of those he wished to see in the government. Born in 1889, Henriot was the son of an infantry officer in Rheims. He studied at several schools, including the Sorbonne, was awarded a *licence ès lettres* and an advanced degree in classical languages, and turned to teaching as a career. He also wrote several books of poetry during the early 1920's but gradually began to focus on the Catholic press and the interwar battle for greater freedom for the church in France. In 1925, Henriot joined General de Castelnau, a proclerical war hero, and became a leading speaker for the Fédération Nationale Catholique, de Castelnau's political organization. Seven years later he was elected in a Bordeaux district to serve in the Chamber of Deputies, and he was reelected in 1936. During the 1930's, Henriot supported Pierre Taittinger's Parti National Populaire, a movement in the Bonapartist tradition, renamed the Parti Républicain National et Social in 1936. The anti-clericalism of the Republicans in the Spanish Civil War turned Henriot against the Popular Front and to a more pro-Axis stand. He supported the Munich appeasement policy and, in 1940, Pétain and Vichy.[26]

For Henriot the decisive event in the war was the German invasion of the Soviet Union, which in his eyes turned the conflict into a holy crusade against Bolshevism. Anti-Communism overcame Germanophobia and led him to support the Axis cause fully. A political lone wolf, Henriot in 1944 embraced a Christian fascism with the

---

may be found in the memoir published anonymously, entitled *La vérité réconcilié... Pour la Milice Justice... par un Chef de Corps de la Milice* (Paris: Etheel, n.d.), pp. 69–74. See also Brissaud, pp. 305–312, Delperrie de Bayac, pp. 308ff., and the more general account of the Milice's war by Dank, pp. 254–257.

[26] For my account of Henriot I am indebted to his former private secretary Charles Filippi, who granted me an interview, July 6, 1974. See also Martin du Gard, pp. 432–433, and Brissaud, pp. 240–242. Henriot, Darnand, and the rally of December 19, 1943 were discussed in Abwehrleitstelle Frankreich, Br. B. Nr. 80594/44g III c A, V-Mann Bericht über Aufnahme der Änderung in der Französischen Regierung to Militärbefehlshaber in Frankreich, Chef des Generalstabs, Ic, Paris, January 31, 1944; CDJC document CDXCIV, 1.

overriding ideal of the church armed and militant. In 1943 he joined the Milice but unlike Darnand, Déat, or Doriot, Henriot exerted an entirely personal influence unrelated to any political party. Déat's journalistic collaborationism was paralleled by Henriot's talks on Radio Vichy. Of all the Ultra leaders, Henriot had the widest impact on the French population, and his radio broadcasts were listened to by friend and foe. In the words of a contemporary:

> Henriot is listened to by everyone, enemies or supporters. Families shift their mealtimes so as not to miss him. There is no one left on the street at the time he speaks. This popularity indicates to what degree the French love oratorical contests, venomous attacks, and talent. If Henriot had had the microphone starting in August 1940, de Gaulle in his London studio would not have played his game so easily. Many things, without doubt, would have happened differently.[27]

Henriot had delivered one radio talk per week prior to joining the government but in his new capacity he spoke twice daily. In his broadcasts he railed against the Jews, the Communists, and the "Anglo-Americans." His most frequent and effective talks, however, were those in which he denounced excesses committed by members of the Resistance or those who acted in their name. He also criticized the Western Allies for their bombing raids against targets in occupied France, which in 1944 caused the deaths of hundreds if not thousands of civilians and brought additional misery to a suffering country. France's most eloquent nay-sayer, Henriot became a collaborationist almost by default.[28]

The last of the triumvirate of Ultra leaders imposed upon the Vichy government by the Germans was Marcel Déat. The process by which Déat ultimately was brought into the government as Minister of

[27]Martin du Gard, p. 433. Additional witnesses, hostile to Henriot, but attesting to his remarkable oratorical skill include Guéhenno, pp. 488–489 and Galtier-Boissière, *Journal*, pp. 231–232, the latter referring also to Pétain's public suggestion to listen to Henriot.

[28]For the themes of Henriot's speeches, see "Discours prononcé par M. Philippe Henriot le 22 avril aux obsèques des victimes du bombardement de la Région Parisienne dans la nuit du 17 au 18 avril 1944" and "Extraits de: 'Libérez-nous des Juifs' par Philippe Henriot" taken from *Gringoire*, issue of June 5, 1942; CDJC Library No. 8085 and Archive document XIV, 17, respectively. Pétain's initial opposition to Henriot's entry into the government is discussed by Martin du Gard, p. 432.

Labor and National Solidarity was long and complicated. By the end of 1943 the RNP leader had turned to open criticism of Laval, in part through the *Plan de redressement*. Despite personal and political failure and the weakening of the RNP, Déat fought on in 1943 and into 1944 in an obstinate fortress mentality depicting the Ultras as a small minority of elite revolutionaries determined to save France in spite of herself. Of all the major collaborationist leaders during the occupation, he seems to have entertained the fewest doubts about the wisdom of his course. He invoked the revolutionary spirit of Valmy of 1792, the defensive aura of Verdun of 1916, and allowed himself to be convinced that the imminent introduction of new German armies and miracle weapons would turn the tide of the war. In the superheated atmosphere of the collaborationist community in late 1943 and early 1944, Deat plotted for the governmental succession.[29]

Under pressure from both Oberg and Abetz, Laval began a long negotiating process with Déat concerning the latter's entry into the government. Déat asked that the government return from Vichy to Paris to facilitate his own participation in its deliberations. He had vowed publicly never to join the government in Vichy after the failure

---

[29]Some of Déat's propagandistic activities are described in Kontrollinspektion der DWStK, Kontrollabteilung, Az. 12, Nr. 1839/43g, Meldungen, Bourges, August 4, 1943, T-77/842/5585913-14 and Muchow, Stabseinsatzführer, Einsatzstab Reichsleiter Rosenberg für die besetzten Gebiete, Hauptarbeitsgruppe Frankreich, Abschrift, June 22, 1944, to Chef des Einsatzstabes Reichsleiter Rosenberg, Stabsführer Utikal, Berlin; CDJC document CXL, 107. The second of these reports also makes clear Déat's anti-Laval stance while still a member of Laval's cabinet. Déat referred to France's revolutionary tradition in demanding the recall of the National Assembly, "Considérations juridiques," *L'Œuvre*, December 10, 1943. His fortress mentality and calls for heroism are in "Entre l'héroïsme et la lâcheté," references to preparations for a long siege of "fortress Europe," "Hypothèse d'une guerre longue," and an exposition of wartime socialism and camaraderie in "Le socialisme et la guerre," *L'Œuvre*, September 23, 1943, December 10, 1943, and February 9, 1944, respectively. In "Puissance des idées," *L'Œuvre*, February 10, 1944, Déat discussed the role of the elite in saving France even against the wishes of the majority of the population in terms similar to those of Henriot. He hinted, in a series of articles from October 9 to 12, 1943, at a separate peace in the East, which would enable the Germans to concentrate their forces against the Western Allies. On November 15, in "Les chevaliers de la conjuncture," also published in *L'Œuvre*, Déat made explicit his preference for a peace with the Soviet Union in order to "prevent the return of the Western bankers." His benevolence toward the Milice and his reactions to the rally of December 19, 1943 are expressed in "Unité militante et milicienne," *L'Œuvre*, December 24, 1943.

of his single-party campaign there in 1940. Oberg had originally wanted Admiral Platon in the government and Déat became a compromise choice, minimally acceptable to both Laval and the SS official. The veteran of Dunkerque, Platon had strong ties to the PPF, and Laval feared that the admiral in the government might become a candidate to replace him as its head. Oberg was unwilling to provoke Laval or risk disorder in France by insisting on a Doriotist. Doriot remained at the Eastern front and his backers were kept out of the government. Laval next attempted to get Déat out of his hair by offering him a ministry to be created, with responsibility for the affairs of all the French then in Germany, including workers and prisoners of war. Déat would have had charge of some two million people and Laval further proposed that he take up his office in Berlin. Déat refused to be sidestepped so easily. The appointment of Darnand and Henriot at the end of 1943 left the Déat question unresolved. In January 1944, Déat was still holding out for more than Laval wished to give, namely the right continue as head of the RNP and write his editorial columns while serving as a minister.[30]

Déat's appointment to the post of Minister of Labor and National Solidarity, the latter job created especially for him, on March 16, 1944 resulted from renewed German pressure, this time from Sauckel. By giving the Labor Ministry to Déat, Laval placed him in a post sure to arouse unpopularity in view of the forced transfers of French workers to Germany. Laval had had long and stormy negotiating sessions attempting to moderate Sauckel's demands for French labor. He now put Déat on the spot and with some relief turned the negotiations over to him. The National Solidarity post was intended by Déat to encompass all aspects of government aid to war victims, who would form a clientele for the RNP leader. From the start, however, the position was an empty one. Pétain insisted that all functions relating

[30]Captain Brunet, Information Ministry in Vichy, report to Militärbefehlshaber in Frankreich, December 27, 1943; CDJC document CDXCIV, 1. See also Martin du Gard, pp. 415–416, and the reports entitled "Information" sent to the military commander in France, January 14, and 26, 1944; CDJC document CDXCIV, 1. The fear of Déat's "socialism" in some entrepreneurial circles was mentioned by Nicolle, 2:366. Déat posed no threat to the established social order and Nicolle pointed out that these business interests were among the most "reactionary." Nicolle also indicated that Oberg had briefly considered Déat as a possible choice for the Interior Ministry before turning to Darnand; see ibid., p. 317.

to prisoners of war be removed from the National Solidarity post. Laval's emasculation of the National Solidarity office by the creation of a labyrinthine bureaucratic infrastructure, taking with one hand what he had given with the other, was the work of a master political infighter. Déat was allowed to continue writing his editorials for *L'Œuvre* but he agreed to stop signing them. In January 1944 a cabinet meeting had been held at the Matignon in Paris and many subsequent meetings were held there so that Déat's refusal to go to Vichy assumed less importance.[31]

By March 1944, Déat had been so thoroughly outmaneuvered that he had little choice but to enter the government on Laval's terms or risk being perceived by the Germans as an obstructionist. Despite his solid collaborationist credentials Déat's support among the Germans in Paris was limited. His relations with Abetz were good but the ambassador was deeply committed to Laval. Oberg, the most powerful German in Paris by the end of 1943, had briefly suggested Déat as a possible interior minister but had then turned to Darnand by the end of December. The RNP chieftain had no strong ties to the Wehrmacht establishment in France. His main source of support came from middle-level officials in the embassy: Dr. Grosse, a former German Socialist whose field was labor questions, and Ernst Achenbach, a counselor at the embassy. According to Brissaud, it was Grosse who suggested to Sauckel that Déat might be more tractible than Laval in labor negotiations. Déat remembered fondly his days as aviation minister in the Sarraut cabinet in 1936 and refusal of a cabinet post would have countered his deepest desires. The acceptance of one seemed a first step toward the presidency of the Council and put Déat back on an even footing with Darnand, already in the government, and ahead of Doriot in the scramble for power.[32]

Since Déat entered a virtually meaningless position as Minister of National Solidarity, it was in the Labor Office that he would have to

[31]For a view of the negotiations that led to Déat's entry into the government, see Martin du Gard, pp. 437–439, and for Pétain's objections to the RNP leader, Tracou, pp. 30–31 and 188–189.

[32]Déat's relations with the various German representatives in Paris is discussed by Brissaud, pp. 293–294. Achenbach's earlier support for Déat is visible in Ritter, Westfalen, telegram to German embassy, Paris, August 12, 1943. T-120/4120/ E071144. For Sauckel's pressure on Laval to accept Déat, see de Brinon, *Mémoires*, p. 211.

make his mark. With internal communications disrupted by Resistance sabotage, civil war, and Allied air strikes, conditions were hardly propitious for any bold moves by the new minister. In addition, Sauckel had to be faced. Administration was not Déat's strength and the Labor Ministry was run in large part by his *chef de cabinet,* Georges Albertini, who had played an analogous role as secretary-general of the RNP. With Déat in the government and many of the top people drawn off from the RNP to serve in his ministry, the decline of the party was accelerated.

Hardly had Déat assumed office when he was confronted with new demands by Sauckel for the transfer of additional French workers to Germany. The new minister was now trapped between public positions taken in years of journalistic bombast and his more humane and patriotic disinclination to send additional French workers into the brutal conditions of labor in Germany. Both Déat and Laval had supported the policy of German Production Minister Albert Speer, who argued that the labor of occupied Europe would be used more efficiently for the Reich if the workers remained home working in war-production plants using local resources. Spread out over a larger area, they would be less vulnerable to Allied air attack. The process of transporting millions of workers from their homelands to Germany was costly, diverting trains and other equipment needed for troop movements and other war-related jobs. Speer had negotiated an agreement with Jean Bichelonne, his opposite number in France, in which French plants working directly for the German war effort were designated *S-Betriebe* (S-Plants) with their workers exempted from service in Germany. Pitted against Speer was Sauckel, who tried to import as much slave labor as he could from the occupied countries.[33]

Laval and later Déat tried at first to promote the *Relève,* an agreement made in 1942 that exchanged one French prisoner of war for three skilled workers volunteering for service in Germany. When the *Relève* had fallen far short of meeting Sauckel's demands, the French had attempted to extend the designation of *S-Betriebe* to cover as many of their factories as possible. French negotiators with Sauckel

[33]The difference of viewpoint and the rivalry between Speer and Sauckel are discussed in Jacques Evrard, *La déportation des travailleurs français dans le IIIe Reich* (Paris: Fayard, 1972), pp. 147–149, in which the *S-Betriebe* are discussed. See also Milward, pp. 121–122 and 158ff.

were caught in an internal struggle between Speer and Sauckel for influence in Berlin and the obvious preference they showed for Speer's ideas did not facilitate their dealings with Sauckel.

An early encounter with Sauckel was a personal disaster for Déat. Promising to act as a decisive fascist leader, Déat told his French colleagues that he would set Sauckel straight in the most direct language. Sauckel, however, exemplified the most brutal, crude, and violent traits of the Nazi personality pattern. Engaged in a continuing struggle against Speer in Berlin, he had little reason to trust the French, especially after months of exasperating negotiation with Laval. He was particularly angry when he met Déat because 91,000 French workers, designated as the transfer contingent for March 1944, had not yet been sent to Germany. Storming into the conference room, Sauckel demanded the immediate transfer of 273,000 French workers, the contingents for the months of March through May 1944. Déat remained silent, but when Darnand pointed out that Sauckel's continuing demands were the single largest factor in the growth of the Resistance, the German exploded in a towering rage and delivered a furious diatribe against what he called French bad faith. Caving in entirely, Déat quickly agreed to the demands. On April 7 he went on Radio Paris to exhort the French to make the sacrifices necessary to preserve "Europe" from the "hordes at the gate" and effectuate a "socialist" community by working in German slave-labor camps. [34]

Defenders of Déat have emphasized the fact that during his tenure as labor minister, few French workers were actually sent to Germany. In addition, 17,000 members of the Chantiers de la Jeunesse, dissolved by Wehrmacht authorities in May and rendered subject to deportation were spared. The Chantiers de la Jeunesse had been established in Vichy after the 1940 armistice as a national labor service to occupy demobilized French soldiers at a time when unemployment was high and they could not readily be reabsorbed into the civilian economy. Gathered in camps in the countryside and run in a

---

[34]De Brinon, *Mémoires*, pp. 218–220. The story is recounted by Brissaud, pp. 301–303. For Albertini's recollection of the incident and his advice that Déat resign rather than accept Sauckel's demands, see Cour nationale de justice, Ministère Public C/M. Albertini, the stenographic account of the December 1944 trial of the former RNP secretary-general, available in the BDIC, p. 102.

kind of boy-scout spirit under General Joseph de la Porte du Theil, the Chantiers by 1944 contained many sympathizers with the Resistance whom the general was suspected of harboring.

Déat appealed to the Armistice Commission in Wiesbaden and suggested that the young Frenchmen be sent into the *Organisation Todt*. Once more, German bureaucratic services were played off against one another. In June, Hitler authorized Déat to create a new French youth labor service and while the bureaucratic wrangling continued, Allied forces swept across France and the issue became moot. It is difficult to evaluate Déat's impact in the saving of the 17,000 Chantier members because Laval also supported his efforts and his staff did much of the difficult negotiating with the Germans. More to the point, by 1944, German policy had shifted away from seeking large contingents of workers from occupied France. The inefficiency of foreign slave labor had been observed and Speer's arguments against the Sauckel policy were beginning to take root. The 1942 argument in favor of greater security for factories in Germany's heartland no longer held two years later when all of Germany had become vulnerable to Allied air power. Millions of foreign workers in Germany also entailed growing security problems when all energies were required for the war effort. Alan S. Milward has shown that the vast majority of all French workers sent to Germany left in two spurts: from October 1942 through March 1943, and again in June and July of 1943. After August 1943, that is during the last year of the occupation, the number of deportees was relatively insignificant.[35]

Déat was also stymied in the sphere of domestic labor reform. He had long called the Vichy Labor Charter reactionary because of its

---

[35]Milward, pp. 123–124. For Albertini's account of the affair of the Chantiers de la Jeunesse, see Ministère Public C/M. Albertini, p. 40, and Varennes, p. 190. Hitler's charge to Déat to create a new youth labor service is discussed by Dr. Ficker, Reichskabinettsrat, note for Jugendführer des Deutschen Reichs, June 9, 1944, T-120/6034H/E444729-30. Déat's position, which might be interpreted as a stalling action to keep the Chantier workers in France, is given in a "Verbalnote," no date, but either June or July 1944, T-77/834/5573661-2. See also Louis Tartarin, of the Labor and National Solidarity Ministry, "Abschrift," to Herr Oberfrontführer Leuthardt, Einsatzgruppe West, Paris, July 21, 1944 and Major Meier-Faust, DWStK Aussenstelle Paris, Abt. II, Nr. 1542/44, "Aktennotiz," Paris, July 24, 1944, T-77/834/5573632-33 and 5573611-12, respectively.

establishment of mixed corporative associations which gave employers substantial power over their workers. Once in the government he tried to alter the labor structure in France and give different form to the Labor Charter. Inspired by Albertini and others with trade-union backgrounds, Déat announced the creation of new interprofessional unions in which employers were not represented. The reestablishment of workers' organizations through the aegis of the Labor Charter was the most significant step taken by Déat as minister but they had insufficient time to prove their mettle. Ludovic Zoretti began to establish trade-union schools for workers but again the landings of the Allied forces in France cut short the execution of all such plans.[36]

Déat was soon conspiring with Admiral Platon against Laval's ministry. On May 16 Platon visited Marshal Pétain to suggest the creation of a new Ultra cabinet and met a stony reception. Déat now requested a personal interview with the marshal, who happened to be in Voisins, not far from Paris. Reluctantly, Pétain acceded. The description of the meeting by Jean Tracou, the director of Pétain's cabinet, aptly characterizes Déat: "He is a squarely built little man, standing well planted on short legs, a kind of Samurai. His face bears, like Paul Reynaud's but in a firmer manner, a reflection of the Far East. He gives an impression of concentrated force and self-assurance. His enemies and even his friends maintain that the impression is deceptive and that all his strength lies in his pen."[37]

By mutual accord the interview was restricted to generalities. Pétain complimented Déat on a speech defending corporatism May 1 at a Labor Day celebration at Trocadero. But after praising the speech, he added: "Monsieur Déat, your speech moves me greatly, and I give you my compliments for it. You call yourself socialist. But there is in you, all the same, something that pleases me less: Monsieur Déat, I do not know if you are human. It is necessary to be human."[38]

Pétain also made an oblique reference to an impending liberation which most of those hearing it took to mean the expulsion of the

[36]Author's interview with Georges Albertini, July 4, 1973; also Varennes, pp. 175–176.
[37]Tracou, pp. 256–258. See also Brissaud, pp. 358–359 and Varennes, pp. 204–206.
[38]Martin du Gard, p. 500.

Germans from France. Déat, however, took the words to mean an imminent sacking of Laval and left the marshal convinced more than ever that his hour was at hand. His isolation and self-delusion had brought Déat to a fantasy land that existed only in his mind. A strange presence in the political world, Déat contributed significantly to the intensification of political passions in 1944 in France. His continued scheming against Laval, Darnand, and Henriot during the weeks preceding the Normandy invasion assumed the dimensions of a tragic and dangerous charade.[39]

The Allied landings on June 6, 1944 on the Norman coast brought to a climax the antagonism between Laval and the Ultras. Upon learning of the invasion Pétain and Laval declared that France was neutral and called for calm. Once more Vichy's policy, long antici-pated by the Germans, worked in favor of the occupation forces who wanted the civilian population to remain calm and not impede the defense effort. For the collaborationists, however, neutrality was in-sufficient. Darnand, Doriot, and Déat issued public calls for the mobilization of their respective forces. Déat instructed his supporters in the RNP to join the Milice which, in contrast to Doriot, he himself symbolically joined.[40] An Ultra onslaught against Laval was now orchestrated by Déat, who again began to sign his daily editorials in *L'Œuvre,* denouncing the government of which he was a member. Giving ground, Laval on June 14 named Darnand Secretary of State for the Interior, an elevation of his rank and an increase in power.

The many weaknesses in the organizational structure of the Milice became evident as mobilization proceeded slowly and many members failed to appear. For the southern zone Brissaud cites figures to show that of 23,000 Miliciens called up in June 1944, only 14,000 appeared and of these nearly 5,000 were over-age. The showing was even worse for the weaker northern zone Milice. Jean Bassompierre in-structed the Milice to fight not at the front in Normandy but behind

---

[39]For discussion of the jockeying for power between Déat and the Milice faction of Darnand and Henriot within the government in May 1944, see ibid., p. 471.

[40]"Marcel Déat à la Milice Française," *Combats,* July 15, 1944. In this article published in the Milice newspaper, Déat gives his reasons for joining the organiza-tion. The responses of the three leading Ultra organizations, the PPF, RNP, and Milice, following the June 6 Allied landings are described in Abetz, Report nr. B 2948/44, to Foreign Ministry, June 10, 1944, T-120/3790H/E042389-90.

the German lines to maintain domestic order. Friedrich Grimm observed, however, that the Milice was too weak to be of any use in the north and that if serious insurrection erupted, German forces would be needed.[41]

The month of June 1944 brought a series of German atrocities committed against civilian populations in a number of towns: Tulle, Rouffignac, Oradour, and Bonneville, by the SS Division Das Reich in transit from the south to the Normandy front. In Oradour virtually the entire population of the village was locked in the church, which was then burned to the ground. Six hundred forty-two were killed.[42] The impassioned atmosphere of civil war was superimposed upon the pent-up anger and frustration of those who had suffered the privations of four years of German occupation. Added to this was the bitterness of the Germans and collaborationists, which had increased with the growing imminence of an Allied landing in France. In late June and early July a series of political assassinations occurred. Within two weeks Jean Zay, Henriot, and Georges Mandel, all prominent in French political life, were murdered. The assassination of Henriot in particular precipitated the last crisis of the Vichy regime.

Zay, a Jew who had been education minister in the Popular Front government, was murdered on June 20. One of the political leaders who in 1940 had attempted to leave on the Massilia for North Africa, Zay had been returned to France, tried, and found guilty of desertion. Interned in a prison near Riom, he was removed by three men in Milice uniforms under pretext of an order to transfer him to another prison. *En route* he was killed. Eight days later, on the night of June 28, a secret Resistance squadron assassinated Henriot in Paris. On July 7, Georges Mandel, the prewar interior minister, who had been held by the Germans after the occupation of the southern zone in November 1942, was assassinated, as with Zay, ostensibly while being transported by the Milice from one place of detention to another. The origin of the order to kill Mandel has never been clarified, but the Miliciens were in a vengeful mood after the execu-

[41]Grimm, Stimmungsbericht, Paris, June 24, 1944, T-120/6442H/E481327. See also Brissaud, pp. 409–410.

[42]The activities of the SS Division Das Reich and the atrocities it committed in its march from southern France to the war front in the north are recounted in great detail by Delarue, pp. 281–493.

tion of collaborators by the Algiers Committee and the assassination of Henriot. Mandel, like Zay, was Jewish.[43]

The assassination of Henriot brought Déat, Darnand, and de Brinon together for what was to be their last assault on Laval's leadership while still in France. Ironically, Henriot seems to have developed some last-minute qualms regarding the rightness of the collaborationist stance. He had criticized German exactions and during a visit to French workers in Germany had been privately critical of the Germans. Henriot had published staunchly anti-German articles before the war, which the Germans had not forgotten. Had he lived and had the Germans won the war, he might have faced a clouded political future. His death brought a stormy outburst by Déat, who complained that Laval did not render sufficient homage to his memory when *pro forma* condolences were sent to Madame Henriot. Already badly strained after the Normandy invasion, relations between Déat and Laval broke with the assassination of Henriot.[44]

The execution of former Vichy Interior Minister Pucheu in March 1944 by the Algiers Committee had tied the Ultra leaders more closely to the Germans and the appearance of the V-1 and V-2 rockets and the antitank *Panzerfaust* gave them reasons for hope. More worldly-wise and able to appreciate the great shifts in the power balance that had occurred by 1944, Pétain was one of many who began to forecast a German defeat.[45] The Ultras could envision only the smartly dressed and well-disciplined German soldiers who had

[43]For the view that the order to kill Mandel came from Darnand, see "Sur la mort de Mandel," an otherwise unidentified report of a secret meeting of July 5, 1944 of the Milice's directing committee, CDJC document CCXXI, 63. See also the discussion of the assassinations of Zay, Henriot, and Mandel in Brissaud, pp. 415–417, 417–427, and 428–438, respectively.

[44]For the protests of Déat and Darnand against Laval's failure to eulogize Henriot, see the untitled and undated report, CDJC document CCXXI, 62, and Tracou, pp. 319–321. Henriot's public opposition to excessive German demands for French manpower and material is mentioned in an undated report, CDJC document CCXXI, 62a, also supported by information provided by Charles Filippi in an interview with the author, July 6, 1974. The split between Déat and Laval on the question of the level of French activity on behalf of the German war effort came to a personal confrontation in a cabinet meeting reported June 26, 1944, hence two days before the assassination of Henriot; see CDJC document CCXXI, 61.

[45]Brissaud, pp. 444–445, recalls an incident in which Pétain predicted imminent German defeat to General von Neubronn, who had been sent by the Germans to Vichy to keep the marshal apprised of military developments on the French front.

marched in victory down the Champs-Elysées in 1940. Such a nation as the one that had so humiliated France four years earlier—and Déat wrote this repeatedly—could never be defeated. An indirect provincialism in the glorification of the German victory minimized the stigma of the French defeat. Crushed by a nation that in turn was headed for total defeat, France would hold a relative position among the world powers that was all the weaker. In their own way the Ultras avoided the painful question of the decline of French power, which de Gaulle would have to face in the years immediately after the Liberation and again after 1958.

While Henriot still lived, Doriot had mocked Darnand as "the furniture mover," in reference to the Milice chief's early trucking days, and exulted in his knowledge of German awareness of the Milice's weaknesses. The assassination of Henriot, however, brought even Doriot behind a new move led by Déat to create an Ultra government. A large rally was held in Paris, its theme and the denunciation of Laval. An open letter to Pétain inspired by Déat and drafted by Dominique Sordet, a military writer friendly with Déat, was essentially a repetition of the *Plan de redressement* drawn up by collaborationist leaders in September of the previous year. On July 10, Platon visited Pétain and presented him with the letter, entitled "Common Declaration on the Political Situation."[46]

Predicting ultimate German military success, the letter castigated the government for "doubt and hesitation" in dealing with the Resistance which, it contended, aimed at the destruction of all organized political authority in France. Five demands were made: the formal taking of a position by the government in favor of the Germans, its return to Paris, the addition of more "reliable" (Ultra) figures to the government, more authority for the Council of Ministers in matters of general policy, and tougher repression of the Resistance. It was signed by four ministers: Déat, Bichelonne, de Brinon, and Abel Bonnard, the education minister. Some thirty others from the Ultra political and journalistic world, including Luchaire, Platon, and Doriot, also signed. Ever loyal to his bosses, Darnand did not sign. After reading the letter to the marshal, Platon praised Déat and

---

[46]Tracou, pp. 324–325. Doriot's contempt for Darnand and his undisguised joy at the failings of the Milice are witnessed in a report catalogued as CDJC document CCXXI, 62a.

suggested a new government of collaborationists which he would head. Pétain in reply advised Platon to retire to a country estate and remain out of politics. Informed of Platon's mission to the marshal, Laval became angry at the insubordination of his own ministers. He called a cabinet meeting for July 12, to crush the incipient Ultra revolt, and declared, "I will immediately send this simpleton Platon off to house arrest in the country."[47]

Admiral Charles-René Platon cut a strange figure in the history of the collaboration. Born in 1886 in Pujols in the Gironde to a Protestant family, Platon was by all accounts an austere man of high personal integrity possessing the most limited political perspectives and questionable judgment. Having played a major role in the evacuation of Allied troops at Dunkerque in 1940, he had developed a deep Anglophobia, traditional in French naval circles but intensified after Dunkerque and Mers-el-Kébir. Platon quickly became a believer in the cause of collaboration. In September 1940, Laval brought him into the government as minister of colonies and in 1941, Platon, who abhorred dissidence, took part in the drafting of plans to retake Chad from the Gaullists in power there. During Laval's second tenure in office Platon was named minister without portfolio and assigned a variety of duties, including the ferreting out of Freemasons in the government, a task which the admiral undertook with vigor. After the Allied landings in North Africa in 1942, Platon was sent by Laval on a special mission to assure the loyalty of the French troops there to Vichy. His mission was apparently for show, a sop to the Germans, for while he was in North Africa other sources informed Darlan that Pétain had approved his negotiations with the Americans. To Laval, Platon was a pawn to be easily manipulated. The admiral made no secret of his own contempt for Laval and desired to replace him as head of the government. He is reported to have said that with the help of the Germans he would preside over a moral regeneration of France. By 1944, Laval had rid his cabinet of Platon, who had become very friendly with Doriot and now participated in the highest councils of the PPF. A German observer in 1941 described Platon as a known user of morphine and the admiral seems to have practiced politics

[47]Tracou, pp. 325–328.

with a naïveté that would almost suggest some sort of dreamlike state.[48]

Laval moved quickly to counter the threat to his leadership. Upon learning of Platon's visit to Pétain, he telephoned de Brinon and Bichelonne in Paris to find out if they had resigned from the cabinet. Both denied this and protested their loyalty to Laval, who then called the cabinet meeting for July 12 in Vichy. Isolated, and no match for Laval, Déat was put on the spot. He hid behind his oath never to return to Vichy to avoid a showdown. The meeting of the twelfth saw Laval at his most formidable and in complete mastery of the situation. For the Ultras it was a humiliating rout. Determined to face down his opposition, Laval opened with a sharp denunciation of Déat for breaking his word by once again criticizing the government openly in *L'Œuvre,* for disloyalty toward the head of the government of which he was a member, and for failing even to attend the cabinet meeting. He then turned to the text of the letter Platon had brought to the marshal. Bichelonne and de Brinon backed off, offering lame excuses. Laval made his labor minister appear foolish as well as hypocritical in the eyes of his colleagues.[49] He then turned to the subject of Platon, who was not even aware that his mail was opened regularly by government agents. In an intercepted letter to his brother, Platon had criticized Laval's neutrality in the battle for France and had expressed his desire to see Laval hung as a common criminal. Laval pointed out that the Ultras' open letter to Pétain mentioned "Europe," but never France. If Déat objected to neutrality, he was free to enlist in the LVF or the Waffen-SS. All present at the cabinet meeting, after hearing Laval's presentation, assented to the policy of neutrality. When Abel Bonnard rose to defend the Ultras as the nucleus of a new France, Laval responded that they were merely

[48]Franz Reuter, report to DWStK, June 18, 1941, T-77/850/5594927. On Platon's relationship with Laval, see Martin du Gard, pp. 323–324 and 341, on which is noted that Laval had Platon arrested in March 1943. Further biographical information on Platon may be found in Albert Kammerer, *Du débarquement Africain au meurtre de Darlan* (Paris: Flammarion, 1949), pp. 28–29, n. 2.

[49]Tracou, p. 333. We are particularly well informed about the cabinet meeting of July 12 because Tracou, in attendance, kept an account of its proceedings, which he published in full in his memoir. His account is reproduced in his deposition of July 29, 1948 in *France during the German Occupation,* 3: 1501–1509.

pawns paid by the Germans. The Doriotist *Groupes d'action pour la justice sociale* he said, were nothing more than paid denouncers. "One day," he continued, "I asked Sauckel: What would you think of Germans who followed this profession? He answered me: I would hold them in contempt. This is what the Germans themselves think of them."[50]

Déat, according to Laval, was either to resign or to accede to power as the new head of the government. In the latter case full-scale civil war would result. Always concerned with the maintenance of public order, Laval seemed to ignore the fact that under his own leadership France was already being wracked by civil war. The cabinet session concluded with unanimous approval of Laval's June 6 message in which he had declared French neutrality. The browbeaten Ultra ministers quietly departed. After the meeting, de Brinon gave an account of its proceedings to Struwe, a German representative in Vichy who let it be known immediately that the occupation authorities would not tolerate the dismissal of Déat. "That's where we are now," Laval told Pétain. Pétain and Laval were totally united against the Ultras.[51]

Laval's victory over the collaborationist leaders was the personal triumph of a skilled professional politician over a group of clumsy and timid amateurs who had lost all touch with reality by June and July 1944. The Ultras returned to Paris to nurse their political and personal wounds. Their revenge was soon to come. On July 30, American forces made a decisive breakthrough at Avranches, opening the road to Paris for the Allies. Laval had one last card to play. He now sought the cooperation of the Radical Socialist leader and former premier Edouard Herriot, who had been interned under house arrest in Maréville, near Nancy. Laval hoped that Herriot, the president of the Chamber of Deputies in 1940, would help him reconvene the National Assembly, which had not met since then. A new government created by the National Assembly would then receive enhanced legitimacy and Laval might yet have a role to play in it. Abetz consented to the plan, which would have shortcircuited Gaullists and Communists but also collaborationists.

[50]Tracou, p. 336.
[51]Ibid., pp. 337–338. See also Nicolle, 2:460.

Hearing of the scheme, de Brinon and Déat informed Oberg's aide Helmut Knochen. Déat assured Knochen that the Ultras could form a new government loyal to Germany in eastern France. He wondered aloud how Hitler might react if a France headed by Laval turned against him in the manner of Badoglio's Italy. Knochen contacted Oberg, who telephoned Himmler and Hitler to ask that Laval's plan be blocked. Abetz was overruled and Oberg given full power in Paris. The Ultras had obtained their revenge for their defeat of July 12 at the hands of Laval. Oberg shattered Laval's plan and ordered that the French government be transferred east and regrouped at Belfort. Laval and Pétain were to be taken, forcibly if necessary, to Belfort.

The revenge of the Ultras was shortlived, however, as events proceeded swiftly in August 1944. Asleep in his office in the Matignon, Laval was awakened by a phone call early on August 17. Albertini, secretary-general of the RNP and *chef de cabinet* in the Labor Ministry, was calling to report that earlier that morning Déat had left for the east. "He's jilted us," said Albertini. "He's a skunk. You judged him correctly."[52]

By August it had become apparent that the Germans were planning to abandon Paris and make their stand somewhere to the east. The Ultras were faced with the choice of fleeing eastward with the departing Germans or remaining to meet an uncertain fate at the hands of the Allies or a new French government. Déat began preparing to leave on August 7 but few of his RNP supporters were ready to follow him. The movement, or what was left of it, was split when Albertini objected to Déat's departure. With Laval discredited in German eyes because of his attempt to reconvene the National Assembly, Déat believed that his hour had arrived.[53]

Doriot was also making his way eastward with the most of the high-ranking officials of the PPF, as was Darnand with many of his Miliciens. Marcel Bucard and some of his Francistes joined what on a much smaller scale was a reversal of the 1940 exodus. Lower-level members of the collaborationist movements often remained home in the belief that they would escape prosecution or fade into anonymity

---

[52]Tracou, pp. 375–378. See also Brissaud, pp. 492–493.

[53]On the split in the RNP between Déat and Albertini in August 1944, see Procès Albertini, pp. 102–103 and Varennes, pp. 231–232.

because of their low status. Some among the Ultras sought refuge in Spain. The leaders, however, joined small columns of refugees heading east.

On August 17, Déat's *L'Œuvre*, Doriot's *Cri du Peuple*, and the other collaborationist newspapers appeared as usual in the streets of Paris. They contained no notices of any kind to indicate that they were appearing there for the last time. The next day brought the emergence of the Resistance press from the clandestinity in which it had been long operating. There was no sign of the collaborationist movements which had so dominated the political life of the capital for four years. For Paris and almost all of France the occupation and with it the collaboration were over by the end of August. The voices of the collaborationists were added to those of Legitimists and Bonapartists in France's museum of lost causes.

11 In German Exile: Sigmaringen

See here, Monsieur Abetz, see here! . . . there's a slight difference! . . . which you pretend not to see! . . . you, Abetz . . . even one hundred percent defeated, crushed, occupied by forty-nine victor powers . . . by God, the Devil, and the Apostles . . . you'll still be the loyal, dutiful German, honor and fatherland! defeated but legitimate! while a damn fool like me will always be a stinking filthy traitor, fit to be hanged!

—Louis-Ferdinand Céline, *Castle to Castle*

To many collaborationists the fall of Paris was merely a transitory event in a war the Germans would eventually win with new armies and miracle weapons. If even Laval still envisioned a compromise peace in the summer of 1944, it is hardly surprising that the more extreme collaborationists could not yet in that August and September imagine the totality of the coming German defeat. The result was a miniature exodus similar to that of June 1940, but in reverse. Once again, files and papers were destroyed and civilians took to the road attempting to escape an oncoming army. The collaborationists who for four years had castigated de Gaulle for taking refuge in a foreign country were about to follow his example. Many left in the belief that only a short period in eastern France would be necessary prior to their return with a newly victorious Wehrmacht, but the swift collapse of German resistance in eastern France in September dashed this hope. The collaborationist refugees were obliged to cross the Rhine.

The exodus of August 1944 included Pétain and Laval, removed from Vichy and Paris, respectively, against their will by the retreating Germans. In protest both renounced the exercise of their government functions but in an attempt to keep the Ultras out neither resigned officially. Their refusal to use their government powers, however, opened the door to the Ultras. Doriot, Déat, Darnand, and de Brinon contemplated the succession as they made their way eastward, dodging *maquisard* ambushes and Allied bombs. By the end of August 1944 the collaborationist leaders represented virtually no one other than themselves and the few thousand Frenchmen who had followed them into exile. The largest group of exiles was three to four thousand Miliciens who felt themselves to have been too heavily compromised in their campaigns against the Resistance. Most lower-ranking members of the PPF and RNP remained in France in the belief or the hope that a Gaullist purge would be limited to the bigger fish.

The leaders, however, continued to aspire to what passed for power in what was rapidly becoming a government in exile. Reciprocal hostility among the PPF, RNP, and Milice did not cease with the retreat into eastern France. Arriving in Nancy, Déat announced that he was heading a new government. Meanwhile on September 6, Darnand authorized the "expropriation" of 300 million francs by his Miliciens from the Belfort branch of the Banque de France. The raid on the Belfort bank was led by Darnand's chief assistant, Bout d l'An. Later arguing that he was simply "requisitioning" money owed the Milice by the government, Darnand contended that the funds enabled the Miliciens to live more independently of German financial support after September 1944. He intended to use his Miliciens as a springboard from which to launch his own drive for the phantom power that leadership of the Ultras conferred in late 1944.[1]

Pushed out of France, the collaborationists were quartered by the Germans in the vast, labyrinthine, faded elegance of the Hohenzollern castle of Sigmaringen, high above the Danube in southwestern Germany. There Pétain, Laval, the French collaborationist leaders, and the German ambassadorial staff lived, each in separate apartments but in very close proximity. The cramped and supercharged surrealistic ambience of the morose castle in which old political enemies could hardly avoid one another has been described in *Castle to Castle* by the collaborationist writer Louis-Ferdinand Céline, who shared its quarters. Gossip flourished and resentments deepened in an atmosphere reminiscent of the close quarters they had left in Vichy's Hotel du Parc. Only Doriot did not inhabit the Sigmaringen

---

[1] The affair of the Milice and the 300 million francs was discussed in *Procès Darnand*, pp. 248 and 266. For reports of Déat's announcement of a new regime headed by himself in Nancy, see Schellenberg, telegram to Wagner, Foreign Ministry, August 27, 1944, T-120/4120H/E071256-7.

castle. He and his entourage were put up at Meinau, an island in Lake Constance. There they were supported by Joseph Bürckel, who as Gauleiter in 1940 had presided over the ruthless Germanizing of Lorraine. Doriot and Bürckel shared an antipathy toward Laval, and Bürckel feared that Himmler might create a greater Burgundy under the leadership of the Belgian Rexist leader Degrelle. Both Doriot and Bürckel, the Westmark Gauleiter in 1944, stood to lose in the creation of a Burgundian political entity. [2]

By September 1944, Doriot had emerged as Hitler's chosen French leader. Ribbentrop had repudiated the Lavalist line of Abetz, whose policy had proven bankrupt upon Laval's refusal to exercise his government powers. Ribbentrop had also gained the ear of Hitler. Accordingly, the collaborationist leaders were summoned to eastern Germany where they met with Ribbentrop and Hitler. In the early days of September 1944, Hitler might have had matters more pressing than to preside at the selection of a French government-in-exile, and his personal involvement in the matter speaks eloquently as to the state of his mind at the time. Laval, invited, refused to go.

On September 1 Hitler received Doriot, de Brinon, Déat, Darnand, and Paul Marion, Vichy's former secretary of state for information and a supporter of the PPF. The German leader, still showing the effects of the July 20 bomb plot that had almost taken his life, rambled on about future German victories and his own "regrets" that France and Germany had ever fought one another. Hitler then turned to his main subject, the formation of a new "national-revolutionary" government to be headed by Doriot. The other Ultra leaders were ordered to assist the PPF leader and collaborate in his government. Hitler wanted the new Doriot cabinet named in a legal manner by Pétain, just as his own cabinet had been nominated legally in 1933 by Hindenburg. To Déat and Darnand, Hitler's nomination of Doriot must have come as a source of shock and dismay. With Hitler standing by, Ribbentrop discussed the details of a new Doriot cabinet and de Brinon promised to gain Pétain's assent to it. When it no longer

[2]The relations between Doriot and Bürckel are discussed in Wolf, pp. 287–289 and Jäckel, p. 355. Louis-Ferdinand Céline's *D'un château l'autre*, published originally in 1957, has been translated into English by Ralph Manheim and published as *Castle to Castle* (New York: Dell, 1968).

mattered, Doriot was to have his chance. His return to his followers in Meinau took place amid wild celebrations.[3]

Even Hitler, however, proved unable to effect unity among the French collaborationist leaders. So loyal in other respects to the Führer, they now set out to undermine the arrangement he had ordered. Déat was convinced that even a German Gauleiter, the *bête noir* of all in France prior to the Liberation, would be preferable to Doriot, and Darnand had no wish to yield control of his Miliciens to the PPF leader. De Brinon had no intention of even trying to win the marshal over to a Doriot government. In addition, Abetz was still ambassador to "France" and he also worked behind the scenes against the plan.[4]

Roughly two million French prisoners and laborers remained in the Reich after the liberation of metropolitan France. Their "interests" were to be looked after by the transplanted "government." Laval's successor, according to collaborationist logic, would govern France when the Allies were finally expelled by the resurgent German forces. After their interview with Hitler, the Ultra leaders returned to Belfort, where their supporters were still encamped during the first week of September. Keeping in mind Hitler's injunction to act within a framework of legality, de Brinon used the authority granted to him in 1940 as Vichy's ambassador to the then occupied zone to create a General Delegation to represent French interests in Germany. Several of Laval's ministers—including Bichelonne, Bonnard, and Marion—followed the example of their chief and refused to engage in any political action. The "actives" who joined de Brinon in the General Delegation were Darnand, Déat, Luchaire, and the secretary of war, General Bridoux. By the end of September a rival organization was in place to keep Doriot and his backers out of the government, or what was left of it.[5]

Although now heading the General Delegation, de Brinon was still under Hitler's order to secure Pétain's approval of a Doriot govern-

[3]Louis Noguères, *La dernière étape Sigmaringen* (Paris: Fayard, 1956), pp. 41–57. Noguères, who presided over the postwar Haute Cour de Justice, which tried many of France's leading political and literary figures for collaboration, utilized the documents of interpreter Paul Schmidt to reconstruct the meetings of the French collaborationists with Ribbentrop and Hitler. See also Jäckel, pp. 355–359.
[4]Noguères, pp. 82–83.
[5]Ibid., pp. 84–95.

ment. In charge for the moment, de Brinon was content to let Doriot wait while giving the Germans the illusion that he was preparing a transition. His maneuvers were supported, naturally, by Déat and Darnand. In notes complaining of the misuse of his name, Pétain protested against the creation of the General Delegation and told de Brinon that he would have nothing to do with it. The prestige of the marshal's name and the fact of his legal appointment as the last premier of the Third Republic still carried weight among the French and Germans in Sigmaringen and Berlin. Through his control of the Sigmaringen media, de Brinon was able to exploit Pétain's prestige by making it appear that his actions had the marshal's support. While de Brinon effectively kept Doriot at bay, Darnand and Déat worked to consolidate their own power bases.[6]

As minister of labor, Déat was theoretically responsible for the French workers in Germany but his real authority over them was nonexistent from the start. His activity in Sigmaringen was confined to writing newspaper articles, giving lectures, pushing papers in his office in the castle, and awaiting his hour of destiny. Darnand had a card to play, the 4,000 Miliciens who had followed him from France, but his freedom of action was severely limited. Even before the convoy of Miliciens had left France, German agents had begun recruiting among them for the Waffen-SS. Morale was sinking rapidly among the exiled Miliciens, many of whom resented German pressure to join the Waffen-SS after having been promised that their service would be in French formations only.[7]

The Milice in Sigmaringen was further weakened by Déat who rescinded his order of June and now told all RNP supporters to leave Darnand's organization. Darnand also encountered trouble on the

[6]Ibid., pp. 134–135. For de Brinon's account of his differences with Pétain, see de Brinon, *Mémoires*, p. 245.

[7]For Darnand's complaints of German recruiters raiding his Milice, see his letter to Himmler, Ulm, October 25, 1944, T-120/3316/E007681-3. The transfer of 1,200 of the 4,000 Miliciens in Germany to the Waffen-SS is discussed in Reichel, report to Gruppenleiter Inland II, Berlin, October 2, 1944, T-120/3316/E007658. Demoralization within the Milice at the time of its transfer to Germany and the many quarrels among the collaborationists there are observed in "Histoire d'une émigration . . . ou d'une déroute" (Limoges: A. Bontemps, 1945), pp. 16–18, 19–21, 27, and passim. This pamphlet was prepared by the Mouvement de Libération National, based on an account by Rouchouze, a Milicien bodyguard of Bout de l'An. Rouchouze had been parachuted as an agent into liberated France, where he was captured.

German side. Not long after the arrival of the Milice in Germany, he met with Himmler and a decision was made to place 1,200 of the Miliciens in the newly formed Waffen-SS Charlemagne Division. The Germans were careful not to assign Darnand too much prominence in the Charlemagne Division, stating explicitly that he was not to receive a position comparable to that of Léon Degrelle, who led the Wallonie Division of the Waffen-SS. Their Foreign Ministry also wished to prevent friction between Darnand and the Doriotists, who had been prominent in the now disbanded LVF which was to comprise a major portion of the new Charlemagne Division.[8]

The factionalism that continued to plague even the French mini-community of Ultras in Germany exasperated Léon Degrelle, who feared the loss of "10,000 to 20,000" otherwise good soldiers for the Axis cause. Describing the composition of the French SS unit as 30 percent followers of Doriot, 30 percent followers of Darnand, and 40 percent "for no one and against everyone," Degrelle proposed that the Miliciens be put under his own control in the Wallonie Division. A revealing example of his own self-confidence, Degrelle's proposal suggested that only a foreign leader could unite the French Ultras.[9]

Darnand had asked to be allowed to join the Charlemagne Division in his capacity as French Secretary-general for the Maintenance of Order, which would have given him command of the unit. He was admitted instead as Sturmbannführer, the rank he had received upon joining the Waffen-SS in August 1943, too low for him to command a division. He then requested permission to join Degrelle's Wallonie Division and with Degrelle create a German "West Corps" of French and Belgians in the Waffen-SS. Degrelle was amenable but the shadow of Doriot again stood in the way. Berger, second in command to Himmler, suggested denial of Darnand's request. According to Berger, the Walloons were to be tied to the Reich, not to the French. Darnand instead was directed to give his support to the PPF chieftain. Berger preferred Doriot, who as an ex-Communist, he reasoned, would know better how to keep French workers in Germany

[8]Strained relations between the followers of Darnand and those of Doriot and the attendant problems for the Charlemagne Division were mentioned in Fritz Bran. "Auf-"zeichnung für Herrn Botschafter Abetz," October 3, 1944, T-120/3316/E007669-70.

[9]Léon Degrelle, "Vermerk über die Französische Waffen-SS," Berlin, December 10, 1944, T-175/130/2656710-11.

from coming under the influence of Communism. Berger also made clear to Himmler his reservations about Darnand's political stability and judgment as evidenced in the request to join Degrelle, whose claims to Burgundy ran counter to French national interests. By the end of 1944 it had been made painfully clear to Darnand that he could not win and that Doriot had become the chosen French tool for Germany.[10]

By October 1944, the French delegation at Sigmaringen had assumed the title "Commission gouvernementale française pour la défense des intérêts nationaux," with de Brinon presiding. The commission was accorded extraterritorial rights by the Germans and on October 1 the French flag was raised officially over Sigmaringen Castle. Pétain refused to attend the ceremony. During the interim, Doriot had become established at Meinau and, predictably, the French exiles in Germany produced rival newspapers and radio stations. The Doriotists brought out an edition of *Petit Parisien* and the Governmental Commission issued *La France,* edited by Luchaire. Both factions beamed radio propaganda intermitently back to liberated France.

The French people were told to resist the general mobilization decreed by General de Gaulle, and both collaborationist factions tried to use the impoverished economic conditions of newly liberated France to turn the population against the provisional government. De Gaulle and his government were characterized as tools of the Communists. In its unending struggle against its collaborationist rivals, the PPF faction was given a boost in December 1944 when Abetz was finally removed as German ambassador and replaced by Otto Reinebeck, a career diplomat already serving as Ribbentrop's liaison with Doriot. Reinebeck was to be far more forthcoming toward Doriot than Abetz had ever been and his nomination was a clear sign, if any were still needed by December, that Doriot was Hitler's man.[11]

[10]Darnand, letter to Berger, December 8, 1944, T-175/130/2656705. Berger stated his objections to Degrelle's solution and his preference for Doriot, whom he called a better leader than Darnand, in a note to Himmler, Berlin, December 16, 1944, T-175/130/2656706-8.

[11]Wolf, p. 298. See also " 'Le devoir des français est de se dresser contre l'ordre de mobilisation,' déclare Jacques Doriot," and "Marcel Déat préside à l'Inauguration du Centre de Forestage de Winterlingen," *La France,* nos. 51 (December 23–26) and 55 (December 30–31, 1944), respectively.

That month brought a sudden burst of hope to the flagging spirits of the French collaborationists in Germany. The early successes of the Rundstedt offensive brought new life to the community at Sigmaringen Castle, whose walls echoed with talk of future cabinets and plans for revenge against personal enemies in an early return to France. Bout de l'An announced plans to turn the Milice into a national revolutionary party, which, he said, would reestablish a parliamentary republican form of government, although with an authoritarian spirit buttressed presumably by a renewed German occupation of France. His plan was nipped in the bud by others in the Milice who were less favorably inclined to a republic and also by the German commitment to Doriot. [12]

Of all the collaborationist leaders in Germany, the most active in the fight against the new government in France was Doriot. The PPF parachuted agents into liberated France to gain intelligence from behind Allied lines and also to sow anti-Gaullist propaganda. Party cells in France, organized for clandestine operation, continued to function but there is no evidence to indicate that Doriotists left behind in France or parachuted in from Germany were able to cause more than occasional nuisances for the new government. On January 6, 1945, Doriot announced the formation of a "Comité de la Libération Française," a paradoxical analogue to the Committee of National Liberation created in 1940 by de Gaulle in London. Doriot's committee became the second Ultra government in exile, in opposition to de Brinon's Governmental Commission but Doriot benefited from stronger German support. [13]

In Meinau Doriot planned the coordination of PPF squads, trained in Germany for sabotage missions, with a clandestine network of "blue maquis," blue the party shirt color, in France. Named president of his committee, Doriot left the program and personnel of a future government in "liberated" France purposely vague in order to give his organization as wide a potential support as possible. Reluctantly, de Brinon joined Doriot's committee. Darnand was still fighting Doriot by trying to secure control of the Charlemagne Division.

[12]Noguères, pp. 222–223.

[13]One of Doriot's many calls for armed resistance to the Allies came in a speech to his Comité de Libération; see "Jacques Doriot, fondateur du comité de libération, adresse un manifeste aux Français," *La France*, no. 60 (January 8, 1945).

Complaining that the creation of the Doriot committee rendered the Governmental Commission and with it his own position powerless, Darnand spoke of resigning. He received no satisfaction from the Germans.[14]

Next it was Déat's turn to reach accord with Doriot by subordinating his ambition to that of his rival. On February 22, Doriot left his party offices at Lindau, where he is said to have passed the previous night in wild and triumphant revelry, to head for Mengen and a meeting of reconciliation with Déat. The RNP leader, the most consistent antagonist of Doriot throughout the entire period after 1940, was now to join Doriot's committee and bring his followers with him. Doriot, however, never reached Mengen. *En route,* his car was strafed by a plane and the PPF chieftain, whose body was riddled with bullets, was killed instantly. The collaborationist phantom died with Doriot. By early 1945 he had become the soul of whatever was left of collaborationism and his death seems to have finally awakened the other Ultras, PPF and rivals alike, to the impending end of their adventure. Doriot's funeral has been described as the funeral of the collaboration.[15]

The circumstances surrounding Doriot's death have remained mysterious and have given rise to a lively controversy over the identity of the attacking plane. His car had been marked clearly with French colors and the official German report on the incident identified the attacking aircraft as a British Mosquito. In view of the clear Allied air superiority in southwestern German skies at the time and the frequency of Allied air attacks, the official German version is credible. Milton Dank has pointed out, however, that there are too many unanswered questions to take the official account at face value. First of all, Doriot was acquainted with military aircraft and according to his secretary, who was present in the car and survived the attack, he

---

[14]Renthe-Fink, Abschrift Büro RAM, Berlin, January 14, 1945 and Reinebeck, telegram, Sigmaringen to Foreign Ministry, Berlin, January 18, 1945, T-120/1755H/404525 and 404526-7, respectively. For mention of plans by the Doriotists to disrupt a rumored visit of President Roosevelt to Paris, see Reinebeck, telegram, Meinau to Foreign Ministry, Berlin, December 8, 1944, CDJC document CXCII, 3. On the formation of the Doriotist committee and the German support for it, see Noguères, pp. 228–231, and Jäckel, pp. 365–366, and for the nomination of Reinebeck as Abetz's successor, Jäckel, p. 367.

[15]Hérold-Paquis, p. 110.

had identified the plane overhead as a Jäger, reassuring her that it was German and that they had nothing to fear.

Dank argues that the death of Doriot would have worth a medal to any Allied pilot responsible but that no one claimed it. Nor were there any reports of such an attack by any American, British, or French planes operating in the area. Furthermore, Doriot's aide Simon Sabiani, when apprised of the attack, hastened to the scene where he found a Gestapo agent holding the dead leader's briefcase. The German officials did not allow PPF representatives to question the driver of the car. Aides of Doriot have since spoken of having received telephone tips to the effect that a German ambush was planned for him on the trip to Mengen.

Several possible hypotheses may explain a German attack against Doriot. Dank points out that Doriot had refused to allow PPF members to fight in the Waffen-SS on the Western front, arguing that the enemy was Bolshevism and that PPF volunteers were to fight solely in the East. In addition, Doriot had recently suspended the parachuting of PPF agents behind the Allied lines in France. He may have made enemies in high places, perhaps including Himmler. Other possibilities, apart from Dank's speculations, involve Darnand and Degrelle. Ever opposed to Doriot, Darnand may have been in league with Himmler and others in the SS in a plot against the PPF leader. It is possible that Degrelle, who also possessed some influence in SS circles, wished to see Doriot eliminated. A strong "national" French movement under Doriot might have precluded the future possibility of an enlarged Burgundian state headed by the Rexist leader. The mystery surrounding the death of Doriot is a fitting capstone to the fractious Byzantine relationships among the French collaborationist groups and the German services with whom they dealt.[16]

The PPF possessed no other leader with the charisma and energy to fill Doriot's place, nor did any of the other collaborationist groups. The Comité de Libération was thus killed just when it had stood on

[16]For his account of Doriot's death, see Dank, pp. 281–283. A recollection of anonymous warnings against the life of Doriot prior to his trip to Mengen was provided me by one of his aides during an interview, July 17, 1974. See also the memoir of the daughter of PPF official Albert Beugras, Marie Chaix, *Les lauriers du lac de Constance* (Paris: Seuil, 1974), p. 118.

the verge of achieving the long-sought unity of the French pro-Axis groups. Many of the collaborationist leaders at Doriot's funeral recognized the end of their dream. The scene was described by Jean Hérold-Paquis, the PPF radio broadcaster who had succeeded the slain Henriot in July 1944. De Brinon and Déat appeared genuinely moved at the funeral, according to Hérold-Paquis, who continued:

> The sky was red toward the west, like a fire devouring the Black Forest. Portent? Literature on this theme would be easy. There will be no literature, any more than there will be a funeral oration. I was a Doriotist. I have friends who were Doriotist. I wore the blue shirt of the PPF. I was a PPF militant, a second-rank militant who... was willing to serve as a voice. In leaving the Mengen cemetery, I knew that the adventure was over, that with Doriot's death the party was dead, and I accepted this as a mysterious sign of Providence. We were many who thought thus. But no one admitted it. And, by evening people were already speaking of other things. Rebatet [author of the sharply anti-Semitic and pro-collaboration book Les décombres in 1942] at least was sincere this time. He was sincere because he told me: "Everything is finished, my friend.... As for me, I no longer believe in anything, no idea, no man, no war."
>
> And grimacing, he disappeared into the night. He had started out again toward Sigmaringen, from whence he had come on foot, like a pilgrim.[17]

The death of Doriot returned a measure of freedom of action to Déat and Darnand, both of whom had agreed to join Doriot only as a result of German pressure. They now turned against de Brinon, whom they blamed for having allowed the Governmental Commission to have come under the influence of Doriot. Darnand was especially bitter, arguing that Doriot's Comité de Libération represented no French interests but was purely a German creation. Forced to follow Doriot, the French collaborationists in Germany had lost precious opportunities to ally with the anti-Communists in the Resistance in France, according to Darnand. Less ideologically oriented than was Doriot and certainly less so than Déat, Darnand seemed inclined on

[17]Hérold-Paquis, pp. 113–114.

occasion to jettison his German ties in an attempt to make common cause with anti-Communist French nationalists of any political persuasion. He blamed de Brinon for aborting this possibility, although it is hard to imagine having been realized in any case.[18]

Unable to appreciate how deeply compromised he was in the eyes of the entire French Resistance, Darnand demonstrated his political naïveté, if also his personal bravery, down to the end. Disgusted with de Brinon, he announced that his political options had been closed and led some of his Miliciens into northern Italy where they joined in the fight against anti-Fascist partisans there. De Brinon tried to gain Doriot's legacy as president of the Comité de Libération, a title he now added to his theoretical presidency of the Governmental Commission. He was opposed by Déat, Luchaire, and Bucard, in addition to Darnand. During the spring of 1945, Déat created a rival "liberation" committee and skirmishes ensued between remnants of the RNP, supporting their leader, and the PPF in support of the committee that had been headed by Doriot. With Germany in ruins and Hitler's *Gotterdämmerung* about to begin, with Doriot already dead, the RNP and PPF were still carrying on their intramural rivalry in Sigmaringen. Hard pressed as they were, the Germans had to intervene to restore order. Finally the anti-de Brinon faction asked Ribbentrop to arbitrate between the contending parties. It no longer mattered for in April 1945, Allied armies were advancing from all sides and the Reich was in a state of collapse. The pressing concern was now flight to avoid capture by Allied and especially French forces. Déat, whose last article, of April 15 in *La France,* forecast quarrels among the victorious Allies, and his two to three hundred remaining RNP backers fled, each on his own to find what refuge he could.[19]

By April 1945 the French collaborationists, along with so many others who had committed themselves to Hitler's New Order, were in

[18]The account of the almost incredible continued strife among the French collaborationists in Germany after the death of Doriot is given in Noguères, pp. 236–237.

[19]Ibid., pp. 237–238. For Déat's activity toward the end of the Sigmaringen episode, see Varennes, pp. 242–243, and for a review by Déat of his own political career in an attempt to justify his pretensions to "power" in early 1945, see "Une action politique: 1914–1944. Le discours de Marcel Déat au Congrès du R.N.P.," *La France,* no. 88 (February 8, 1945). The speech had been delivered four days earlier.

flight for the second time in less than a year. The four-year adventure, during which they had spent the greater portion of their energies fighting one another, was over. Their fate was to be the usual fate of those on the losing side of a civil war: flight, retribution, suffering, and finally, oblivion.

12 Conclusion:
Collaborationist Profiles

> We were soldiers. Many [members of the middle classes] were struck by the fact that only the uniform permitted them to be fully accepted by and on an equal footing with young workers and young peasants. We were astonished in exercising the profession of arms to feel vibrating in us tones we did not suspect existed.
> —François Gaucher, *Combats*, April 15, 1944

By all accounts the collaborationist movements represented a very small if vocal proportion of the French population during the German occupation. During the later months of 1943 and into the first half of 1944, however, they constituted one side of what has been called the "Franco-French" war. Despite a statement made in 1944 by General de Gaulle to the effect that there was no civil war in France at the time of the Liberation, the Axis had its supporters to the end. In Paris, Marseilles, Nice, and other cities, collaborationist party memberships ran into the thousands. By comparison, at the peak of Popular Front strength in 1937, the Socialist party counted fewer than 3,000 members in most of its *fédérations*. Membership in French political parties has traditionally been small, with the exception of the Communists, but even here Gounand has pointed out, for example, that the RNP membership in the Loiret department approximated that of the Communist party of 1935. Add to the RNP figures those of its rivals, the PPF, Francistes, and MSR, and the picture of a significant collaborationist faction in the Loiret emerges.[1]

Including the figures for Châteaubriant's Groupe Collaboration, a rough estimate puts the total figure in the range of 150,000 to

[1]For the comparison of RNP with Communist party membership figures in the Loiret, see Durand and Bohbot, pp. 64–65. Figures for the *fédérations* of the Socialist party in 1937 come from Greene, p. 163; see also pp. 307–314. De Gaulle's statement on the absence of any civil war in France was made shortly before the Liberation when Admiral Auphan attempted to deliver to him a message from Marshal Pétain asking for an orderly transition of power to avoid civil war. "Where is the civil war?" de Gaulle had asked caustically and had shown his visitor to the door. See Charles de Gaulle, *Mémoires de guerre*, 3 vols. (Paris: Plon, 1954–1959), 2:319–321.

200,000 for those involved in the movements of the collaboration over the entire four-year period. Although this figure includes some duplicate memberships, it clearly shows the importance of organized collaborationism in occupied France. Seen in this perspective, the Franco-French war must be viewed as a part of the larger European civil war between fascist and antifascist forces, both with roots deep within the Western cultural tradition. The defeat suffered by the collaborationists in 1944 and their total obliteration as a political force after 1945 constituted but one facet of the massive defeat suffered by fascism in World War II.[2]

Wherever fascism developed it was spawned by crisis: rapid modernization and fears of social revolution, postwar economic and social dislocation after 1918, and real and imagined national grievances and ethnic resentments.

After 1934, France experienced demographic and economic decline, foreign threats, and a progressive discrediting of her parliamentary system which weakened her morale and social cohesion in advance of the 1940 collapse. Many in the aspiring middle classes saw avenues closed to them after 1934 by the depression, which the revolving-door cabinets of the Third Republic appeared unable or unwilling to curb. Younger, more enterprising Frenchmen often criticized a social order stalled by preindustrial economic structures and values with control in the hands of a generation that had come of age before 1914. As the moderate consensus cracked, France like other countries experienced a strengthening of the Left, in the form of the Popular Front, and the Right, in reaction.

By 1936 a new radical Right had formed, a coalition of outsiders who wanted to open wider the avenues to power and wealth in France without undermining the social order or threatening their private holdings. Included were new and dynamic business interests blocked by the petty proprietary economic structure of France, veterans and peasants in protest against deflationary policies, students who saw opportunities being closed to them, and intellectuals in quest of a

---

[2]The concept of the "era of Fascism," upon which my conclusion is in large part based, is developed by Nolte, p. 6. The "Franco-French" civil war is discussed by Hoffmann, "Collaborationism," p. 376 and more recently by Dank, p. 250. For one rather simplistic characterization of the Paris-based Ultras as a "gang of desperadoes," see Herbert Luethy, *France against Herself: The Past, Politics and Crises of Modern France* (New York: Meridian, 1957 [original edition, 1955]), p. 98.

political order with more panache. Added to these were elements of the white-collar middle and artisan lower-middle classes in fear of Communism and no longer trusting the parliamentary leadership to maintain social order. Some workers, confused and disillusioned by the gyrations of the Communist party which took on the cast of a Soviet tool, were also ready for the radical Right. It is hardly surprising that some began to look for solutions to the models provided by the fascist powers or that others might question the wisdom of and even the motives behind a strong anti-Axis foreign policy.

Fascism is a product of a society in deep crisis, and the shocks of the interwar years were insufficient to produce a movement in France with the strength of German National Socialism. The moderate consensus, although shaken, held when Daladier succeeded the Popular Front with a more conservative government. Many who had been won over to the leagues and parties of the radical Right deserted them in 1938, indicating less intense a disaffection in France than in Weimar Germany after 1929. The potent combination of modernizing business forces and antimodernist lower-middle classes which historically gave fascist movements their strength was mitigated by the relative economic backwardness of interwar France. In addition, the social conservatism of the radical Right offered little new to majority French opinion, which preferred the less turbulent and more traditional parties that comprised the centrist consensus. Their scope of effective activity circumscribed, the new radical Right movements of the interwar years dissipated much of their energy in fruitless internecine quarrels. A similar process was repeated during the occupation.

When the collapse of 1940 further discredited the parliamentary regime and the German occupation gave new life to the radical Right, the tendency toward political fragmentation inherited from the Third Republic was used by Vichy and the Germans to kill any potential chances for effective collaborationist action. By a political education that induced ideological rigidity and by their own interwar experience, the collaborationists were prepared only for oppositional dissidence. Unable to overcome their sectarian origins, Doriot and his rivals showed how weak a common ideology could be in the face of their own national traditions of political behavior.

The components of a strong fascist movement were all present within the collaborationist camp under the occupation. Big business, technocracy, and social engineering were represented prominently in Deloncle's MSR and were present in the other movements, particularly the Groupe Collaboration. Déat's RNP attracted white-collar and professional support, as did the Groupe Collaboration, and some workers. All the parties had lower-middle-class backing. The organizational skills of Doriot and his men combined with the social and academic respectability of the Groupe Collaboration and the doctrinal and propagandistic skills of Déat and Henriot would have produced a powerful force. Add the terrorists of Deloncle and PPF, Milice, and Franciste paramilitary forces and the result would have been potent. Speculation that all who actually joined the various factions would have also joined a unified movement is a luxury afforded the historian but it shows how French factionalism facilitated the work of the Germans in exploiting occupied France.

The inability of the collaborationist groups to unite was assured by Doriot's sectarian strategies. Doriot was the only Ultra leader with the political skill and personal charisma to play the role of fascist leader in the style of Mussolini or Hitler, and the PPF alone among its rivals possessed the will to power and the seasoned political cadres of a powerful fascist movement. Yet Doriot was unable to unify the radical Right, let alone the rest of France during the occupation. A source of political strength, the Communist origins of Doriot and his immediate entourage were also responsible for their political undoing. Their most natural clientele after 1940 consisted of anti-Communists but too many of these were unable to forget Doriot's past and a large number of his potential constituents perceived the PPF, whether correctly or not, as a turncoat opportunist movement. Anti-Communism, after all, was the hallmark of the French radical Right in general and the collaboration in particular. In his recent study of the collaboration, Pascal Ory points out that the French formed no anti-English legion as a parallel to the Anti-Bolshevik Legion, despite the direct attack by English ships upon the French fleet at Mers-el-Kébir in 1940. Radical Right anti-Communism was of a different order than were their other passions.[3]

[3] Ory, *Les collaborateurs*, p. 152. Those who had been active in Ultra organizations other than the PPF repeatedly cited in the interviews I conducted their mistrust of Doriot and his Communist past as the reason for their aversion to his party.

329

Career military men and others whose experiences in the trenches of the First World War oriented them toward the far Right could not forgive Doriot his leadership of the Communist campaign against the French military effort in the 1925 war against Abd-el Krim in Morocco. They preferred movements led by military heroes such as Darnand, Bucard, Costantini, and Jean Boissel. The military element was a vital component of fascist movements which Doriot was in general unable to attract. Another weakness of the PPF leader in terms of appeal to the Right was his well-known anticlericalism. Although Doriot attempted with some success a rapprochement with the church during the occupation, many of those who viewed the struggle against Communism as a latter-day Christian crusade opted for the more openly Christian warrior image of Darnand's Milice and to a lesser extent Bucard's Francistes. Paradoxically, while Doriot maintained a firm control over the policies of the PPF, refusing to cooperate with Ultra rivals except on his own terms, he was unable or perhaps unwilling to exert a similar control over his own more extreme and violent followers. The result drove some potential recruits to the milder and more respectable RNP and Groupe Collaboration. The RNP attraction for teachers is a case in point. The ability of Doriot's rivals to attract followings, however small, was a reflection of the PPF leader's inability to unite the radical Right into a single unified movement.

The failure of Doriot to unify the collaborationist camp gave free rein to the fractious tendencies at work in the French radical Right and facilitated the growth of rival movements. Several distinct although related profiles of collaborationism were allowed to emerge. Déat's RNP, especially after the departure of Deloncle, was a combination of professional, academic, and trade-union groups seeking to preserve at least some of the working-class gains made under the Popular Front and the secular French educational system against big business and clericalist interests in Vichy.

The temperamental affinity of the RNP for the more sedate Groupe Collaboration was manifested in the frequent sharing of public podiums by Déat and Châteaubriant at jointly sponsored cultural events. The Déatist activist was less likely to engage in political violence than was his PPF or Milice counterpart, a tendency borne out by the relatively lower proportion of RNP militants volunteering for service in the German armed forces. There were no RNP equivalents of the Milice campaigns against the maquis, campaigns that were sometimes joined by units of the PPF. RNP members who wished to fight against the Resistance had to join the Milice after 1943. Unlike its rivals, the RNP under Déat was not organized for combat. It did not pressure the Germans for arms with the kind of urgency put forward by the Milice, the PPF, and even some elements of the Groupe Collaboration after 1943.[4]

The PPF scored more success among elements of the lower-middle classes, traditionally anti-big business, and prone to associate industrialization and finance capitalism with the Jews. The more dynamic personality of Doriot was reflected in the higher level of aggressiveness in PPF ranks as compared with the RNP. PPF militants, especially among the leadership corps, were more likely to be ex-Communists, although veterans of the Communist party were also found among the Francistes and the RNP. Nonetheless, the higher proportion of former Communists in PPF ranks gave the party a political militancy and sophistication together with the cynicism of the disillusioned and the fervor of the newly converted unmatched in any of its rivals. Doriotist and also Franciste street brawlers were reminiscent of incipient fascism in other countries and the German observer Grimm compared them to early Nazi fighters in Germany.[5]

RNP leaders, in contrast, paid greater attention to organization of subsidiary affiliates and matters of party doctrine, called "national socialist" by Déat. Repeatedly during the occupation Déat pointed to his national socialism as a logical development of his interwar Neo-Socialism. Affected by his experience in the trenches, Déat shared with Doriot a pacifism which in the interwar years was directed primarily toward Franco-German relations. Interwar pacifists who later joined the collaborationist movements, more the leaders than the rank-and-file, might be called militarized pacifists. Pacifist by

[4]For arms requests of the Groupe Collaboration, see above, Chap. 8, n. 1; for the PPF, Chap. 10, n. 8; and for the Milice, Chap. 5, nn. 16 and 18. An evaluation of the RNP as incapable of effective armed action against the Resistance was made in 1943 by Grimm, who characterized the men of the RNP's militia as too old to make effective fighters. The real street fighters, he reported, were to be found among the ranks of the PPF and the Francistes. See Grimm, Bericht über meine Reise nach Paris vom 12.-26. Juli 1943, Berlin, July 27, 1943; T-120/6442/E481242.

[5]Grimm, Bericht, July 27, 1943; T-120/6442/E481242.

doctrine, at least with regard to Germany, they had become militarized in temperament by their experiences in the First World War. The phenomenon of the militarized pacifist was described aptly by the British psychologist Peter Nathan, who wrote in 1943:

> Who has not noticed the ferocity of our pacifists, who clench their teeth and fists when one argues with them?... Pacifism is the preoccupation with war and its horrors. It is true to say that the horrors of war are more ever-present to the pacifist than they are to the average soldier. May I tell you how to enrage a pacifist? Just tell him what I have been telling you, dig a little hole in his repressive armour. Then you will see with your own eyes the truth in what I have been saying, then you will see the fury, hate and temper which lie behind the total denial of oppression. It is almost the same thing: whether we make war on aggression or whether we indulge in it. [6]

The ambiguities within the RNP closely paralleled those within its leader. Radical in rhetoric yet moderate in practice, Déat was a timid man, a model of ascetic behavior both as platoon leader in World War I and party leader during the occupation. His unwillingness to place the RNP in direct opposition to Laval until almost the end of the occupation marked Déat's timidity in action and his own personal motivation, largely the securing of a cabinet post. Similarly, intellectual timidity on the part of Darnand placed his Milice in the ambiguous position of defending Laval and Vichy while calling for a new fascist order. Unwilling to use the Milice in a real strike for power, Darnand allowed himself and his friends to be exploited in the interest of others. Recruited to preserve order against the Resistance and especially the Communists in the latter stages of the occupation, Milice paratroopers incarnated the contradictory ideals of social order and the incipient fascist spirit of revolt. This contradiction weakened a Milice circumscribed by identification with Vichy, association with the German occupation authorities, and the growing strength of a Resistance associated with the ideal of a renascent independent France. The most discerning Miliciens may have been those who sought to use the organization for their own personal gain. The visceral collaborationism practiced by the Milice lacked the intellectual vision of Déat and his *instituteurs* in the RNP.

[6]Nathan, pp. 124 and 128.

Opposed in temperament to Déat was Deloncle, who with his MSR supporters was among the most reckless within the collaborationist camp. Recruited in large part, although not exclusively, from the ranks of the conspiratorial *Cagoule,* the MSR in the image of its leader comprised the *condottieri* of the collaboration in 1941. During the brief period of Deloncle's association with Déat and the RNP, the more adventurous and violent members looked to the MSR chieftain, whom they followed out of the RNP in November 1941. In its combination of the Saint-Simonian technocratic tradition, the Blanquist proclivity toward coups and terrorism, and Renaissance *condottiere* adventurism, the MSR most clearly combined the modernistic and atavistic traits that gave fascist movements much of their appeal to Europe's counterrevolutionaries.

Having acquired a certain allure from his days as head of the *Cagoule,* Deloncle attracted urban brawlers and mad bombers, giving to his movement the quality of technology gone wild. The dynamiting of Parisian synagogues, which alienated many whose support Deloncle would need in a mass movement, was the work of a gang rather than an organized political party such as Déat's RNP or the PPF. No movement headed by Deloncle could seriously hope to govern France, but the existence of his MSR and Bucard's Francistes deprived Doriot of potentially valuable cadres and shock troops. An excellent military tactician, Deloncle would have functioned most effectively heading the paramilitary arm of a party, as he did briefly with the RNP. Egotism and paranoia prevented him from attracting and retaining the men he needed to build a party organization and provide it with even a rudimentary political doctrine.

The virulence and violence of the MSR were matched, although in a different way, by Bucard's Francistes. They were street fighters and marchers, practitioners of minor acts of violence in public view, compared with Deloncle's bombers and conspirators, who practiced major acts of violence in secret. The Francistes developed the cult of personality to its highest degree. Virtually all that kept the small band together was a fierce loyalty to Bucard, the man "who was never wrong" according to their slogan during the occupation years. Resplendent in his uniform with ten medals, Bucard was nonetheless an ineffectual leader, and his followers were limited primarily to peddling copies of the party newspaper on the streets of Paris and the other large cities of France. Selling newspapers gave them ample opportunity for scuffling with Jews, anti-Germans of all kinds, and most frequently the members of rival collaborationist groups.

Organized in 1933 as an openly fascist party, the Francistes felt events had proven their wisdom and resented newer and larger rival groups, whom they called opportunists. More than their rivals, the Francistes retained the violent spirit of the early Italian Fascist slogan "me ne frego" (I don't care), and their combativeness earned for them the grudging respect even of their rivals in the Ultra camp. Bucard, however, did not know what to do with his troops, who even more than the militants of the RNP and PPF came from the ranks of those without prior political experience. To a greater degree than their larger rivals, the Francistes were openly imitative of the Axis parties and lacked roots in French political traditions.

The collaborationist groups whose centers were in Paris shared a clientele there and in the other cities and towns of the northern zone. Although the PPF, Francistes, and some of the smaller Ultra parties extended into the southern zone before 1942, the presence of the German forces favored their development north of the demarcation line. The north was also more industrialized, producing more of the rapid social transformations that were conducive to the growth of the radical Right in Europe. In contrast, Darnand's Milice, a southern zone product, even after many of the original SOL personnel had dropped out in opposition to the move toward collaboration, continued to reflect a more provincial spirit and a more pronounced Catholic traditionalism than its northern rivals. The mission of the Christian crusader was manifested in a more pronounced fashion in *Combats,* the Milicien newspaper, than elsewhere in the Ultra camp. The good soldier Darnand and the anti-Bolshevik crusader Henriot well represented the Milice ideal, although by 1944 Milicien ideals, like those of the Paris-based Ultra groups, had been radically compromised by the actions of many of the members. The political naïveté of Darnand and his lieutenants, which allowed the Milice on occasion to be infiltrated by the PPF, was an indication of the difference in the worldliness of the Milice as contrasted to the PPF. Darnand's men never aroused in German circles the fears expressed concerning Doriot and the PPF.

334

Despite differences in political origins, doctrinal nuance, and style, the collaborationist movements resembled one another far more than they differed. Generalizations about the composition of camps in civil wars are always difficult in view of the influences of personality, connections, and opportunity in directing the orientation of individuals. Jean Bassompierre, a leader of the Milice who also fought in the Anti-Bolshevik Legion, lost a brother fighting against the Germans.[7] Most members of the collaborationist parties came from the so-called "popular" classes of the cities and towns. These included artisan and merchant lower-middle-class elements who during the interwar years had supported Action Française and the Croix de Feu but after 1940 were more willing to follow Germany than were Maurras and de la Rocque. Drawn to collaborationism by anti-Communism and often anti-Semitism, they formed large proportions of all the Ultra groups with the exception of Châteaubriant's Groupe Collaboration. These were the historically moderate centrist elements, which threatened by industrialization turned sharply to the Right in France, as elsewhere in Europe.

The RNP was able to make some limited inroads in its recruitment of workers with its appeals by Georges Dumoulin and others who had opposed the prewar CGT's alliance with the Communists under the Popular Front. Those workers who did join the RNP, however, did so as individuals rather than in groups and although Déat's party drew a higher proportion of workers than did its rivals, they remained a minority within the ranks of the movement. Doriot's PPF showed more success in attracting some big names from the Communists after 1939 but relatively few rank-and-file Communists followed them. The social composition of the PPF did not differ markedly from the make-up of its smaller rivals. Indeed, the fact that so many within the collaborationist camp switched parties during the four-year occupation and the numerous instances of cooperation among the Ultra parties on the local level, most prominently in Tunisia but also in metropolitan France reflect the basic similarities in their constituencies. The collaborationist cause attracted the middle-class outsiders of interwar French political life: dissidents of the Right, anti-

[7]See *Freres ennemis* in Charles-Ambroise Colin, p. 173. See also Luethy, p. 98.

335

Communist dissidents of the Left, the young, some businessmen on the make, all those who wished to replace the social and political elites without restructuring the social order.

The collaborationist movements shared certain traits which separated them intellectually and politically from the Resistance and resembled those of other fascist movements in Europe. They all stood for social order and paid at least lip service to conventional moral norms in France even if these were sometimes honored in the breach. Many came from families in which the father had had a military career, leading to a staunch Pétainist paternal political outlook after 1940. Intolerant of ambiguity, some of the sons and daughters of these military men took off from Pétainism to full ideological collaborationsim, undoubtedly further than the cautious old marshal wished to go. Nonetheless, Pétain's call for collaboration at the time of the Montoire meeting with Hitler in October 1940 cloaked even the most fanatic of the collaborationists in his mantle. Darnand and many other collaborationists, especially in the Milice and Francistes, believed that they possessed the open approval of the marshal.[8]

Another characteristic of many of the collaborationists was their Catholic fervor, which more often than not was translated into support for the struggle against Communism on the Eastern front and at home. Henriot, Darnand, and many of their Milicien followers from the smaller towns of the southern zone represented a Christian fascism, different in tone from the more secular spirit of Doriot's PPF and Déat's RNP. It is not surprising that in Catholic France, there were many Catholics in the collaborationist movements but there seems to have been a proportionately large number of collaborationists strongly grounded in Catholic education. Darnand and Bucard are examples from among the leaders.

---

[8]For Darnand's loyalty to the marshal, see Bruckberger, p. 93. Pétain's support of the Francistes is mentioned in Chap. 7 above, n. 6. Many former collaborationists whom I interviewed placed great emphasis on Pétain's public support of collaboration at Montoire. His name was invoked in virtually every collaborationist publication during the occupation. The phrase "intolerant of ambiguity" was used originally by the Else Frenkel-Brunswik in 1949. Frenkel-Brunswik participated with several others in putting together *The Authoritarian Personality,* the landmark work written by Theodor W. Adorno et al. (New York: Harper, 1950). See also Fred I. Greenstein, *Personality and Politics: Problems of Evidence, Inference, and Conceptualization* (Chicago: Markham, 1969), p. 104 and p. 104, n. 24.

Fascism in general held a special appeal for renegade Catholics searching for a total world view and ritual they could substitute for that of the church. The Milice was particularly oriented toward Catholic ritual and tradition and even pronounced anticlericals such as Doriot and Déat made their peace with the church. (Déat died in exile in the arms of the church ten years after the war ended.) The concept of the Christian warrior or the medieval crusader, evident in the Waffen-SS and movements such as the Rumanian League of the Archangel Michael, was most manifest in the Milice, whose ceremonies and oaths taken on one's knees recalled those of the church. While many members of the Resistance opposed Vichy and the Germans on the grounds of Christian conscience, the image of the crusading Christian knight belonged to the Milice. Milice ideologues called for a rejuvenation of "decadent" France through the appropriation of the Christian crusading tradition and an emulation of the Spartan society they saw in Nazi Germany.[9]

Writers such as Drieu la Rochelle and Brasillach looked toward a new homo fascista to be generated by the Axis conquest of Europe, but they were exceptional and their ideas cannot be said to have been representative of the rank-and-file or even the leaders of the collaborationist parties. Among the volunteers for the Waffen-SS, the number who wanted to become Nietzschean supermen in a Wagnerian New Europe were in the minority. The neopagan Nietzschean warrior fought side by side in the Waffen-SS with the Milicien Christian crusader. The French Ultras reflected as a whole the ambivalence of fascism with respect to the Christian tradition.

Most of those who turned to collaborationism did so in order to improve their situations in France or perhaps gain a measure of revenge against local political enemies. Most were political outsiders, either totally inactive politically or frustrated in their political endeavors during the years between the wars. Examples of the latter include virtually all the collaborationist leaders. Doriot and Déat had failed to convert the Communist and Socialist parties, respectively, to

---

[9]A postwar fascist reflection of Sparta appears in Maurice Bardèche, *Sparte et les sudistes* (Paris: Les Sept Couleurs, 1969). The theme of lapsed Catholicism came up repeatedly during my interviews with collaborationists. For a discussion of the same phenomenon in regard to Hitler and many of the Nazi leaders, see Alan Cassels, *Fascism* (New York: Thomas Y. Crowell, 1975), p. 141.

their views and had been expelled. Darnand, denied an officership after World War I, and Bucard, who failed as a political protégé of Tardieu in 1924, both turned against a Republic which had thwarted their ambitions.

Although many in France collaborated with the Germans under the occupation, collaborationism as an ideal was unable to make substantial progress among the public even during the heady days of 1940 and 1941. Large numbers of Frenchmen blamed the Republic for the military defeat and the alleged moral and spiritual decay that had preceded it. They were ready for something new. Pétain and Laval, however, were able to capture the support of most of those who claimed that France required an authoritarian state based on conservative values to repair the damage of 1940. The National Revolution enunciated by Vichy in 1940 incorporated many of the values of the collaborationists and had the appearance of being more French and less under the influence of the occupying power. Indeed, none of the collaborationists attacked the National Revolution as such; rather they argued as late as 1944 that it was yet to be achieved and could be accomplished only under their auspices.

The concepts of the National Revolution themselves were never fully clarified and were subject to a variety of interpretations. There was sufficient identity, however, between the goals of the National Revolution and those of the Ultras—the authoritarian state, a corporate society into which the proletariat was to be "reintegrated" without revolution, a moral renovation of France, and some degree of integration into the New Order—for Vichy and not the Ultras to attract the traditional elites and the majority of French opinion in 1940. Pétain belonged to the men of Vichy and not the Ultras who had nothing to counter his personal prestige. Collaborationism could attract only those who shared many of the goals enunciated in Vichy but were for various reasons dissatisfied with the men or policies of the regime. It was, so to speak, a legal opposition, but when large-scale opposition to Vichy did develop, it took the direction of the Resistance. As German pressure for French wealth and manpower intensified, the prospect of increased collaboration offered little to most Frenchmen. The collaborationists remained a small group of ideologues, adventurers, and bandits.[10]

[10]See Paxton, pp. 352–357.

338

Those who argued for collaboration in 1940 were strengthened by the "correct" behavior of the Wehrmacht, which came as a relief to many terrified French civilians. The apparent totality of the German victory made even the most ardent collaborationists seem prudent in the summer of 1940. As the war progressed, opportunists of all kinds were attracted to the movements of the collaboration and each undoubtedly had its share. Denunciations and profiteering were commonplace. The many letters secretly denouncing Jews, Freemasons, and other enemies of Vichy and the Axis reflected a society in disarray. The loss in social cohesion during the interwar period had been manifested in a similar wave of epistolary denunciation at the time of the revelations of *Cagoulard* conspiracies in 1937. Hundreds of letters, many written anonymously accusing people of concealing bombs and guns, were received by the Paris Police Prefecture alone.[11]

Members of the Ultra movements informed on the Resistance and, as was pointed out in many postwar trials, facilitated German police action. The most sinister manifestations of collaboration, for example the Bonny-Lafont gang which blackmailed Frenchmen and served the Germans as an auxiliary police in Paris, usually functioned independently of the political parties, although individuals may have been involved in both. The ranks of those who collaborated with the Germans included criminals in it for the money or for personal revenge but also men such as Jean Fontenoy of the MSR, François Sabiani, the son of the PPF mayor of Marseilles, Noël de Tissot of the Milice, and other personally disinterested warriors who lost their lives at the Eastern front. For some, especially the leaders who had been excluded from positions of power before the armistice, enhanced opportunities for wealth and careers went hand in hand with political beliefs.[12]

If Vichy has been called the "revenge of the minorities" of the traditional Right against the Republic, the collaborationists repre-

[11]Examples of the denunciatory letters sent to the Paris police in response to the revelation of the *Cagoule* conspiracy may be found in folio B^A/344 (79501.2156.1), in the Archives de la Préfecture de Police in Paris. The various folios in the CDJC archive contain a large number of denunciatory letters sent during the occupation years to French and German authorities.

[12]The Bonny-Lafont clique and the notorious police office at 93 rue Lauriston, together with others who engaged in police work, intelligence gathering, the procurement of materiel, and even more sinister work for the Germans, are discussed in

sented a new plebeian radical Right, claiming intellectual roots going back to Rousseauist ideas interpreted by the Jacobins of 1793. Déat repeatedly evoked the totalitarian qualities of Jacobin rule while ignoring its message of liberty. Collaborationists often pointed to intellectual roots in the ideas of Proudhon, La Tour du Pin, Sorel, Péguy, Barrès, and Maurras. The Bonapartist tradition was invoked by most collaborationists, who found Napoleon particularly to their liking, seeing in him a precursor to Hitler's attempt to unify Europe and defeat Russia. Concepts of plebeian dictatorship, charismatic leadership, nationalism, militarism, and social welfare without revolution were all present in the Bonapartist tradition to which Barrès and others brought ethnocentric anti-Semitism. Ultra anti-Semitism looked also for inspiration to Drumont and the enemies of Dreyfus. In the words of Robert Soucy, a leading student of French fascism:

> If French fascism was influenced by other fascisms, it also had a national past of its own; consequently, in many instances developments abroad merely served to fortify a set of pre-existing attitudes at home. Moreover the fact that fascism failed to achieve mass public backing in France hardly demonstrates that it was an ideology non-indigenous to that country. A political party need not win popular support to be rooted in several of its country's political traditions. Were this not so it might be said that Hitler's Nazi party was "un-German" because it lacked mass public support before the onset of the depression.[13]

The radical Right became the terrain for a group of old Left and old Right dissidents against the elites of the parliamentary system and their own oppositional movements. The ex-Communist Doriot, who opposed the 1925 war against a colonial revolt in Morocco, went off to fight Communism in the Soviet Union and spoke out repeatedly for French imperial interests. Déat could not countenence the spilling of French blood over Danzig in 1939 but four years later his position had

---

detail bv Delarue, pp. 15–143, and Cathelin and Gray, *Crimes et trafics de la Gestapo française.* More recently there has appeared a memoir by Bonny's son, Jacques Bonny, *Mon père l'Inspecteur Bonny* (Paris: Robert Laffont, 1975).

[13]Soucy, "The Nature of Fascism in France," p. 30. The relationship between Bonapartism and fascism generally is examined by Jost Dülffer, "Bonapartism, Fascism, and National Socialism," *Journal of Contemporary History,* 11 (October 1976), 111–112.

changed diametrically. The same Déat who had participated with the Grand Rabbi of Paris in a 1935 rally to protest German harassment of Jews took a very different stand after 1940 when German anti-Semitic policies had been vastly increased in tenor and scope. His progression away from human rights may be read in his journalistic campaign against Château, his former colleague who had remained more true to his earlier ideas. Doriot allowed his anti-Communism after 1934 to consume him to the point where his PPF hardly differed in its goals after 1940 from its rivals of a more rightist pedigree. [14]

The collaborationist movements all described their goals in terms of "socialism," as did most interwar and wartime fascist and national socialist movements. Their socialism was to be moralistic and spiritual rather than structural. All classes were to transcend their differences and work together in harmony for the greater good of the fatherland. Making such socialism attractive was more difficult for the collaborationists in France as their concept of the national good entailed working for or with a hostile occupying power, perceived as a national enemy by the majority of the French. It is one of the ironies of the occupation that the collaborationist movements, seen as treasonous by many of their compatriots, referred to themselves collectively as the "national opposition."

Having inverted the term "national," the collaborationists did the same to the word "socialism." To them it became an emotive word, a call for unity in difficult times. Suffering from a kind of anomie, a feeling of powerlessness and of being cast adrift in a rapidly changing

[14]The leftist political origins of Doriot, Déat, and many of their followers are emphasized by Eugen Weber, "Nationalism, Socialism, and National-Socialism in France," pp. 285–287, and *Varieties of Fascism*, pp. 135–137. Plumyène and Lasierra, p. 150, point out that the revolutionary language of the PPF and RNP covered counterrevolutionary intentions. Robert Soucy, "French Fascism as Class Conciliation and Moral Regeneration," *Societas*, 1 (Autumn 1971), 292, also argues that the French collaborationists whose political roots had been in the Left did in fact change camps in their transition to fascism.

For a view of the plebeian character of fascism, see Barrington Moore, p. 447. The almost exclusively urban nature of the French collaborationist movements, however, argues against Moore's attempt to relate fascism to the peasantry. Vichy is described as a "great revenge of minorities" by Stanley G. Hoffmann, "The Vichy Circle of French Conservatives," in Hoffmann, *Decline or Renewal? France since the 1930's* (New York: Viking, 1974), p. 5, and by Paxton, p. 249. Hoffmann's article was published originally as "Aspects du régime de Vichy," *Revue française de science politique*, 6 (January–March 1956).

341

mass society with traditional human ties destroyed, many in the middle classes subconsciously envied what they perceived as proletarian cohesiveness and sense of historical mission. In his statement quoted at the beginning of this chapter, the Milicien François Gaucher articulated a middle-class sense of social dislocation that only a uniform could overcome. As part of a revolutionary political party or a trade union, the worker appeared to have a sense of belonging, knowing his place in the larger unfolding of history. This human solidarity or, more accurately, the perception of it, had a powerful appeal to frightened members of the middle and lower-middle classes, the "losers" in the process of industrialization, to use Wolfgang Sauer's term.[15]

Among the fragmented middle classes of twentieth-century Europe, many hoped to appropriate working-class solidarity without proletarian status. They hoped to emulate the "revolution from above" made when a defeated Prussia under Baron vom Stein had borrowed the mobilizing power without the liberty and equality of the French Revolution. The key word was "socialism," which fascist and national socialist ideologues and propagandists freely used. They transformed the meaning of the word, using it for their own purposes as the Prussians did with the meaning of the French Revolution. In so doing they stripped "socialism" of its revolutionary content and gave it a moralistic meaning acceptable to middle-class outsiders seeking to climb rather than discard the social ladder. Tamed in this way, "socialism" became an acceptable substitute for the far more threatening Communism of Marx and Stalin.

In France after 1940 "socialism" offered the added benefit of providing a point of unity for a society riven by deep political divisions

---

[15]Sauer, 417. A provocative discussion of the lower-middle class's role in history is in Arno J. Mayer, "The Lower Middle Class as Historical Problem," *Journal of Modern History,* 47 (September 1975), in particular p. 418, at which lower-middle-class feelings of superiority over blue-collar manual workers are discussed. A related consideration of "anomie" appears in J. Milton Yinger, "Anomie, Alienation, and Political Behavior," in Jeanne N. Knutsen, ed., *Handbook of Political Psychology* (San Francisco: Jossey-Bass, 1973), p. 192. The moral as opposed to structural nature of reform in German Nazism and French fascism are elucidated respectively by Schoenbaum, pp. 244–245 and 283, and Robert Soucy, "French Fascism as Class Conciliation and Moral Regeneration," p. 293. Schoenbaum discussed the Nazi "revolution" as a transformation in status, unaccompanied by changes in the social structure of Germany.

and needing to unite in the face of the German occupation. Each collaborationist faction preached "socialism" to unite the French under trying conditions but the very multiplicity of their organizations and the way in which they were used by the Germans worked in the opposite direction. In France as in Italy, the unity sought vainly by fascism was achieved only in resistance to it.[16]

The PPF evoked the tradition of the Communards of 1871 who had also attempted to strike for power while under German guns. In 1871, however, socialists of many different kinds had fought together and no one ethnic group was targeted for opprobrium. The rights fought for in 1871 were still universal, transcendent, to use the concept of Ernst Nolte. By 1940 the situation had changed drastically. A generation of French who had known the privations of the 1914–1918 war had come of age in a society that offered at best limited prospects for material and social advancement in the interwar years. To the middle-class popular base of the Ultra factions, collaboration offered the right balance between adventure and protection under the occupation. Those who joined the PPF and its rivals were no longer trying to make a revolution but rather trying to stave one off, although employing the means used by "red" revolutionaries. For the collaborationists were France's fascists, far more clearly than the members of Action Française, which Nolte saw exemplifying fascism in France.[17]

To the radical Right in occupied France, those who wished to abort the "red" revolution by means of a dynamic countermovement of their own, Germany provided an example, especially formidable after 1940. France would be given a hierarchical society in which opportunity would be open to talent, like the army. A new toughened generation would take its rightful place at the helm of the French state and in the positions of economic control. The colored shirt or uniform symbolized youthful camaraderie: all would belong to the community.[18]

[16]The theme of Italian unity forged in the resistance against Mussolini rather than by the Fascists is brought out by Alan Cassels, p. 111.

[17]See the definition of fascism in Nolte, p. 429. For PPF evocation of the Communard spirit of 1871, see Sicard, *La Commune de Paris contre le Communisme,* pp. 24–33.

[18]On the subject of the role of uniforms for collaborationist groups in Holland and in Europe generally, see Littlejohn, pp. 122–123.

Those excluded before 1940 would receive their just rewards in the new society; presumably Darnand would receive his previously denied military commission. France's martial tradition, tarnished in 1940, would be restored and enhanced, primarily through the service of volunteers in the German armed formations and also through France's colonial empire. All of this was to be achieved in a New Europe of united and virile peoples, led by the Germans, who, the collaborationists repeated ceaselessly, would "dominate" their victory, that is, use their military victories for the good of all Europeans. In defeat France would find a European if not a world mission which, according to the collaborationists, she had been unable to do in victory in 1918. Solutions to the problems of 1940 were all too easy for the collaborationists. Their plans required gaining for France the respect of the Germans but this could be won only through a cohesiveness and strength which neither the collaborationist parties nor France as a nation possessed after 1940.

Even without the impediments placed in their way by the Germans, the collaborationists could have expected at best a difficult time after 1940. The reasons for the relatively poor showing of fascism in interwar France as compared with Central Europe are well known. France had been spared the worst of the economic ills that had befallen Italy after World War I and Germany in 1923 and again six years thereafter. French society was more stable than her neighbors' in Central Europe and there were fewer déclassés in France than in Germany. The French lacked the keen edge of resentment caused after 1918 by Italian "mutilated peace" and German "stab in the back" legends. More basic was the political culture of France, steeped in the revolutionary principles of 1789.

Déat's attempt to tie twentieth-century totalitarianism to Rousseau and the spirit of 1793 and PPF associations with Communard traditions failed to overcome the libertarian and egalitarian ideals so closely associated with France. The precepts of 1789 had been inculcated for generations into French school children in the lay schools of the Republic and had become an integral part of France's national identity. The Axis regimes were perceived increasingly as antipathetic to French political traditions and a threat to her national interests as well. The parliamentary regime had absorbed the impact of the right-wing threat by 1938, and when toppled in 1940 was replaced by

344

the Vichy regime, less fascist-inspired and more deeply rooted in the traditions of the mainstream French Right.

As strident as their calls for national strength might be, it was impossible for collaborationists to avoid the stigma of being perceived as in the service of an enemy with whom France was still legally at war after 1940. They might have been installed as puppet rulers by the Germans but it is difficult to imagine them winning any more popularity in that fashion than Quisling did in Norway. The French collaborationist leaders shared with confrères such as Quisling the quality of being so far beyond the mainstream in their view of Germany as to have been entirely incapable of understanding the anti-German mood of the majority of their compatriots, especially as the war progressed.[19]

From Hitler down, the German leaders outfoxed their would-be allies in France. To win their new world the collaborationists were required to strike a Faustian bargain, selling their souls to the devil. The German Mephistopheles in 1940, however, was far shrewder than his French acolytes. Hitler's offer of an armistice and a measure of sovereignty to the French government went a long way toward compromising much of France's social and political elite, but they at least held real domestic power in the southern zone until 1942. The collaborationists were proportionately more compromised and received far less in return. They got none of the power they had anticipated after the armistice, but the days of reckoning came anyway, after August 1944, with the liberation of France and the explosion of the pent-up wrath of their compatriots. Hitler had played a monstrous hoax on those whose desire had been to bring France into his New Order. He had undermined their very reason for existence, as in his refusal to support Doriot's quest for power in 1942. Small wonder that many of the collaborationists simply refused to believe the reality of German policy, a reality whose existence is still denied today by some survivors of the Ultra camp.

Hitler's policy toward France was consistent in the years before the war and after the armistice. Playing shrewdly upon the fragmentation he knew existed in the French body politic, Hitler exploited divisions

[19]See John M. Hoberman, "Vidkun Quisling's Psychological Image," *Scandinavian Studies*, 46 (Summer 1974), 255.

within the collaborationist ranks to prevent any one movement from becoming too powerful. He used the entire collaborationist camp as a lever with which to exert pressure when needed upon official Vichy and turned to the collaborationists only when Pétain and Laval refused to cooperate. The significance of the collaborationists lay not in their strength but in the fact of their existence, demonstrating the presence of fascism, even if in a weakened form, in France.

As the war continued and German pressure for French manpower and wealth was intensified, the Resistance grew and collaborationists were targeted for elimination. Some tried to slip quietly back into private life; the more militant and aggressive ones took up arms and fought in the Milice or the PPF formations. Some of the younger ones, especially those who fought in the German armed forces and after August 1944 no longer had a homeland to which to return, took pride in the ostracism they received from their compatriots. In the Milice at home and in the Charlemagne Division fighting in eastern Germany, the younger brothers and associates of the "realists" of 1940 had become the wild-eyed romantic fanatics of 1944, no closer than ever to real political power.[20]

Some one or two hundred thousand French, the manifestation of an evolving radical Right during the occupation, actively identified their own interests and those of France with Hitler's New Order. Anti-Communist, anti-Freemason, anti-Semitic, opposed to the direction taken by modern history in France and Europe, they looked to the National Socialist New Order to open doors previously closed to them. Shaken less severely than her neighbors by the economic disruptions and social dislocations that followed World War I, France remained more resistant but hardly immune to the growth of fascism. The 1940 disaster opened up new possibilities promptly squandered by the radical Right. Half a dozen competing political parties claimed the inheritance of the radical Right in France. Each asserted its native roots, intellectual and political, in the French soil. The existence of so many of them, in view of the fractious political tradition of Republican France, justified their claims.

[20]A recent study of German Nazis concludes that many young recruits, early in the party's history, apparently discovered their own identity in disputatious conflict with majority opinion in Weimar Germany and in their sense of being castigated for their minoritarian political beliefs. See Merkl, p. 259.

13 Epilogue: The Collaborationists since the War

> You have no blood on your hands, nor did you sell yourself for money nor affirm an idea in which you did not believe. Your only crime is to have appeared at a moment in history in the camp of the defeated. All events will only confirm your vision and justify the attitudes that you dared propose to your country and to Europe.
> —Déat, "Méditation sur l'existence," 1945

> If in 1939–1940, the German-Soviet pact had been played out to the end and we had been defeated and occupied by the Russians, how many patriots and partisans of liberty would have done for Russia as much as and more than Darnand did for Germany?
> —R. Bruckberger, *Si Grande Peine*

The defeat of Germany in April 1945 brought on the final obliteration of the parties of the French collaboration. With Allied armies closing in toward the last citadels of the Reich, the French collaborationists in exile there fled in a spirit of *sauve qui peut*. Most of their leaders ultimately fell into the hands of the Allies and were returned for trial in liberated France. Even before the Liberation the various elements of the Resistance had decided that a renovation of French political life necessitated a thoroughgoing purge of Vichyites and collaborationists. With most of the metropole under the control of the de Gaulle Government, a start was made in September 1944 with the establishment of special courts to try the cases of those accused of having collaborated with the enemy. By the time these trials ended five years later, they had aroused widespread controversy. Resistance purists argued that the courts had been too lenient and that the purge had not been sufficiently extensive. Judicial inconsistencies arose from factors beyond anyone's control, not the least of which was that many of the collaborationists were beyond the reach of French justice in the fall of 1944 and could be tried only after the final defeat of Germany when passions had cooled in France. [1]

[1] The concept of renovation (*renouvellement*) as it related to Resistance thought is

347

Many of those affected by the purge denied that the trials had any legality at all and termed them "victor's justice," a critique also voiced about the Nuremberg trials. They argued that in serving and obeying the government of Marshal Pétain, they had followed the directives of a legally installed government, approved by the vast majority of the French people in 1940. Vichyites and collaborationists asserted their patriotism and high-minded intentions, arguing that by interposing themselves between their compatriots and the occupation authorities they had been able to save much for France. The more extreme collaborationists often contended that their goal was simply the ending of the apparently interminable Franco-German hostility that had caused so much bloodshed since 1870. They claimed to have been playing the German "card," that is, providing representation for France in the camp of the Axis which would later have served the French well had the Axis won the war. Some attempted conciliation by arguing that just as they had played the German "card," de Gaulle and his supporters had played the Allied "card." Both sides, they said, had served France well by providing representation for her in whichever camp ultimately won the war.

Collaborationists who had wielded political influence were often able to show that they had intervened successfully with the Germans to save French lives. Theirs, they sometimes said, was an "internal" resistance, an attempt to soften German rule from within and many successful instances of this type of behavior were produced during the postwar trials. To be effective in their "internal" resistance, however, they needed to fool the Germans. In so doing they also fooled and demoralized their compatriots and aided the occupation authorities in many ways. Their postwar defense sought to direct the trials to the question of motives, virtually impossible to ascertain in the courtroom. Former collaborationists have argued that they countermanded German-inspired written orders by telephone or in personal conversations with subordinates, all impossible to verify. They contended that the entire trial process was an illegal exercise in political vengeance conducted *ex post facto*.[2]

---

discussed in Peter Novick, *The Resistance versus Vichy: The Purge of Collaborators in Liberated France* (New York: Columbia University Press, 1968), p. vii.

[2]The theme of "internal resistance" was repeated in virtually every postwar trial of the collaborationists and was often reiterated to me during interviews by col-

In a study of the purge of Vichyites and collaborationists, Peter Novick has shown that in proportion to total population the French purge was significantly milder than corresponding purges in other Western European countries and that progressive amnesties starting in 1951 led to the liberation of most of those imprisoned. By 1956 only sixty-two persons remained in prison, and eight years later, at the time of the twentieth anniversary of the Liberation, there were no longer any people imprisoned in France as a result of the postwar trials. The figures for those executed in the purge vary widely from estimates of over 100,000 given by rightist sources to the official government figures of 2,853 death sentences, of which 767 were carried out. Another 3,910 received death sentences *in absentia*. Approximately 38,000 prison sentences were handed down of which slightly fewer than 3,000 were life terms with hard labor, the remaining being for varying periods of detention. Nearly 50,000 persons received the penalty of "national degradation," entailing the loss of all civic rights. Comparing France with other newly liberated countries, Novick shows that there 94 of every 100,000 of the population were imprisoned for collaboration, whereas the corresponding figures in the Netherlands, Belgium, and Norway were 419, 596, and 633, respectively.[3]

Consideration of the figures alone, however, can lead one to overlook the way the postwar purge was perceived by its victims who survived and their political successors in the French radical Right. To them it was an ideological purge, orchestrated by the Communists who, they argued, concocted a myth of "Résistantialisme" to hide their own subversive activities of 1939–1941 and plans for power after 1944. Traumatized by the purge, the radical Right more than thirty years later has still not fully overcome the shock. In the words of two students of French fascism, the purge made antifascism a

---

laborationists of all shades of opinion. Their bitterness in respect to the postwar trials has been manifested in many memoirs. See, for example, Charbonneau, 2:337–338; Labat, pp. 585–587; and the accounts of two former PPF members, Hérold-Paquis, p. 170 and Saint-Paulien, *Les maudits*, 2: *Le rameau vert*, p. 11. Hérold-Paquis was executed for collaboration in 1945. For the accounts of disillusioned pacifist ex-Socialists who suffered retribution after the war, see Paul Faure, *De Munich à la Cinquième République* (Paris: Elan, n.d. [approx. 1959]), pp. 240–250, and Jean-Pierre Abel [René Château], *L'age de Caïn*.

[3]Novick, pp. 186–188.

"state theology," producing a political and moral order that silenced the Right for years thereafter. Large numbers of collaborationists had to live clandestinely for a time and others sought refuge in Spain and South America. "Now we are the clandestine ones," said a Milicien in August 1944.[4]

In its drive against those involved in the collaboration, the new government decided to mete out the severest penalties to the leaders, as quickly as possible, and then get on with the task of building a new political order in France. With the collapse of Germany in April 1945, Vichyites and collaborationists previously inaccessible to French justice became the objects of the purge. Pétain, whose return to France was voluntary, and Laval, whose return was not, were both tried and sentenced to death. Laval's execution was carried out, Pétain's sentence was commuted. Of the collaborationist leaders, most fell before firing squads after having been found guilty of "intelligence with the enemy." These included Darnand, Bucard, de Brinon, and Luchaire. Doriot's death in Germany had taken him out of the picture. Two major collaborationist leaders escaped: Déat and Châteaubriant. Déat and his wife successfully made their way across the Tyrolian Alps into northern Italy, where they were given refuge in a Catholic convent in Turin. The former RNP leader died of natural causes there in 1955.[5]

---

[4]Plumyène and Lasierra, p. 197. For further consideration of the quantitative severity of the purge, see Robert Aron, *Histoire de la Libération de France: juin 1944–mai 1945* (Paris: Fayard, 1959), pp. 216–219 and 325–326, and Novick, p. 68. On pp. 77–78 of his book, Novick discusses summary justice meted out to Doriotists and Déatists at Gap in southeastern France. The ideological nature of the purge is brought out by Plumyène and Lasierra, p. 173. "Résistantialisme" as a myth is discussed by Paul Sérant, *Les vaincus de la Libération. L'épuration en Europe occidentale à la fin de la Seconde Guerre mondiale* (Paris: Robert Laffont, 1964), p. 385, and Alfred Fabre-Luce, *Au nom des silencieux* (Bruges and Paris: La Diffusion du Livre, 1945), p. 153. For rightist use of the word "trauma" to describe the purge, see Bernard Vorge, "Les intellectuels et l'épuration," in *L'épuration*, a special issue of *Défense de l'Occident*, January-February 1957, p. 127. A more complete consideration of the effects of the purge in the development of the postwar French Right is available in my unpublished paper, "'*Les prisons de la Quatrième*': The Purge of Vichyites and Collaborators in the Formation of the Postwar French Radical Right," presented at the meeting of the American Historical Association, San Francisco, December 30, 1978.

[5]Novick, p. 157, discusses de Gaulle's desire to limit the extent of the purge and to get it accomplished as quickly as possible.

The years of inactivity enforced upon Déat in Turin gave him time to reflect and write. He left an extensive body of unpublished writings at the time of his death. Although the erudition of the RNP leader differentiated him from other collaborationist leaders and most of their followers, the thoughts he expressed after 1945 represented many of their ideas as well. He argued that his activity during the war had been entirely honorable. He had been, he claimed, a personally disinterested supporter of a united Europe, an ideal he stated would yet be realized. His "crime," he wrote, was to have appeared at the wrong moment in history, to have had the misfortune of being on the losing side. Knowing that he had been tried *in absentia* and sentenced to death in 1945 in France, Déat denied all moral and legal legitimacy to this judgment. Reports of his postwar activities in Italy occasionally filtered back to France. He was said to have participated in clandestine fascist meetings of the "maquis noir" with former SS men and Italian Neo Fascists in 1946 in Scorza. Some liaisons were said to be maintained between Déat and his former supporters in France but it would appear that if such ties existed, they were used more in attempts to protect the ex-RNP followers than to organize concerted political action. In his postwar writings, Déat regretted "excesses" committed against Jews and other enemies of Hitler's Germany but he, along with many other former collaborationists, believed that he needed to make no apologies for his political activity during the occupation. Gradually, Déat's health deteriorated in Italy and he turned to the church, a thorough departure from the anticlericalism that had characterized his political career in France. The tendency of many lapsed Catholics to turn to fascism was reversed in the spiritual odyssey of Déat.[6]

Châteaubriant lived the remainder of his life in seclusion in the Austrian Tyrol, dying there in 1951. His followers in the Groupe Collaboration had been less violent in their pursuit of the New Order and it was easier for larger numbers of them to slip back into anonym-

[6]For Déat's reflections on his political career, see his "Méditation sur l'existence," *Courrier de l'Ouest*, February 12, 1957, and "Ce dévot barbu, c'était l'Anticlérical Déat, homme de peine, chez les bonnes soeurs," *France Dimanche*, no. 449 (1955), both brought to my attention by Emily Goodman, at whose suggestion they have been microfilmed and made available at the Library of the Hoover Institution. For earlier accounts of Déat's postwar activity, see "Pierrot le Fou et Marcel Déat se retrouvaient au 'Maquis Noir'," *Libération*, November 24, 1948.

ity than for those of the Milice or the PPF, the two groups whose members seem to have borne the brunt of the popular wrath where it appeared in late 1944 and early 1945. Many of the medium-level collaborationist party personnel found safety in exile in 1944 and 1945. Madrid became a center for refugees from the Milice, the PPF, and the collaborationist press of Paris. Most of the collaborationists, especially the rank-and-file, had remained in France in 1944, refusing to follow their leaders to Germany. Believing in their own good motives and patriotism, they were sometimes surprised to see themselves visited with penalties no different from those meted out to their fellows brought back from German exile after the defeat of Hitler's Reich. The progressive amnesties issued starting in 1951 brought many exiled collaborationists back to France, where most of them resumed quiet private existences. Others chose to remain abroad in countries where they had established new lives. Some undoubtedly feared the possibility of private revenge taken by those who felt the collaborationists had been insufficiently punished. The Franco regime made Spain a museum of sorts for the debris of Hitler's Europe.[7]

In France the former collaborationists tended to stick together, forming a closed society, a subculture within the larger French community. Although party differences were not forgotten, the former "collabos" kept in contact with one another. Frequently, the better-placed ex-collaborationists helped their less fortunate comrades find jobs in libraries, publishing houses, educational institutions, and a wide variety of other enterprises. It is difficult to generalize about the lives and thoughts of collaborationists since the war because some refuse to discuss their prior activities. Others recall with affection the sense of camaraderie they felt in the parties of the collaboration but now maintain that collaborationism was an error based on a misreading of German intentions during the occupation. Many others who continue to defend their wartime activities live in a subculture produced by what they perceive as the overly severe and unjust postwar purge.

[7]On the rift within the RNP between those who left for exile in Germany and those who remained in France, see Chap. 10 above, n. 52. Descriptions of the flight of collaborationists and their activities after the war in Spain and elsewhere may be found in Saint-Paulien, *Les maudits*, volume II, and Saint-Loup [Augier], *Les nostalgiques* (Paris: Presses de la Cité, 1967). In many interviews I was given embittered accounts of experiences in the "prisons of the Republic."

Collaborationists who survive in the 1970's were young during the war and their feelings of indignation for their treatment since its end are often combined with nostalgia for their youth and the adventures they shared as part of the collaboration. Those who were most militant during the war have by and large preserved their truculence to a greater degree than have the more moderate collaborationists. Once a month a small dinner party attended by a dozen or so survivors of the Milice, Anti-Bolshevik Legion, and French Waffen-SS and their families takes place at a Paris restaurant. Old war maps are broken out and pored over, old songs sung, and the shibboleths of Hitler's New Order repeated. A black SS helmet is playfully placed upon the head of a young boy, the son of one of the old warriors in attendance. Nearby in Paris another group of aging men and women gathers at a monument erected to an unknown Jew, killed during the 1939–1945 war. The monument stands in front of the shining new building erected in Paris' Marais district to memorialize the Jews killed in Hitler's holocaust. It is July 16, the anniversary of the herding of 16,000 Jews of Paris into the Vélodrome d'hiver for transportation to the death camps in 1942. A candle is lit and a service is held for the dead. In many ways does France remember the war.

Most of the collaborationists did not return to political activity after the war. A small number, however, emerged from clandestine political activity into an assortment of extreme Right movements after 1946. A few looked briefly in 1951 to de Gaulle's oppositional Rassemblement du Peuple Français and others to Poujade in 1955. The Algerian war brought a number of Algerians of European stock into fascist-type groups, notably the Organisation de l'Armée Secrète, transplanted to metropolitan France at the time of the granting of Algerian independence. Throughout the postwar period a multitude of radical Right splinter groups have come and gone in France. One of the more recent and better known, Ordre Nouveau, created in November 1969, was dissolved by the government following the June 1973 street disorders in Paris. It has been succeeded by a new formation, Œuvre Française. Both of these groups represent a new generation of radical Right activists, too young to have been involved in wartime politics.[8]

[8]Bernard Brigouleix, "L'extrême droite à la recherche d'un avenir," *Le Monde*, June 12–15, 1976. On Ordre Nouveau, see François Duprat, *Les mouvements*

Some of the postwar groups have called for a united Europe, for which Nazi-dominated Europe served as the prototype, which alone, they argue can make Europe a third force, independent of the United States and the Soviet Union. Others have been oriented more toward traditional French nationalism of the Right. All have demanded strong authoritarian states and hierarchical social orders. Still marginal, split among "nationalists" and "Europeanists," monarchists and neofascists, the radical Right perpetuates its factionalist tradition in France. Some of its members have been involved in bank robberies which in 1976 gained widespread publicity in attempts to build up war chests for future political activity. On the fringes now, they await the crisis that they hope will come and drive millions of the French middle classes into their arms as the last bulwark against the Left. Collaborationism died in 1945. Most of its supporters either adapted to the new political system after 1944 or quietly retired from the political arena. They have taken their historical place as one of the stages in the evolution of the radical Right, which lives on in France.

---

d'extrême-droite en France depuis 1944 (Paris: Les Editions Albatross, 1972), p. 168. Duprat provides a thorough discussion of virtually all the extreme Right movements from the time of the Liberation until the early 1970's.

Appendix A: Milice Française Membership

Figures as of June 30, 1943. Source: Kontrollinspektion der DWStK. Kontrollab-teilung Az. 20. Nr. 1900/43g, Bourges, August 11, 1943; T-77/842/5585903.

Region	Department	Milice	Franc-Garde	Total
Clermont-Ferrand	Puy de Dôme	610	240	850
	Cantal	150	110	260
	Haute-Loire	320	160	480
	Allier	390	310	700
Total		1,470	820	2,290
Limoges	Haute-Vienne (and			
	part Charante)	560	170	730
	Dordogne	120	185	305
	Corrèze	95	70	165
	Creuse	48	107	155
	Indre-et-Loire	100	160	260
	Cher	50	60	110
Total		973	752	1,725
Lyons	Ain	110	240	350
	Ardèche	140	260	400
	Drôme	150	270	420
	Isère	210	410	620
	Jura	100	200	300
	Loire	225	475	700
	Rhône	325	675	1,000
	Saône-et-Loire	200	400	600
	Savoie	120	230	350
	Haute-Savoie	220	430	650
Total		1,800	3,590	5,390
Marseilles	Bouches-du-Rhône	8,100	2,100	10,200
	Vaucluse	800	600	1,400
Total		8,900	2,700	11,600
Montpellier	Hérault	200	800	1,000
	Aude	350	600	950
	Pyrénnées-Orientales	400	600	1,000
	Aveyron	150	200	350
	Lozère	30	20	50
Total		1,130	2,220	3,350

Collaborationism in France during the Second World War

Toulouse	Haute-Garonne	1,240	385	1,625
	Ariège	130	153	283
	Basses-Pyrénnées	238	207	445
	Hautes-Pyrénnées	187	309	496
	Lot	125	169	294
	Lot-et-Garonne	750	845	1,595
	Tarn-et-Garonne	176	260	436
	Tarn	163	250	413
	Gers	185	285	470
Total		3,194	2,863	6,057
Grand total: entire south zone		17,467	12,945	30,412

Appendix B: The Lesser Movements of the Collaboration

Ligue Française

Leader: Pierre Costantini.

Interwar history: None, the Ligue was established by Costantini after the armistice.

Party organ: *L'Appel*.

German attitude: Legally recognized.

Outstanding characteristics: The Ligue was the largest of the lesser movements. Costantini, a Corsican, tried to infuse it with a Bonapartist ideology. In 1942 he allied with Doriot; see Chapter 4, above. The Ligue was able to attract 8,000 to its November 1942 party congress in Paris.

Parti Français National-Collectiviste

Leader: Pierre Clémenti.

Interwar history: Following the February 1934 Days, Clémenti established a small radical Right group called National Communism, which attacked Freemasons, Jews, and the Popular Front. He later changed the name to National Collectivism.

Party organ: *Le Pays Libre*.

German attitude: Tolerated rather than recognized. The Germans felt they possessed insufficient evidence to judge Clémenti's group.

Outstanding characteristics: The PFNC was the parent organization of Charles Lefebvre's Garde Française, which embarrassed the Germans by its anti-Semitic rampage along the Champs-Elysées in August 1940. Lefebvre later left Clémenti, who was one of the few collaborationist politicians actually to serve in the Anti-Bolshevik Legion. Clémenti also announced that he intended France to secure the Francophone territories of Belgium, which brought him into direct conflict with the Rexist movement of Léon Degrelle.

Le Feu

Leader: Maurice Delaunay.

Interwar history: None; le Feu was created in 1941 by Delaunay.

Party organ: *La Tempête*.

German attitude: Legally recognized.

Outstanding characteristics: This movement was the work of Delaunay, the deputy from Caen, who called himself "Maître du Feu" and wrote under the nom de plume François-Henry Promethée. A lone wolf, Delaunay was even more moralistic than most in his writings.

Le Front Franc

Leader: Jean Boissel.

Interwar history: In 1934 Boissel founded a newspaper called *Racisme International Fascisme* and a small group, the Légion Frontiste which called for the establishment of an authoritarian right-wing regime and the expulsion of Jews and Freemasons from France.

Party organ: *Réveil du Peuple*.

German attitude: Legally recognized

Outstanding characteristics: Boissel was a heavily decorated hero of World War I who attracted a few veterans to his side. As tiny as the Front Franc was, it was wracked with internal dissension and constant quarrels with the other collaborationist grouplets.

Les Energies Françaises: Led by a certain Cayla, this was an ephemeral moralistic pressure group that tried in 1943 to gain influence in French army circles.

La Croisade Française: Led by someone named Gatinais, this organization was closed down by the Germans after it brawled with the rival Parti National Socialiste Français.

Parti National Socialiste Français

Leader: Christian Message.

Interwar history: None.

Party organ: None.

German attitude: At first favorable, but the party was proscribed when it proved too turbulent. Message was jailed in 1941 by the Germans.

Outstanding characteristics: Tinier than the movements of Clémenti and Boissel, the PNSF wanted to expel all Jews and "anti-fascist foreigners," and wanted the state to control all church properties. Also called for France to join the Axis.

Parti Français: A dissident offshoot of the Parti National Socialiste Français which was born and died in 1941. Led by Henri Ours, a patron of sporting events and former member of the steering committee of Message's group.

Centre d'Action et de Documentation: Run by Henry Coston as an investigative agency exposing Jews and Freemasons. Coston had revived Drumont's *La Libre Parole* in the 1930's but the Germans refused to let him publish a newspaper during the occupation.

La Communauté Française: An obscure racist group.

Comité d'Epuration de la Race Française: Headed by Louis Deseutre-Poussin, it sought the exclusion of Jews from the national life of France. Among its activists were Châteaubriant of the Groupe Collaboration and Abel Bonnard, the minister of education after 1942.

Parti Ouvrier et Paysan Français
  Leader: Marcel Capron.
  Interwar history: None.
  Party organ: None. A series of "open letters to workers and peasants" was
    published.
  German attitude: Legally recognized but only for Paris.
  Outstanding characteristics: The Parti Ouvrier was a small group of
    prominent ex-Communists who defected after the signing of the Nazi-
    Soviet pact. It was founded by Marcel Gitton, a former member of the
    Communist Political Bureau assassinated in 1941. These dissident
    Communists might have been expected to support Doriot, and Gitton
    eventually did, but most distrusted Doriot and seemed unwilling to
    follow him to fascism.

Comité d'Action Anti-Bolchévique: Headed by the naval historian Paul Chack, this committee served as a clearing house for anti-Communist propaganda, which it shared with all political movements interested.

Les Amis du Maréchal: A pro-Vichy (as opposed to collaborationist) group, which was tolerated rather than legally recognized by the Germans. It functioned in Bordeaux, where it was led by a Dr. Cantorne, and in Rouen, led there by Maurice Durame.

Cercles Pétain: Clandestine French political organizations functioning within German prisoner-of-war camps. They were staunchly Pétainist, but they did produce some ideological collaborationists who were released to become active in the Ultra movements. Brasillach was the most prominent alumnus of the Cercles Pétain.

Parti National Breton

Leader: Olier Mordrel, succeeded in November 1940 by Raymond Delaporte.

Interwar history: The PNB predated the war as a Breton autonomist movement.

Party organ: *L'Heure Bretonne*.

German attitude: The PNB was the leading one of several autonomist Breton movements that was not necessarily fascist but began to assume fascist trappings after 1940. It was openly opposed by Bishop Duparc of Quimper.

Vlaamsche Verbond voor Frankrijk: A Flemish separatist movement established in the two northern departments under the German military command in Brussels. Its leader was a certain Abbé Gantois.

The most important sources for the lesser collaborationist movements are: Deutsche Waffenstillstandskommission, "Übersicht über die politischen Vereinigungen (Parteien) im besetzten französischen Gebiet," August 28, 1941, T-77/850/5594887-94; Der Militärbefehlshaber in Frankreich, Anlage 32 zum Lagebericht für die Monate Februar-März 1942, CDJC document CDXCV, 10; and the *French Basic Handbook*, pp. 152–155.

Bibliographical Note

The student of the collaborationist movements of France during World War II will find them elusive and often shadowy phenomena. Their history is the history of losers in a deeply embittered civil confrontation and there are many survivors who prefer to let the past remain buried. One can only guess at the magnitude of the destruction of party rosters and other documentation, now sorely missed by the historian, in August 1944. I have interviewed several dozen of those involved in the collaboration and some of my interlocutors were kind enough to show me unpublished materials from their own private archives. One wonders how much of interest is still hidden in attics, basements, and the like. Precious documentation may appear only by freakish accident in the distant future or may be lost forever due to carelessness, forgetfulness, or a conscious desire to conceal embarrassing information. It has always been the lot of the historian, however, to depend for source material on forces beyond his control. Recent events present problems of partisanship and lack of historical perspective, but these are balanced by the great quantities of written source material and the availability of living participants to discuss their experiences. Oral testimony given by a former collaborationist over a glass of cognac in a comfortable apartment in a fashionable district of Paris requires the same careful scrutiny demanded by an ancient scroll from a long dead civilization: no more, no less.

More than thirty years after the end of World War II, the collaboration is still a sensitive subject in France. The National Archives are closed to researchers beginning with the year 1940, which, as Robert Paxton has pointed out, speaks eloquently to the fears of exposure that still exist in France.[1] A voluminous quantity of published material devoted to the study of the war years has appeared in France but very little of it has been addressed to the problem of the collaboration. Perhaps, as suggested by Stanley Hoffmann, one may

[1] Paxton, p. 392.

write about Vichy in terms of "internal resistance" and thereby salvage something for national pride, but collaborationism offers no such possibilities.[2]

In the light of the postwar revelations of Nazi brutality, the subject of collaboration undoubtedly raises questions of guilt, particularly as some have defined even going about one's daily life as tacit collaboration in occupied France. A few works appeared in the 1960's purporting to deal with the collaboration in France. One, Saint-Paulien, *Histoire de la collaboration* (Paris: L'Esprit Nouveau, 1964), is an apologia for the PPF rather than a thorough study of the entire phenomenon of collaborationism, written by Maurice-Ivan Sicard, who was in charge of PPF propaganda in the southern zone. Another is a systematic but limited study of the collaborationist press in occupied Paris by Michèle Cotta, *La collaboration, 1940–1944*, one of the Kiosque series (Paris: Armand Colin, 1964). The only really systematic attempt until recently to analyze collaborationism was that of Stanley G. Hoffmann, "Collaborationism in France during World War II," *Journal of Modern History*, 40 (September 1968), 375–395.

In recent years, however, the French have started to take a more careful look at collaboration during the Second World War. A new generation has come of age and it has begun to question the roles of its parents under the occupation. The film *Le chagrin et la pitié*, directed by Marcel Ophuls in 1968, stirred the extensive controversy that was to be expected but it was a long step toward the removal of taboos against the discussion of the collaboration. Other films, such as Louis Malle's *Lacombe Lucien* (1974) followed.

Some young devotees, bored with the prosaic and conventional life of urban France in the late 1960's and 1970's, have cultivated a renewed taste for fascism and collaborationism. Popular literature dealing with the French Waffen-SS has become commercially profitable, and at one time the flea market just north of Paris had to ban the sale of Nazi and collaborationist memorabilia, which were becoming highly prized. The renewal of interest in the collaboration has also been manifested in a scholarly direction by the government-supported Comité d'Histoire de la Deuxième Guerre Mondiale, which has devoted three recent issues of its *Revue* to the collabora-

[2]Hoffmann, "Collaborationism," pp. 375–376.

tion. One of the issues is devoted to regional studies of the collaboration. It includes P. Gounand, "Les groupements de collaboration dans une ville française occupée: Dijon," *Revue d'histoire de la deuxième guerre mondiale*, 23 (July 1973), 47–56, in addition to other regional studies in the same issue, cited in the relevant sections below. The issues of January 1975 and October 1977 contain several articles devoted to the various Ultra parties, also cited in the relevant sections below.

The growing scholarly interest in collaboration in France is reflected in three books published there in the past few years. A short summary of the collaboration with excerpts from collaborationist speeches and writings is available in Jean-Pierre Azéma, *La collaboration, 1940–1944* (Paris: Presses Universitaires de France, 1975), covering Vichy as well as the Ultras. Pascal Ory, *Les collaborateurs, 1940–1945* (Paris: Seuil, 1976), studies the entire Ultra camp with emphasis on the literary collaboration. It is the most important book yet to appear on the subject in France. Another book edited by Ory, *La France allemande: paroles du collaborationisme français (1933–1945)* (Paris: Archives Gallimard/Julliard, 1976), is a collection of collaborationist writings.

Study of the French collaborationist movements is made possible by the availability of the huge quantity of German archival material seized by advancing Allied armies at the end of the war. Many of these papers have been microfilmed, with copies available from the National Archives in Washington. These documents view events through German eyes, although they often contain French reports prepared for or intercepted by the Germans. The proliferation of German offices in occupied France provided increased quantities of correspondence and reports, extremely useful to the historian. Contemporary with the events of the occupation, they provide a picture that the more self-conscious and self-serving statements made in postwar trials and memoirs cannot.

The various guides to the literally hundreds of thousands of captured German documents on microfilm are discussed by Paxton, who made extensive use of them in his masterful study of the Vichy government.[3] Of particular use in examining the German views of

[3]Paxton, pp. 395–396.

the collaborationist groups are the collections T-77, T-120, and T-175, materials from the Supreme Wehrmacht Command (OKW: Oberkommando der Wehrmacht), the Foreign Ministry, and the various police services united under Himmler, respectively. Friedrich Grimm's reports to the Foreign Ministry, included among the German documents microfilmed, have been collected and published in book form by a group of his friends as Friedrich Grimm, *Frankreich-Berichte 1934 bis 1944, herausgegeben vom Kreis seiner Freunde* (Bodensee: Hohenstaufen, 1972). A substantial quantity of captured German material gathered to prepare the cases against those on trial at Nuremberg after the war is also available at the archive of the Centre de Documentation Juive Contemporaine (CDJC) in Paris. The Centre also holds some official French documentation relating to the collaborationists and a scattered assortment of correspondence, leaflets, and published speeches from the collaborationist movements themselves.

The richest sources for published collaborationist material—newspapers, pamphlets, and books—are the Bibliothèque de Documentation Internationale et Contemporaine, located at the University of Paris X in Nanterre, and the Bibliothèque Nationale in Paris. The Hoover Institution Library at Stanford University also has a good collection of collaborationist publications. In the French tradition, the collaborationists were usually prolific writers, and a thorough perusal of the press just at Paris during the occupation could take years. Much of it becomes repetitious and it is condensed and summarized in Cotta's book, *La collaboration*. Her discussion is limited to the Paris press, however, and should be supplemented by a look at several newspapers not included. Notable among those absent from Cotta's book are the Milice's *Combats*, published in Vichy; *Rassemblement*, the RNP weekly while Déat and Deloncle were united in that movement; the Anti-Bolshevik Legion's *Combattant Européen*; the Waffen-SS *Devenir*; *La France*, the paper edited by Luchaire on behalf of the Governmental Commission at Sigmaringen; and *Jeune Force de France*, which represented the thought of young militants such as Merlin, who ended up in the Waffen-SS.

For discussion of the collaborationist press, see Jacques Polonski, *La presse, la propagande et l'opinion publique sous l'occupation* (Paris: Centre de Documentation Juive Contemporaine, 1946); Jean Quéval

[Jacques Dormeuil], *Première page, cinquième colonne* (Paris: Fayard, 1945); Marcel Baudot, *L'opinion publique sous l'occupation* (Paris: Presses Universitaires de France, 1960); and two more recent studies by Claude Lévy, "La presse de collaboration en France occupée: conditions d'existence," *Revue d'histoire de la deuxième guerre mondiale*, 20 (October 1970), 87–100 and *Les Nouveaux Temps et l'idéologie de la collaboration* (Paris: Fondation Nationale des Sciences Politiques, 1974). The *Nouveaux Temps* was edited by Jean Luchaire. Of related interest in studying one of the significant right-wing publications is Pierre-Marie Dieudonnat, *Je suis partout, 1930–1944: Les maurrasiens devant la tentation fasciste* (Paris: La Table Ronde, 1973). The ways in which the French media were fed German propaganda during the occupation is studied by R. G. Nobécourt, *Les secrets de la propagande en France occupée* (Paris: Fayard, 1962).

One of the most useful sources of information concerning the various collaborationist parties, as well as many other aspects of life in occupied France is the *French Basic Handbook, Parts III and IV* (London: Foreign Office, 1944). Prepared to equip British forces with a broad knowledge of conditions in France just prior to the invasion, this book was part of a series on the occupied countries put together by the British Foreign Office. Information was gathered by teams of experts who made extensive use of reports of agents returning from missions to the Continent as well as information from refugees who had fled their homelands. The American equivalent of the British report on French collaboration is the mimeographed United States Office of Strategic Service, Research and Analysis Branch, R and A No. 1694, "French Pro-Fascist Groups," available in the Hoover Institution Library.

For German policy toward occupied France, see in addition to the microfilm series cited above the collection of German Foreign Ministry archives published as *Akten zur deutschen Auswärtigen Politik 1918–1945. Aus den Archiv des deutschen Auswärtigen Amts*, Series D, vols. X-XIII (various publishers, 1963–1970) and Series E, vols. I-II (Göttingen: Vandenhoeck and Ruprecht, 1969–1972). See also the collection of documents in Otto Abetz, *Pétain et les allemands: Memorandum d'Abetz sur les Rapports Franco-Allemands* (Paris: Gaucher, 1948). Ambassador Abetz also wrote memoirs, *Das offene Problem. Ein Rückblick auf zwei Jehrzehnte deutscher Frankreichpolitik*

(Cologne: Greven Verlag, 1951). Of further help in studying the collaboration is the memorandum of Elmar Michel, in charge of economic aspects of collaboration as Chief of Staff to the Administration of the Military Command; see "Rapport Final au Gouvernement du Reich du Doctor Michel, Chef de l'A.M. sur la Collaboration Franco-Allemande (1940–1944)," *La France intérieur, Cahiers*, no. 50 (November 15, 1946), 4–13 and no. 51 (December 15, 1946), 3–18. The most thorough study of German attitudes and policies toward occupied France is Eberhard Jäckel, *Frankreich in Hitlers Europa: Die Deutsche Frankreichpolitik im zweiten Weltkrieg* (Stuttgart: Deutsche Verlags-Anstalt, 1966). More specific studies of German policy toward occupied France are Alan S. Milward, *The New Order and the French Economy* (Oxford: Clarendon Press, 1970), and Hans Umbreit, *Der Militärbefehlshaber in Frankreich 1940–1944* (Boppard-am-Rhein: H. Boldt, 1968). See also Patrick Facon and Françoise de Ruffray, "Aperçus sur la collaboration aéronautique franco-allemande 1940–1943," *Revue d'histoire de la deuxième guerre mondiale*, 27 (October 1977), 85–102.

The best treatment of the Vichy government is Robert O. Paxton, *Vichy France: Old Guard and New Order, 1940–1944* (New York: Knopf, 1972). Paxton's work may be supplemented with Stanley G. Hoffmann, "Aspects du régime de Vichy," which first appeared in the *Revue française de science politique*, 6 (Jan.–March 1956) and has been translated into English as "The Vichy Circle of French Conservatives," in Hoffmann, *Decline or Renewal? France since the 1930s* (New York: Viking, 1974), pp. 3–25. For a provocative examination, emphasizing the fascist characteristics of the Vichy government, see Roger Bourderon, "Le régime de Vichy était-il fasciste? Essai d'approche de la question," *Revue d'histoire de la deuxième guerre mondiale*, 23 (July 1973), 23–45. A standard account of the complex history of Vichy is Robert Aron, *The Vichy Regime*, translated from the French by Humphrey Hare (Boston: Beacon, 1969) [original edition, 1955]). See also Paul Farmer, *Vichy Political Dilemma* (New York: Columbia University Press, 1955).

The various institutions of the Vichy government during its period of relative independence, up to the occupation of the southern zone in November 1942, are studied by a group of French scholars, published as Fondation Nationale des Sciences Politiques, *Le gouvernement de*

Vichy, 1940–1942: institutions et politiques (Paris: Armand Colin, 1972). For a discussion of the political Left within the Vichy government, see Françoise Laurent, "Les hommes de gauche," a typewritten manuscript prepared for a colloquium of March 6 and 7, 1970 under the auspices of the Fondation Nationale des Sciences Politiques and now available at the BDIC.

For Colonel de la Rocque's rightist but not collaborationist Progrès Social Français, see Philippe Machefer, "Sur quelques aspects de l'activité du colonel de la Rocque et du 'Progrès Social Français' pendant la seconde guerre mondiale," *Revue d'histoire de la deuxième guerre mondiale*, 15 (April 1965), 35–56, and on the subject of the "synarchy" legend which touched all the collaborationist movements, see Richard F. Kuisel, "The Legend of the Vichy Synarchy," *French Historical Studies*, 6 (Spring 1970), 365–398.

Life in occupied France, an understanding of which is important in examining the collaborationists, has been described by many writers. Especially helpful are the memoirs of Jean Galtier-Boissière, the editor of the muckraking magazine *Crapouillot* which had to suspend publication during the occupation, *Mon journal pendant l'occupation* (Paris: La Jeune Parque, 1944); Jean Guéhenno, *Journal des années noires* (Paris: Gallimard, 1947); and the memoir of a Russian press correspondent in occupied Paris, Vassili Soukhomline, *Les hitlériens à Paris*, translated from Russian into French by Lily Denis (Paris: Editeurs Français Réunis, 1967). Of related interest is the misnamed memoir of Hans E. Lichten, *Collaboration Phantom und Wirklichkeit* (Zurich: Aero-Verlag, 1948). A German consular official in Paris, Lichten was fired by the Nazis in 1933 but chose to remain as a businessman in France.

Postwar descriptions of life under the occupation include Henri Amouroux, *La vie des Français sous l'occupation* (Paris: Fayard, 1961) and Gérard Walter, *La vie à Paris sous l'occupation, 1940–1944*, one of the Kiosque series (Paris: Armand Colin, 1960). Also useful are Henri Michel, *La France sous l'occupation* (Paris: Presses Universitaires de France, 1968) and Alexander Werth, *France: 1940–1955* (Boston: Beacon, 1966). The invasion of 1940, collapse, and establishment of the Vichy regime are discussed at length in many works, including Michel, *Vichy année 40* (Paris: Robert Laffont, 1966), Jean Marc de Foville, *L'entrée des allemands à Paris* (Paris: Calmann-Lévy,

1965), and William L. Shirer, *The Collapse of the Third Republic: An Inquiry into the Fall of France in 1940* (New York: Simon & Schuster, 1969).

Literature dealing with the individual collaborationist movements is still relatively sparse. David Littlejohn, *The Patriotic Traitors: A History of Collaboration in German-Occupied Europe, 1940–45* (London: Heinemann, 1972) devotes a lengthy section to the French parties but is based on too uncritical a reliance upon the *French Basic Handbook* and does little more than catalogue the various movements. More analytical are Jean Plumyène and Raymond Lasierra, *Les fascismes français, 1923–63* (Paris: Seuil, 1963), which provides a very brief discussion of the three major collaborationist groups and places them in the tradition of the French radical Right. Stressing the leftist origins of many of those in the RNP and PPF is Eugen Weber, "Nationalism, Socialism, and National-Socialism in France," *French Historical Studies*, 2 (1962), 273–307, and *Varieties of Fascism* (New York: Van Nostrand Reinhold, 1964). Weber's *Action Française: Royalism and Reaction in Twentieth Century France* (Stanford, Cal.: Stanford University Press, 1962) should be consulted for the history of Maurras' movement.

For Marcel Déat's RNP, in addition to the literature above, the party's *Bulletin des Cadres*, published in 1943 and 1944, is most instructive. Déat's unpublished memoirs may be consulted, although with some difficulty, in Paris. See also Claude Varennes [Georges Albertini], *Le destin de Marcel Déat* (Paris: Janmaray, 1948). Recent studies of Déat and the RNP include J.-P. Cointet, "Marcel Déat et le parti unique (été 1940)," Yves Durand and David Bohbot, "La collaboration politique dans les pays de la Loire moyenne: étude historique et socio-politique du R.N.P. en Indre-et-Loire et dans le Loiret," and Stanley Grossmann, "L'évolution de Marcel Déat," all three published in the *Revue d'histoire de la deuxième guerre mondiale*, 23 (July 1973), 1–22; 57–76; and 25 (January 1975), 3–29, respectively. See also the doctoral dissertation of Emily H. Goodman, "The Socialism of Marcel Déat" (Stanford University, 1973). Of related interest in view of Déat's stint as labor minister in 1944 are Edward L. Homze, *Foreign Labor in Nazi Germany* (Princeton, N.J.: Princeton University Press, 1967) and Jacques Evrard, *La déportation des travailleurs français dans le IIIe Reich* (Paris: Fayard, 1972). For an evaluation of Déat by one who joined and then left the RNP, see Jean-Pierre Abel [René Château], *L'age de Caïn: Premier témoignage sur les dessous de la libération de Paris* (Paris: Editions Nouvelles, 1947).

For Doriot and the PPF, see the doctoral dissertation of Fred J. Carrier, "Jacques Doriot, a Political Biography" (University of Wisconsin, 1968) and Gilbert D. Allardyce's articles: "The Political Transition of Jacques Doriot," *Journal of Contemporary History*, 1 (1966) 56–74, reprinted in Walter Laqueur and George L. Mosse, eds., *International Fascism, 1940–45* (New York: Harper Torchbooks, 1966); "French Communism Comes of Age: Jacques Doriot, Henri Barbé, and the Disinheritance of the *Jeunesses Communistes*, 1923–1931," *The Durham University Journal*, 46 (March 1974), 129–145; and "Jacques Doriot et l'esprit fasciste en France," *Revue d'histoire de la deuxième guerre mondiale*, 25 (January 1975), 31–44; all relating to different periods in the career of Doriot. For Doriot's split from the Communist party, see Jean-Paul Brunet, "Réflexions sur la scission de Doriot (février-juin 1934)," *Mouvement Social*, no. 70 (January-March 1970), 43–64. Of limited use in describing the latter stages of Doriot's career is the anonymously published "La vérité sur la mort de Doriot," *Europe-Amérique*, November 1, 1945, pp. 18–26; November 15, 1945, pp. 12–17; and November 29, 1945, pp. 18–23.

The fullest study of Doriot's career with a considerable section on the PPF during the occupation is Dieter Wolf, *Die Doriot-Bewegung. Ein Beitrag zur Geschichte der französischen Faschismus* (Stuttgart: Deutsche Verlags-Anstalt, 1967). The roles of the PPF and the Milice in Tunisia in 1942 and 1943 are discussed in René Pellegrin, *La Phalange Africaine: La L.V.F. en Tunisie, 1942–1943* (Paris: published by the author, 1973) and the memoir of the special German envoy sent there, Rudolf Rahn, *Ruheloses Leben Aufzeichnungen und Erinnerungen* (Düsseldorf: Diederichs Verlag, 1949).

Joseph Darnand's Milice has been studied by Jacques Delperrie de Bayac, *Histoire de la Milice* (Paris: Fayard, 1969) and Monique Luirard, "La Milice Française dans la Loire," *Revue d'histoire de la deuxième guerre mondiale*, 23 (July 1973), 77–102. Darnand is considered in my article, "Un soldat du fascisme: L'évolution politique de Joseph Darnand," *Revue d'histoire de la deuxième guerre mondiale*, 27 (October 1977), 43–70. Discussing the "Franco-French" war, Milton Dank, *The French against the French: Collaboration and Resistance* (Philadelphia and New York: Lippincott, 1974) devotes some attention to the Milice and also to the Anti-Bolshevik Legion. A number of memoirs have been written by former Miliciens. These include Henry Charbonneau, *Les Mémoires de Porthos*, 2 vols. (Paris: Clan and Robert Desroches, 1967–1969), which also treats Charbonneau's activity in the MSR prior to his joining the Milice. See also Jean Bassompierre, *Frères ennemis* in Charles-Ambroise Colin, *Sacrifice de Bassompierre* (Paris: Amiot-Dumont, 1948), in which Bassompierre also discussed his service in the Anti-Bolshevik Legion. There is also an anonymously written memoir by a former Milicien with a preface by General G. L. Lavigne-Delville, *La vérité réconciliée... Pour la Milice Justice... par un Chef de Corps de la Milice* (Paris: Etheel, n.d.).

Some of the seamier sides of the collaboration and the civil strife, although not the Milice per se, are discussed in Jacques Delarue, *Trafics et crimes sous l'occupation* (Paris: Arthème Fayard, 1968), Jean Cathelin and Gabrielle Gray, *Crimes et trafics de la Gestapo française*, 2 vols. (Paris: Historama, 1972), Philippe Aziz, *Au service de l'ennemi. La gestapo française en Province* (Paris: Fayard, 1972), and Jacques Bonny, *Mon père l'Inspecteur Bonny* (Paris: Robert Laffont, 1975). As Secretary-general for the Maintenance of Order after January, 1944, Darnand was responsible for all segments of the French police, not only the Milice.

The smaller movements of the collaboration have attracted even less scholarly attention than have the larger ones. For Eugène Deloncle and the MSR, see Philippe Bourdrel, *La Cagoule: 30 ans de complots* (Paris: Albin Michel, 1970), which concentrates on the interwar *Cagoule*; Pierre Bourget, *Histoires secrètes de l'occupation de Paris (1940–1944)* (Paris: Hachette, 1970), volume 1; and Jean-Raymond Tournoux, *L'histoire secrète* (Paris: Plon, 1962); the two latter touching briefly on Deloncle and the MSR. A fuller treatment of the MSR may be found in my article "The Condottieri of the Collaboration: *Mouvement Social Révolutionnaire*," *Journal of Contemporary History*, 10 (April 1975), 261–282.

The Francistes have been studied by Arnaud Jacomet, "Marcel Bucard et le mouvement Franciste, 1933–1940," Maîtrise, University of Paris X, 1970 and "Les chefs du francisme: Marcel Bucard et Paul

Guiraud," *Revue d'histoire de la deuxième guerre mondiale*, 25 (January 1975), 45–66. Post war trial accounts, which must be used with special care, include a summary of the stenographic account of Bucard's trial published in *Quatre Procès de trahison devant la cour de justice de Paris. Paquis. Bucard. Luchaire. Brasillach. Réquisitoires et plaidoiries* (Paris: Les Editions de Paris, 1947). The tiny collaborationist movements have found no historians, nor has the much larger Groupe Collaboration of Châteaubriant.

The literature concerned with the French in the German armed forces is more extensive than that devoted to the collaborationist parties at home as the French volunteers abroad provided better bases for romanticized accounts. The most scholarly treatments are those of Owen Anthony Davey, "The Origins of the Légion des Volontaires Français contre le Bolchévisme," *Journal of Contemporary History*, 6 (October 1971), 29–45, and Delarue, *Trafics et crimes sous l'occupation*, cited above. See also Albert Merglen, "Soldats français sous uniforms allemands," *Revue d'histoire de la deuxième guerre mondiale*, 27 (October 1977), 71–84. More romanticized accounts include the trilogy of Saint-Loup [Marc Augier], *Les volontaires*, *Les hérétiques*, and *Les nostalgiques* (Paris: Presses de la Cité, 1963–1967), narrating respectively the campaigns of the Anti-Bolshevik Legion, those of the French Waffen-SS, and their postwar fate. On the French SS, see also Saint-Paulien [Maurice-Ivan Sicard], *Les maudits*, 2 vols. (Paris: Plon, 1958) and Jean Noli, *Le choix: Les marins français au combat, 1939–1945* (Paris: Fayard, 1972), discussing among others the French sailors who volunteered for service with the Axis. See also Jean Mabire's three-volume *Les SS Français* (Paris: Fayard, 1973–1975).

Memoirs of those who enlisted to fight for Germany include Marc Augier, *Les partisans* (Paris: Denoël, 1943), Eric Labat, *Les places étaient chères* (Paris: La Table Ronde, 1951), and the anonymously written *Vae Victis ou deux ans dans la L.V.F.* (Paris: La Jeune Parque, 1948), all by veterans of the Anti-Bolshevik Legion. For accounts of veterans of the French SS, see Serge Mit, *Carcasse à vendre* (Paris: Dominique Wapler, 1950), and Christian de la Mazière, the former SS man interviewed in the film *Le chagrin et la pitié*, *Le rêveur casqué* (Paris: Robert Laffont, 1972). To understand some of the sources of inspiration of the *engagés* in the Anti-Bolshevik Legion and the Waffen-SS, one should examine the writings of Montherlant and

Giono. See also Jacques Pugnet, *Jean Giono* (Paris: Éditions Universitaires, 1955). The Spanish equivalent of the Anti-Bolshevik Legion, the "Blue Division," has been studied by Raymond L. Procter, *Agony of a Neutral: La Division Azul* (Moscow, Idaho: Idaho Research Foundation, 1974), and the Waffen-SS is examined in its entirety by George H. Stein, *The Waffen-SS: Hitler's Elite Guard at War, 1939–1945* (Ithaca, N.Y.: Cornell University Press, 1966).

Special attention is devoted to the entry of Darnand, Henriot, and Déat into the Vichy government and their impact on it in 1944 by André Brissaud, *La Dernière année de Vichy (1943–1944)* (Paris: Librairie Académique Perrin, 1965). The Sigmaringen episode is treated by Louis Noguères, *La dernière étape Sigmaringen* (Paris: Fayard, 1956) and Brissaud, *Pétain à Sigmaringen* (Paris: Librairie Académique Perrin, 1966). See also the memoir by Marie Chaix, the daughter of PPF Politbureau member Albert Beugras, *Les lauriers du lac de Constance: Chronique d'une collaboration* (Paris: Seuil, 1974), and G. T. Schillemans, a doctor procured by the Germans for Pétain, *Philippe Pétain: Le prisonnier de Sigmaringen* (Paris: MP, 1965), which is full of portraits of the collaborationist leaders at Sigmaringen. The memoir of the PPF radio broadcaster Jean Hérold-Paquis, *Des illusions... Désillusions: 15 août 1944–15 août 1945* (Paris: Bourgoin, 1948), is also helpful, especially in following the attitudes and activities of the PPF camp in German exile. For Hérold-Paquis see J. Goueffon, "La guerre des ondes: Le cas de Jean Hérold-Paquis," *Revue d'histoire de la deuxième guerre mondiale*, 27 (October 1977), 27–42. The spirit of the exiles in Germany can be seen in the novel *D'un château l'autre* by one of them, the author Louis-Ferdinand Céline. It has been translated into English by Ralph Mannheim as *Castle to Castle* (New York: Dell, 1968 [original French edition, 1957]).

Some light is shed on the personalities and movements of the collaboration by the large number of memoirs that have appeared since the war. These include Vichy Foreign Minister Paul Baudouin, *The Private Diaries*, translated from the French by Sir Charles Petrie (London: Eyre and Spottiswoode, 1948), Finance Minister Yves Bouthillier, *Le drame de Vichy*, 2 vols. (Paris: Plon, 1950–1951), and Transport Minister Jean Berthelot, *Sur les rails du pouvoir (1938–1942)* (Paris: Robert Laffont, 1968). Of particular value are Henry

Du Moulin de Labarthète, of Pétain's civil cabinet, *Le temps des illusions: souvenirs (juillet 1940–avril 1942)* (Brussels: Cheval Ailé, 1946); Pierre Nicolle, an economics counselor to the government at Vichy, *Cinquante mois d'armistice: Vichy, 2 juillet 1940–26 août 1944: Journal d'un témoin*, 2 vols. (Paris: André Bonne, 1947); and Maurice Martin du Gard, *La chronique de Vichy*, 1940–1944 (Paris: Flammarion, 1948). Indispensable for the events of 1944 is the memoir of Pétain's cabinet director in that year, Jean Tracou, *Le maréchal aux liens* (Paris: André Bonne, 1948).

Among other memoirs are those of Fernand de Brinon, *Mémoires* (Paris: L.L.C., 1949) and those of collaborationist writers Robert Brasillach, *Journal d'un homme occupé* (Paris: Les Sept Couleurs, 1955), published after his postwar execution, and Pierre Drieu la Rochelle, *Chronique politique, 1934–1942* (Paris: Gallimard, 1943), *Ne plus attendre (Notes à leur date)* (Paris: Bernard Grasset, 1941), and *Récit secret, suivi de journal (1944–1945) et d'Exode* (Paris: Gallimard, 1951). A biting collaborationist account of the early history of the occupation appears in the staunchly pro-German and anti-Semitic work by Lucien Rebatet, *Les décombres* (Paris: Denoël, 1942). Additional memoirs of some interest include the account of the movie starlet who was the daughter of Jean Luchaire, Corinne Luchaire, *Ma drôle de vie* (Paris: Sun, 1949). Finally, the views of Pierre Laval appear in *Laval parle... Notes et mémoires rédigés à Fresnes d'août à octobre 1945* (Paris: Cheval Ailé, 1948).

Two military men involved in interwar *Cagoule* plots and later in Vichy before joining the Resistance are Colonel Georges A. Groussard, *Chemins secrets*, volume 1 (Paris: Bader-Dufour, 1948) and his updated *Service secret, 1940–1945* (Paris: La Table Ronde, 1964), and Georges Loustaunau-Lacau, *Mémoires d'un Français rebelle, 1914–48* (Paris: Robert Laffont, 1948). The inspiration of at least some of the militants in movements such as the MSR may be found in part in the memoir of the German *Freikorps* veteran Ernst von Salomon, *The Outlaws*, translated from the German *Die Geächteten* by Ian F. D. Morrow (London: Jonathan Cape, 1931).

Trial accounts published are *Procès du Maréchal Pétain* (Paris: Journal Officiel, 1945); *Procès Laval* (Paris: Albin Michel, 1946); *Quatre Procès de trahison*, cited above; and *Les Procès de Collaboration* (Paris: Albin Michel, 1948), which contains the stenographic accounts of the trials of de Brinon, Darnand, and Luchaire. Of related interest are *Les Procès de la Radio: Ferdonnet et Jean Hérold-Paquis* (Paris: Albin Michel, 1947); *Le Procès de Charles Maurras* (Paris: Albin Michel, 1946); and *Le Procès de Xavier Vallat*, Vichy's first Commissar for Jewish Affairs (Paris: Conquistador, 1948). See also Jacques Isorni, *Le Procès de Robert Brasillach* (Paris: Flammarion, 1946) and Louis Noguères, *Le Véritable Procès du Maréchal Pétain* (Paris: Robert Laffont, 1955) and *La Haute Cour de la Libération* (Paris: Robert Laffont, 1965).

In addition to the published trial accounts, the BDIC has a number of unpublished typewritten trial accounts of collaborationists and Vichyites, and all the trials were followed closely in the press of postwar France. Several collections of documents, some relating to the collaboration, have been published since the war. These include Jacques Baraduc, *Les archives secrètes du Reich. Tout ce qu'on vous a caché* (Paris: Elan, 1949); Claude Gounelle, *Le dossier Laval* (Paris: Plon, 1969); and the three-volume collection of testamonial statements put together by Laval's daughter and son-in-law, Josée and René de Chambrun, *France during the German Occupation, 1940–1944: A Collection of 292 Statements on the Government of Maréchal Pétain and Pierre Laval*, translated from the French by Philip W. Whitcomb, 3 vols. (Stanford, Cal.: Hoover Institution Press, 1957). A lengthy postwar parliamentary investigation of the 1940 collapse and the Vichy regime produced little on the collaborationist parties as such. See Assemblée Nationale, *Rapport fait au nom de la commission chargée d'enquêter sur les événements survenus en France de 1933 à 1945*, 11 vols. (Paris: Presses Universitaires de France, 1951).

The published writings of the collaborationists were voluminous, and only a few representatives of the various parties can be mentioned here. For the RNP, see Déat, *Le parti unique* (Paris: Aux Armes de France, 1942), and for the PPF, Doriot, *Je suis un homme du maréchal* (Paris: Bernard Grasset, 1941) and *Réalités* (Paris: Editions de France, 1942). Franciste values were elaborated by party doctinaire Paul Guiraud, *Codréanu et la Garde de Fer* (Rio de Janeiro: Colectia Dacia, 1967 [original publication, 1940]). From MSR circles came André Mahé and Georges Soulès, *La fin du nihilisme* (Paris: Fernand Sorlot, 1943) and Eugène Schueller, *La révolution de l'économie* (Paris: Robert Denoël, 1941). A few collaborationist writers are included in the anthology edited by Germaine Brée and Georges Bernauer, *Defeat and Beyond: An Anthology of French Wartime Writing (1940–1945)* (New York: Pantheon, 1970). The richest source for published collaborationist writings is, of course, the press under the occupation.

There is a vast literature on the subject of fascism, but little specifically related to the political movements of the French collaboration. The various different schools of thought concerning fascism in general and the relevant bibliography are summarized by Alan Cassels, *Fascism* (New York: Thomas Y. Crowell, 1975). The important study by Ernst Nolte, *Three Faces of Fascism: Action Française, Italian Fascism, National Socialism,* translated from the German by Leila Vennewitz (London: Weidenfeld & Nicolson, 1965) merits special mention as perhaps the single most influential work on the subject. In his concept of resistance to transcendence, Nolte includes Action Française in the fascist tradition, a view at variance with that of René Rémond, who argues that fascism was alien to France; see "Y a-t-il un fascisme français?" *Terre Humaine* 2 (July-August 1952), 37–47, and *The Right Wing in France: From 1815 to de Gaulle,* translated from the French by James M. Laux (Philadelphia: University of Pennsylvania Press, 1969 [original French edition 1963]). Also to be considered are Henri Lemaitre, *Les fascismes dans l'histoire* (Paris: Cerf, 1959) and the collections of articles in two books edited by S. J. Woolf, *The Nature of Fascism* (New York: Vintage, 1969) and *European Fascism* (New York: Vintage, 1969), and Hans Rogger and Eugen Weber, eds. *The European Right: A Historical Profile* (Berkeley and Los Angeles: University of California Press, 1966). The works of Eugen Weber discussed above are also significant in the general discussion of fascism, as is A. James Gregor, *The Fascist Persuasion in Radical Politics* (Princeton, N.J.: Princeton University Press, 1974).

Psychological insights into fascist personality types were made in the landmark book by Theodor W. Adorno, et al., *The Authoritarian Personality* (New York: Harper, 1950). Later works on the subject are Fred I. Greenstein, *Personality and Politics: Problems of Evidence, Inference, and Conceptualization* (Chicago: Markham, 1969) and the collection edited by Jeanne M. Knutsen, *Handbook of Political Psychology* (San Francisco: Jossey-Bass, 1973). Also helpful in his discussion of fascist personality traits is Peter Nathan, *The Psychology of*

375

Fascism (London: Faber & Faber, 1943) and, more recently, Peter Loewenberg, "The Psychohistorical Origins of the Nazi Youth Cohort," *American Historical Review*, 76 (December 1971), 1457–1502, the latter a study of the deprivations caused by the First World War and the subsequent economic dislocations to the cohort of children who grew up to become Hitler Youth.

For the study of the development of interwar French fascism and its relation to the historical Right in France, there are several useful works in addition to those of Rémond cited above. Fascism before the February Days of 1934 is discussed by Claude Willard, "Quelques aspects du fascisme en France avant le 6 février 1934," in Jacques Chambaz, *Le Front Populaire pour le pain, la liberté et la paix* (Paris: Editions Sociales, 1961), pp. 190–223. See also William D. Irvine, "French Conservatives and the 'New Right' during the 1930's," *French Historical Studies*, 8 (Fall 1974), 534–562, and the more general guide to the interwar radical Right, Philippe Machefer, *Ligues et fascismes en France (1919–1939)* in the series Dossiers Clio (Paris: Presses Universitaires de France, 1974). A more recent study of the modernizing tendencies within French fascism is Klaus-Jürgen Müller, "French Fascism and Modernization," *Journal of Contemporary History*, 11 (October 1976), 75–107.

The relationship of the radical Right to war veterans is discussed by René Rémond, "Les anciens combattants et la politique," *Revue française de science politique*, 5 (April-June 1955), 267–290, and more recently by Robert J. Soucy, "France: Veterans' Politics between the Wars," in Stephen R. Ward, ed., *The War Generation: Veterans of the First World War* (Port Washington, N.Y.: Kennikat Press, 1975), pp. 59–103. Antoine Prost, *Les anciens combattants et la société française, 1914–1939* (Paris: Presses de la Fondation des Sciences Politiques, 1977), and Soucy both argue for the political moderation of most of France's veterans in the years between the wars. The relationship of the radical Right to the peasants is studied by Pascal Ory, "Le Dorgérisme: institution et discours d'une colère paysanne (1929–1939)," *Revue d'histoire moderne et contemporaine*, 22 (April-June 1975), 167–190.

Several works are helpful in understanding the background of the stalled society and the fragmentation in French political life, so important in the development of the interwar radical Right and its failure under the occupation. These include the studies of Stanley Hoffmann, the most relevant of which are his "Paradoxes of the French Political Community," in Stanley Hoffmann, et al., *In Search of France: The Economy, Society, and Political System in the Twentieth Century* (New York: Harper Torchbooks, 1965 [1963]), pp. 3–117 and "Protest in Modern France," in Morton A. Kaplan, ed., *The Revolution in World Politics* (New York: Wiley, 1962), pp. 69–91. See also François Goguel, *La politique des partis sous la IIIe République* (Paris: Seuil, 1946), and Pierre Sorlin, *La société française, II, 1914–1968* (Paris: Arthaud, 1971). A useful encyclopedia of personalities and parties is Henry Coston, *Dictionnaire de la politique française* (Paris: La Librairie Française, 1967).

The French fascist literati have attracted more study than the political movements of the collaboration because their writings have been more readily accessible and personally self-revealing. The careers and writings of several leading fascist literary figures are summarized by Paul Sérant, *Le romantisme fasciste: étude sur l'oeuvre politique de quelques écrivains français* (Paris: Fasquelle, 1959). See also Robert J. Soucy, "The Nature of Fascism in France," *Journal of Contemporary History*, 1, (1966), 27–55, reprinted in Laqueur and Mosse, eds., *International Fascism*; "Le Fascisme de Drieu la Rochelle," *Revue d'histoire de la deuxième guerre mondiale*, 17 (April 1967), 61–84; "French Fascism as Class Conciliation and Moral Regeneration," *Societas*, 1 (1971), 287–297; and *Fascism in France: The Case of Maurice Barrès* (Berkeley: University of California Press, 1972). A useful survey of fascist literati is Alastair Hamilton, *The Appeal of Fascism: A Study of Intellectuals and Fascism, 1919–1945* (New York: Discus/Avon, 1973 [1971]), which contains a section on France, and Raoul Girardet, "Notes sur l'esprit d'un fascisme français, 1934–1939," *Revue française de science politique*, 5 (July-September 1955), 529–546. For a more specialized treatment of a literary personality, see J. Mièvre, "L'évolution politique d'Abel Bonnard," *Revue d'histoire de la deuxième guerre mondiale*, 27 (October 1977), 1–26.

An understanding of French collaborationism may be enhanced by the study of analogous movements elsewhere. Collaborationism throughout occupied Europe is discussed in Littlejohn, *Patriotic Traitors*, noted above. For specific collaborationists and their political organizations, see Werner Warmbrunn, *The Dutch under German Occupation, 1940–1945* (Stanford, Cal.: Stanford University Press, 1963); Vojtech Mastny, *The Czechs under Nazi Rule: The Failure of National Resistance, 1939–1942* (New York: Columbia University Press, 1971); John M. Hoberman, "Vidkun Quisling's Psychological Image," *Scandinavian Studies*, 46 (Summer 1974), 242–264; Wilfried Strik-Strikfeldt, *Gegen Stalin und Hitler. General Wlassow und die russische Freiheitsbewegung* (Mainz: Von Hase und Koehler, 1970); and a non-European example, Gerald E. Bunker, *The Peace Conspiracy: Wang Ching-wei and the China War, 1937–1941* (Cambridge, Mass.: Harvard University Press, 1972). Two significant examinations of German National Socialism are also helpful for comparative study: Wolfgang Sauer, "National Socialism: Totalitarianism or Fascism?" *American Historical Review*, 73 (December 1967), 404–422, and Peter H. Merkl, *Political Violence under the Swastika: 581 Early Nazis* (Princeton, N.J.: Princeton University Press, 1975).

Studies dealing with the trials of the collaborationists and Vichyites and their fate after the Liberation include Robert Aron, *Histoire de la Libération de France: juin 1944–mai 1945* (Paris: Fayard, 1959) and *Histoire de l'épuration*, 4 vols. (Paris: Faynard, 1967–1975); Paul Sérant, *Les vaincus de la libération* (Paris: Robert Laffont, 1964); and, most important, Peter Novick, *The Resistance versus Vichy: The Purge of Collaborators in Liberated France* (New York: Columbia University Press, 1968).

The radical rightist perception of the purges in the postwar years is discussed in my unpublished paper, "'*Les prisons de la Quatrième*': The Purge of Vichyites and Collaborators in the Formation of the Postwar French Radical Right," presented at the meeting of the American Historical Association, San Francisco, December 30, 1978. For more general treatments of the radical Right since the war, see Plumyène and Lasierra, *Les fascismes français*, listed above, and François Duprat, *Les mouvements d'extrême-droit en France depuis 1944* (Paris: Albatross, 1972). The extreme Right under the Fifth Republic is considered in René Chiroux, *L'extrême-droit sous la Ve République* (Paris: Librairie Générale de Droit et de Jurisprudence, 1974).

Index of Published Sources

To assist the reader in following up citations, an index of most of the published primary and secondary sources used in this book has been compiled. Only works actually cited appear below.

Most of the references are listed alphabetically by author. Where more than one article or book by an author is cited, a short title indicates the appropriate reference.

Index of Published Sources

Index

General Index

**Collaborationism in France
during the Second World War**

Designed by Richard Rosenbaum.
Composed by The Composing Room of Michigan, Inc.
in 11 point VIP Fairfield Medium, 2 points leaded,
with display lines in Helvetica Bold Condensed.
Printed offset by LithoCrafters, Inc.
on 50 pound Warren's Number 66 Antique Offset.
Bound by LithoCrafters
in Holliston book cloth
and stamped in All Purpose foil.

Library of Congress Cataloging in Publication Data

Gordon, Bertram M   1943-
  Collaborationism in France during the Second World War.

  Bibliography: p.
  Includes index.
  1. World War, 1939–1945—Collaborationists—France. 2. France—History—
  German occupation, 1940–1945.
I. Title.
D802.F8G67   940.53'24'44   79-25281
ISBN 0-8014-1263-3